The Mulatto in the United States

Including a study of the role of mixed-blood races throughout the world

Edward Byron Reuter

Alpha Editions

This edition published in 2020

ISBN : 9789354039737

Design and Setting By
Alpha Editions
www.alphaedis.com
email - alphaedis@gmail.com

As per information held with us this book is in Public Domain. This book is a reproduction of an important historical work. Alpha Editions uses the best technology to reproduce historical work in the same manner it was first published to preserve its original nature. Any marks or number seen are left intentionally to preserve its true form.

THE MULATTO IN THE UNITED STATES

INCLUDING A STUDY OF THE
RÔLE OF MIXED-BLOOD RACES
THROUGHOUT THE WORLD

BY

EDWARD BYRON REUTER

BOSTON
RICHARD G. BADGER
THE GORHAM PRESS

PREFACE

OF the social problems before the American people for solution, there is none perhaps of more fundamental importance than that created by the presence of some ten million persons of a race and color different from that of the major part of the country's population. The future of the nation is in a degree conditioned by the treatment which this race problem receives. Is the amalgamation of the races in contact to be regarded as an ideal? If so, there remains the problem of working out a technique by means of which some degree of harmony and good will can be established between the racial groups during the period that mongrelization is in progress. Or would the infusion of ten per cent of Negro blood so materially lower the ideals and the intellectual and cultural capacity of the population as to cause the country to drop out of the group of culture nations? If so, there is the problem of checking the fusion already in progress, as well as the problem of establishing some sort of harmonious working relations between the races while they separately work out their racial destiny. In regard to the fundamental question there is as yet no concensus of scholarly opinion; the problem has scarcely been attacked in a scholarly way. The more immediately practical problem has as yet received little intellectual consideration: for the most part it still arouses emotion rather than thought.

At the same time that the social problem created by the presence of the race in America challenges the careful study of scientific men and taxes the ingenuity of the statesman and the administrator, the racial group itself presents the richest field for study of a people in evolution of any group in the modern world. Every stage in the social evolution and in the intellectual and moral development of a people is present in the American Negro group. Yet the study of the Negro and his American environment—his reaction and responses to that environment and the effect of that reaction and response on his intellectual growth and social development, as well as the influence which his presence and peculiar racial traits have had in modifying or determining the direction and the degree of development of American customs and institutions—has received but a trifling amount of attention from scholars. Discussion of the Negro and the American race problem has for the most part been left to the doctrinaire and the demagogue, neither of whom has accomplished much toward the discovery of truth, even toward the discovery of those relatively simple truths which must be known and acknowledged before any rational program looking toward a more harmonious relation between the races can be advanced.

The following study is not a brief in behalf of, nor in opposition to, racial amalgamation; yet it presents certain of the facts which must be known before any pronouncement of scientific value can be made upon that subject. Neither is it a study of the race problem, in the narrow sense in which that phrase is popularly understood, yet it presents certain facts which must be taken into account in any intelligent dealing with that problem. The book is an attempt to state one sociological problem arising when two races, divergent as to culture and distinct as to physical appearance, are brought into contact under the conditions of modern life and produce a hybrid offspring whose characteristic physical appearance prevents them from passing as either the one or the other. Under such conditions physical appearance becomes the basis for class and caste distinctions; a biological phenomenon gives rise to a sociological problem. It is with the sociological consequences of race intermixture, not with the biological problems of the intermixture itself, that the present study has to do. The investigation proceeds throughout on the assumption that no permanent good can accrue to the Negro people as a whole and that unfortunate and avoidable discord in interracial relations is promoted by the concealment of truth and the denial of fact.

The writer takes this opportunity to acknowledge his indebtedness to Dr. Robert E. Park, at whose suggestion the work was begun and to whose friendly encouragement and generous criticism during the progress of the investigation much of the merit of the study is due. In no respect, however, is Dr. Park to be considered responsible for any errors of fact or interpretation which may appear in the text. To Dr. William I. Thomas the writer is indebted—to mention but one way—for mediation in publication, always a difficult matter where a study deviates either in method or content from the strictly conventional.

It was through the courtesy of Editor R. S. Abbott and the other members of the staff of the *Chicago Defender* that the writer had placed at his disposal, during the entire period of investigation, some sixty odd of the best and best known Negro newspapers. He here acknowledges his indebtedness and expresses his appreciation. Finally to a large number of other prominent Negroes, who may not here be mentioned by name, the writer is indebted for information on many matters of race sentiment and attitude and especially for information concerning the racial ancestry of members of their race. E. B. R.

Palo Alto, California
   February, 1918.

CONTENTS

CHAPTER		PAGE
I.	INTRODUCTION	11
II.	MIXED-BLOOD RACES	21
	In Primitive Times	21
	In Spain	23
	The Eurasians	26
	The Eskimos	31
	In Spanish America	33
	In the Philippines	51
III.	MIXED-BLOOD RACES (concluded)	55
	In Cuba, Porto Rico and Santo Domingo	55
	In Haiti	61
	In Jamaica	65
	In South Africa	71
	North American Indians	77
IV.	THE MULATTO: THE KEY TO THE RACE PROBLEM	86
V.	THE AMOUNT OF RACE INTERMIXTURE IN THE UNITED STATES	105
VI.	NATURE OF RACE INTERMIXTURE IN THE UNITED STATES	127
	Intermarriage	127
	The Concubinage of Colored Women by White Men	139
	Unlawful Polygamy	144
	Intermarriage with Indians	155
	Intermixture During Slavery and at Present	158
VII.	THE GROWTH OF THE MULATTO CLASS	166
VIII.	LEADING MEN OF THE NEGRO RACE	183
IX.	THE HISTORY AND BIOGRAPHY OF THE NEGRO	216
X.	THE NEGRO AND THE MULATTO IN PROFESSIONAL AND ARTISTIC PURSUITS	246
XI.	THE NEGRO AND THE MULATTO IN BUSINESS AND INDUSTRY	293
XII.	THE RÔLE OF THE MULATTO IN THE INTER-RACIAL SITUATION	315
XIII.	THE RÔLE OF THE MULATTO IN THE UNITED STATES	338
XIV.	SUMMARY: PRESENT TENDENCIES	375
	INDEX TO NAMES OF MEN WHOSE ETHNIC ANCESTRY IS ANALYZED	399
	GENERAL INDEX	413

THE MULATTO IN THE UNITED STATES

CHAPTER I

INTRODUCTION

THE mulatto, as the term is used in this study, includes all those members of the Negro race with a visible admixture of white blood.[1] Thus used, the word is a general term to include all Negroes of mixed ancestry regardless of the degree of intermixture. It includes all persons who are recognized, in the communities in which they live, as being of mixed blood. It is in this sense that the word is most widely used and best understood in this country.[2]

[1] The United States Census Office has not been consistent in its definition of the term. ". . . the fact that the definition of the term 'mulatto' adopted at different censuses has not been entirely uniform may affect the comparability of the figures in some degree." In 1870 and 1910, however, the term was applied to all persons having any perceptible trace of Negro blood, excepting, of course, Negroes of pure blood. In 1850 and 1860 the term seems not to have been defined. In the returns for 1890 the Negroes of mixed-blood were classified into mulattoes, quadroons and octoroons. U. S. Census Report 1910: *Population,* Vol. 1, p. 129.

[2] "The offspring, . . . of a negress by a white man, or of a white woman by a negro; in a more general sense, a person of mixed Caucasian and negro blood, or Indian and negro blood." Webster, International Dictionary.

"Loosely used for any half-breed resembling a mulatto." Murray, Dictionary.

Strictly defined, the word designates the first generation of hybridization between the Negro and the Caucasian races.[3] The hybrid may be the offspring of a white father and a Negro mother or the child of a Negro father and a white mother. Both ancestral elements, however, must be of racially pure lineage else the offspring resulting from the union will not be a first generation hybrid and hence not a mulatto in the biological sense.[4] The word thus delimited becomes a biological concept unavailable for use except in a technical, biological sense. It designates a particular and scientifically interesting but relatively infrequent type of human hybrid. It is, in this usage, coördinate with the words *mango, sambo, quadroon, octoroon, mustifee* and the like [5]

[3] In its derivation the word is from the Spanish *mulato,* the diminutive of *mulo,* a mule. So *mulato* is literally a young mule—so called because of hybrid origin. Century Dictionary.

[4] The first cross, for example, between the Negroes and the North European races gives a mulatto in the true and accurate biological sense. The offspring shows definite predicable physical characteristics. This is not true in the case of crossings between the Mediterranean peoples and the Negro. The offspring here may show in the first generation the variability that appears in the second generation cross of North European and Negro. The ancient intermixture of black blood in the South European peoples makes the effect of their crossing with the Negro that of the crossing of a pure and a hybrid race.

[5] Olmsted, writing about 1854, states that the French of the Southern States classify the colored people, according to the greater or less preponderance of Negro blood, as follows:

Sacatra	griffe and negress
Griffe	Negro and mulatto
Marabon	mulatto and griffe
Mulatto	white and Negro
Quadroon	white and mulatto
Metif	white and Quadroon
Meamelouc	white and metif
Quarteron	white and meamelouc
Sang-mele	white and quarteron

Frederick Law Olmsted, *A Journey in the Seaboard Slave States,* p. 583.

Introduction

each of which connotes a specific type of racial cross.[6]

But for purposes of sociological study it is the mixed group as a whole, not the degree of hybridization nor the particular types of hybrid, that is of prime importance. So

Davenport gives the following classification:

Mulatto	Negro and white
Quadroon	mulatto and white
Octoroon	quadroon and white
Cascos	mulatto and mulatto
Sambo	mulatto and Negro
Mango	sambo and Negro
Mustifee	octoroon and white
Mustifino	mustifee and white

C. B. Davenport, *Heredity of Skin Color in Negro-White Crosses*, p. 27.

[6] The mulatto, of course, differs in certain marked ways from other types of intermixture. He is the product of the cross between pure races and, like all first generation hybrids, shows an unvarying uniformity and a universal instability of physical type. The Negro characters are always dominant and appear prominently; the Caucasian characters are recessive and for the most part remain concealed. It is possible to predict with scientific certainty the characters that will appear in the first generation hybrid.

In the second and subsequent generations the Caucasian and Negroid characters combined in the mulatto, *i.e.*, the first generation hybrid, segregate in almost infinitely variable ways. Individuals appear with the typical characters—skin color, hair color, hair length, eye color, body odor and the like—redistributed in endless new combinations. Individuals appear with light skin and tufted hair, black skin and blue eyes, with dark skin and lank hair, with fair skin and light but curly hair, with the skin coloration and hair formation of the white man and the body odor of the Negro; so with hundreds, perhaps thousands, of other human characters. The uniformity of the first generation hybrid becomes an almost infinite variety as further generations appear.

But however wide the variations, however numerous the varieties, the mixed race can never become, biologically, either Negro or white. Interbreeding or further crossing produces new hybrids. No amount of interbreeding or of crossing can ever produce a white man or a Negro from a hybrid ancestry. The hybrid individual is a biologically unstable type and he and his descendants remain hybrid and physically unstable to the extermination of the group.

if the biological terminology be adhered to, it becomes necessary to adopt some other term to include all individuals of mixed ancestry. No term more satisfactory than *mulatto* has been suggested. The word *coloured* is used in this sense in the English publications, but, as this word is widely used in the United States as synonymous with Negro, it is not available here. The term *mulatto* will therefore be used in the following pages in its more general and popular sense as defined above. When it is used in the more restricted sense to designate the first generation offspring of a Negro-white cross, the fact will be so indicated.

The mulatto, then, is a man of mixed blood. But it is not that alone that makes the mulatto a matter of sociological importance. Mixture of blood is a characteristic of all races.[7]

Man always has been a restless animal moving to and fro in search of food or adventure, to escape his enemies or merely in response to a nomadic impulse. Ratzel,[8] speaking of the "innumerable wanderings" of certain Pacific primitive peoples, says that this should not be considered as an exception but rather as the rule, "for none of these races was ever at rest." Again he says [9] that "It would hardly be possible

---

[7] The term "race" is to be understood in its popular rather than in its ethnological sense. Ethnologically it means a human group which owes its distinctive traits to the selective forces of nature acting upon biological mutation and which invariably breeds true to type. As used here it refers to peoples rather than to biological races. Practically all the present day races are the products of intermixture in varying degrees of previously more or less well established types, and the adaptation of the hybridized stock to the special environment. For the purpose in hand we are not concerned with race as a physical concept but with race as a social unity which arises by and through social development.

[8] Friedrich Ratzel, *The History of Mankind*, English Translation by A. J. Butler, Vol. I, p. 174.

[9] *Ibid.*, Vol. I, p. 446. Speaking here of the Malays.

to name a race, however small, the traditions of which are not based upon a migration."

Migrations brought contacts with new and strange peoples resulting, in some cases, in an intermingling of blood, which, combined with environmental adaptation, produced modified racial types. Johnston [10] summarizes the early mixture of races in these words:

> ... Ever since the existing human species diverged into its four or five existing varieties or sub-species, there has been a constant opposite movement at work to unify the type. Whites have returned southwards and mingled with Australoids, Australoids have united with Negroids, and produced Melanesians, and Papuans, and these, again, have mixed with proto-Caucasians or with Mongols to form the Polynesian. The earliest types of White man have mingled with the primitive Mongol, or directly with the primitive Negro. There is an ancient Negroid strain underlying the populations of Southern and Western France, Italy, Sicily, Corsica, Sardinia, Spain, Portugal, Ireland, Wales and Scotland. Evidences of the former existence of these negroid people are not only to be found in the features of their mixed descendants at the present day, but the fact is attested by skulls, skeletons, and works of art of more or less great antiquity in France, Italy, etc., ... There are few Negro peoples at the present day —perhaps only the Bushmen, the Congo-Pigmies, and a few tribes of forest Negroes—which can be said to be without more or less trace of ancient White intermixture.

Old races have been constantly broken up and new ones formed from the fragments.[11] Powerful groups have conquered smaller groups or imposed themselves as a ruling

[10] Sir Harry H. Johnston, "Racial Problems and the Congress of Races," *Contemporary Review*, Vol. 100, pp. 159-60.
[11] Ratzel, *History of Mankind*, Vol. I, p. 129.

16   *The Mulatto in the United States*

class on weaker but more numerous peoples and absorbed or been absorbed by the conquered group. No primitive group has remained long in the form peculiar to it; all were being constantly modified by the fusion with other types.[12]

Reinsch [13] shows that in modern times the intermixture of races has been greatly increased as a result of the great advance in the safety and rapidity of communication which made possible the contact in large numbers of races heretofore far distant from each other. At the present time there are no pure races in Europe [14] and few of any consequence elsewhere in the world.[15]

If the attention be turned from races to the composition of nationalities the mixture of blood is even more apparent. European nations, without exception, are a medley of imperfectly blended types.

> . . . The modern Italian, Frenchman, and German is a composite of the broken fragments of several different racial groups. Interbreeding has broken up the ancient stocks, and interaction and imitation have created new national types which exhibit definite uniformities in language, manners and formal behavior.[16]

Mayo-Smith [17] says that "There has never been a state whose population was not made up of heterogeneous ethnical

[12] Ratzel, *History of Mankind*, Vol. I, p. 395.
[13] Paul S. Reinsch, "The Negro Race and European Civilization," *American Journal of Sociology*, Vol. 11, p. 145.
[14] William Z. Ripley, *The Races of Europe*, pp. 109-10, 597 ff.
Edward Westermarck, *The History of Human Marriage*, pp. 282 f.
[15] The mixtures are, of course, generally of nearly allied races. They are rather mixtures within a single race, as the different groups of the white race or different tribes of the Negro race, than between races.
[16] R. E. Park, "Racial Assimilation in Secondary Groups," *Publications of the Sociological Society*, Vol. 8, p. 66.
[17] Richmond Mayo-Smith, "Theories of Mixture of Races and Nationalities," *Yale Review*, Vol. 3, p. 175.

elements," while Luschan would even have it that the advance of civilization is dependent upon this process of racial intermixture. He says: [18]

> We all know that a certain admixture of blood has always been of great advantage to a nation. England, France, and Germany are equally distinguished for the great variety of their racial elements. In the case of Italy we know that in ancient times and at the Renaissance Northern "Barbarians" were the leaven in the great advance of art and civilisation; and even Slavonic immigration has certainly not been without effect on this movement. The marvellous ancient civilisation of Crete, again, seems to have been not quite autochthonous. We know also that the ancient Babylonian civilisation sprang from a mixture of two quite different national and racial elements, and we find a nearly homogeneous population in most parts of Russia, and in the interior of China associated with a somewhat low stage of evolution.

Normally the intermixture of the diverse racial elements of a population, especially in a cosmopolitan situation, goes on without arousing comment or opposition. Except in a pathological situation, it does not become a social problem. Rather, it tends toward the elimination of any problem that the presence of the unassimilated alien element may have created. Any distinguishing racial marks which the parents may have borne are partly effaced in their mixed offspring. Superficially at least, the mixed-blood individuals are like all other members of the community in that they generally bear no obvious marks of their origin.

It is not, then, the mere fact of a mixed ancestry that makes the mulatto a problem in the community and an ob-

[18] Felix von Luschan, "Anthropological View of Race," *Inter-Racial Problems*, pp. 22-3.

ject of sociological interest. But when the crossing of races produces an offspring readily distinguishable from both the parent races of which it is a mixture, the situation may become the basis for class distinctions; the bi-racial ancestry of the individual may determine his status in the community.

This would seem to be true especially in those cases where there already exists a condition of racial ill-will, of jealousy or hatred between the groups in contact; where the two groups are on different cultural levels, and where the distinctive appearance of the lower [19] race gives a hold around which prejudice may crystallize.[20]

This race problem, that is, the problem of arriving at and maintaining mutually satisfactory working relations between the members of two non-assimilable groups which occupy the same territory, is primarily a matter of difference of physical appearance.[21] The color, or other racial marks, of one race may come to be a symbol of its inferior culture and so come to stand, in the thinking of the culturally superior group, for poverty, disease, dirt, ignorance, and all the undesirable concomitants of a backward race. It is this that makes it impossible for individuals to escape the status of the lower group. Any person bearing the physical marks of the lower group is assumed to embody the traits that are supposed to be typical of the lower race. The individual cannot pass in the opposite group on his merits as an indi-

---

[19] The terms "lower," "backward," etc., do not assume anything and do not prejudice anything biological or fundamental. They are purely cultural designations. A backward race is one backward in culture. "Race as such has nothing to do with the possession of civilization." Yet, "It would be silly to deny that in our time the highest civilization has been in the hands of the Caucasian, or white race." Ratzel, *History of Mankind*, Vol. I, p. 20.

[20] Mayo-Smith, *Yale Review*, Vol. 3, p. 185.

[21] Compare, T. P. Bailey, *Race Orthodoxy in the South*, pp. 40 ff.

vidual, but must pass as a member of the opposite race.

The half-castes who appear in such a situation are an easily distinguishable physical variety. This characteristic physical appearance classifies them; it separates them from both groups and makes them alien in both. It makes it impossible for them to escape the stigma which attaches itself to a tainted ancestry. The half-caste individual cannot, therefore, be a mere individual; he is inevitably the representative of a type. He is not merely a biological product; he is a sociological phenomenon.

Under such conditions, the half-castes tend to develop peculiar mental traits and attitudes which are not racial but are determined by the social situation in which they find themselves. To the extent that this takes place, the differences that normally exist between individuals are suppressed and the mental and moral characteristics of the group approach uniformity. In a word, they tend to form a distinct class or caste in the community and one based fundamentally on physical appearance.

The problem of the mulatto, then, is not something unique and local: it is the problem of the mixed-blood wherever blood has been made the basis of caste. It seems desirable, therefore, before coming to the specific and detailed study of the mulatto in the United States and as a preliminary to that study, to pass in review the chief mixed-blood races that have appeared in other countries as a result of the contact of advanced and backward races and have constituted distinct types and distinct problems in other situations. It is actually to determine to what extent they have arisen under similar social situations, or what the situations are under which they have arisen; to determine to what extent they have developed the same type of mind in different groups, or what the types of mind are if they differ; and to see what are the reactions they have made to the different social and racial environments; what accommodation they have made or caused to be made in the different social situations in which they have been placed, that a summary of the origin and development, the psychological condition and the social status of the chief of these mixed-blood races is here given. Such a survey will furnish a necessary background to an understanding of the mulatto situation in the United States. It will serve to put in proper perspective what might otherwise appear to be a detached and an isolated phenomenon.

CHAPTER II

MIXED-BLOOD RACES

In Primitive Times

AMONG primitive peoples, a mixed-blood race as a separate caste or class in the community seems nowhere to have existed. Primitive peoples, especially those near enough together geographically to come into contact with each other, did not differ very widely. The various culture stages were not markedly different and the ethnological contrasts were not generally such as distinguish one group sharply from another. Where exogamy existed, it was between related groups. Moreover, where two races were on sufficiently friendly terms for intermarriage to take place between them, there seems to be little reason to suppose that the appearance of mixed-blood offspring would cause a social problem. Strange groups were mutually exclusive groups with a state of potential warfare always existing among them. Where there was intermixture it was the blending of a conquering with a conquered group to produce a single mixed-blood group.[1]

In numberless instances, the ruling classes were of an origin different from that of their subjects. But the conquering and the conquered groups very soon became bound together by ties of interest.[2] Pride of race was but a feeble

---
[1] See Franz Oppenheimer, *The State; Its History and Development Viewed Sociologically.* Translation by J. M. Gitterman, pp. 60 ff.
[2] See F. Stuart Chapin, *Social Evolution,* pp. 201 ff.
Friedrich Ratzel, *The History of Mankind,* Vol. 2, pp. 165-66.

sentiment, if indeed, it existed at all. The prestige of the ruling class attracted the maidens of the conquered race, and the choicest of these became the auxiliary wives of the conquerors. But the mixed-bloods produced, did not form a separate caste. The primitive state nowhere possessed the cohesive strength to withstand for long the disorganizing force of a mixed-blood caste. It would lead quickly to a dissolution of the group though there seems no adequate ground for assuming that the incessant decay and reorganization of primitive tribes was anywhere due to this cause. The mixed-bloods were seldom an outstanding physical type. Their appearance in the situation tended to bind yet more intimately together the conquerors and their subjects. Their production was the first step toward a new racial homogeneity.[3]

In the ancient world, contacts seem nowhere to have resulted in the production of a mixed-blood race with a distinct social and psychological status.[4] The Phoenicians, interested above all else in material prosperity, sacrificed every national and racial trait that interfered with their commercial prosperity. Their colonies very soon lost their national character through a fusing with their ethnic environment.[5] The Greeks with a stronger sense of nationality than the Phoenicians, better maintained their national identity. Their colonists felt strongly the distinctions between themselves and the barbarians, and so kept themselves free from any large-scale miscegenation with the natives. "The

[3] In Africa there are, in general, two regions of pure Negro and two regions of Caucasian-Negro mixed-blood races. See Ratzel, *The History of Mankind*, Vol. 2, pp. 245 ff., 257. A map showing the mixed-blood races of North and East Africa is given in Vol. 2, pp. 336-37.

[4] See G. Elliot Smith, "The Influence of Racial Admixture in Egypt," *Eugenics Review*, Vol. 7, pp. 163-83.

[5] A. G. Keller, *Colonization*, p. 35.

barbarians became Greek less through contact with Greek settlements than through the dissemination of the Greek tongue and culture—they became Greek by adoption, not by the infusion of Greek blood."[6] The Romans mixed, no doubt, with their subject peoples, but there was on the part of these peoples, no very clearly defined sentiment of race diversity. The Romans were not looked upon as enemies of the race. There was no sentiment of nationality; as for the state, it simply did not exist. All was disorder and continual struggle between petty groups. There existed no very marked outstanding external differences that would serve as a basis for race separation and discrimination.[7] Keller[8] speaking of the Gauls remarks upon "the absence of wide racial diversity in these ancient times." He adds:[9]

> ". . . The superiorities of Roman ideas and systems were self-evident because the grades of civilization were not so distant one from another as to prevent easy passage from the lower to the higher. This was particularly noteworthy in respect to Gaul, but not untrue in the case of other lands."

In Spain

In Spain there has always been much intermixture of the blood of different ethnic stocks but no purely racial problem or distinctive half-caste population. The Phoenicians fused with the Iberians who were already modified by intermixture

---

[6] *Ibid.*, p. 48.
[7] ". . . The contrast between the culture represented by the modern white and that of primitive man is far more fundamental than that between the ancients and the peoples with whom they came in contact. . . ." Franz Boaz, *The Mind of Primitive Man*, p. 12.
[8] *Colonization*, p. 59.
[9] *Ibid.*, pp. 59-60.

with the Celts.[10] Following the Phoenicians, the peninsula was overrun successively by the Carthaginians, the Romans, the Visigoths, the Vandals and finally by the Arabs and the Moors.[11] In addition to these there was a large infusion of Jewish blood and, with the Moors, came some admixture of the Negroid.[12] In spite, however, of this extensive mixing of blood, there was little alteration in the original type.[13] Most of the invaders, like the original stock, were dolichocephalic, short of stature and dark of skin and hair and eyes. The stages of culture were not widely contrasted. Class distinction between noble and not-noble, between town and countryman were everywhere rigidly drawn. There was little to create a permanent racial problem and there was no emergence of a half-caste group. The persecution of the Moriscoes after the fall of the Moorish Empire was not primarily, nor even largely, racial. During the flourishing period of the Moorish Empire, the line of demarcation between the races was but faintly drawn.[14] "Openly, at least, they did not consider each other as enemies."[15] Intermarriages were frequent especially those of Spanish women [16] with the men of the dominant group. Intermarriage was, however, contrary to the policy of Islam and such alliances

[10] Appleton's *Encyclopedia:* Spain.
[11] *New International Encyclopaedia:* Spain.
[12] Sir Harry H. Johnston, "The World-Position of the Negro and Negroid," *Inter-Racial Problems*, p. 330. The Moors of course are members of the white race though much mixed. They have "more Arab than Berber blood." *Encyclopaedia Britannica:* Moors.
[13] *New International Encyclopaedia:* Spain.
[14] S. P. Scott, *History of the Moorish Empire in Europe*, Vol. 3, p. 197.
[15] *Ibid.,* Vol. 3, p. 197.
[16] ". . . The harems of the Moslems were filled with Christian maidens who had, without hesitancy or compensation, renounced the faith of their fathers." *Ibid.,* Vol. 3, p. 200.

were discouraged [17] although no stigma attached to either party of such union. It was, however, this attitude on the part of the Arabs that was chiefly responsible in preventing a complete amalgamation of the races. With the decline of the Moorish Empire and more especially with the rise of the Castilian power in Spain, an antipathy grew up between the races. The latent or repressed feeling gradually grew into an open hostility. The prejudice was sedulously nourished until the Spanish came to consider the Moors as their hereditary [18] and implacable enemy. They asserted the superiority of their race and considered their enemies as barbarians in spite of the wide and obvious superiority of the latter in knowledge and culture. The smallest drop of Moorish blood became a taint that nothing could remove.[19] But behind this hostile attitude, was the Church and the impoverished condition of the national treasury. In the sixteenth century, Spain subordinated everything to the Church; [20] she sacrificed everything to the idea of religious unity. Moreover, the Moriscoes were industrious and frugal; they were prosperous and wealthy. The Castilian subsisted by rapine. The wealth of the Moriscoes attracted the cupidity of the authorities.[21] Like the Jews of a previous period, their wealth brought upon them the suspicion of heresy.[22] The institution of the Inquisition was put into operation against the inoffensive and prosperous class,[23]

[17] *Ibid.*, Vol. 3, p. 212.
[18] *Ibid.*, Vol. 3, p. 199.
[19] "A taint of Moorish blood was sufficient to prevent the holding of any public office, even in the smallest municipality." Chambers' *Encyclopaedia:* Spain. See, also, Scott, *History of the Moorish Empire*, Vol. 3, p. 224.
[20] *Ibid.*, Vol. 3, p. 304.
[21] *Ibid.*, Vol. 3, p. 245.
[22] *Ibid.*, Vol. 3, p. 226.
[23] *Ibid.*, Vol. 3, p. 260.

and the persecution ended only with their final expulsion. The persecution, however, was a religious festival; it was only incidentally racial.

The Eurasians

The mixture of races is by no means a modern phenomenon, but it is only within recent centuries that the half-breed appears as a psychological type and as a social problem. Keller, placing the emphasis on the more tolerant attitude of the culture races and the absence of wide cultural or ethnical differences of the races in contact, summarizes the situation as follows: [24]

> For similar reasons the "native policy" of ancient times was constructed to subserve the purposes of exchange, or was directed simply toward the maintenance of such subordination and order as a wider administrative experience had proved to be socially beneficial, if not indispensable. There was no idea of "culture-mission" or the like, and consequently no dogma, . . . of "assimilation." No moral or religious crusades were carried on through the colonies; diversity of customs and morals was regarded as natural and a matter of course,—though both customs and religions were nationally less differentiated than they have come to be in the eyes of later ages. The predominant commercial motive, and the imperial policy as well, counseled respect for the social forms of an alien people; . . . between the races that were brought into contact, especially around the borders of the Mediterranean, there existed few contrasts of any significance. The like was true in the case of the Chinese and their ethnic environment. There was no obvious ethnological differences such as distinguish one race sharply from another, and the various stages of culture were separated

[24] *Colonization*, pp. 76-77.

by no impassable or discouraging chasms. . . . Even slavery was an institution totally different from that with which later ages have made us familiar: there was no "color-line"; the system was one of "domestic slavery" in the main; and the passage from freedom to servitude was easy. . . . Hence that eternally vexatious and unsolved question of the treatment of a "lower race" was but faintly represented. . . . [With these colonies] instead of native wars and annihilation, an auspicious large-scale miscegenation, mainly of closely allied races, took place, . . . no such barriers to intermarriage existed as appeared in later times, when racial distinctions were more marked. . . .

It was the mass meeting of the cultured and primitive peoples, brought about as a result of the period of the discoveries, that gave rise to the mixed-blood races with a status different in some respects from that of either of the parent races; and so gave rise, in some cases at least, to special social and racial problems.

Chief among these mixed-blood races are the "Eurasians," a mixture of Hindu and European living in the port cities of India; the mixed-blood race of Eskimo-Dane living off the West Coast of Greenland; the so-called "coloured peoples" of South Africa, a mixed-blood race of complicated ancestry; the *metis* of Brazil, a mixture of Portuguese with Amerindian and Negro; the *mestizo*, a mixture with varying proportions of Spanish and Indian blood found in most parts of South and Central America; the Spanish mulatto in Cuba and Porto Rico; the "coloured people" and "whites by law" in Jamaica; the Spanish *mestizo* and the Chinese *mestizo* in the Philippines; and the mulatto in the United States. In lesser numbers, are the English-Eskimo mixtures on the Newfoundland Coast; the European and Oriental mixtures in the port cities of China and Japan; half-caste Arabs in East Central Africa; various mixtures of Indian-White, Indian-Negro and Indian-Negro-White in the United States; French-Indian mixtures in Canada; and a great variety of other mixtures in various regions but in lesser numbers or forming less acute problems.

The Eurasians or Indo-Europeans are a people of mixed European and Asiatic blood born and raised in Asia. This population had its origin in the miscegenation of Hindu women with the early Portuguese traders and resident Portuguese. There was never any considerable immigration of Portuguese women into India and illicit relations with the native women were common.[25] The Portuguese, accustomed to such mixed unions in their home country, had no racial repugnance to overcome.[26] The policy was fostered by the Portuguese governors; Albuquerque himself was the father of a mulatto son.[27] But the effort to build up a half-caste group was only partially successful. The mongrel type, in the absence of a regular infusion of Portuguese blood, failed to hold its own. It has now pretty thoroughly reverted to the native type.[28] Perhaps a half million of the population show traces of this early hybridization, but they are distinguishable from the natives mainly by virtue of a distinctive dress.[29]

With the coming of the English into India, there was a new intermixture of European and Indian blood. Concubin-

[25] Keller, *Colonization*, p. 122.

[26] *Ibid.*, p. 104.

[27] *Ibid.*, p. 122.

[28] ". . . The Portuguese have left behind a monument of their Indian dominion in a very numerous race of half-breeds, . . . They enter largely into domestic service and in Bombay all the best cooks and waiters are of Portuguese extraction. Nor will you find, in the whole of India, any better servants than these, . . ." Herbert Compton, *Indian Life in Town and Country*, pp. 208-10.

[29] Élisée Reclus, *Asia*, Vol. 3, pp. 389-90.

Mixed-Blood Races 29

age with the native women was the usual and manly thing.[30] The new body of half-breeds number in all somewhat over one hundred thousand and are confined almost exclusively to the large port cities where the foreign trade of India is largely concentrated.[31] It is, for the most part, these English Hindu hybrids alone who are responsible for the so-called Eurasian question.

Physically the Eurasians are slight and weak.[32] Their personal appearance is subject to the greatest variations. In skin color, for example, they are often darker even than the Asiatic parent.[33] They are naturally indolent and will enter into no employment requiring exertion or labor. This lack of energy is correlated with an incapacity for organization.[34] They will not assume burdensome responsibilities, but they make passable clerks where only routine labor is required.

The native woman is inordinately proud of her half-caste offspring. In infancy he is nursed, and in youth pampered by his native servants upon whom he is dependent. "As a consequence, all the stronger traits of manhood are feebly

---

[30] Recently the anti-nautch movement has resulted in forcing this relationship into the dark. "Concubinage, which was esteemed as rather a manly fashion twenty years ago, has largely disappeared among the more enlightened classes; and even among the less enlightened it is regarded as a thing rather to be ashamed than to be proud of." "The Indian Social Reformer." Quoted by J. P. Jones, "Conditions in India," *Journal of Race Development*, Vol. 2, p. 201.

[31] Madras 26,000; Bengal 20,000; Burma, Bombay and the United Provinces 8,000 to 11,000; total 100,451. This is an increase of 15 per cent since 1901. The increase seems partly due to "the growing tendency amongst certain classes of Indian Christians to pass themselves off as Anglo-Indians." Census of India 1911, Vol. 1, Part 1, p. 140.

[32] Mary Helen Lee, *The Eurasian: A Social Problem*, p. 13. See, also, Ellsworth Huntington, "Geographical Environment and Japanese Character," *Journal of Race Development*, Vol. 2, pp. 158-59.

[33] Compton, *Indian Life*, p. 208.

[34] Lee, *The Eurasian*, pp. 11, 13.

developed in him."[35] In manhood he is wily, untrustworthy [36] and untruthful.[37] He is lacking in independence and is forever begging for special favors. Yet supersensitiveness is a characteristic of the whole Eurasian community. They recklessly "resign from any and every post when, for some reason or without reason, their feelings are hurt."[38] The girls, in some cases at least, are sold into prostitution.[39] The men are employed for the most part by the government in subordinate clerical positions.

Socially the Eurasians are outcaste. They are despised by the ruling whites and hated by the natives.[40] In the words of one of their class: "To the European we are half-caste, among ourselves we are no caste, and to the Indians we are outcaste."[41] They are extremely sensitive on the point of color.[42] They object to the term *nigger;* it is even necessary to avoid the term Eurasian in their presence.[43]

---

[35] Lee, *The Eurasian,* pp. 12, 17. See, also, Ethel Hunter, *The Y.W.C.A. in India, Burma and Ceylon,* 1911.

[36] "Industrially a Christian native is preferred to an Eurasian, for he is more trustworthy." Lee, *The Eurasian,* p. 10.

[37] Reclus, *Asia,* Vol. 3, pp. 389-90.

[38] "They frequently appeal to ministers especially and to all charitably disposed people. Lord Curzon . . . gave their memorials special attention, and as a result delivered a reply of the most searching kind and urged the people of the community to carve out something worthy themselves, instead of being continually memorializing for special favors; and refused to aid in the special class regulations. The delegates retired, 'thanking His Excellency for his sarcastic remarks.'" J. Smith, *Ten Years in Burma,* p. 117.

[39] See J. S. Dennis, *Christian Missions and Social Progress,* Vol. 2, p. 273.

[40] Reclus, *Asia,* Vol. 3, pp. 389-90.

[41] Quoted by Lee, *The Eurasian,* p. 10.

[42] "Especially if very dark the Eurasian is overmuch pained that he has not a white skin." *Ibid.,* p. 13.

[43] Catering to this idiosyncrasy the British government has changed their official designation to "Indo-Europeans."

They wish to be called Europeans.[44]

They have no part in the racial situation. They aspire to be English, but they do nothing to consolidate British rule, as neither the Indian nor the white man considers them as Englishmen. They have equally little standing with the Indian. They stand between two civilizations but are a part of neither. They are miserable, helpless, despised and neglected.

The Eskimos

In Greenland, the half-breed Eskimos date their origin from the establishment of the Danish missionary settlements on the West Coast in 1721. The European interest always has been trade and missions. The number of Scandinavians has at no time been large, and the colony is composed almost exclusively of men. In the early days, it was used as a penal colony, and from time to time, there was a compulsory immigration of orphan boys to recruit the teaching force and the inferior clergy. The present white population is about two hundred and never has exceeded that number very greatly. At first there were no white women in the colony; even now the number is very small. The relations between the races always have been friendly in spite of the missionary interference with the native customs, and in spite of the feeling of superiority of the Europeans over the natives.

Miscegenation went on from the first and so extensively that the native Eskimo is practically extinct in the territory

---

[44] ". . . Some special enquiries made in certain towns . . . showed three-tenths of the persons returned as Europeans were in reality Anglo-Indians." "The number of Eurasians who returned themselves as Europeans is perhaps somewhat less than at former censuses owing to the use of the term 'Anglo-Indian.' . . ." Census of India 1911, Vol. 1, Part 1, pp. 139, 140.

under the influence of European civilization. A hundred years after the settlement, the half-breeds composed fourteen per cent of the population. In 1885 the proportion had increased to thirty per cent. At present the intermixture has gone so far that the various mixed types are no longer distinguishable but blend into one another in almost imperceptible degrees from the pure Dane, on the one extreme, to the pure Eskimo, on the other. This intermixture, for the most part, has been extra-matrimonial, though there have been some unions of a semi-regular sort. The stupid interference of the missionaries with the fundamental native customs brought about a disorganization of the native habits which, in the presence of their severe climate, proved destructive to the native population. In the presence of a declining pure-blood population, the Danish government has favored the policy of intermixture and requires the Danish official on his return to Denmark on pension to leave his native wife and children in the colony.[45]

In comparison with the native Eskimo the mixed-bloods are in reality superior men.[46] They are an improvement, especially in physical appearance, over the native stock.[47] Socially the status of the mixed-blood man is superior to that of the native, but the social distinctions are not so much dependent upon the presence or absence of white intermixture as they are upon the amount of that intermixture. "The native women prefer the worst Dane to the best Greenlander, and the half-breeds are the more eligible for their

[45] At present there are from thirty to forty Danes so married to native women. *Encyclopaedia Britannica:* Greenland.

[46] *Handbook of the American Indians,* Bureau of American Ethnology, Bull. 30, Part 1, p. 913.

[47] Keller, however, says: "The mongrels resulting from these mixed unions appear to form no very great improvement on the native stock." *Colonization,* p. 515.

strain of white blood; illicit relations with white men are rather a glory than a disgrace."[48] The young native woman, says Nansen, "positively glories" in illicit relations with white men and gains a considerable prestige among her female friends as a result of having been so honored.[49]

In Spanish America

From the first coming of the Portuguese to Brazil, there was a wholesale miscegenation with the Indian women. The *mestizo* group soon became a numerically important element in the population. Later, there were introduced large numbers of black slaves from the West Coast of Africa. Unions between the Portuguese and the black women began with the first introduction of the Negroes. As a result, the mulattoes presently appeared as a second mixed-blood race in the population. Moreover, the Negroes mixed readily with the Indians, giving rise to a race of Negro-Indian hybrids—the *zambos*. There were thus six distinct racial groups in the population each with a clearly defined status. Crosses between these various hybrids and between the hybrids and the pure races took place with even more readiness than between the pure stocks. The mixed-blood groups gradually blended into one another to form a single mixed-blood race, the relative ethnic composition of which is entirely indeterminable.

It was this triangular mixture in unknown proportions of the blood of Portuguese, Indian, and Negro that produced the so-called *metis*,[50] who compose somewhat above one-third

---

[48] *Ibid.*, p. 515.

[49] F. Nansen, *Eskimo Life*, pp. 12, 20, 163-5. See, also, A. N. Gilbertson, *Some Ethical Phases of Eskimo Culture*, p. 73. He quotes Trebitsch as expressing an opposite opinion.

[50] The *metis* differ from the *mestizos* of other parts of South America

of the present population of Brazil.⁵¹ Of the fifteen million whites, a considerable number are so by law rather than because of an entire absence of Indian or Negro blood.⁵²

Biologically the *metis* are an unstable type.⁵³ Their physical traits vary with each new crossing sometimes toward one and sometimes toward the other parent though there is a general tendency toward the white type.⁵⁴ They are not muscular, and have little power to resist disease.

Tuberculosis is common among them.⁵⁵ Some of the women are graceful and well proportioned, but they are

principally in that there is a considerable amount of Negro blood in their ethnic composition. It would seem to be an error, however, to say that this term is a synonym for mulatto. See W. E. B. DuBois, *The Negro*, p. 166.

⁵¹ P. F. Martin, *Through Five Republics of South America*, p. 155 gives the population as follows:

15,000,000	total
3,500,000	Negroes
6,000,000	mixed
1,300,000	Indians
900,000	Portuguese
520,000	Germans
1,800,000	Italians

James Bryce, *South America; Observations and Impressions*, pp. 433-34, 564-65, estimates the Negro and Negro mixture to be about 8,000,000 or two-fifths of the total population. The number of *zambos* he puts at 300,000.

⁵² Martin, *Through Five Republics*, p. 155. Bryce, *South America*, pp. 564-65.

⁵³ "Their physical characteristics are not fixed." Jean Baptiste de Lacerda, "The *Metis*, or Half-breeds, of Brazil," *Inter-Racial Problems*, p. 378.

⁵⁴ "Continuous infusions of Portuguese blood, due to an immigration . . . have gradually overcome the native strain of what was a largely mongrel population, and a fortunate reversion toward the more developed ethnic component, with its happier adaptation to modern conditions, has ensued." Keller, *Colonization*, p. 164.

⁵⁵ Lacerda, *Inter-Racial Problems*, p. 380.

in no sense a beautiful people. In color they vary from a dark yellow to a dull white. Their hair is usually dark and nearly always curly. Their eyes are chestnut, brown, or greenish. Their lips are thick. Their teeth are irregular, though less protruding than the Negroes'. On the whole they seem to be an improvement upon both the Negro and the Indian elements of their ancestry,[56] though the evidence on this point is by no means uniform.[57] As agricultural laborers, they are inferior to the blacks and they show no capacity for commercial or industrial life.[58] Lacerda[59] asserts that they are ostentatious, unpractical, talkative, intemperate, and lacking in veracity and loyalty but admits that they are intelligent, have some literary ability and show great cleverness as politicians.

In Brazil the *metis* form a sort of middle-class between the white aristocracy, on the one hand, and the Negro and the Indian, on the other. The Indians are passive and, so far as political affairs are concerned, are outside the nation. The black Negroes are inferior in education[60] and enter-

---

[56] ". . . if these half-breeds are not able to compete in other qualities with the stronger races of the Aryan stock, . . . it is none the less certain that we cannot place the *metis* at the level of the really inferior races. They are physically and intellectually well above the level of the blacks, who were an ethnical element in their production." *Ibid.*, p. 381.

[57] "In Brazil . . . his [the Indian's] successor is a decidedly inferior being. . . ." Martin, *Through Five Republics*, p. 1.

[58] Lacerda, *Inter-Racial Problems*, p. 380.

[59] *Ibid.*, p. 380. Compare the Chileans. E. A. Ross, *South of Panama*, pp. 113, 213-14, 219, 221.

[60] Eighty per cent of the total population is illiterate. The ratio among the blacks is far higher. See Martin, *Through Five Republics*, p. 155. Of recent attempts to provide education adapted to the needs of the situation, see H. E. Everly, "Vocational Education in Brazil," *Manual Training Magazine*, June, 1915.

prise to the Negro of the Southern States of America.[61] They take life very easy, exerting themselves just sufficiently to provide the few necessities of life in a tropical climate.[62] The whites are the ruling class,[63] though for political and social purposes, the upper grade of the *metis* and the whites are practically one class.

At the founding of the republic, the numerical preponderance of the mixed-blood race enabled them to secure an equal share in the governmental affairs of the country. Many of them secured political offices, and they exert a considerable influence on the government of the country.[64] Many of the mixed-blood race are men of property [65] and are influential in the affairs of the community.

In social affairs, the color line between the whites and the mixed-blood race is neither hard nor fast.[66] Many of the so-called whites are tinged with Negro or Indian blood.[67] Intermarriage is forbidden neither by law nor by custom, and mixed unions are not uncommon. To the Portuguese, the idea of personal contact with an Indian or a Negro excites little feeling of physical repulsion. The aristocracy here, as elsewhere in South America, are pure white; and marriages between them and the pure Indians or Negroes do

[61] Bryce, *South America*, pp. 479-80.
[62] *Ibid.*, pp. 404-05.
[63] *Ibid.*, p. 565.
[64] Lacerda, *Inter-Racial Problems*, pp. 381-82.
[65] Not so many as is sometimes asserted. "Bahia . . . has a population of 250,000 and is rapidly growing. Most of the population are real Negroes. . . . The city is so prosperous that there are 10,000 Negroes who are millionaires. . . ." The *Chicago Defender*, A Negro Paper, 1-15-1916.
[66] It seems to be the observation of this fact that has led certain superficial observers to announce an entire absence of color prejudice in Brazil. See The *Chicago Defender*, 12-11-1915, 1-22-1916.
[67] Bryce, *South America*, p. 565.

not occur.[68] "The Brazilian lower class intermarries freely with the black people; the Brazilian middle class [69] intermarries with the mulattoes and the quadroons."[70]

The color line—so far as there is a color line—is drawn with the Negro and the Indian on the one side and the white man and the *metis* on the other.[71] The mixed-blood man is as contemptuous of the native and the Negro, as is the white man.[72] The aspiration of the half-breed is to be like the white man.[73] He calls himself white, consciously models himself on the white man, tries to think and act as a white man and, if possessed of education and property, is so treated.[74] He is free to intermarry with the whites and his ambition is to do so. With each such crossing, the offspring approximate more and more to the pure white type. Aside from reversions, they are sometimes able to pass as white in their Portuguese community by the third generation. Lacerda [75] sums up the racial situation in these words:

> The mulatto himself endeavours, by marriage, to bring back his descendants to the pure white type.

[68] See Theodore Roosevelt, "Brazil and the Negro," *Outlook*, Vol. 106, pp. 409-11.

[69] Largely mixed. Officially white. See Bryce, *South America*, p. 492; *South American Year Book*, 1915, p. 216.

[70] Bryce, *South America*, pp. 479-80. Bryce counts as white all individuals having three-fourths or more white blood.

[71] In southern Brazil in the expanding German, Swiss and white Portuguese settlements the color line is drawn separating the whites from the colored and the mixed. See Sir Harry H. Johnston, *The Negro in the New World*. See, also, D. P. Kidder and J. C. Fletcher, *Brazil and the Brazilians*, pp. 132-33.

[72] Bryce, *South America*, p. 565.

[73] Lacerda, *Inter-Racial Problems*, p. 382. Bryce, *South America*, pp. 460-67.

[74] The same thing is theoretically true of the Indian and the Negro. See Roosevelt, The *Outlook*, Vol. 106, pp. 409-11.

[75] *Inter-Racial Problems*, p. 382.

Children of *metis* have been found, in the third generation, to present all the physical characters of the white race, although some of them retain a few traces of their black ancestry through the influence of atavism. The influence of sexual selection, however, tends to neutralise that of atavism, and removes from the descendants of the *metis* all the characteristic features of the black race. In virtue of this process of ethnic reduction, it is logical to expect that in the course of another century the *metis* will have disappeared from Brazil. This will coincide with the parallel extinction of the black race in our midst. When slavery was abolished, the black, left to himself, began to abandon the centres of civilisation. Exposed to all kinds of destructive agencies, and without sufficient resources to maintain themselves, the negroes are scattered over the thinly populated districts, and tend to disappear from our territory.

Aside from Brazil, most of Central and South America was colonized by the Spanish. The early immigration was of a poor quality, being composed chiefly of clergy and of adventurers who came with an intention of acquiring a competence if possible and then returning to Spain. Another large group of immigrants were convicts, sentenced to death or mutilation, whose sentences were commuted on condition that they emigrate to the colonies. The objects of the early colonists were adventure and trade rather than settlement.[76] Consequently there were few women of good character though, unlike the Portuguese, the Spanish government never foisted their objectionable women upon the colonists. There was, therefore, a dearth of Spanish women either married or marriageable.

The Spanish interest was centered in the mines and for

[76] See James Bryce, "Migrations of the Races of Men," *Contemporary Review*, Vol. 62, p. 134.

three centuries the plantations and agriculture in general was a failure in Spanish America.[77] The healthful and wealth-producing regions of the tropics were the interior highlands, and it was there alone that a considerable population grew up. But even there, it was made up mostly of useless individuals, adventurers, and functionaries but not of workers, as is shown by the fact that it was almost exclusively a town population.

The Indians and the Spanish were not so temperamentally constituted as to be able to come to any mutually satisfactory working relations. They never reached anything remotely approaching kindly feeling and unity of purpose. The Indians were not adapted to slavery; the Spanish had an exaggerated idea of their own superiority. The situation worked itself out on the single and simple principle of relative power.[78] The attitude of the Spanish was ruthless and savage. They seized the public and private wealth of the natives, appropriated their women, and finally levied upon their vital force. To develop the mines, they needed a large labor supply; to get the labor supply, they drove the natives in crowds to the mountains, where the unwonted labor and the scanty nourishment combined with the effects of the climatic change and the broken family life, to bring about a rapid decline in the population.[79] To supply the place of the decreasing native labor, African slaves were introduced and grew rapidly in numbers.[80]

Intermixture with the natives began with the first landing of the Spanish explorers on American soil.[81] and so exten-

[77] Keller, *Colonization*, p. 223.
[78] *Ibid.*, p. 259.
[79] *Ibid.*, pp. 256 ff.
[80] *Ibid.*, pp. 280-82.
[81] Syphilis, which spread like a plague over the whole of Europe during the sixteenth century, dates its origin as a disease of civilized man from

sive was this mixture of races that it has been characterized as the "prime phenomenon in the contact of races in Spanish America."[82] After the introduction of the Negro, there grew up several new varieties of half-breeds and each of the races and half-races came to have a more or less clearly and definitely defined status in the community life.

The main constituents, taken as ethnic and social types, were six in number.[83] The Peninsular Spaniards, those from Europe, were of course the aristocracy; next in order came the white creoles, descendants of Europeans settled in America; a third class was the *mestizos*, mongrels resulting from the association of Europeans with the native women; a little later in time and lower in status, came the mulattoes; next in the social rank came the Negroes, and last of all, the natives.

Between these main groups were many other mixtures approximating one or the other of the main groups, or forming separate groups apart. The *mestizos* multiplied with such rapidity that they came to form and still form a very considerable portion of the population of Spanish America.

The association of these various ethnic groups was marked by hatred, bitterness and strife.[84] The Spanish officials held

the return of the first Columbian expedition from America. It was the red man's one contribution to civilization. See Iwan Bloch, *The Sexual Life of Our Time,* M. Eden Paul's Translation, pp. 351-56.

[82] Keller, *Colonization,* p. 295.

[83] Perhaps seven or even more. See H. C. Morris, *The History of Colonization,* Vol. 1, pp. 252-53.

[84] "The different shades were classified with minute attention, not only by the force of custom but also by the law. When there was only a sixth of negro or Indian blood in the veins of a colonist, the law granted him the title of white: *que se tenga por blanco.* Each caste was full of envy for those above and of contempt for those below." Leroy-Beaulieu, i, II; cf. Roscher, *The Spanish Colonial System,* pp. 149-50. Keller, *Colonization,* p. 220, f. n.

in contempt the creoles and, especially, the *mestizos* who formed the industrial elements of the Colonies. The mixed-blood races felt superior to the native and the Negro stock from which they had sprung.[85] The Negroes had an implacable hatred for the natives and, secure in their greater physical strength and the approval of their masters, mistreated the natives at every opportunity. The natives in their pitiable condition hated all their oppressors in varying degrees.

Time and further mixed breeding reduced the various mongrel types to a relative uniformity in physical appearance and mental characteristics. Immigration being restricted for a long time, the number of incoming Spaniards was small and this, together with the scarcity of Spanish women, kept the natural increase of the white race very limited. Consequently the native element was the determining factor in the biological situation. The very fact of relative numbers made it inevitable that the mixed-blood race should tend toward the Indian type. The caste feeling was not sufficient to preserve them from this fate and, in spite of a larger later immigration from Europe, the reversion has partly taken place.[86]

[85] "The aversion between mulattoes and negroes was as great as that between whites and negroes. The civil position of each class depended mainly and naturally upon the greater or less whiteness of their complexion. 'Todo blanco es caballero.'" Roscher, *The Spanish Colonial System*, p. 21. Keller, *Colonization*, p. 220 f. n.

[86] Earl Finch states that it is the American Indian who declines in the process of miscegenation of the Negroes, Spanish, Portuguese and Indians. See "The Effects of Racial Miscegenation," *Inter-Racial Problems*, p. 109. This is true in the sense that the introduction of foreign blood into a population tends to diffuse in a culturally downward direction, and the lower strata of the population tend to become contaminated by traces of it. But the decline in numbers of a pure-blood native race is due to disease and the failure or inability of the primitive folk to accommodate themselves to civilized habits and manners of life. In an

42   *The Mulatto in the United States*

Such is the racial background for the latter day situation in the various Spanish-American Republics.

There are no general censuses of the Spanish-American countries, and consequently no accurate numerical knowledge of the various racial groups in the different republics. Bryce estimates the total population at 45,000,000, of whom approximately one-fifth are pure Indians, one-third *mestizos*, one-third white with much Indian blood and the remainder Negroes, mulattoes and *zambos*.[87] Of the 15,000,000 whites, more than half are in the Republics of Argentine and Uruguay, which republics contain no native or Negro elements,[88] and in the southern part of Brazil which is also free from the colored races. The Negroes and their various intermixtures with the white and Indian races are chiefly in northern and eastern Brazil, though there are a goodly number in Guinea and some in Venezuela.[89] In insignificant numbers, they are found in the cities of the other South American countries. The population of Paraguay is nearly all Indian: the white and mixed elements are so small as to be negligible. Colombia is approximately fifty per cent so-called white. The

[87] inter-racial situation in which there is intermarriage between the races the result is determined exclusively by the relative members of the two groups. In a caste situation, Finch is right: there the lower groups receive a continual admixture of blood from the castes above them while the superior caste receives no blood from the inferior groups.

Whites	15,000,000	Whites	15,000,000
Indians	8,000,000	Indians	8,000,000
Negroes	3,000,000	Negroes	3,000,000
Mestizos	13,000,000	Mixed	19,000,000
Mulattoes	5,700,000		
Zambos	300,000		

South America, pp. 564-65.

[88] There is a substratum of Indian *mestizos* in North Argentine but no country in the western hemisphere with the single exception of Canada is so nearly racially white. See E. A. Ross, *South of Panama*, pp. 119-20.

[89] White 10 per cent; *mestizo* 70 per cent; Indian and Negro 20 per cent. *South American Year Book*, 1915, p. 742.

actual whites form a much smaller per cent.[90] Equador is approximately ten per cent white.[91] Peru has ten per cent or less of white and near-white, thirty-five per cent mixed, and fifty-five per cent Indian.[92] Bolivia has a somewhat larger percentage of pure Indian stock.[93] Chile has a small white aristocracy and a very few Indians; the population is nearly all mixed though they claim to be white and the tendency is to so classify them.[94] The Central American states are about fifteen per cent white or what passes for white in the Spanish-American states.[95] The Mexican census of 1900 returned nineteen per cent of the total population as "white or nearly white," forty-three per cent as Indian and white intermixture and thirty-eight per cent as Indian out of a total population of 13,607,259.[96]

[90] *Ibid.*, 1915, p. 503.

[91] *Ibid.*, p. 562.

[92] *Ibid.*, p. 638. The Lima Geographical Society, 1896, estimated the population of Peru as white 20 per cent, Indian 57 per cent and mixed 23 per cent. Quoted by P. F. Martin, *Peru of the Twentieth Century*, p. 42. Bryce estimates that the pure whites of Peru do not number as much as 5 per cent. See *South America*, p. 66. Ross, *South of Panama*, pp. 39-40, 260, gives the population as 2,000,000 Indians, 1,500,000 *mestizos* and 500,000 white or near-white.

[93] Bryce gives the population of Peru and Bolivia as follows:

6,000,000	total
3,500,000	Indian
1,500,000	*mestizo*
1,000,000	Spaniards, more or less pure.

South America, pp. 458-59.

[94] *Ibid.*, p. 232.

[95] Martin, *Through Five Republics*, p. 237. N. O. Winter, *Guatemala and Her People of To-day*, p. 109.

[96] Bryce is disposed to materially modify these proportions. He gives:

Total	15,000,000
Indian	8,000,000
Mixed	6,000,000
Spaniards	1,000,000

South America, p. 459.

44   *The Mulatto in the United States*

These numbers are at best only a rough approximation. There are no data available which justify any close estimation either of the total population or of the various racial elements of which it is composed. Moreover, it is not possible to make any accurate distribution of the population into racial categories because color is a badge of inferiority and is always denied or if too obvious to be denied, the amount is understated. Further there is no agreement as to what proportion of Negro or Indian blood must be present to rule an individual out of the white class to which every one strives to belong. Bryce, for example, in his estimates counts as "white" all whose racial ancestry is as much as three-fourths white.[97] The tendency of the official statistics is to count as white all educated *mestizos*.[98]

Despite the fact that they constitute but a small percentage of the total population in most of the Spanish-American republics, the whites are in all cases the ruling class.[99] They form the social aristocracy, they practically control the political and governmental situation,[100] and they comprise the educated class so far as such a class exists.[101]

The census of 1910 gave a total population of 15,160,369 distributed as follows:

    15,160,369   total
    15,043,842   Mexican birth
        116,527   foreign birth of whom 29,541 were Spanish

[97] Bryce, *South America*, p. 565.
[98] *Ibid.*, p. 460.
[99] Bolivia, for example. "Politics is left to the few whites and Mestizos in four or five towns. Politically the Bolivian nation shrinks from two million to some thousands." *Ibid.*, p. 529. See, also, Ross, *South of Panama*, pp. 331 ff.
[100] *South American Year Book*, 1914, pp. 561-62.
[101] *Ibid.*, p. 508.

Speaking in particular of the women: "So far as the northern republics of dusky and mixed races are concerned, one can only deal with the few white women of each republic, since all the rest may, for the pur-

Mixed-Blood Races

In the southern and more progressive republics, the white element has been reinforced continuously by a considerable immigration from western Europe. This is especially true of Argentine and Uruguay and to a somewhat lesser extent of Chile and of south and central Brazil,[102] where the whites are numerically the dominant group. In the northern republics, however, it is only a small white aristocracy that is comparable with the general population of Argentine and the other white states of the south.[103] As a consequence, the whites have been able to maintain a republican form of government in the southern republics; in the north, it is only by compromising with the mixed elements that they have been able to maintain any government at all.[104]

Everywhere throughout Spanish America, the Indians form the lowest strata of the population and but seldom rise out of their degraded position.[105] In the remoter central regions and in the mountains, the race is still relatively

---

poses of generalization, really and truly be placed in one category—that of the completely unintellectual." W. H. Koebel, *The South Americans*, p. 31. See, also, pp. 13, 16.

[102] Argentine, for example, has received an immigration in excess of four million during the past fifty years. *Ibid.*, p. 17. There is much Germanic blood in the upper classes of Chile and this fact is said to be reflected in the political life. Ross, *South of Panama*, pp. 109, 110.

[103] "To the North of these countries [Argentine, Chile, Uruguay, South Brazil and Central Brazil] . . . we get for the most part territories where a small white and educated aristocracy governs of necessity the population of Indians, Mestizos, or even Negroes; and thus we enter into a new and different phase which does not permit of comparison with European circumstances." Koebel, *The South Americans*, p. 13.

[104] Venezuela, for example, with her 10 per cent of white and near-white and her 90 per cent of Negroes, Indians and *mestizos* has never in her whole history had a president who attained office through a legally conducted election. *South American Year Book*, 1915, p. 742.

[105] Bryce, *South America*, pp. 478-79. He is speaking here of the northern republics.

unmixed. There are no European settlers and even the infiltration of Negro blood has been small.[106] The Negro, aside from Brazil and the northern tropic regions, has not persisted.[107] The Indians in general perform all the lower forms of work and come but little into contact with the white people, except in the capacity of servants and employees. They are in general wholly illiterate,[108] and socially and otherwise form a group apart—within the nation but not of it. "By the constitution they are, in many states, citizens and have votes. But they never think of voting, having, although free, no more to do with the government than the slaves had in the Southern United States before the Civil War." [109]

Between the small white upper class and the illiterate and largely uncivilized natives, stands the *mestizo* who is, taking Spanish America as a whole, the numerically dominant group. While the status of the *mestizos* varies within rather wide limits in different states and even within the same state, they form, in general, a sort of middle class in the population. Exception must here be made of the white Republics of Argentine and Uruguay, the native Republic of Paraguay and of Brazil, the southern parts of which are white, and the northern parts largely Negro and mulatto.[110] The upper class *mestizos* are in many cases small property owners and compose most of the small shop-keeping class; from the

[106] ". . . the distinctions which undoubtedly exist, and are often supposed to be of race, are in fact only between Indians who are Catholic and speak Spanish and Indians, who are grouped by the other Indians, 'as savages' . . ." Sir Charles W. Dilke, "Forced and Indentured Labor in South America," *Nationalities and Subject Races,* p. 101.

[107] Koebel, *The South Americans,* p. 92.

[108] The same might be said of most of the mixed and a good per cent of the white population. Eighty per cent of South America is illiterate.

[109] Bryce, *South America,* p. 529. Ross, *South of Panama,* p. 331.

[110] *Ibid.,* p. 492.

Mixed-Blood Races 47

lower grades of the *mestizo* come the artisan and the servant classes.[111]

But the ethnological distinctions seldom are clearly drawn. A certain per cent of the white race have preserved their racial integrity intact[112] and these everywhere form the social and intellectual aristocracy. But the bulk of the so-called whites are tinged with a greater or less amount of Indian blood.[113] The upper class *mestizos*, in manners and customs and habits of life, often compare not unfavorably with their white neighbors. They are, to the extent of their ability, Spaniards. In education, they are Spanish; in religion, they are Christians; and in their ideas and habits of thinking, they are faithful imitations of the white aristocracy.[114]

Between the white man and the educated *mestizo* there is no color line in the sense in which that term is understood in the United States. For social and political purposes they form virtually one class. All *mestizos*, and increasingly so as their color decreases and their education increases, claim to be white men, and in general they are so treated.[115] It is, in fact, by compromising thus with the mixed element that the white has been able to maintain some semblance of orderly government in many of the Latin American republics. But the *mestizos* are not all educated, and by no means all

[111] *South American Year Book,* 1915, p. 503.
[112] *Ibid.,* pp. 638, 503, 562.
[113] ". . . ethnologically there is no dividing line to be drawn in South America between the white, the Indian, and the Savage. The so-called whites are largely Indian, the Indians are largely negro, and the savages are partly Indian, partly negro and partly an amalgam of races older in the country than the principal Indian tribes." Dilke, *Nationalities and Subject Races,* p. 103.
[114] Bryce, *South America,* p. 433. Ross, *South of Panama,* p. 168.
[115] "Every one wishes to be reckoned as a white man. . . ." Bryce, *South America,* p. 460. See, also, pp. 478-79, 473-74, 232, 472-73.

are able, even in a South American community, to pass as white men. It is frequently as difficult to determine who should be deemed an Indian and who a *mestizo*, as it is at the other end of the scale to say who is to be deemed a white man and who a man of mixed-blood.[116] Between the lower class *mestizo* and the Indian, there is little intellectual or social distinction.[117]

While there are thus mixed-blood men in both the white and the Indian groups, it is not to be understood that the *mestizo* forms, in any other than a physiological sense, a connecting link between the races. He is, rather, a member of one or the other group depending upon his color, education, and economic status. The break between the upper-class *mestizo* and the Indian group is frequently a sharp one. They sometimes differ as widely as do the native and the white with the additional consideration that the *mestizo* constantly emphasizes the fact of his white blood by his hatred of and contempt for the native.[118] "The Indians," says Bryce, "have nothing, except the worship of the saints and a fondness for liquor, in common with the class above them."[119]

There is nothing in law or custom to prevent the intermarriage of the races. The educated *mestizo* endeavors to marry a white woman and is successful in proportion to his economic status in the community. The lower-class *mestizos* intermix readily with the Indians.[120] Between the whites and the near-

[116] Bryce, *South America*, p. 458.

[117] "The Indians . . . absorb or are absorbed by the Mestizo." *South American Year Book*, 1915, p. 503.

[118] [He] "has repeatedly shown himself to be very cruel toward the Indians, whom he despises much more than the better class man would do." *Ibid.*, p. 7.

[119] *South America*, p. 474. See, also, pp. 438, 185-86.

[120] The mixed-blood women in Peru bear a goodly number of children to the Chinese coolies. See Ross, *South of Panama*, pp. 39-40.

whites, on the one hand, and the Indian and the lower-class *mestizo*, on the other, there is no intermarriage; but this fact seems to be due more to social than to racial causes. It is class separation rather than a racial antipathy.[121] Says Bryce:[122]

> To understand the social relations of the white and Indian races one must begin by remembering that there is in Spanish and Portuguese countries no such sharp colour line as exists where men of Teutonic stock are settled in countries outside of Europe. As this is true of the negro, it is even more true of the Indian. He may be despised as a weakling, he may be ignored as a citizen, he may be, as he was at one time, abominably oppressed and ill treated, but he excites no personal repulsion. It is not his race that is against him, but his debased condition. Whatever he suffers, is suffered because he is ignorant or timid or helpless, not because he is of a different blood and colour. . . . The distinction between the races is in Spanish America a distinction of rank or class rather than of colour. Against intermarriage there is, therefore, no more feeling than that which exists against any union palpably below a man's or woman's own rank in life. If it is rare for a pure white to espouse a pure Indian, that is because they are of different ranks, just as it is rare for a well-born Englishman to marry a peasant girl. There is nothing in the law to oppose such a union, and though whites seldom marry pure Indians, because the classes come little into contact, the presence of an unmistakable Indian strain in a mestizo makes no difference to his acceptability to a white woman of the same class. . . .

[121] However, Meredith Townsend states that the years "during which Spaniards and Indians have dwelt together in South America have not softened their mutual antipathies; . . ." *Asia and Europe*, pp. 217-18.
[122] *South America*, pp. 470-71.

The state of almost entire absence of racial or color prejudice thus pictured seems, at times,—between revolutions and race wars—to approach realization in some of the South American countries. In how far this racial harmony is real and in how far it is merely a temporary accommodation to the exigencies of the situation, is still a matter of some doubt.

But wherever the Negroes and mulattoes are found even in small numbers, there is also found an unmistakable race question. In Guiana, for example, there is a marked antipathy toward and avoidance of the black man by every other race and color in the community. There was formerly some intermarriage between the Portuguese immigrants and the blacks and mulattoes, but there is now an avoidance of association even of the low-class Europeans and the Negroes. There is still some intermarriage between the Portuguese and the near-white mulattoes.[123] The Negroes have a wholesome fear of the Chinese, and the latter freely and without hesitation use the mulatto and Negro women as concubines though the relation is hardly one of marriage.[124] The East Indians intermix to some extent with the mulattoes, but they have the greatest antipathy for the blacks and refuse to cohabit with them.[125] The American Indian detests and despises the Negro.[126] The whites, even where they show no particular prejudice against the presence of Indian blood, have an entirely different attitude toward the Negro and the

---

[123] Johnston, *The Negro in the New World*, pp. 333-34.

[124] *Ibid.*, p. 332. The Negroes are "entirely 'unmoral' in their sexual relations" and have no repugnance toward intermixture with any of the other races. *Ibid.*, p. 334.

[125] "An Indian kuli would ordinarily prefer to live unmarried sooner than cohabit with a negress: they are not perhaps so squeamish about marriage with mulattoes." *Ibid.*, p. 334. See, also, p. 332. They intermarry with the Amerindians.

[126] *Ibid.*, p. 332. Bryce, *South America*, pp. 473 f. n., 566-67.

mulatto. The greatest antipathy, however, is that existing between the near-white mulattoes on the one hand and the Negroes and mulattoes of darker hue on the other.[127]

In the Philippines

In the Philippine Islands at the present time, there are two mixed-blood races in considerable numbers and of different race parentage—the Chinese *mestizo* and the Spanish *mestizo*. The former is the product of the intercrossing of the Chinese and the Malay; the latter is the offspring of the Peninsular Spaniard or the Spanish creole with the native Malay woman. A great variety of other mongrels is found, but not in numbers sufficient to assume the proportions of a problem.

When the Spanish entered the Islands in 1521, they found the productive valleys occupied by a race of uncivilized Moros. They subjugated this race, and undertook the business of conversion. To the Spaniards, the Islands were always rather a mission than a colony. There were no mines to be worked and no plantations calling for a large body of servile labor. There was no decline in the native population as was elsewhere true of the Spanish colonies [128] and there was no introduction of a substitute labor supply. The Islands were too far away and offered too little in the way of immediate and large returns to attract the Spanish mer-

---

[127] "There is a slight 'color question' in Guiana, but the sensitiveness lies rather between the 'near-whites' of pale ivory complexion and the darker tinted mulattoes or negroes. There is now practically no intermarriage between whites and blacks; on the other hand, numerous unions take place between whites, especially Portuguese, and the lighter-skinned negroids, many of whom would almost sooner perish in celibacy than intermarry with the negro or mulatto." Johnston, *The Negro in the New World*, p. 337.

[128] Keller, *Colonization*, p. 350.

chant. The number of Spaniards on the Islands was always small and consisted almost exclusively of the military and priestly classes.[129] Other foreigners were excluded.

During the four centuries of the Spanish occupancy of the Islands, there grew up a Spanish *mestizo* mixture that numbers at present about two per cent of the population. A small per cent of this mixed-blood race is the product of intermarriage between the Spanish creoles, who now number about three hundredths of one per cent of the population, and the native women of mixed parentage. The bulk of the mixed-blood race, however, owe their origin to less conventional and less permanent unions. Another considerable number of the mixed-blood race trace their ancestry back to a priestly origin. Officials and other Spaniards usually formed no permanent unions with the native girls.

The second mixed-blood race, the Chinese *mestizos*, number about two per cent of the population. They are more often, perhaps generally, the offspring of a fairly permanent union.

The civil and social status of the various races and half-races follows for the most part the lines of race and color. Color prejudice and class hatred are everywhere a factor in the situation. At one extreme of the social scale are the foreign white and the white creoles. Below them in the social scale, come the Spanish half-breeds, envious of the classes above them, contemptuous of those below. Every mixture of foreign blood has tended to raise them above the native. Now, as during the last two centuries of Spanish rule, they are the dominant class in the native affairs. The prominent

---

[129] In 1820 there was one white to 1,600 natives. The whites were mostly in Manila. In 1864 there was a total of 4,050 Spaniards in the Islands. Of these 3,280 were government officials, 500 were clergy, 200 were landed proprietors and 70 were merchants.

Mixed-Blood Races 53

Filipinos are probably without exception from this mixed-blood class.[130] "No Filipino ever has become known in America, either through his attainments or his political prominence, who was more than a few generations removed from a foreign ancestor."[131] It is from this class that most of the higher Filipino officials come. They are the discontented and troublesome element in the population.[132] "They are always hoping for recognition as equals by the foreigners with whom they are brought into contact and to whom they may be related."[133] They despise the native element and ignore the ties by which they are bound to them. The present administrative problem in the Islands is to prevent the half-breed official from oppressing the despised Malay.[134]

The vigorous, thrifty, enterprising Chinese share with the Chinese half-breeds the monopoly of the trade in the Islands. The Chinese are despised by all the races, even by the Chinese half-breed and the Filipino, as bitterly as by the creoles and

[130] "Rizal, the most famous man—and one might say the only famous man—produced by the islands was the direct descendant of a Chinese trader, and his mother was of Filipino-Chinese-Spanish descent with a little Japanese blood." Carl Crow, "What About the Filipinos?" *World's Work*, Vol. 26, p. 519. See, also, J. A. Robertson, "Notes from the Philippines," *Journal of Race Development*, Vol. 3, p. 470, and Keller, *Colonization*, p. 350 f. n. The best discussion of Rizal's personality is by Ferdinand Blumentritt, *Internationales Archiv für Ethnographie*, Bd. X, Heft 2. There is a brief abstract of this article in *Pop. Sci. Mo.*, July, 1902. An inaccurate and laudatory appreciation by his personal friend, Sir Hugh Clifford, appeared in *Blackwood's Magazine*, Vol. 172, pp. 620-38. Rizal married a white woman of English birth. See James A. LeRoy, *The Americans in the Philippines*, p. 117 f. n.

Sergio Osmena, former speaker of the Philippine Assembly, was a Chinese *mestizo*. Crow, *World's Work*, Vol. 26, p. 523.

[131] *Ibid.*, Vol. 26, p. 519.

[132] LeRoy, *The Americans in the Philippines*, p. 76.

[133] Crow, *World's Work*, Vol. 26, p. 519.

[134] Charles E. Woodruff, "Some Laws of Racial and Intellectual Development," *Journal of Race Development*, Vol. 3, p. 175.

foreign whites, and this is a situation of long standing.[135] The quiet, industrious Chinese half-breed is perhaps the best man on the Islands.[136] He is classed with and despised as a Chinaman by the races above him, while, in his turn, he shares with the white the white man's bitter hatred for the Chinese and contempt for the Filipino. At the bottom of the social scale, comes the Filipino who is economically inefficient and despised by every one, while he in turn hates in varying degrees the various classes above him.

[135] ". . . It is also noteworthy that the Filipinos and even the Chinese half-breeds (*mestizos de sangley*) exhibited this hatred in as bitter a form as did the Spanish themselves." Keller, *Colonization*, p. 355. LeRoy, *The Americans in the Philippines*, p. 279, speaks of the "traditional hostility between the Filipinos and Chinese."

[136] ". . . During the latter days of my residence in the Islands in 1905 Governor-General Wright one day told me that he had recently personally received from one of the most distinguished Filipinos of the time, and a member of the Insular Civil Commission, the statement 'that there was not a single prominent and dominant family among the christianized Filipinos which did not possess Chinese blood.' The voice and the will of the Filipinos to-day is the voice and the will of these brainy, industrious, rapidly developing men whose judgment in time the world is bound to respect. . . ." A. E. Jenks, "Assimilation in the Philippines, as Interpreted in Terms of Assimilation in America," *American Journal Sociology*, Vol. 19, p. 783. Ratzel, *The History of Mankind*, Vol. 1, p. 397, says that the Chinese half-breed in the Philippines is superior to the European half-breed. See, also, LeRoy, *The Americans in the Philippines*, p. 76.

CHAPTER III

MIXED-BLOOD RACES (CONCLUDED)

In Cuba, Porto Rico, and Santo Domingo

THE Islands of the West Indies were colonized by Spain during the first quarter of the sixteenth century. During this period Spain was at the height of her national power, and the Islands were the centers of trade and commercial activity.

The Spaniards found the Islands inhabited by a numerous population of peaceful Indian tribes whom they conquered, enslaved, converted, and worked to death on the plantations and in the mines on the mainland. So disastrous to the natives was the Spanish policy of slavery, concubinage, and catholicism that, with the exception of some infusion of Indian blood in the Spanish part of Santo Domingo and in Cuba, the native element is totally extinct.[1]

It was to save the native element from total extinction that

---

[1] The population of Santo Domingo decreased two-thirds in the first three years of Spanish occupancy. The population was estimated as follows:

1492	3,000,000
1508	60,000
1510	46,000
1572	20,000
1574	14,000
1648	under 500

A similar fate befell all of the other Islands. See A. G. Keller, *Colonization*, p. 226.

the introduction of Negroes was first recommended. The Spaniards had intermixed freely with the natives during the two centuries that their extermination was in process. With the Negroes they intermixed with almost equal readiness.[2] A mulatto race soon sprang up and increased rapidly in numbers. In Porto Rico, at the time of its cession to the United States in 1898, approximately one-third of the population was returned as colored.[3] The colored element included a few Chinese and the Negro-white mixture as well as the pure Negroes. Of the total returned as colored eighty-four per cent were of mixed-blood. In Cuba the per cent of mixed-bloods in the Negro population is yet larger as is to be expected from the fact that the ratio of Negroes to the white population is much smaller.[4] From the other Islands, the Spanish were expelled before the mixture had gone so far.

Cuba, Porto Rico and Santo Domingo, Spanish until 1898 and in spirit and civilization Spanish still, have the race problem in much the same form as it is found on the mainland of South America. The mixed-blood race is of Spanish, Negro, and Indian blood. On the mainland, the Indian blood is vastly in excess of the Negro; on the Islands, it is the Negro blood that predominates; the Indian blood is but a

[2] Johnston attributes the fact that the Spanish have never shown the same repugnance as have the Northern nations of Europe to sexual intercourse with Negroes, to the ancient strain of Negro blood in their ethnic composition. Sir Harry H. Johnston, "The World-position of the Negro and Negroid," *Inter-Racial Problems*, pp. 329-30.

[3]
Total	953,243
White	589,462
Colored	363,817

[4] White 1,067,354 or 67.9 per cent; Colored 505,443 or 32.1 per cent. The few Chinese are here counted as white as has been the Spanish custom in all previous censuses. United States War Department *Census of Cuba*, 1899, p. 97.

trace.

In Cuba the opportunities and personal privileges of the Negro people have been somewhat greater than in most other parts of the West Indies. They are and always have been sufficiently below the whites in numbers effectually to prevent any wide-spread reversion to their ancestral African customs. During the slave period, though cases of barbarous mistreatment were not infrequent, the Spanish laws were highly favorable to the slave. It was easy for him to purchase his freedom and there were a large number of free Negroes throughout the slavery period.[5] After the abolition of slavery in 1880, the rights of the black man were of course much greater and his status much higher, the Spanish government giving the same consideration to the colored as to the white Cuban. The rebellions of 1868-78 and of 1895-98 and the threatened uprising in 1906 all operated to raise the status of the Negro. At present all civil, military and ecclesiastical positions and honors are open to members of the race.[6]

The mulattos have responded to these conditions in a way that differentiates them from the Negroes elsewhere. Though the race is behind the whites in education, morals, and economic advancement, many individuals have made advances along these lines. They are found in all professions and

Census Year	Free Colored	Slaves
1775	41.0	59.0
1792	45.6	54.4
1817	36.7	63.3
1827	27.1	72.9
1841	25.9	74.1
1861	37.4	62.9
1877	55.7	44.3

[5] *Ibid.*, p. 98. See, also, H. C. Morris, *The History of Colonization*, Vol. I, p. 278.

[6] U. S. War Dept. *Census of Cuba*, 1899, p. 69.

58   *The Mulatto in the United States*

in all trades. Bullard says:[7] "Though found in more professions than in America, they are less industrious than here. They show disposition but no aptness for commerce, and their inclination in this direction must perhaps be looked upon more as a desire to avoid the hard labor of the fields than as any serious effort to try fortune in trade." However this may be, a few have distinguished themselves [8] and a goodly number have made a reasonable success; they show more self-respect and self-possession than is found elsewhere among Negro people. Speaking of this self-respecting attitude Bullard says:[9]

> . . . Everywhere—in public, in the streets, in the theatres, on steamers and cars—our man of negro blood carries himself with confidence and self-possession. It is his marked characteristic in Cuba. Looking at him, one cannot but be impressed with his great gain in dignity in consequence. He feels himself a worthier man. In rural guard, police and other official positions occupied by him, he conducts himself with steadiness and dignity. Placing him in such offices seems not in Cuba, as in America, to make him foolish and giddy. These are noteworthy things for Cuba and the negro race.

During the slavery period the black and mulatto females sought the white and disdained the black men as fathers of their children. So extensive and long continued has been this intercrossing that it is now impossible to draw any clear distinction between the races. At either extreme the colors are unmixed. The aristocracy and the middle-class towns-

[7] Lieutenant-Colonel R. L. Bullard, U. S. A., "The Cuban Negro," *North American Review*, Vol. 184, p. 629.

[8] Antonio Maceo of the Cuban Army, 1895-98, was a mulatto. See U. S. War Dept. *Census of Cuba*, 1899, p. 69.

[9] *North American Review*, Vol. 184, p. 626.

folk are quite free from Negro intermixture; some blacks, especially the rural folk of the interior, are still of unmixed African blood. But between the extremes is an unbroken gradation through all the tints from the swarthy complexion of the Spaniard to the glossy black of the West African Negro. Yet few of those who pass as Negroes are without some admixture of the white man's blood. "Few of the Negroes are black; some of the blackest have the regular features of the Caucasian; and racial mixtures are everywhere evidenced by color of skin and by physiognomy."[10]

There is no hard and fast color line separating the colored and white races of the Cuban population. In politics, the Negro is the equal of the white man. In resorts, in places of amusement, and in public conveyances, there is no separation of the races. Negroes have held some minor political offices and members of some of the higher governmental bodies have been tinged with Negro blood. In social affairs there is little ostensible inequality but only in the army, if anywhere, has there been recognized any condition of real social equality.[11] Socially and politically, however, the Negro is constantly losing ground as the white race increases in numbers.[12] Nowhere else in the West Indies is there so much tenderness on the point of color. Bullard says on this point:[13]

[10] *Encyclopaedia Britannica:* Cuba. See, also, Sir Harry H. Johnston, *The Negro in the New World,* p. 59, and William Z. Ripley, "Race Problems in Cuba," *Publications of the American Statistical Association,* Vol. 7, pp. 85-89.

[11] U. S. War Dept., *Census of Cuba,* 1899, p. 69.

[12] "Yet the negro is losing ground, politically and socially, and unless he is content with his present status of farmer, labourer, petty tradesman, minor employé, and domestic servant, there will arise a 'colour' question here as in the United States." Johnston, *The Negro in the New World,* p. 60.

[13] *North American Review,* Vol. 184, p. 628.

> ... The earliest negroes brought to Cuba had a sad, faint little belief that after death they should be born again into another land, white men. "Negro" and even "mulatto" must be softened into *"gente de color"* ... and "pardo" ... while the house-maid becomes "Señorita" ... and the cook "Señora." ... These, and the tendency, in the face of manifest aversion, to push themselves as equals upon another race, are discouraging signs of weakness, showing a lack of that genuine independence, self-respect and pride that indicate strength and real worth.

It is, however, between the blacks and the mixed-bloods that the lines of social demarcation are most clearly drawn. The mixed-blood man desires to be white, and imitates the white man's virtues and the white man's faults. Bullard[14] points out the difference in the social life of the blacks and the mixed-bloods and illustrates the difference by a description of the two dances which are more or less peculiar to the Negroes of the Island:

> There are two dances, the "Congo" and the "Creole," both protracted perhaps through many nights. The first is a memory or tradition of Africa. In it, men and women, black, real negroes, sing the songs and dance the dances of Africa to the sound of rattles and rude drums, genuine savage instruments. The dance is always significant. It takes many forms of war, love, tradition and conjury, yet it is most addressed to the sexual passions and can but lead to their indulgence. The "Congo" may be seen to-day in any country town in the cane regions.
>
> The "Creole" aspires to be very different. It is a modified waltz by the more mixed generation, far less interesting, more modern, but not more moral than the "Congo." One needs but to see it to be impressed with its sensuality.

[1] *North American Review*, Vol. 184, pp. 625-26.

In Haiti

After some two centuries of occupancy Spain lost Haiti to the French. It remained a French province for nearly a hundred years, during which time the mulattoes came to be a distinct caste and to occupy a separate status in the community. On the one hand they were generally free from bondage; on the other they were excluded from citizenship. When, at the time of the French Revolution, the slaves were liberated, the mutual antipathies of the whites, blacks, and mulattoes blossomed into a triangular warfare, the final result of which was the massacre of the entire European population.[15] After several costly and unsuccessful attempts on the part of the French and later of the English to restore orderly government, the Island was abandoned, became a black, independent state, and has been for a century free to work out its salvation without interference.

The abandonment of the Island by the civilized powers so soon after the emancipation of the blacks was fatal to Haitian prosperity. The civil wars had destroyed property and capital of every description and left labor in a hopelessly demoralized state. The effect was as disastrous politically as it was economically: the political history of the hundred years is simply a narrative of revolutions. The country, nominally a republic, has in practice alternated between anarchy and military despotism. The actual power has been in the hands of the president who almost always rode into office as the momentary favorite of the major division of the army.[16] Below the forms of civilized government

---

[15] J. A. Froude, *The English in the West Indies*, pp. 182-83.

[16] "... Scarcely a President in the history of Haiti has not been a military man, and the favorite leader for the time being, of the major portion of the army...." Johnston, *The Negro in the New World*, p. 197.

there always has existed in every department of the official life every conceivable form of political corruption, official dishonesty, and judicial murder. "Justice is venal and the police brutal and inefficient." [17] The Roman Catholic religion has degenerated into a thin disguise for the practice of the rites of Voodooism in which cannibalism and the sacrifice of children in the Serpent's honor has, at least at times, played an important part.[18] The forms of marriage are disregarded or forgotten.[19] Polygamy prevails in the interior and the frequent orgiastic dances are accompanied by promiscuous sexual debauchery.[20] On the whole, the Island, during the century of independence and self-government, has made no progress along any line, has retrogressed in some

[17] *Encyclopædia Britannica:* Haiti.
[18] See H. V. H. Prichard, *Where Black Rules White; a Journey Across and About Hayti,* Chapter IV. For a more apologetic account see General Légitime, "Some General Considerations of the People and Government of Haiti," *Inter-Racial Problems,* pp. 183-84.
[19] "In most of the country districts polygamy is openly practiced. The rite of marriage—civil and religious—is probably confined to about an eighth of the total adult population. . . ." Johnston, *The Negro in the New World,* p. 194.
[20] "The 2,500,000 Haitian peasants are passionately fond of dancing, will even sometimes dance almost or quite naked. And following on this choregraphic exercise is much immorality. . . ." Johnston, *The Negro in the New World,* p. 194. It is interesting to compare this statement with his description of the dance of the Brazilian Negro. "The dances to which negro slaves were trained . . . usually began with a slow movement of two persons, who approached each other with a shy and diffident air, and then receded bashful and embarrassed. By degrees, the time of the music increased, the diffidence wore off, and the dance concluded with 'indecencies not fit to be seen nor described.' Sometimes it was of a different character, attended by jumping, shouting, and throwing their arms over each other's heads, and assuming the most fierce and stern aspects. The indecent display was a 'dance of love,' but the shouting dance was a mimicry of war." *Ibid.,* p. 93. As a further stage in the evolution of the race and the dance compare the American Negro's "cake-walk."

Mixed-Blood Races 63

lines and in others the "republic has gone back to the lowest type of African barbarism." [21]

No census ever has been taken, and consequently there are no accurate figures as to the population. The population, however, is made up almost entirely of Negroes, about nine-tenths of whom are full-blood Africans. The ten per cent of mulattoes is said to be a rapidly diminishing class.[22] The number of whites is very small and of negligible influence in the affairs of the country. They are, by a provision of the constitution, prohibited from holding real estate.[23]

There is a sharp contrast between the black and the mulatto inhabitants. The blacks, who form the peasantry of the country, are peaceable, kindly, and hospitable people. They are constitutionally lazy,[24] almost entirely uneducated [25] and they preserve their ancient snake worship and cannibalistic rites under the forms of Roman Catholicism.[26] Their sex relations are of a frankly natural sort. "Mar-

[21] Chambers' *Encyclopædia:* Hayti. See, also, *Encyclopædia Britannica:* Haiti, and *New International Encyclopaedia:* Haiti.

[22] *Encyclopædia Britannica:* Haiti. For a contrary opinion see Earl Finch, "The Effects of Racial Miscegenation," *Inter-Racial Problems,* pp. 109-10.

[23] Johnson's *Cyclopædia:* Haiti.

[24] "The island is one of the most fertile in the world, and if it had an enlightened and stable government, an energetic people, and a little capital, its agricultural possibilities would be boundless." *Encyclopædia Britannica:* Haiti.

[25] "The plain fact remains that something like 2,500,000 out of the 3,000,000 of Haitians cannot read or write, and are as ignorant as unreclaimed natives of Africa:" Johnston, *The Negro in the New World,* p. 187.

"But what use is it talking of the 'country' doing this or willing that when no more than 200,000 out of 3,000,000 Haitians have the slightest approach to education? . . ." *Ibid.,* p. 204.

[26] "At least two out of the three millions of Haitian negroes are only Christians in the loose statistics of geographers. They are still African pagans, . . ." *Ibid.,* p. 193.

riage is neither frequent nor legally prescribed." [27] Polygamy is openly practiced and the African dances lead to a more or less wholesale and promiscuous sexual indulgence. They speak a patois of French origin which is known locally as creole. The one man of first-class ability produced by the black group was the insurgent chief, François Dominique Toussaint.[28]

The mulattoes are economically, socially, and intellectually far in advance of the black Negroes. They compose the professional classes and own most of the property. They are frequently educated in Paris and many do not materially differ in education from Europeans of the same class.[29] In regard to the educational system, Johnston says:[30]

> . . . Unhappily, the weak point in all this superior education of the Haitians is its utterly unpractical relation to a useful and profitable existence in the West Indies. . . . But the education which she gives to the youth of Haiti is perversely useless in its nature. It is apparently only adapted to life in Paris or in a French provincial town, and the adepts thus trained show a singular tendency on returning to Haiti to cast off their European learning. Young doctors, sent to France for education in medical science, come back and discard any modern aseptic or antiseptic theories in their practice, in fact almost revert to the position of negro charlatans. Lawyers can think of nothing but the meticulous intricacies of the Code Napoléon,

[27] *Encyclopædia Britannica:* Haiti.

[28] In middle life Toussaint acquired the nickname L'Ouverture because, having lost the most of his front teeth, there was a marked opening in his mouth when he spoke. See Johnston, *The Negro in the New World*, p. 157. Toussaint was a leader of the Negroes and is generally considered to be a full-blood Negro. That this is the case, however, is at least doubtful.

[29] *New International Encyclopædia:* Haiti.

[30] *Negro in the New World*, p. 188.

and seem incapable of devising a simple civil and criminal jurisprudence applicable to the essentially African race which inhabits Haiti. . . .

In dress, manners, and habits of life, they imitate the French and exaggerate upon their models.[31] Though comparatively few in numbers, they occupy most of the prominent positions in the political and governmental affairs of the Island and generally manage to control the political situation. The majority of Haiti's score or more of Presidents, and all of the better ones, have been mulattoes.[32] They form the more enlightened and less brutal class of the population.

Between the two groups there exists and has existed throughout the entire history of the Republic the bitterest type of race hatred. The hatred of the Negro for the mulatto is equaled only by the mulatto's contempt for the Negro.[33] The mulattoes hate and despise the black man with all the bitterness of a superior caste which lacks the power, but not the desire, to reduce the black man to the status of a slave.[34]

In Jamaica

Jamaica became an English province in 1658. The century and a half of Spanish occupancy, except for the annihilation of the native Arawak Indians, had no permanent

[31] "As to the dress of the two hundred thousand educated people, though less exotic than it was, it is still, as in Liberia—a worship of the tall hat and frock-coat. In the streets of Port-au-Prince, as of Monrovia, in a temperature 95 degrees in the shade and something under boiling-point in the sun, you may see Haitian statesmen cavorting about in black silk hats of portentous height and glossiness, with frock-coats down to their knees, and wearing lemon kid gloves. . . ." *Ibid.*, p. 190.

[32] Prichard, *Where Black Rules White*, p. 82.

[33] Johnston, *The Negro in the New World*, p. 159. See, also, *Encyclopædia Britannica:* Haiti.

[34] Johnston, *The Negro in the New World*, p. 159.

66 **The Mulatto in the United States**

effect upon the Island. When taken by the British, the total population, slave and free, did not number above three thousand. After the formation of the Royal African Company in 1672, with a monopoly on the slave trade, Jamaica became one of the great slave marts of the world. The English emancipation act was passed in 1834 and, subject to a short apprenticeship, the slaves were free.

The present total population of Jamaica is approximately 830,000. Of these, 15,000, in round numbers, are pure white, 17,000 are East Indian coolies, and about 2,000 are Chinese; a total of some 34,000 non-African people. The remaining 796,000 are Negro and Negro mixtures.[35] The mixed-bloods number about one-fifth of the total number of the race.

The various classes in the population seem to correspond exactly to the race and color lines. Needham [36] says that

> ... The inhabitants are divided into three classes which are comparable, except as to numbers, to the three classes existing in England. The pure whites correspond to the aristocracy; the "coloured" ... are in a social sense relatively like the English middle class; the darks or blacks—meaning those who have no evidence of white ancestry—are the laboring or peasant class. These three mingle freely in many of

[35]
Races	Numbers	Percentage
White	15,605	1.88
Colored	163,201	19.63
Black	630,181	75.80
East Indians	17,380	2.09
Chinese	2,111	0.25
Not specified	2,905	0.35
Total	831,383	100.00

Census of Jamaica, 1911.

[36] Charles K. Needham, "A Comparison of Some Conditions in Jamaica with those in the United States," *Journal of Race Development*, Vol. 4, p. 190.

Mixed-Blood Races

the affairs of life, but in certain other matters there is a distinction well recognized by an individual when coming in contact with one who is his social superior. . . .

There is a hard and fast color line between the whites and the Negroes and mulattoes.

The blacks are the laboring class. There has been some effort to settle them as independent peasant proprietors but the effort has not been a marked success. The conditions of life are such as to require but little work in order to live; the Negroes do the little that is required.[37] They are without education or the desire for education.[38] They have little part in the government and in general show little desire to participate.[39] The relations of the sexes are of the most elastic sort, well over half of the births being illegitimate.[40]

---

[37] It was the impossibility of getting the Negroes to do any regular work that led to the importation of the Chinese and the Indian coolies. Froude, *The English in the West Indies*, pp. 50, 73 ff.

[38] "At the present day only about one-quarter of the total colored population of Jamaica can read and write." The fact that there is little agricultural or industrial education suited to the race offered in the schools perhaps accounts in part for their indifference to education. Though free and liberally supported by the government, the education is not suited to the needs of the race. See Johnston, *The Negro in the New World*, p. 270.

[39] "The black does not want representative government; he prefers to rely on the impartial, despotic rule of trained officials, . . ." "The blacks . . . always prefer a white man. . ." William Thorp, "How Jamaica Solves the Negro Problem," *World's Work*, Vol. 8, p. 4910.

[40] ". . . No negress could bear the idea of growing to old age without being a mother; she would deem herself slighted. Therefore the negro and mulatto men are much run after; the marriage rate is not only low, but tends to decrease (it is just now about 3.8 per 1000 persons), and with its decrease rises the percentage of illegitimate births, which now [1906] stands at the figure of sixty-five children out of every hundred." Johnston, *The Negro in the New World*, p. 275.

The mulattoes are officially separated from the blacks by applying to them the special racial designation *coloured*. This class includes the majority of those engaged in the trades and professions and they fill most of the minor governmental positions and some of the higher positions in the public service.[41] The press of the country, though owned by white men, is, for the most part, run by mulattoes. Johnston[42] states that

> The negroid in this island enters into all the professions and careers and fills nine-tenths of the posts under Government. The coloured population, besides residing as cultivators in the country, frequents the towns and earns a living as doctors, dentists, ministers of religion, teachers, waiters, tradesmen, skilled artisans, clerks, musicians, postal employés, press reporters, the superior servants of the State railways, overseers of plantations, hotel-keepers. . . . The pure Negro in Jamaica is mainly a peasant and a countryman.

Between the blacks and the mulattoes, there is a sharp social as well as official distinction.[43] The social position of a member of the race is conditioned by the lightness of his skin and the absence of other racial marks.[44] The mu-

---

[41] "On the Legislative Council of to-day only *four* of the elected members are of *unmixed* Nordic-European descent; *four* are of well-known Jamaican-*Jewish* families descended from the Spanish and Portuguese Jews of Guiana and Brazil; *one* member is an absolute negro (of Bahaman birth), and the remainder (*five*) are octoroons and mulattoes of Jamaican birth." Johnston, *The Negro in the New World,* p. 268.

[42] *Ibid.,* p. 280.

[43] ". . . I am told that in the West Indies the 'coloured' man despises the 'nigger' and feels himself immeasurably his social superior." William Archer, *Thro Afro-America,* p. 273. See, however, Froude, *The English in the West Indies,* p. 155, for the attitude of the blacks toward the mixed-bloods.

[44] See Needham, *Journal of Race Development,* Vol. 4, pp. 193-94.

lattoes refuse to intermarry with the blacks [45] except in cases where the black individual is possessed of large fortune or holds a high government position; even in this case the children of the union will be barred, because of their color and features, from the upper class mulatto society.[46]

The same views on the subject of intermarriage of the races are held by the white people of Jamaica as are held by the white people of the Southern United States. Mixed marriages are approved by the ambitious mulattoes and by the "whites by law." The exceptionally light-colored girls of this latter class are occasionally able to secure white husbands from the immigrants to the Island, whom they have deluded into the belief that they are really white.[47] A few other pretty, well-educated and wealthy girls of this class are able to marry white because of their wealth and of the scarcity of white girls on the Island.[48] The number, however, is very small, and sexual association between the white men and the mulatto girls goes on without the for-

---

[45] The same thing is true of the East Indian coolies. "They are proud, however, and will not intermarry with the Africans. . . . The black women look with envy at the straight hair of Asia, and twist their unhappy wool into knots and ropes in the vain hope of being mistaken for the purer race. But this is all. The African and the Asiatic will not mix. . . ." Froude, *The English in the West Indies*, pp. 73-74.

[46] ". . . When such a child [a mulatto with Negro features] appears in the Jamaican upper class—let the skin be ever so irreproachable in color—that individual is almost doomed to step down when he or she settles under a roof separate from the parents. Of course all such obstacles are sometimes counterbalanced when an abundant dowry is provided; but we are now considering only general rules." Needham, *Journal of Race Development*, Vol. 4, p. 192.

[47] Thorp, *World's Work*, Vol. 8, p. 4912.

[48] ". . . Out in the country it is not uncommon to find a white man married to a woman of mixed ancestry, for the same reason that white men go to Oklahoma and marry squaws or half-breed girls. . . ." Needham, *Journal of Race Development*, Vol. 4, p. 195.

70   *The Mulatto in the United States*

mality of a legal marriage.⁴⁹ Marriages between mulatto or "white by law" males and white women almost never occur. The few on record are those of light-colored men of wealth who have gone to England and married white women there, where a man is lionized not in spite of his color but because of it, or where the fact of his Negro blood is not known.⁵⁰ The native families on the Island never marry outside their race; any British officer or official would ruin his career by taking a colored wife.

Racial feeling is everywhere present in Jamaica though the insignificant number of the whites and the political recognition of the mulattoes have, in general, kept it from assuming the proportions of a problem.⁵¹ The blacks are socially, economically, and intellectually inferior and contentedly accept the inferior status assigned them.⁵² Except in the

⁴⁹ Needham, *Journal of Race Development,* Vol. 4, p. 195. Some students at least recognize this as a desirable phenomenon. ". . . There is no such reason against the begetting of children by white men in countries where, if they are to breed at all, it must be with women of coloured or mixed race. The offspring of such breeding, whether legitimate or illegitimate, is, from the point of view of efficiency, an acquisition to the community, and, under favourable conditions, an advance on the pure-bred African. . . ." Sir Sidney Olivier, *White Capital and Coloured Labour,* p. 38.

⁵⁰ Thorp, *World's Work,* Vol. 8, p. 4913. See, also, W. P. Livingstone, "The West-Indian and American Negro: A Contrast," *North American Review,* Vol. 185, p. 647.

⁵¹ ". . . I am convinced that this class [mulatto] as it at present exists is a valuable and indispensable part of any West Indian community, and that a colony of black, coloured, and whites has far more organic efficiency and far more promise in it than a colony of black and white alone. . . . The graded mixed class in Jamaica helps to make an organic whole of the community and saves it from this distinct cleavage." Olivier, *White Capital and Coloured Labour,* pp. 38-39. See, also, Livingstone, *North American Review,* Vol. 185, p. 647.

⁵² "The whites regard the negro as a primitive being, incapable as yet of standing alone, and adopt the attitude of trainers and teachers: the negroes are conscious of their inferiority and willingly fall into the po-

In South Africa

In South Africa the native population is everywhere far more numerous than the Europeans; the mixed element is generally small. It is, speaking generally, only in Cape Colony that a very considerable half-caste population is found.[53]

The half-breed race is of very complicated ancestry. In the early days, the Dutch mixed to some extent with the Hottentot women of the Cape, giving rise to the so-called Bastaards.[54] Later, as they withdrew into the interior, they came into contact with the Abantus, who at that time were migrating from the Northwest, and produced a second type of hybrid.[55] In 1658 came the first introduction of Negro

---

sition of learners." Livingstone, *North American Review*, Vol. 185, p. 647. See, also, Johnston, *The Negro in the New World*, p. 279. So universal is this feeling of inferiority on the part of the blacks and mulattoes that it is claimed that white women can go about unprotected in perfect safety.

[53] "In British South Africa the colored races are nearly five times as numerous as the whites." *Encyclopædia Britannica:* South Africa. In 1904 the white population was 1,149,336 and the colored 7,111,329. In 1911 the white population was 1,305,531 and the colored 6,890,693. By colonies H. E. S. Fremantle, *The New Nation; A Survey of the Conditions and Prospects of South Africa*, p. 179, gives the following:

Colonies	European	Colored	Total
Cape Colony	579,741	1,830,063	2,409,804
Orange R. Colony	142,679	244,636	387,315
Transvaal	297,277	972,674	1,269,951
Natal	97,109	1,011,645	1,108,754
Total	1,116,806	4,059,018	5,175,824

See, also, *Encyclopædia Britannica Year Book*, 1913, pp. 702-12.

[54] Keller, *Colonization*, p. 444.

[55] The Bushmen appear to have been the original South Africans. The

slaves from the West African Coast;[56] shortly afterwards began the importation of Asiatic convicts from the East Indian Archipelago. These Mohammedan Malays mixed with the slave women from the Guinea Coast as well as with the native Hottentot women. There were also slaves from Mozambique and natives from Madagascar, the injection of whose blood further complicated the ethnic mix.[57] Speaking of the present-day conditions in Cape Town and Colony as a result of an incomplete fusing of these divergent ethnic types, Evans says:[58]

> ... Equally, to a Natal resident visiting Cape Town the mixed colored population of that city and neighborhood is a feature that deeply impresses him. He sees a mixture of races to which he is quite unaccustomed. Hottentot, Bushman, Mozambique black, Malay, and other peoples from the Far East, liberated slaves from West and East, Abantu, and European all fused, in varying proportions, to make the colored Cape people of to-day. At one end of the scale he sees men and women almost white, well educated, well spoken, well dressed, courteous and restrained in manner, and at the other end of this color scale some whom he considers inferior to the ordinary native or Indian coolie of his home. ...

These mixed-blood people are at the present time the intellectual class among the blacks. The blacks are on their native soil and never have had the advantage of a period of

Hottentots were the dominant race at the time of the settlemnt. The Kafir (Bantu) is a conqueror in South Africa. These people have never been enslaved and are keenly conscious of that fact; they have the instincts of a race with a proud history. Fremantle, *The New Nation*, pp. 181-82.

[56] James Bryce, *Impressions of South Africa*, p. 104.
[57] *Encyclopædia Britannica:* South Africa.
[58] Maurice S. Evans, *Black and White in South East Africa; A Study in Sociology*, p. 296.

industrial training such as the Negroes in the New World received during the slave regime. They are practically all heathen and handicapped by the lack of a culture language. In point of natural ability, the Abantus probably are considerably superior to West African Negroes who made up the bulk of the importations to the Americas.[59] Moreover, the blacks are such an overwhelming majority in South Africa that they have little opportunity to acquire, or to have thrust upon them, the white man's culture; their numerical preponderance operates to their serious disadvantage. The mixed-bloods form separate groups apart from the native and from the white, and live a life similar to their European neighbors. In general their aims and ideals are white, though they grade off by almost imperceptible degrees into the native groups who form the great mass of the population. Freemantle considers them as doubtfully superior to the Abantus. He says:[60]

> The half-castes, or coloured people, as they are generally called, have more civilization though not more character. They are showing good capacity as artisans, and although their position as the lower class in the towns, the dubious origin of their race, and the absence of such primitive but effective discipline as controls the Kafirs in their tribal state do not conduce to high standards of life, it cannot be said that they have proved that they are essentially lacking in the moral qualities which distinguish strong and virile peoples. . . .

Mr. Finot, however, has asserted that the Bastaards are in no sense inferior to the pure whites,[61] but this seems not

[59] Bryce, *Impressions of South Africa*, pp. 378-79.
[60] *The New Nation*, p. 182.
Finch, *Inter-Racial Problems*, p. 109, says that they have "multiplied and prospered while the pure Hottentots have rapidly decreased."
[61] "The Griquas [Bastaards], mixed products of Hottentots and Dutch,

to be the opinion of those with most knowledge of the actual facts. Evans, for example, says: [62]

> ... It is utterly contrary to fact to say they [Griquas] are equal to Europeans; either physically, mentally, morally, as a whole, neither are they equal in any single character of value. ... The Griquas are a degenerate, dissolute, demoralized people, weak and unstable, lazy and thriftless. They appear to be constitutionally immoral, far more so than either the European or Bantu people among whom they live. The branch of these people with whom I am best acquainted live in Griqualand East, just south of the Natal border. They came to this land, then unoccupied owing to native wars and thus called No Man's Land, under Adam Kok their chief, some half century ago. It is one of the best parts of South Africa, well grassed and well watered, with fertile arable land, a glorious climate, with good rainfall, and healthy for all kinds of live-stock. This goodly land was parcelled out to the Griqua families in farms of from 2000 to 3000 acres. Never had a people a better start in life. To-day the land has passed from them and they live miserably as squatters, as herds for Europeans, or without definite employment, and the farms they once held are owned and occupied by Europeans, who are prosperous and thriving, and constantly advancing in the amenities of life. The Griquas were not dispossessed by force; excepting for one short-lived outbreak the country has been in peace. They are simply constitutionally unable to hold; gin, immorality, laziness, debt, the lack of foresight and inability to forego present gratification

or the Cafusos, are quite equal to pure whites, just as the cross breeds of Indian and Spanish are at least as good as the Spaniards themselves." Finot, *Race Prejudice*. Quoted by Maurice S. Evans, *Black and White in the Southern States*, pp. 25-26.

[62] *Black and White in the Southern States*, pp. 26-27. See, also, Friedrich Ratzel, *The History of Mankind*, Vol. 2, p. 295, and Élisée Reclus, *Africa*, Vol. 4, p. 149.

for future well-being, are the reasons for their race failure. The methods of the incoming European were sometimes not justifiable, but the hopeless weakness of the Griqua was his undoing.

Between the races in South Africa there is a complete separation on the basis of color. The white inhabitants recognize no difference between the various shades of Negroes, but draw an impassable color line with the whites on one side and all grades of the colored population on the other.[63] No colored man ever enters the house of a white man except it be as a servant. Intermarriage, though permitted in the English colonies, does not occur in South Africa, and illicit relations between the races are pretty effectually tabooed by an intolerant public opinion.[64] "Each race goes its own way and lives its own life." [65] Black children are not admitted to the schools attended by white children,[66] with the exception of a very few mission schools to which a few families of the poorer whites send their children because of the low fees.[67] The superiority of the white man must be maintained even at the expense of his sense of humor.[68]

[63] Bryce, *Impressions of South Africa,* p. 368.

[64] "I suppose, in the opinion of the average South African, the admixture in blood of the races is the worst thing that can happen, at least for the white race, and possibly for both . . . he can see the degradation of the white man, the ambiguous position of the children, often the resentment of the native in cases of miscegenation; . . ." Evans, *Black and White in South East Africa,* p. 223. See, also, Fremantle, *The New Nation,* pp. 217-18.

[65] Bryce, *Impressions of South Africa,* p. 375.

[66] Evans, *Black and White in South East Africa,* p. 299.

[67] Bryce, *Impressions of South Africa,* p. 378.

[68] "Sometimes the usual relations of employer and employed are reversed, and a white man enters the service of a prosperous Kaffir. This makes no difference as respects their social intercourse, and I remember

The attitude of the white man is one of aversion towards colored people. He dislikes and despises the black. The attitude of contempt is to be found in all classes though strongest in the rougher elements. The Dutch are more bitter than the English, and more disposed to treat the native harshly. There is no community of ideas and no sympathy between the races.[69] "The black man accepts the superiority of the white man as a part of the order of nature."[70] He submits patiently to the stronger race.

But there is no serious friction between the white and the black people of South Africa. The native is too far removed from the white man to appreciate or resent the white man's attitude.[71] The mixed-bloods, here as everywhere, chafe against the social ostracism from the white group with which it is their ambition to be identified, and resent the attitude of the white group which identifies them with the native side of their ancestry which they are anxious to conceal and forget. Speaking of the half-castes Fremantle says:[72]

> . . . In varying degrees he possesses white blood. He is permanently conscious of the fact that the infusion of that blood differentiates him completely from the natives who surround him. He feels that he has a right to a definite place in the social structure of South Africa, and he is embittered by finding that no such place is accorded to him. He has a definite place in each Colony but, as has already been stated, he is subjected to different rules in the different Colonies. South Africa, as such, does not recognize him. And he,

to have been told of a case in which the white workman stipulated that his employer should address him as 'Boss.'" Bryce, *Impressions of South Africa*, p. 367.

[69] *Ibid.*, pp. 365-68.
[70] *Ibid.*, p. 375.
[71] *Ibid.*, p. 375.
[72] *The New Nation*, pp. 319-20.

who ought to be a permanent support to the influence of white rule, is tempted to turn his face backwards to a more sympathetic understanding with that native population from which he is, in so large a part, derived.

North American Indians

The contact of the North European races with the North American Indians more often resulted in the extermination of the Indian by slaughter or disease, than in an amalgamation of the races. During the period of settlement and colonization, there generally existed a state of potential if not of actual warfare between the races. The Indian was dispossessed and driven farther and farther into the interior, rather than absorbed into the new life of the country.

However, there was from the first some intermingling of the blood of the races which has continued to the present day. The French mingled freely with the Algonquian tribes both on the coast and in the interior. They furnished fathers for the great group of present-day French-Canadians. The Catholic missionaries, especially in the interior, favored these unions and they took place to such an extent that to-day few French families in the Missouri-Illinois region are entirely free from any trace of Indian blood. Of the fifteen thousand persons of French-Canadian descent in Michigan, few are without some trace of Indian intermixture.[73] In Manitoba at the time of its admission to the Dominion, there were some ten thousand mixed-bloods, the result of the Hudson Bay Company's activities in the Canadian Northwest. A considerable per cent of the mixed-bloods of the Northwest are the descendants of English and Scotch fathers. The Iroquois are largely mixed with both

[73] Bureau of American Ethnology, *Handbook of the American Indians*. Part I, p. 913.

French and English blood, an appreciable amount of which came from the captives in the wars of the seventeenth and eighteenth centuries and from their tribal institution of adoption. In the Apache, Comanche, and other warlike tribes of the Southwest, is also some admixture of captive white blood. In such cases the offspring are, in a larger percentage of cases than is elsewhere true, the children of white mothers and Indian fathers.[74]

In the early days, the unions of the whites and Indians were usually temporary alliances formed and broken at the pleasure of the conquering white man. Almost exclusively they were unions between white men and Indian women. Occasionally, and much more frequently during the past half century, there have been alliances of a different sort. Educated individuals of some Indian blood and whites occasionally have intermarried; some of these unions have been between white women and men of Indian blood. In how far these mixed marriages have been dictated by economic motives, it is of course not possible to say.[75]

At the present time the Indian population of the United States is about forty per cent mixed-bloods, and considerably over nine-tenths of the mixed-bloods are Indian-white crosses. The actual numbers and percentages are as follows:[76]

Indian Population, Continental United States, 1910

Racial Ancestry	Number	Per cent of Total
Full blood	150,053	56.5

[74] See *Handbook of the American Indians*, Part I, pp. 913-14.
[75] Charles Alexander Eastman, "The North American Indian," *Inter-Racial Problems*, pp. 367-76.
[76] *Indian Population in the United States and Alaska*, United States Census 1910, Supplement 1915, p. 31.

Mixed-Blood Races

Racial Ancestry	Number	Per Cent of Total
Mixed blood	93,423	35.2
⎡White and Indian a	88,030	33.1 ⎤
⎢Negro and Indian	2,255	0.8 ⎥
⎨White, Negro and Indian	1,793	0.7 ⎬
⎢Other mixtures	80	0.1 ⎥
⎣Unknown	1,265	0.5 ⎦
Not reported	22,207	8.3
Total	265,683	100.0

a Includes Mexican and Indian.

More than four-fifths of those in the "not reported" group are scattered through the white population and the great majority are probably individuals of mixed blood.[77] Moreover, the degree of the intermixture is appreciably greater than appears on the face of the table. Of the total number of mixed white and Indian blood about twenty per cent are less than half white, nearly twenty-eight per cent are one-half Indian and one-half white, while approximately one-half of all the mixed-bloods are more than one-half white. About four-fifths of the total number of mixed-bloods are at least one-half white.[78]

Degree of Mixture	Number	Per cent
Less than one-half white	18,169	20.6
One-half white, one-half Indian	24,353	27.7
More than one-half white	43,937	49.9

In regard to the geographical distribution of the mixed-bloods, the report gives the following table:[79]

[77] *Ibid.*, p. 31.
[78] *Ibid.*, p. 35.
[79] *Ibid.*, p. 32.

State	Full-blood	Mixed-blood	Per cent mixed
Arizona	27,087	414	1.4
Oklahoma	25,887	44,288	62.6
New Mexico	20,085	175	0.9
South Dakota	13,247	5,408	28.7
California	10,493	4,217	28.1
Montana	6,204	3,895	37.5
Washington	6,770	3,019	30.6
Wisconsin	5,249	4,330	45.1
Nevada	4,287	508	10.3
Minnesota	3,859	4,886	55.8
Michigan	3,528	3,218	47.6
Oregon	2,901	1,668	36.4
Utah	2,900	105	3.4
Idaho	2,864	514	15.0
New York	2,850	2,028	38.9
Nebraska	2,294	939	28.4
North Dakota	2,499	3,561	57.7
Wyoming	1,174	284	19.5
North Carolina	1,394	5,855	80.3
Mississippi	1,077	90	7.7
Colorado	718	50	6.5
Kansas	516	889	62.9

It is of importance to note that the proportion of mixed-bloods is high in the regions where the total Indian population is small as compared to the whites, or where it is scattered through the white population; and that the proportion of full-bloods is high in the regions with a large total Indian population, or where the Indian tribes live in relative isolation.

The Hopi Indians of Arizona, for example, are 99.9 per cent pure, while the Croatan Indians of North Carolina are 7.8 per cent pure. The former is an isolated group of some 2,009; they are but little in contact with the whites. They

Mixed-Blood Races 81

live in a region sparsely populated by the whites. The Croatans, a small group of composite origin, have been in contact with the whites and Negroes since the colonial days, in a region of relatively dense white population.

The St. Regis, a tribe of mixed Iroquoian origin living in the state of New York, are the second most mixed group.[80] Out of a total of 1219, there are 1140 mixed-bloods. The Navajo, a large nomadic tribe of New Mexico and Arizona, is next to the Hopi in the purity of their blood. Out of a total of 22,304, there are but 99 mixed-bloods. [81]

Oklahoma is the only notable exception to the rule that the number of mixed-bloods is inversely proportional to the number of full-bloods in the region. With a large number of Indians, it also has a small proportion of full-bloods. In explanation of this anomaly the report says: [82]

> . . . This low proportion in Oklahoma is no doubt due in part to the fact that the possession of valuable lands by the Indians encourages intermarriages between whites and Indians, and that persons with very little Indian blood are anxious to establish their claims as members of the Indian tribes, in order that they may be entitled to participate in the distribution of lands and moneys belonging to the Five Civilized Tribes in Oklahoma.

It should also be noted that some, at least, of the Oklahoma tribes were enormously mixed before being settled in their present home; also that the number of white people is relatively large in the Oklahoma region.

[80] *Indian Population in the United States and Alaska,* United States Census 1910, Supplement 1915, p. 84.
[81] *Ibid.,* p. 78.
[82] *Ibid.,* p. 32.

The Negroes and the Indians of most tribes have freely intermixed. There never has been any legal barrier to their intermarriage and positively there exists some fundamental grounds of sympathy between them. In the early days, they were frequently slaves together associating on terms of social equality. In these cases, the Indians eventually disappeared by absorption into the larger body of blacks, and were counted with the Negro slaves. Throughout the slave period, there is occasional mention made of slaves of mixed Indian and Negro blood. Many of the broken coast tribes have been completely absorbed into the Negro race.[83] All these mixtures, however, now appear in the American mulatto rather than in the American Indian groups.

In certain of the tribes, notably those who formerly lived in the Gulf States and on the Atlantic seaboard, there is a large admixture of Negro blood. The five civilized tribes [84] were large slave holders and, at the close of the Civil War, they were required to free their Negro slaves and admit them to equal Indian citizenship. There were over twenty thousand of these adopted Negro citizens in the five tribes in addition to those of various degrees of intermixture.

The number of Indians who reported Negro blood was doubtless far less than the actual number.[85] The degree of Negro blood in those reporting is relatively very much less than the amount of white blood in the Indian-white crosses.

---

[83] *Handbook of the American Indians*, Part I, p. 914.

[84] "The Seminoles at this time, 1834, owned perhaps 200 slaves, their people had intermarried with the maroons, . . ." Minnie Moore-Willson, *The Seminoles of Florida*, p. 14.

[85] "The number of Negro and Indian mixed-bloods reported, 2,255, is probably an understatement, owing to disinclination to admit Negro blood." *Indian Population in the United States and Alaska*, United States Census 1910, Supplement 1915, p. 38.

Amount of Negro Blood in the Indian-Negro Crosses [86]

Degree of Mixture	Number	Per cent of total
Less than one-half Negro	717	31.8
One-half Negro, one-half Indian	729	32.3
More than one-half Negro	780	34.6
Unknown proportions	29	1.3

In all cases the fertility of the mixed unions is higher than the unions of the full-blood Indians. The greatest amount of sterility is found in the marriages between the full-bloods; in cases of miscegenation it is considerably less common. The per cent of issueless marriages decreases directly with the decrease in the amount of Indian blood in the married couple. In cases of fertile marriages the number of children is also less in the Indian marriages than in those that were mixed. The marriages between mixed-blood Negroes and Indians show the highest degree of fertility.[87]

Such study as has been made of the Indian-white mixtures in America, shows the mixed-blood race to be physically superior to the Indian type. Boaz [88] in a study of the French-Indian mixtures, found the offspring to exceed both parents in height, to be more variable than the Indian parents and also to be more fertile. "We observe in the mixed-blood race that the fertility and the laws of growth are affected, that the variability of the race is increased, and that the resultant stature of the mixed-blood race exceeds that of both parents." [89] In other respects, notably in the color of skin, texture of the hair and the facial features,

[86] *Ibid.*, p. 38.
[87] *Ibid.*, pp. 157-58.
[88] Franz Boaz, "The Half-Breed Indian," *Popular Science Monthly*, Vol. 45, pp. 761-70. See, also, Eugen Fischer, *Die Rehobother Bastards und das Bastardierungsproblem beim Menschen.*
[89] *Ibid.*, p. 766.

the mixed-blood race is much nearer to the Indian than to the white ancestry. In the case of the Negro intermixture, the offspring incline much more to the Indian than to the Negro type.[90]

In general, the mixture of other blood with the Indian has not given rise to a special racial problem. The increasing amount of white blood in the Indian race simply has decreased the gap between the races, not by the creation of an intermediate caste, but by a modification of the temperament and appearance of the Indian group.[91] The mixed-blood Indian, dressed in the clothes of civilized man, loses most of his distinctive Indian characteristics. Moreover, a trace of Indian blood is not considered a taint which it is necessary to conceal and of which the individual need feel ashamed. As a consequence, the man of mixed Indian-white ancestry who desires to do so, may escape from the Indian group and identify himself with and become lost in the culture group.

Most frequently, however, the half-breeds have elected to remain with the mother race and to become the leaders of the race. The Five Civilized Tribes are to-day far more Anglo-Saxon than they are Indian. The Wyandots have not a single full-blood. For over a century, to take a single example to illustrate the status of the half-breed, every leading man of the Cherokee Nation has had more white than

[90] *Handbook of the American Indians,* Part I, p. 365.

[91] Possibly also by causing his intellectual advance. At any rate "The families that have made Cherokee history were nearly all of this mixed descent. The Doughertys, Galpins, and Adairs were from Ireland; the Rosses, Vanns, and McIntoshes, like the McGillivrays and Graysons among the Creeks, were of Scottish origin; the Waffords and others were Americans from Carolina or Georgia, and the father of Sequoya was a [Pennsylvania?] German. . . ." See James Mooney, "Myths of the Cherokee," *19th Report of the Bureau of American Ethnology,* Part I, p. 83.

Indian blood. John Ross, their most noted man, was one-eighth Indian and seven-eighths white.[92]

Where a race problem has appeared, it has been due in most cases to an antipathy toward the Negro and Negro mixtures, or to an effort on the part of these mixtures to escape classification with the Negro race. The Croatan Indians of North Carolina, a mixed-blood race of Negro and white around an Indian nucleus whose identity has been completely lost, were for years classed with the free Negroes. They persistently refused to accept the classification or to attend the Negro schools or churches, claiming special privileges on the ground that they were descended from native tribes and early settlers. In 1885, they were given separate legal existence on the baseless theory that they were descended from Raleigh's lost colony of Croatan, and separate school provision was made for them.[93] In some of the more distinctly Indian tribes, notably the Cherokee and Osage, there is a bitter rivalry between the mixed-bloods and the full-bloods, and they have formed rival factions. The Cherokees, too, draw a color line against their Negro citizens and refuse to intermarry with them.

[92] *Handbook of the American Indians,* Part I, p. 914.

[93] They are a mixture of wasted Indian tribes, forest rovers, runaway slaves and other Negroes. There are a number of other similar groups, the "Redbones" of South Carolina, the "Melungeons" of West Virginia and East Tennessee and the "Moors" of Delaware, but like the "Croatan Indians" they are rather mulatto than Indian mixtures. See *Ibid.,* p. 365.

CHAPTER IV

THE MULATTO: THE KEY TO THE RACE PROBLEM

THE foregoing summary review of the origin and status of the chief half-caste races has necessarily been brief and more or less unsatisfactory. It does not include a sketch of all such groups, and makes no pretense of being an adequate treatment of any.

Little more can be done, however, in the present state of knowledge concerning these peoples. Of the score or more of mixed-blood races scarcely one has been made the subject of objective scientific study.[1] The whole work on this important subject remains to be done. Any wide observation or comparison, or any thoroughgoing analysis of a single situation, has not been made.

The little that is known concerning most of these racial groups comes from the reports of travelers and officials who

[1] Dr. Eugen Fischer's *Die Rehobother Bastards und das Bastardierungsproblem beim Menschen* is the only adequate, objective, scientific study that has been made of the amalgamation of two diverse racial groups. Fischer's general conclusion is to the effect that the interbreeding of the first generation of bastards and their crossing with the pure parent races have given rise to a group in which the physical characters of the pure-blood parent races reappear in endless new combinations and that no new race with approximately uniform characters has arisen. On the mental side the bastards show an intellectual capacity and variability superior to that of the Negro side of their ancestry but are as lacking in the mental energy and fixedness of the European as is the full-blood primitive group. Fischer's general position would seem to be that two diverse races cannot amalgamate to a new ethnic unity. See note 6, p. 13 above.

The Mulatto: the Key to the Race Problem   87

are dealing primarily with other matters. These observers frequently disagree concerning even the most obvious objective facts. Their opportunity to observe generally is limited; they see one phase of a situation, seldom the whole. Moreover, individual interest determines what the non-scientific observer of a social situation will see. His preconceptions lead him to see the things for which he is looking. His prejudice may prevent him from giving an unbiased report of what he observes if, indeed, it does not actually prevent him from seeing certain facts of first-rate importance. Sweeping generalizations are made on the basis of the most partial and inadequate observation. Seldom is any account taken of the part played by different factors at work in the situation. The amental influences behind the observed conditions are never gotten at and there is seldom a consciousness on the part of the writers that such influences exist.

On the basis of such data as are available, the object has been to give in brief space as accurate a statement as possible concerning the main facts of the miscegenation of the advanced and backward races for the light that such a comparison would throw on the mulatto type and problem existing in the United States. Incomplete as are the data, and tentative as the conclusions must consequently be, enough has been said to reveal the fact that the mulatto is the key to the racial situation. Any scientific study of a race problem that fails to take account of the man of mixed ancestry and the special and important part he plays, falls short of a complete analysis of the situation. Any program of racial adjustment that does not recognize and provide for this special factor fails at the most vital point. Broadly speaking, the review seems to bear out the conclusion that in its acute and troublesome form, the "race problem" is the problem of the mulatto.

It remains for this section to summarize in general terms certain facts in regard to the origin, growth, and status of the mixed-blood races; to point out certain similarities in the psychological type developed, and to show the sociological problem that the type creates.

In every case the half-caste races have arisen as the result of illicit relations between the men of the superior and the women of the inferior race.[2] In India it was the Portuguese and later the English men who mixed with the native women; in Greenland it was the Danish men and the native women; on the Labrador coast it was the English fishermen and the native women; in Brazil it was the Portuguese immigrant men with the native and later with the Negro women; in other parts of South America and the Spanish West Indies, it was the Spanish males with the native and later with the Negro females; in Haiti it was the French settlers with the Negro women, and so it has been in all other cases. There is no mixed-blood race which is the result of intermarriage between culturally unequal races and none where the mothers of the half-castes are not of the culturally inferior race.

While all the advanced races have, under certain conditions, mixed with the women of the lower races they have not done so with anything like equal readiness. Of the white races, the Spanish and the Portuguese have mixed most easily and in largest numbers. They have mixed, moreover, with almost equal readiness with the Malay, the American Indian, and the African Negress; and with less repugnance than any other people with whom these lower races have come in contact. "They had never acquired, or

[2] Sir Harry H. Johnston, "Racial Problems and the Congress of Races," *Contemporary Review*, Vol. 100, p. 159.

The Mulatto: the Key to the Race Problem 89

had lost as the result of experience, any aversion to race mixture."[3] The French mixed readily with the American Indians but in contact with the Negroes in Haiti they mixed relatively little. The English have crossed with all the lower races, but much more slowly than have the Latin peoples. Moreover, the English mix less readily with the Negroes than with the Indians, and more slowly with these than with certain of the brown races.[4] Bryce summarizes the situation in these words:[5]

> . . . Roughly speaking . . . we may say that while all the races of the same, or a similar, colour intermarry freely, those of one colour intermarry very little with those of another. This is most marked as between the white and the black races. The various white races are, however, by no means equally averse to such unions. Among the Arabs and Turks the sense of repulsion from negroes is weakest, . . . The South European races, though disinclined to such un-

[3] A. G. Keller, *Colonization*, pp. 104, 216, 219. See, also, H. C. Morris, *The History of Colonization*, Vol. 1, p. 249.

[4] B. L. Putnam Weale [Weale is the pseudonym of Mr. B. L. Simpson], "The Conflict of Color," *World's Work*, Vol. 19, p. 12,328, points out the same preference on the part of the Chinese. They mate readily with "many varieties of brown maidens" but avoid the black. See, also, U. G. Weatherly, "A World Wide Color Line," *Popular Science Monthly*, Vol. 79, p. 480.

[5] James Bryce, *Relations of Advanced and Backward Races*, pp. 18-19. See, also, Bryce, "Migrations of the Races of Men," *Contemporary Review*, Vol. 62, p. 130. ". . . Whether in each case of dispersion the migrating population becomes fused with that which it finds, depends chiefly on the difference between the level of civilization of the two races." Luis Cabrera, "The Mexican Revolution—Its Causes, Purposes and Results," *Annals of the American Academy of Political and Social Science*, Supplement, Jan. 1917, p. 5, states the order of ease with which civilized races fuse with the Mexican mixed-blood race as follows: 1. Spanish and Italian, 2. German, 3. French, and 4. American and English. The first two races "nearly always" blend; the last two "hardly ever."

ions, do not wholly eschew them. . . . In modern times the Spanish settlers in the Antilles and South America, and the Portuguese in Brazil, as well as on the East and West coasts of Africa, have formed many unions with negro women, as the Spaniards have done with the Malayan Tagals in the Philippines, and the Portuguese with the Hindus in Malabar. There is to-day a negro strain in many of the whites of Cuba, and a still stronger one in the whites of Brazil. The aversion to color reaches its maximum among the Teutons. The English in North America and the West Indies did, indeed, during the days of slavery, become the parents of a tolerably large mixed population, as did the Dutch in South Africa. But they scarcely ever intermarried with the free coloured people: . . . So the English in India have felt a like aversion to marriages with native women, and even such illicit connections as were not rare a century ago are now seldom found.

Where a white race comes into contact with the so-called "red" or "yellow" race . . . the sense of repulsion is much less pronounced. The English settlers intermarry, though less frequently than the French did, with the aborigines of America. . . . The Spaniards have been still less fastidious. All over Central and South America they have become commingled with the aborigines, especially, as was natural, with the more advanced tribes. . . .

Another element that conditions the amount of miscegenation that takes place between the members of two divergent races is the class of the superior race that comes into contact with the native race. In most of the early contacts of the white race with the darker races, the white race has been represented by its adventurer and outcast classes.[6] In Cen-

[6] "Most race crossing has occurred on the outskirts of civilization, . . ." Earl Finch, "The Effects of Racial Miscegenation," *Inter-Racial Prob-*

The Mulatto: the Key to the Race Problem 91

tral and South America, the adventurers and the clergy were reinforced by convicts sentenced to death or mutilation who had their sentences commuted on condition that they emigrate to the colonies. Greenland was practically a Danish penal colony with a forced immigration of orphan boys to recruit the teaching force and the inferior clergy. South Africa was made the dumping ground for Asiatic convicts. Portugal unloaded on her Brazilian colony not only her convicts but her prostitutes as well. Aside from the criminal and the vicious, however, the military and the adventurer classes are hardly more typical of the moral sense of a community, but they usually have been the first representatives of the superior race with whom the nature peoples have come in contact.

Of more importance, perhaps, than either race or class considerations is the matter of the presence or the absence of women of the higher race. In the absence of their own women, men of all divisions of the white race have intermixed, though not with equal readiness, with the women of the lower races. Where women have been present some intermixture has still gone on, but never in the wholesale way that characterizes the trading, as distinguished from the settlement, colony. It is to this fact—the presence or absence of women of the culture race—that Keller seems inclined to attribute the differences in the amount of intermixture with the native races in the North American and the South American colonies. White women were present in the former; and few in number, or entirely absent, in the latter.[7]

---

lems, p. 111. See, also, Felix von Luschan, "Anthropological View of Race," *Inter-Racial Problems*, p. 23.

[7] *Colonization*, p. 14. See, also, E. A. Ross, *South of Panama*, pp. 109 ff.

Comparison is likewise challenged in respect to marriage and the family. The fundamental factors which rendered the conditions of the tropical colonies so different from those, say, of the New England settlements, were the great preponderance of males, and the feeble economic efficiency of such females as were present. The former factor led to formal celibacy, intermixture of races, and aberrations all but unknown in societies of the other type,—all this amounting to a negation of matrimony in the sense characteristic of the temperate colony. The other factor, economic inefficiency, minimized the importance of woman's status; the materfamilias had no such independent and influential position in the tropics as in the cooler regions. And where woman was absent or of little significance, there could be little of the family life and solidarity characteristic of many settlement colonies. . . .

With the increase of women and the consequent equalizing of the sexes of the white race, the miscegenation with the native women everywhere has tended to decrease. But the coming of women, usually as the members of immigrating families, has meant, also, a change in the class of men who were immigrating to the colony. It has indicated that the settler and the home seeker was displacing the adventurer so that a difference in the sexual relations of the races is to be expected quite apart from whatever influence the presence of women might have.

It is sometimes held that the institution of slavery was responsible for the origin of the mixed-blood races through the compulsory concubinage of the slave women by the master class. But mixed-blood races have arisen where the institution of slavery has not prevailed. The North American Indians were never successfully enslaved, yet they have intermixed with every other race with whom they have come in contact. The same fact is to be noted in other regions.

Slavery did not exist in Greenland, nor in the Philippines, nor in India or elsewhere in Asia. The simple fact of the case seems to be that the women of the lower races everywhere seek sex relations with the men of the superior race or caste. Ratzel [8] comments upon "the ease with which Malay women form transitory alliances with foreigners," and adds that "nearly all the so-called Chinese women in Banca are half-breeds from Malayan mothers." Keller [9] says of the Eskimo women that "illicit relations with white men are rather a glory than a disgrace." Of the Indian women, Lee [10] says "she is the seducer and it is the proudest moment of her life when she has allied herself with a man of a superior race," while Crooke [11] points out the fact that a failure on the part of girls of certain castes to attract the attention and have sex relations with men of a higher class ruins their chances to secure husbands in their own group, and that for a girl to claim such an honor falsely is legal grounds for divorce on the part of the outraged husband.[12] It seems to be the usual situation everywhere that the women of the lower races or the lower castes desire, seek, feel honored by the attention of the higher class men, and are enormously proud of their light-skinned, half-caste children. The effect of slavery, so far as any effect can be shown, seems to be to lessen the amount of intermixture by separating and restraining the vicious elements, and so preventing an indiscriminate sexual relation.

Once started, the half-caste races everywhere increase

[8] Friedrich Ratzel, *The History of Mankind*, Vol. 1, p. 438.
[9] *Colonization*, p. 515.
[10] Mary Helen Lee, *The Eurasian: A Social Problem*, p. 5.
[11] W. Crooke, "The Stability of Caste and Tribal Groups in India," *Journal of the Royal Anthropological Institute*, Vol. 44, pp. 270-81.
[12] Edward Westermarck, *The History of Human Marriage*, pp. 65-67, 76-77, 81.

rapidly in numbers and always at the expense of the backward race. Illicit relations between the half-breed women and the men of the superior race are the normal situation after the mixed-blood race has become sufficiently large to allow the forces of sexual selection to operate. The half-breed men in their turn prey upon the women of the pure-blood native race. Both result in additions to the mulatto group. Moreover, the marriage of the mixed-blood individuals is in nearly every case with their own or a lighter color, hence the natural, legitimate increase is normal or nearly so.[13]

In some cases, especially after the earlier crosses have produced a somewhat choicer type of female, there has come to be some intermarriage. A small number of Danes form temporary marriage unions with the mixed-blood Eskimo women in Greenland, though the women and children are deserted when the man retires from official life. The unions of the Chinese with the native women in the Philippines is a form of marriage very similar to that practiced by the Danes and Eskimo women of Greenland. There is some intermarriage between the middle-class or low-class whites and the mixed-breed races of Latin America. In Brazil the wealthy and near-white mulattoes and *metis* sometimes marry immigrant and other white women. Occasionally among the Indian tribes in the United States, are to be

---

[13] It would be quite normal except for the illegitimate children that the women of the mixed-blood race bear to white men. These, however, cannot all be counted as substitutes for children of a mixed-blood father. They are usually born before the girl forms a regular sexual union with one of her own class and are in general to be looked upon as extra-matrimonial additions to the class. Such relations seem generally not to be a bar to the girl forming a regular matrimonial alliance with one of her own class and in some cases at least gives her a decided prestige.

found white men and women married to wealthy Indians and half-breeds.

In most of these situations if not in all, intermarriage is the exception and not the rule. Where it takes place, the compelling motive is to be looked for in the economic status of the colored man or woman, in the scarcity of women of the advanced race, or in a combination of the two. In all other situations, mixed marriages are very rare though isolated cases occur in all countries. All in all, the number of mixed marriages that occur in any country with an advanced race and a backward race in the population, is very trivial as compared to the amount of amalgamation that takes place between the races outside the marriage bond.

In general, the half-breed children are disowned by their fathers though this is not always the case. Where the unions take the form of a fairly permanent marriage, as with some of the Danish-Eskimo and many of the Chinese-Malay unions, the offspring are acknowledged and cared for. The Chinaman is even said to be inordinately proud of his half-breed progeny. In the colonial days, the Spanish and the Portuguese in South America in some cases acknowledged their mixed-blood offspring by the Negro and native women, and provided for their education and training. In general, however, the child followed the status of the mother.[14] The French in Canada in the colonial days often showed much fondness for their offspring by the Indian women. In Haiti their unions with the Negro women were of a casual sort; the fathers showed little concern for their mulatto progeny. The British never have acknowl-

---

[14] "The amalgamation of the negroes by the Mohammedans is facilitated particularly by the institution of polygamy, the conquerors taking native wives, and raising their children as members of their own family." Franz Boaz, *The Mind of Primitive Man*, p. 15.

edged their offspring by a lower race. In India and the sea-port cities of Asia, the offspring in many cases are the result of a casual meeting; the father may not know his offspring or even know of their existence. In general it may be said that individual fathers, more frequently in some places than in others, have acknowledged and cared for their half-caste children but that this has at no time or place been the rule.

The status of the mixed-blood race tends to differ from that of either of the parent races. It is not everywhere the same, however, and the status of a single group is not the same at different times. The operation of the two prime factors—the racial differences and the cultural differences of the pure-blood groups—is modified by historical factors and by the prevailing social situation.

There are almost infinite gradations of both color and culture. There are, however, four different combinations in which these factors may appear. The two races in contact in a given geographical situation may be practically alike both as to color and as to culture. There may be an essential equality of culture, but a wide diversity in color or other physical characteristics. They may be widely different as to cultural development, yet essentially alike as to color and other ethnic characters. Finally they may diverge both in cultural and in racial characteristics. The inter-racial situation differs in each case and the status of the half-caste race likewise differs. The first situation ordinarily does not give rise to a lasting racial problem. The third case may or may not do so. In the second, a characteristic form of the race problem appears. It is in the fourth, however, that the problem emerges in its most characteristic present day form and presents the most troublesome social situation. Each of the phases will be noted in turn.

Of the innumerable bastard races produced by the commingling of primitive groups, none seems to have acquired a distinct status in the community life. Where there exist no fundamental differences in culture and no wide ethnic divergence, there soon comes to be an intermingling of the cultures of the two groups in contact, or a cultural assimilation of the one by the other. As friendly intercourse increases, the original separation on race lines gives way little by little to a class division. The individuals of mixed ancestry who practically always appear are a help in this direction. They serve as a tie between the originally hostile groups and their lack of a distinctive appearance militates against their being made into a special class in the community. In the process of racial amalgamation, the group of lesser numerical strength presently loses itself within the larger—becomes an integral part of the community—without greatly altering the ethnic type of the larger group. Where the numerical strength of the two groups is more nearly equal, the intermixture of the two races leads to the formation of a homogeneous hybrid race in which the distinctive features of the parent races blend and disappear. Between closely related ethnic groups, as different branches of the same race, intermarriage is governed by much the same rules as govern the marriage of individuals within the same branch. It is a question of association and of sufficient time to allow of mutual understanding and appreciation.

Oppenheimer,[15] discussing the formation of the primitive state through the subjugation of one group by another and their gradual reduction to an ethnic and cultural unity,

[15] Franz Oppenheimer, *The State; Its History and Development Viewed Sociologically*, pp. 80-81.

says:

> ... The two groups, separated to begin with, and then united on one territory, are at first merely laid along side one another like a mechanical mixture, as the term is used in chemistry, until gradually they become more and more of a "chemical combination." They intermingle, unite, amalgamate to unity, in customs and habits, in speech and worship. Soon the bonds of relationship unite the upper and the lower strata. In nearly all cases the master class picks the handsomest virgins from the subject races for its concubines. A race of bastards thus develops, sometimes taken into the ruling class, sometimes rejected, and then because of the blood of the masters in their veins, becoming the born leaders of the subject race. In form and content the primitive state is completed.

Where each of the two races in contact possesses a culture and a civilization, yet differ markedly in physical appearance, the mixed-blood race tends to become an outcast group. A distinctive physical appearance makes it impossible for the hybrids to pass as individuals of either race. They cannot rise, as a group, superior to either of the parent races. Both races despise and reject them.

This appears to be the status of the Eurasian of India and of the various European-Asiatic half-castes. The Orientals, as the East Indians, have a civilization in which they believe, and a pride of race that is often more intolerant than that of the Caucasian. They do not consciously admit the superiority of European culture. The civilizations are not serially arranged; one is not so much higher than the other as that they are different civilizations. In this situation there is no place for the half-castes. They are neither Asiatic nor European. They are accepted by neither race and they can rise superior to neither.

The Mulatto: the Key to the Race Problem

Where the two peoples, essentially alike as to ethnic characters but different as to cultural development are brought into close contact and association, a permanent race problem may or may not arise. Even though color and other physical features are not sufficiently divergent to create, or serve as a basis for, an antipathy; the peoples may be so tempermentally constituted as to make it impossible for them to arrive at any mutually satisfactory working relations. Their interests may so clash as to keep them even from approaching anything like kindly feeling and unity of purpose. Their political ideas may diverge. Their religious beliefs may differ. Their distinctive manners, customs, and habits of life may be at variance. The differences may be so marked that toleration may be impossible and accommodation come about only by the elimination of the one or the other or a more or less complete separation along racial lines. The established customs and the habits of thought and action, differences in speech, dress, religion, and the like that set them off as a distinct people, may be nursed and deified and every effort made to prevent assimilation of the one by the other. This, however, is the problem of the immigrant; it is the problem of nationalities. It, for the most part, falls outside the present discussion. The half-races that appear, differ too slightly from either of the parent races for them to be easily distinguishable. Individuals may therefore pass in either group and be judged according to their personal ability and worth. They do not represent a type. Individual initiative and opportunity are the things required to raise the individual to a higher class.

When color differences coincide with differences in culture levels, then color becomes symbolic and each individual is automatically classified by the racial uniform he wears.

If the proportions of the two groups be such that the racial purity and cultural traits of one group are potentially threatened, the initial conflict may settle down into a chronic state of racial contempt or hatred. The more widely the races differ in appearance, culture, language, religion, anything that serves to distinguish them, the more bitter will be the feeling existing between them. The more unalterable the differences, the more permanent will be their mutually hostile attitude. The greater the danger the backward group is felt to be to civilized standards, the greater will be the intolerance of the culture group.[16]

Where the two groups in a racial situation thus have differed widely both in culture and in color, they everywhere have tended toward an adjustment on the basis of superiority and subordination. The Portuguese and the Spanish enslaved or exterminated the natives of the West Indies and on the mainland of South America. In the Philippines, the Spanish subjugated the native Moros. The Danes reduced the Eskimos to a dependent status. The settlers of North America exterminated the Indians or drove them into the interior as did the English settlers in Australia. The Negro has been reduced to the status of a slave by every people with whom the race has come in contact.

Where the status of one race is absolutely inferior to that of the other and the social separation complete, the adjustment of the races is frequently a harmonious one. The accommodation of the races under a slave regime, for example, is in general marked by a singular lack of racial friction. Under the condition of freedom with its consequent greater differentiation within the ranks of the backward group, the racial superiority and inferiority become less

[16] See Bryce, *Relations of Advanced and Backward Races*. See, also, Weatherly, *Popular Science Monthly*, pp. 478-79.

absolute and the social separation less complete. Friction arises and prejudice becomes active when, and to the extent that, the unlike races come into association and competition.

Where there has been this absolute separation of superior and inferior groups, the half-castes, as a class, have tended to acquire a distinct status in the life of the community. This status is, in general, above that of the colored race, and inferior to the position occupied by the dominant race. They everywhere tended to become a middle class between the races and a connecting link between the extremes of the population. In the Philippines, the Spanish *mestizo* stood midway, socially, between the parent elements.[17] The Chinese-Moro half-breed was superior to the Moro and not markedly inferior to the Chinese. The same midway position was reached by the mulatto races of the English possessions,[18] the *metis* of Brazil,[19] the mixed-blood race of South Africa [20] and the various Indian-white mixtures in Mexico and in Central and South America.[21]

This tendency of the mixed-blood group to rise superior to their racial status generally has been modified by the circumstances of the social situation. In South Africa, because of their numerical insignificance and because of the racial intolerance of the small white group,[22] the tendency

[17] Carl Crow, "What About the Filipinos?", *World's Work*, Vol. 26, p. 519.

[18] W. P. Livingstone, "The West-Indian and American Negro," *North American Review*, Vol. 185, p. 646.

[19] Jean Baptiste de Lacerda, "The *Metis*, or Half Breeds, of Brazil," *Inter-Racial Problems*, p. 381.

[20] Maurice S. Evans, *Black and White in South East Africa; A Study in Sociology*, pp. 298 ff.

[21] James Bryce, *South America; Observations and Impressions*, pp. 481, 492. Ross, *South of Panama*, pp. 29-30, 40-41, 92, 111.

[22] This intolerant attitude finds its explanation in the fact that the

was to thrust them back upon the lower race. In Brazil and in general throughout Spanish America, the numerical strength of the mixed-blood group, in the presence of a relatively weak sense of either race or national pride on the part of the ruling group, has enabled them to claim social recognition from the whites. In some cases, they apparently have risen to the upper class standards; in other cases, they have debased the higher standards to the level of the mongrel group. In Jamaica the insignificant number of the ruling race has counseled the "divide and rule" policy. The natural tendency of the mulatto to rise above the blacks has been fostered, while a rigid separation from the whites has been maintained. Thus they occupy a distinct middle-class status in the community life.[23]

Psychologically, the mulatto is an unstable type.

In the thinking of the white race, the mulattoes generally are grouped with the backward race and share with them the contempt and dislike of the dominant group. Nowhere are they accepted as social equals. The discrimination varies all the way from the more or less successfully concealed contempt of the Brazilian white for the socially ambitious

whites were a small, isolated group in the presence of an overwhelming number of primitive peoples. "That cry, which unceasingly for generations has rung out from the Boer woman's elbow-chair, 'My children, never forget that you are white men! Do always as you have seen your father and mother do!' was no cry of weak conservatism, fearful of change; it was the embodiment of the passionate determination of a great, little people, not to lose the little it possessed and so sink in the scale of being. To laugh at the conservatism of the Boer is to laugh at the man who, floating above a whirlpool, clings fiercely with one hand to the only outstretching rock he can reach, and who will not relax his hold on it by one finger, till he has found something firmer to grasp." Olive Schreiner, "The African Boer," *Cosmopolitan,* Vol. 29, p. 602.

[23] Their caste feeling of superiority tends to keep them a separate type. See Finch, *Inter-Racial Problems,* p. 110.

metis, to the open and bitter hatred of the South African for the "coloured man" and the Native boy, but it seems to be present everywhere. The origin of the half-castes was everywhere an irregular one; this is a point about which prejudice can always center. Their nearer approach in physical appearance to the white type is simply taken as evidence of additional irregularities in ancestry. The two things—the lower ancestry and the presumption of a dubious origin—are the focal points about which the white man's contempt for the mixed-blood group centers.

By the native race, the mixed-blood group is generally accepted as superior. The possession of white blood is an evidence of superiority. The ancestral blot excites no prejudice. The mulattoes are envied because of their color and enjoy a prestige among the darker group because of it.

Between these two groups, one admiring and the other despising, stand the mixed-bloods. In their own estimation, they are neither the one nor the other. They despise the lower race with a bitterness born of their degrading association with it, and which is all the more galling because it needs must be concealed. They everywhere endeavor to escape it and to conceal and forget their relationship to it. They are uncertain of their own worth; conscious of their superiority to the native they are nowhere sure of their equality with the superior group. They envy the white, aspire to equality with them, and are embittered when the realization of such ambition is denied them. They are a dissatisfied and an unhappy group.

It is this discontented and psychologically unstable group which gives rise to the acute phases of the so-called race problem. The members of the primitive group, recognizing the hopelessness of measuring up to the standards of the white race, are generally content and satisfied with their lower status and happy among their own race. It is the mixed-blood man who is dissatisfied and ambitious. The real race problem before each country whose population is divided into an advanced and a backward group, is to determine the policy to be pursued toward the backward group. The acute phase of this is to determine the policy to be adopted toward the mixed-bloods. To reject the claims and to deny the ambition of the mulattos may cause them to turn back upon the lower race. In this case, they may become the intellectual leaven to raise the race to a higher cultural level, or they may become the agitators who create discord and strife between the pure-blood races. To form them into a separate caste between the races, is to lessen the clash between the extreme types and, at the same time, to deprive the members of the lower race of their chance to advance in culture by depriving them of their natural, intellectual leaders. To admit the ambition of the mulattoes to be white and to accept them into the white race on terms of individual merit, means ultimately a mongrelization of the population and a cultural level somewhere between that represented by the standards of the two groups.

The actual policy that has been adopted towards the mixed-blood race in different countries and the consequent rôle that the mulatto plays in different situations will be made the subject of a later chapter.[24]

The tentative conclusions here reached by a review of the mixed-blood races outside the American mulatto group, will be further verified or modified by a closer investigation into the origin, growth, status, and rôle of the mulatto in the United States.

[24] Chapter 12.

CHAPTER V

THE AMOUNT OF RACE INTERMIXTURE IN THE UNITED STATES

IN Negro-white crosses, the characteristic negroid features persist with noticeably greater relative tenacity than do the characteristic Caucasian features.[1] In the mixed-blood population, therefore, the great majority of those individuals in whom Negro blood predominates pass as Negroes of pure blood, while in crosses where the white blood largely predominates, the Negro characteristics are still quite noticeable.[2] As a result, that part of the population commonly classed as mulatto contains far more white than Negro blood, and the actual number of mixed-bloods is

[1] Boaz, in studying Indian-white crosses, found similar results. "We find ... the remarkable fact that the Indian type has a stronger influence upon the offspring than the white type. The same fact is expressed in the great frequency of dark hair and of dark eyes among the half-breeds." Franz Boaz, "The Half-Breed Indian," *Popular Science Monthly*, Vol. 45, p. 768. See, also, *The Mind of Primitive Man*, pp. 78 ff; and "Zur Anthropologie der nordamerikanischen Indianer." *Verhandlungen der Berliner Gesellschaft für Anthropologie, Ethnologie und Urgeschichte.* 27:366 ff.; and F. von Luschan, "Die Tachtadschy u. andere Ueberreste der alten Bevölkerung Lykiens," *Archiv für Anthropologie*, 19:31 ff., who points out the same fact as regards the mixed population of Southern Asia Minor. See James Oliver, "The Hereditary Tendency to Twinning," *Eugenics Review*, Vol. 4, p. 40.

[2] H. Grégoire estimated that five generations with no Negro blood after the original cross were necessary to make it possible for a Negro to pass as a white man. *Literature of Negroes*, p. 29. "Where the proportion is less than one-eighth of African blood the distinction of class begins to be obscured, ..." *The Compendium of the Seventh Census of the United States*, 1850, p. 62.

likely to be greater than a set of census figures shows.[3] The desire, too, of the Negroes themselves to claim as full-blood all dark mulattoes of prominence tends further to obscure the facts.

Moreover, the actual statistics of race intermixture in the United States [4] are of the most meager sort, and those available are not always wholly dependable.[5] This is more especially the case as investigation is pushed toward the beginning of the group. The only general statistics are those of the Federal Censuses of 1850, 1860, 1870, 1890 and 1910. No other general census made a distinction in the returns between the full-blood and the mixed-blood Negroes. Prior to 1850, that is for four-fifths of the period that the Negro has been in America, there are only occasional estimates and partial statistical reports of sections, states, or cities made for special purposes.

The institution of slavery is indigenous to Africa, and the slave trade has been carried on there since time immemorial. At the time of the American colonization and development, the traffic in African slaves, captured on the West Coast, or purchased from the native African slave

[3] C. K. Needham, "A Comparison of Some Conditions in Jamaica with those in the United States," *Journal of Race Development*, Vol. 4, p. 192, calls attention to the fact that in Jamaica the sambos—individuals about three-fourths Negro blood—usually do not return themselves as mixed bloods. It is notorious that in this country many brown Negroes call themselves full bloods and so pass in their group. It is the exceptional Negro, of course, who knows what his ancestry was for more than a generation. See, for example, William Pickens, *The Heir of Slaves*, p. 4.

[4] In South America and Central America and Mexico the statistics are wholly unreliable as the tendency is for every one to call himself white if he has any trace of white blood. See p. 47 above.

[5] "The censuses of mulattoes, as distinguished from full-blooded negroes, taken in 1850, 1860, 1870 and 1890, though subject to a far greater and wholly indeterminate probable error, have shown a general agreement of results." United States Census, 1890, *Population*, Vol. I, Part 1, p. 185.

Amount of Race Intermixture in United States 107

dealers, was an important and profitable business carried on with the sanction of the more important nations of Europe. American colonization opened a new market for the slave dealers and slavery was introduced into most of the colonies almost as soon as they were founded.[6] Georgia was the only exception. This colony started with ordinances against the institution, but political pressure from the mother country, combined with business competition and social pressure at home, overcame the first intention so that slavery was introduced into the colony and legalized seventeen years after its founding.

For a century there was a very slow increase in the number of Negroes in the colonies.[7] Increased importations began after about the middle of the eighteenth century, and the number of Negro slaves grew rapidly. For three-quarters of a century, the natural increase was being constantly added to by an ever and ever greater importation. The actual number of importations, as well as the actual number of slaves, can only be estimated.[8]

[6] Virginia 1619; Massachusetts before 1633; Connecticut from the first settlement of the colony; Maryland 1634 or earlier; Delaware probably in 1636; Georgia 1749; Rhode Island and each of the remaining colonies had slaves from their founding.

[7] *The Compendium of the Seventh Census of the United States*, 1850, p. 83, quotes from Mr. Carey's work on the Slave Trade as follows: ". . . the trade in negro slaves to the American colonies was too small before 1753 to attract attention."

[8] Carey's estimate of slave importations:

Prior to 1715	30,000
1715—1750	90,000
1751—1760	35,000
1761—1770	74,000
1771—1790	34,000
1791—1808	70,000
Total	333,000

"It is claimed, however, that this total is too small, and that a closer

The number of the Negroes was very different in the different colonies, though there was an increase in number in all sections of the country until at least the middle of the century. "At the beginning of the eighteenth century, negro slavery was considered by the settlers of the colonies as a usual and routine matter, and in the New England and Middle Colonies, as well as in the South, the possession of slaves was generally accepted as an evidence of wealth and importance in the community." [9] By the middle of the century it existed by legal sanction in each of the colonies.[10]

estimate would bring the number to 370,000 or even 400,000." "Mr. Carey's figures indicate that the average annual importation was about 2,500 between 1715 and 1750, and 3,500 for the period between 1751 and 1760. The following decade was the period of greatest activity, the importations reaching an average of 7,400 a year. For the 20 years from 1771 to 1790 the average fell to 1,700, but for the period immediately preceding the legal abolition of the slave traffic in the United States it was more than double that number." *A Century of Population Growth,* United States Census, 1890, p. 36.

[9] *Ibid.,* p. 37.
[10] Slave population:

Colonies	1715 a	1775 a	1790 b
Connecticut	1,500	5,000	2,648
Delaware	...	9,000	8,887
Georgia	...	16,000	29,264
Maryland	9,500	80,000	103,036
New Hampshire	150	629	157
New Jersey	1,500	7,600	11,423
New York	4,000	15,000	21,193
North Carolina	3,700	75,000	100,783
Pennsylvania	2,500 c	10,000	3,707
Rhode Island	500	4,373	958
South Carolina	10,500	110,000	107,094
Virginia	23,000	165,000	292,627
Massachusetts	2,000	3,500	...

a G. W. Williams, *History of the Negro Race in America,* Vol. 1, p. 325.
b *A Century of Population Growth,* p. 132.
c Includes Delaware.

Amount of Race Intermixture in United States 109

The crossing of the races began from the very first introduction of the Negroes into the country. The first law in regard to slavery was an act not to establish, or even to provide a legal basis for, the institution but to "fix a rule by which the status of mulatto children could be determined." [11] This was in 1662, forty-three years after the Dutch traders had sold to the planters of Jamestown the first African Negroes brought to America. The total population at the time probably did not exceed one thousand.[12]

In Maryland the first statute concerning slavery was in 1663.[13] It had for its object the deterring of English women from marrying with slaves and had to do with the offspring of Negro slaves who had intermarried, or in the future should intermarry, with white women.[14] This was twenty years after the first introduction of slavery into the colony.

Massachusetts already was requiring military service of certain classes of her free Negroes and mulattoes by 1707, though the total number of Negroes at the time scarcely exceeded half a thousand, most of whom had come in during the quarter of a century just preceding.[15] Intermix-

[11] J. H. Russell, *The Free Negro in Virginia*, p. 19.

[12] In 1648 the number was about 300; in 1670 it was given as 2,000. See Chambers, *American Colonies*, Vol. 2, p. 7.

[13] Slavery seems to have been mentioned incidentally in a law proposed in 1638. See J. W. Cromwell, *The Negro in American History*, p. 3.

[14] Williams, *History of the Negro Race in America*, Vol. 1, p. 240.

[15] In 1676 there were said to be some two hundred Negroes, chiefly from Guinea and Madagascar in the colony. Four years later Governor Bradstreet estimated that ". . . there may be within our Government about one hundred or one hundred and twenty . . . there are very few blacks borne here. . . ." In 1708 Governor Dudley estimated the number at 550. G. H. Moore, *Notes on the History of Slavery in Massa-*

ture must have begun early in order that there could be a body of mixed-bloods at this time sufficiently numerous to be made the object of legislative enactment. Eleven years later, another act was passed having for its object the fixing of the status of mulatto slaves and mulattoes who were servants for a term of years.

In Pennsylvania intermixture was already going on before the colony was ceded to William Penn in 1681. A white servant was indicted in 1677 for having sexual intercourse with a Negro.[16] A settlement in Sussex County bore the name of "Mulatto Hall."[17] In 1698 the County Court of Chester County forbade the mixture of races.[18] Again in 1722, a woman was punished for "abetting a clandestine marriage between a white woman and a negro."[19] The same year the Assembly received a petition praying for relief from the "wicked and scandalous practice of Negroes cohabiting with white people.[20] A general law of 1725-26 forbade the mixture of the races. By the close of the colonial period, one hundred years after the colony was ceded to William Penn,—1681—the mulattoes constituted twenty per cent of the slave population of Chester County. Nearly half the Negroes in Pennsylvania were free at that time.[21] The percentage of mulattoes was doubtless greater among them than among the total Negro population or among the slaves.

What was true in this respect in regard to Virginia, Maryland, and Pennsylvania was equally true of the other colo-

chusetts, pp. 49 ff. See, also, Williams, *History of the Negro Race in America*, Vol. 1, pp. 183, 184.

[16] E. R. Turner, *The Negro in Pennsylvania*, p. 29.

[17] *Ibid.*, p. 30.   [18] *Ibid.*, p. 30.   [19] *Ibid.*, p. 30.

[20] *Ibid.*, p. 30.

[21] In 1790 the slaves numbered 3,707 and the free Negroes 6,531. *A Century of Population Growth*, pp. 222-23.

Amount of Race Intermixture in United States 111

nies. In New York, in 1706, twenty-two years after the first introduction of Negroes, mulattoes were sufficiently numerous to be made the subject of legislative enactment. Connecticut began her black code in 1690 by passing a series of measures in which mulattoes were enumerated with Negroes and Indians.[22] The first act of Rhode Island was one recognizing the manumitting or setting free of mulatto and Negro slaves.[23] New Hampshire never legally established slavery, but as early as 1714 passed several laws regulating the conduct of "Indian, Negro and mulatto servants or slaves."[24] The first legislation of Delaware in 1721 mentions mulattoes.[25] North Carolina was settled from Virginia and as some of the settlers brought slaves with them into the new territory, there were probably mulattoes in the colony as soon as there were Negroes. The first statutory recognition of slavery was in an act against intermarriage passed in 1715.[26] South Carolina's first positive slave act, 1712, mentions [27] *mestizos* as well as mulattoes, Negroes, and Indians, and implies that there were members of these classes who were free as well as members who were slaves. In New Jersey the usual formula including Negro, Indian, and mulatto slaves appears in the legislation at least as early as 1714.[28]

[22] B. C. Steiner, *A History of Slavery in Connecticut*, pp. 12-13. Williams, *History of the Negro Race in America*, Vol. 1, p. 254.

[23] *Ibid.*, Vol. I, pp. 262-63.

[24] *Ibid.*, p. 310.

[25] *Ibid.*, p. 250.

[26] J. S. Bassett, *Slavery and Servitude in the Colony of North Carolina*, p. 15.

[27] Williams, *History of the Negro Race in America*, Vol. 1, p. 290.

[28] H. S. Cooley, *A Study of Slavery in New Jersey*, p. 39. "In 1704 'An Act for regulating negroe, Indian and mulatto slaves within the province of New Jersey,' was introduced, but was tabled and disallowed." Williams, *History of the Negro Race in America*, Vol. 1, p. 285.

While it is thus clearly evident that the mixture of the races went on in all the colonies from a very early date, no definite information exists as to the number of mulattoes at any time during the colonial period.[29] There is every reason to believe that it was relatively more rapid than during the period that slavery existed as a national institution [30] and this seems to be borne out by the few statistics available.

A census of Maryland in 1755 returned eight per cent of the Negroes as mulattoes. Out of a total Negro population of 42,764, the mixed-bloods numbered 3,592.[31] At that time, Maryland had about one-sixth of the total Negro population of the country.[32] On the assumption that Maryland was a typical average of the colonies so far as racial intermixture was concerned—and this would seem to be a fairly reasonable assumption—there would have been 21,552 mulattoes in the country at that time. Allowing twenty-five years for the mulatto population to double [33] by natural increase, that is, by interbreeding and intermarriage with the blacks, they would have numbered approximately sixty thousand by 1790. Assuming that intermixture went on during the years between 1755 and 1790 as it had during the preceding decades, and allowing for the enormously greater number of both the white and the black population, the number would easily double the above figure by the beginning of the national period.

The statistics of free Negroes throw no light upon the subject. Of the 3,608 mixed-bloods in Maryland in 1755,

[29] See *A Century of Population Growth*, p. 91.
[30] See pp. 128, 147 ff., 158 f., 163 below.
[31] *A Century of Population Growth*, p. 6. See, also, p. 185.
[32] The total Negro population of the English Colonies in 1754 was 260,000. That of Maryland in 1755 was 42,764.
[33] This has been the approximate rate of increase since 1860.

1,460 were free Negroes and 2,148 were slaves.[34] The percentage of mulattoes among the free Negroes was apparently higher everywhere than it was among the slaves, but there were mulattoes in considerable numbers among the slaves and by no means all of the free Negroes were mulattoes.[35] The situation differed greatly in different regions. In 1860 in the South, 10 per cent, roughly, of the slaves and 40 per cent of the free Negroes were mulattoes.[36] In Richmond, there were more free blacks than free mulattoes, while in Charleston the great bulk of the free Negroes were mulatto.[37] The growth of the free Negro class was constant and rapid throughout the period that slavery existed as a national institution.[38]

Concerning the distribution of the mulatto population at any time before the census of 1850, not much can be stated definitely. The relative number of mulattoes was greatest in the Northern colonies especially during the latter colonial period and during the entire national period.

---

[34] *A Century of Population Growth*, p. 185. In 1752, Baltimore County had 116 mulatto slaves and 196 free mulattoes, 4,027 Negro slaves and 8 free Negroes. See, J. R. Brackett, *The Negro in Maryland*, pp. 175-76.

[35] Free Negroes 1850:

```
        Black   .................... 275,400
        Mulatto ....................  159,095
        Total   ....................  434,495
```
The Compendium of the Seventh Census of the United States, 1850, p. 52.

[36] See p. 116 below, notes, 45, 47.

[37]   Free black   891
       Free mulatto 4,587

[38]

1790	59,557	1830	319,599
1800	108,435	1840	386,293
1810	186,446	1850	434,495
1820	233,634	1860	488,070

A Century of Population Growth, p. 80.

The ratio of Negroes to the white race was less there than in the Southern colonies; the relative number of free Negroes was greater. As a result of these two conditions, there was always a relatively greater admixture of white blood to the Negro group in the Northern states than in other sections of the country.[39] The later and heavy importation of slaves was into the Southern colonies, hence the newer and darker Negroes were in the South as against a relatively larger ratio of the older importations in the North. The determination of the Northern colonies late in the eighteenth century to free the slaves, further increased the difference. The percentage of blacks among the slaves sold South when these laws began to go into effect, was greater than their percentage in the general Negro population of the North. The free Negroes, who had a larger percentage of mixed-bloods, were not effected by the emancipation laws and so remained behind and became, relatively, a more important part of the Negro population. Of the actual numbers North and South, however, no definite facts are ascertainable.

As between the urban and the rural situation, the mulattoes were largely a city product. Not only did the intermixture go on chiefly in the towns, but the free Negroes, always with a large percentage of mulattoes, tended to drift to the urban centers. For example, the slave register of Chester County, Pennsylvania, in 1780 showed twenty per cent of the slaves to be mulattoes—a percentage reached by the whole country only after one hundred and thirty years of further intermixture. There were probably between four

---

[39] At the time of the first census the ratio of slaves to the white population in the, then, Southern States was fifty-three to one hundred; in New England less than one to one hundred, and five to one hundred in the Middle States. *A Century of Population Growth*, pp. 139-40.

and five thousand Negroes in the state in the year mentioned.[40] This preponderance of mulattoes in the city as against the rural districts was especially the case in the South, but the difference was marked in all sections of the country.[41]

[40] Turner, *The Negro in Pennsylvania*, p. 197. Russell, *The Free Negro in Virginia*, pp. 14-15, points out the larger per cent of free Negroes in the urban population in colonial days and during the whole period of slavery.

[41] Per cent of mulattoes in total Negro population of a chief city and of the rest of the state of typical Southern, Border and Northern States in 1860.

Area	1860	
Georgia		
Savannah City	18.1	
Rest of State	8.2	
Louisiana		
New Orleans City	48.9	
Rest of State	11.0	
South Carolina		
Charleston City	25.2	
Rest of State	5.5	
Kentucky		
Jefferson Co. (Louisville)	21.8	
Rest of State	20.0	
Missouri		
St. Louis County (St. Louis)	32.7	
Rest of State	19.2	
Virginia		
Richmond City	21.4	
Rest of State	16.9	
New York		
King's County (Brooklyn)	19.5	(N. Y. City 3.3)
Rest of State	20.3	
Illinois		
Cook County (Chicago)	49.3	
Rest of State	46.8	
Massachusetts		
Suffolk Co. (Boston)	38.3	
Rest of State	29.9	

United States Census, 1890, *Population*, Vol. 1, Part 1, p. 191.

The first Federal Census to make separate returns of the mixed-bloods was that of 1850. At that time, they constituted something over eleven per cent of the Negro population of the country.[42] Of the total mulatto population approximately forty per cent were free and the remaining sixty per cent slaves.[43] Of the free mulattoes approximately two-thirds were in the slave states.[44] Of the total slave population about eight per cent were mixed-bloods [45] while about thirty-seven per cent of the free Negro population were mulattoes.[46] Among the free Negroes, the per cent of mulattoes was considerably higher in the slave than in the free states.[47] But as the whole Negro population of

[42] Blacks 3,233,057; Mulattoes 405,751. United States Census, 1910, *Population*, Vol. 1, Part 1, p. 129.

[43]
Free	159,095
Slave	246,656

The Compendium of the Seventh Census of the United States, 1850, pp. 64, 82.

[44]
Free mulatto		
Slave states		105,945
Free states		53,150

Ibid., p. 83.

[45]
Slave population	3,204,313
Black	2,957,657
Mulatto	246,656

Ibid., p. 82.

[46]
Free Negroes	434,495
Black	275,400
Mulatto	159,095

Ibid., p. 62.

[47]
Free Negroes	
Slave States	
Black	151,076
Mulatto	105,945
Free States	
Black	124,334
Mulatto	53,150

Ibid., p. 83.

Amount of Race Intermixture in United States 117

the North was free at this time, the only comparison with any point is that between the total Negro population of the two regions. Nearly one-half the Negroes of the Northern States were mixed-bloods, as against about one-ninth of those in the slave-holding states. In summarizing the distribution in different regions, the Census Report of 1850 says:[48]

> The mulattoes in the United States are about one-eighth as numerous as the blacks—the free mulattoes are more than half the number of the free blacks, whilst the slave mulattoes are only about one-twelfth of the slave blacks. Between the states the ratios are very remarkable. Whilst nearly half of the colored in the non-slaveholding states are mulatto, only about one-ninth in the slaveholding states are mulatto, excluding New Jersey. In Ohio and the Territories there are more mulattoes than blacks. In nearly all of the slave states, except Kentucky, Arkansas and Missouri, etc., the free mulattoes greatly preponderate over the free blacks. Kentucky, Arkansas, Missouri and Texas have the largest portion of slave mulattoes, and in the District of Columbia they are about one-fourth of the whole.

Since the emancipation of the slaves, the census figures show an immensely more rapid increase among the mulattoes than among the darker members of the race. The returns for the United States as a whole for the five census periods for which there was a separate enumeration of the mulattoes is as follows:[49]

[48] *The Compendium of the Seventh Census of the United States*, 1850, p. 82.

[49] United States Census, 1910, *Population*, Vol. 1, Part 1, p. 129. There is a constant effort on the part of the mulattoes to make the proportion appear larger. "The figures as to mulattoes have been taken from time to time and are officially acknowledged to be understatements. Prob-

CONTINENTAL UNITED STATES
NEGRO POPULATION

Census Year	Total Negro	Black	Mulatto	Per cent Mulatto
1850	3,638,808	3,233,057	405,751	11.2
1860	4,441,830	3,853,467	588,363	13.2
1870	4,880,009	4,295,960	584,049	12.0
1890	*7,488,676	6,337,980	1,132,060	15.2
1910	9,827,763	7,777,077	2,050,686	20.9

* Includes 18,636 Negroes enumerated in Indian Territory not distinguished as black or mulatto.

Doubtless these figures contain inaccuracies, but there seems to be no reason for the opinion often expressed that they are fundamentally misleading.[50] The Census itself

ably one-third of the Negroes of the United States have distinct traces of white blood." W. E. B. DuBois, *The Negro*, pp. 184-85. He adds: "There is also a large amount of Negro blood in the white population." See, also, *Inter-Racial Problems*, p. 350. Fortune's statement is even more absurd: "The blood of all the ethnic types that go to make up American citizenship flows in the veins of the Afro-American people so that of the ten million of them in this country, accounted for by the Federal census, not more than four million are of pure negroid descent, while some four million of them, not accounted for by the Federal census, have escaped into the ranks of the white race, and are reënforced very largely by such escapements every year." T. T. Fortune, "Place in American Life." In Booker T. Washington, *The Negro Problem*, pp. 214-15.

[50] Question as to the accuracy of these Census figures is frequently raised. A good deal of this popular skepticism seems to have had its origin in a widely read book by Mr. Ray Stannard Baker. Mr. Baker says: "In the last census (1900) the government gave up the attempt in discouragement of trying to enumerate the mulattoes at all, and counted all persons as Negroes who were so classed in the communities where they resided. The census of 1870 showed that one-eighth (roughly) of the Negro population was mulatto, that of 1890 showed that the proportion had increased to more than one-seventh, but these statistics are confessedly inaccurate; the census report itself says: 'The figures are of little value. Indeed as an indication of the extent to which

Amount of Race Intermixture in United States 119

says:

> ... The only available test of the trustworthiness of the results reached in 1850, 1860, 1870 and 1890 would be the degree to which they corroborated and confirmed one another.

And again:[51]

> ... the censuses of mulattoes, as distinguished from full-blood negroes, ... though subject to a greater [*i. e.*, greater than the returns of the Negro] and wholly indeterminate probable error, have shown a general agreement of results.

This increase in the mulatto population has been general throughout all sections of the country; each division has shown a marked increase from census to census. Not only have numbers increased, but the percentage of mulattoes to full-blood Negroes has increased everywhere except in the Mountain, Pacific and East North Central divisions. While the number of mulattoes has of course been far

the races have mingled, they are misleading.'" *Following the Color Line*, p. 153.

Mr. E. B. DuBois, "The Negro Race in the United States of America," *Inter-Racial Problems*, p. 350, and elsewhere, apparently following Mr. Baker, reiterates the same error.

The Census Report (Eleventh Census of the United States, 1890, Vol. 1, Part I, p. xciii. See, also, United States Census, 1900, *Population*, Vol. 1, Part 1, p. cxi.) does use the words quoted by Mr. Baker but in a context which wholly changes their significance. The census of 1890 undertook to divide the Negroes into Negroes, mulattoes, quadroons, and octoroons. Regarding the results of this last inquiry the census report used the words quoted by Mr. Baker. To acknowledge that the attempt to make a minute subdivision of the race into Negroes, mulattoes, quadroons and octoroons was not considered successful is quite a different matter from asserting that the enumeration of mulattoes as distinct from the blacks is "of doubtful validity and officially acknowledged to be misleading."

[51] U. S. Census, 1890. *Population*, Vol. 1, Part 1, p. 185.

120   *The Mulatto in the United States*

greater in the Southern sections of the country at all periods covered by the census returns, the percentage of mulattoes always has been greater in the Northern sections. The following tabulation shows both the numerical and percentual increase in the different divisions thus allowing a comparison between different sections of the country.

NUMBER OF MULATTOES AND THE PERCENTAGE THEY FORMED OF THE TOTAL NEGRO POPULATION
1870 1890 1910[52]

DIVISIONS	1870 Total	1870 Per cent	1890 Total	1890 Per cent	1910 Total	1910 Per cent
New England	9 080	28.6	14 579	32.7	22 150	33.4
Middle Atlantic	21 989	14.9	48 152	21.4	81 969	19.6
E. N. Central	38 125	29.2	76 999	37.2	99 809	33.2
W. N. Central	22 880	16.0	56 782	25.2	69 631	28.7
South Atlantic	230 721	10.4	438 785	13.4	855 819	20.8
E. S. Central	162 228	11.1	289 035	13.6	507 055	19.1
W. S. Central	96 755	13.1	197 124	14.5	397 986	20.1
Mountain	473	30.0	4 637	35.7	6 135	28.6
Pacific	1 798	37.0	5 967	42.3	10 132	34.7
Total U. S.	584 049	12.0	1 132 060	15.2	2 050 686	20.9

While there has thus been a general and a decided increase in all sections of the country since the emancipation of the slaves, the actual increase, of course, has been greatest in the former slave states. The percentage of mulattoes to blacks has also increased more rapidly in the Southern states. Many of the Northern states show a decrease in the mulatto percentages during the half-century of freedom.[53] The following tabulation shows the num-

[52] *Negroes in the United States,* United States Census Bulletin 129, 1915, p. 60.

[53] The decrease in the percentage of mulattoes in certain of the Northern States seems to be indicative of nothing except a migratory movement of the Negro population. The movement of the Northern Negroes, who have a high percentage of mixed-bloods, tends to increase the mulatto percentage of the Southern states, while the migration of the southern Negroes, with a smaller percentage of mixed-bloods, tends to decrease the mulatto percentages in the North. Owing to the great number of the race in the Southern States the effect of the movment is scarcly noticeable there but in the states where the actual number of

ber of mulattoes and their percentage of the total Negro population of the state as enumerated in 1860 and 1910.

NUMBER AND PERCENTAGE OF MULATTOES IN DIFFERENT STATES
1860 AND 1910

	1860 [54]		1910 [55]	
	Number of Mulattoes	Per cent	Number of Mulattoes	Per cent
Arkansas	14,136	12.7	81,371	18.4
Alabama	36,428	8.3	151,410	16.7
S. Carolina	28,314	6.9	134,381	16.1
Connecticut	1,901	22.0	3,746	24.7
N. Carolina	44,798	12.4	144,123	20.7
California	1,526	37.7	7,858	36.3
D. of C.	5,433	28.0	32,952	34.9
Delaware	2,979	13.8	3,706	11.9
Florida	5,896	9.4	49,511	16.0
Georgia	38,904	8.4	204,205	17.3
Illinois	3,587	47.1	36,828	33.8
Indiana	5,447	47.7	14,553	24.1
Iowa	568	53.1	3,644	24.3
Kansas	268	42.7	16,141	29.9
Kentucky	47,359	20.1	65,943	25.2
Louisiana	47,781	13.6	152,577	21.4
Massachusetts	3,071	32.0	13,955	36.7
Maryland	24,913	14.6	43,152	18.6
Missouri	23,588	19.9	44,690	28.4
Minnesota	169	65.3	2,616	36.9
Maine	634	47.8	626	45.9

Negroes is very small the immigration or emigration of a few families is sufficient to change the percentage of the colors. It is just those states with a small Negro population where the effect of migrations would most quickly show in statistical tables which show a decreased percentage of mulattoes to Negroes.

[54] United States Census, 1860, *Population*, pp. 598-99.
[55] *Negroes in the United States,* United States Census, Bulletin 129, 1915, p. 60.

	Number of Mulattoes	Per cent	Number of Mulattoes	Per cent
Michigan	3,375	49.6	8,036	47.0
Mississippi	37,219	8.5	171,005	16.9
New York	7,781	15.9	30,608	22.8
New Jersey	3,462	13.7	14,207	15.8
New Hampshire	253	51.2	208	36.9
Oregon	62	48.4	434	29.1
Ohio	16,691	45.5	39,249	35.2
Pennsylvania	19,142	33.6	37,154	19.2
Rhode Island	997	25.2	3,179	33.4
Texas	25,260	13.8	124,695	18.1
Tennessee	41,878	14.8	118,697	25.1
Vermont	192	27.1	436	26.9
Virginia	93,464	17.0	222,910	33.2
Wisconsin	737	62.9	1,143	39.4

The distribution of the mulatto population, at all times for which the facts are known, has been in general accord with the ratio of the races. Where the proportion of whites in the total population is highest, the mulatto population, as a rule, is highest; and where the proportion of Negroes in the general population is highest, there as a rule, the percentage of mulattoes is lowest. The minor divisions ranked in the order of increasing per cent of mulattoes in the Negro population is seen in the tabulation (p. 123) from the census returns of 1890 to parallel, in general, the decreasing per cent of Negroes in the general population.

The tabulation shows that the per cent of mulattoes increases as the proportion of Negroes decreases. From the great black belt of the South to the Northern States, there is a decreasing proportion of Negroes in the general population and an increasing percentage of mulattoes in the Negro population. "The general conclusion seems warranted that the proportion of mulattoes to total negroes

RANK OF MINOR DIVISIONS IN ORDER OF INCREASING PER CENT MULATTO TO NEGRO POPULATION

Minor divisions having at least 1000 negroes in 1850	Rank in order of increasing per cent mulatto in total negro population				Per cent negro in total population
	1890	1870	1860	1850	
Southern S. Atlantic	1	1	1	1	45.5
Eastern S. Central	2	2	2	2	33.0
Western S. Central	3	3	3	3	29.1
Northern S. Atlantic	4	4	4	4	25.6
Southern N. Atlantic	5	5	6	7	1.8
Western N. Atlantic	6	6	5	5	2.5
New England	7	7	7	8	0.9
Eastern N. Central	8	8	9	9	1.6
Pacific	9	9	8	6	0.8

was found by the enumerators to be high or low, according as the proportion of whites to negroes is high or low."[56] The figures of the separate states bear out this conclusion in some detail.[57]

Commenting upon this distribution of mulattoes Stone

---

[56] United States Census, 1890, *Population,* Vol. 1, Part 1, pp. 190, 191. Also, "The figures also indicate that this admixture was found to be most prevalent in sections where the proportions of negroes to whites was smallest, and least prevalent where the proportion of negroes to whites was largest." *Ibid.,* p. 190. And again, "The table seems to show that as a rule the states with the largest proportion of negroes to total population have the smallest reported proportion of mulattoes to total negroes. To this general rule Louisiana is a notable exception, that being third in order of proportion of negroes to population, but ranging from eighth to sixteenth in order of proportion of mulattoes to negroes." *Ibid.,* p. 190. The exception in the case of Louisiana is to be accounted for by the fact of the early French and Spanish occupation, by the fact of it being an older settlement and by the fact that the transfer of the territory to the United States created a large population of free Negroes.

[57] See table p. 122. Compare pp. 79 ff.

says:[58]

.... A separate enumeration of mulattoes has been made four times, in the censuses of 1850, 1860, 1870, and 1890. The results disclosed the fact that where the proportion of Negroes to whites was lowest, the proportion of mulattoes to total Negroes was highest. For example: in 1890, in the South Central States of Kentucky, Tennessee, Alabama, Mississippi, Louisiana, Arkansas, Oklahoma, and Texas, the mulattoes were but 14 per cent of the total Negro population. On the other hand, they were 32.7 per cent in the New England group. Expressed differently, of all the so-called "Negroes" whom a white man would see in Mississippi, only 11.5 per cent would be of the mulatto type, while of all those observed in Massachusetts 36.3 were mulattoes. In Maine 57.4 per cent were mulattoes, and in Michigan they were 53.8 per cent; while in Georgia and South Carolina they were respectively 9.9 per cent and 9.7 per cent. . . .

The proportion of mulattoes is higher in the cities than in the rural districts. This is especially the case in the Southern States. In the cities of the Border States the percentage of mulattoes is still noticeably higher than it is in the general population of the states though the difference is not so marked as in the distinctly Southern States. In the Northern group of states the per cent of mulattoes is enormously higher in both the cities and the general population of the states, and the difference between the two is less noticeable though the difference still exists.[59]

The data available seem to show that intermixture of the races began with the first coming of the Negro to the

[58] A. F. Stone, *Studies in the American Race Problem*, pp. 40-41.

[59] Unfortunately there seems to be no figures upon which a quantitative statement can be based. The census gives the proportion of mulattoes to Negroes in the cities of over 5,000 inhabitants. It also gives

English colonies. It seems to have been a phenomenon in no way characteristic of any particular section of the country. Mulattoes appeared in all of the colonies and the increase seems to have been rapid during the greater part of the colonial period. With the decline of the slave system in the North and the consequent freeing of large numbers of Negroes, the mulatto population correspondingly increased and its growth has continued to be rapid. With the firmer establishment of the slave system in the South, the relative amount of racial intermixture probably de-

the proportion of mulattoes in the general population of the states. For example:

State and city	Per cent of mulatto
Georgia	17.3
Atlanta	32.4
Louisiana	21.4
New Orleans	34.1
South Carolina	16.1
Charleston	23.6
Kentucky	25.2
Louisville	36.6
Missouri	28.4
St. Louis	34.0
Virginia	33.2
Richmond	39.9
New York	22.8
New York City	24.9
Illinois	33.8
Chicago	41.6
Massachusetts	36.7
Boston	34.3

This is a comparison of the chief city in the state with the Negro population of the state as a whole. Were it possible to separate the urban from the rural regions the differences shown here would be enormously increased. It would probably be found that the mulatto population is exclusively or almost exclusively urban and that the rural population with rare exceptions is black. United States Census, 1910, *Population*, Vol. 1, Part 1, pp. 159, 230.

creased greatly. Since the emancipation of the slaves, the number of mulattoes, especially in the former slave states, has increased rapidly. The decades from 1890 to 1910 show an enormous increase in the number of mixed-blood individuals. The ratio of mulattoes to Negroes has been greater in the North than in the South, at all periods for which the facts are known. The present forces operating tend to decrease this difference. At all periods, the mulatto formed a larger per cent of the Negro population of the towns and cities than of the rural population. This is particularly the case at the present time in the southern section of the country but is not untrue of any region. If the facts could be known the mulatto would probably be found to be almost an exclusively urban phenomenon.

The nature of the racial intermixture and the forces operating to produce the observed conditions are considered in the following chapter.

CHAPTER VI

NATURE OF RACE INTERMIXTURE IN THE UNITED STATES

Intermarriage

IN many of the Negroes brought as slaves to America, there was already some infiltration of Caucasian blood. The great majority, well above fifty per cent, came from the West Coast. A few came from the Congo and other regions toward the interior; a few were Hottentots and Bushmen from the southern part of Africa. These latter, however, like the Pygmies of the interior, were mostly of a physical type too low to serve the purposes of slave labor. In general the higher Negroes were not taken.[1] It has been estimated that possibly one per cent of the Negroes imported were able to speak an Arabic dialect. Possibly fifty per cent had some trace of a previous intermixture with a white race. But of all the Negroes brought the Guinea Negroes were the purest and they constituted above half of the total importations.

[1] Edward Wilmot Blyden, one of the ablest men of the Negro race, maintains the thesis that white intermixture "has been the salvation of the Negro in the New World, for the black man who was weak enough to be caught and shipped away as a slave was naturally inferior in mind and body to the black man who possessed ingenuity enough to escape from the toils of slavery and remain at home as a slave hunter." Quoted from The *Crisis*, Sept. '13, pp. 229-30. See, also, G. W. Williams, *History of the Negro Race in America*, Vol. 2, pp. 544-45, for a variation of Blyden's thesis.

Further crossing began as soon as the Negroes landed on American soil, if, indeed, it did not begin before the Negroes were landed.² The race never has shown any hesitancy about crossing with other races in any time or country. Their women have mixed with every race and people with whom they have come in contact in the ancient, as in the modern world. The scarcity of white women all through the Colonial period doubtless was an immense factor tending to overcome any hesitancy the whites may have had toward sexual association with the members of a strange race.³ This mixture, as we have seen, has increased as the race has gained the rudiments of civilization and come to a better appreciation of Western culture.

While the crossing of the Negro and the white races in America has for the most part not been within the bounds of conventional marriage, some small part of the actual intermixture has received the sanction of law and social tolerance.

In the colonies, the marriage of Negroes with white persons was considered highly undesirable and from an early date was usually prohibited by severe laws.⁴ The public disapproval seems generally to have got itself enacted into legal prohibitions as a result of the first unions of the kind

---

² "Indeed, in those early days many a negress was landed upon our shores by her captors already pregnant by one of the demoniac crew that made up the company of the slave ship that brought her over." R. W. Shufeldt, *The Negro: A Menace to American Civilization*, p. 80.

"The first mulatto children were born off the coast of Africa, and their fathers were the first white men the black princesses of that country ever saw. . . ." Anonymous, The *Independent*, Vol. 54, p. 2226.

³ J. H. Van Evrie, *White Supremacy and Negro Subordination*, p. 153.

⁴ "In the French, English and Dutch colonies, the laws, or public opinion, so prevents marriages between individuals of different colors, that those who would contract them, would be considered as degraded by their alliance, . . ." H. Grégoire, *Literature of Negroes*, p. 66.

that took place.⁵ The first act of Maryland establishing slavery, passed in 1663, forbade the practice of intermarriage and, from its wording, seems to show that such marriages had already taken place.⁶ North Carolina in 1715 passed an act carrying a heavy penalty on any white man or woman who should marry a Negro, mulatto, or Indian and also provided a heavy penalty on any minister who should officiate at such a marriage.⁷ Within two years of the passing of the act, two persons were indicted for performing such a marriage ceremony.⁸ A further law in 1723 recites that certain free Negroes, mulattoes, and other persons of mixed blood had moved into the colony and, in defiance of the laws to the contrary, several of them had intermarried with the white inhabitants.⁹ Pennsylvania passed a similar law in 1725-1726, partly the result, apparently, of a clandestine marriage between a Negro and a white woman.¹⁰

Similar laws in the other colonies were passed at an early date usually as a reaction and a protest against some mixed marriage. How many such marriages there were, we have no way of knowing; but that they were anywhere more than

⁵ The law of Maryland, 1681, for example, seems to have been called forth by the marriage of "Irish Nell," a servant of the Lord Proprietor, who had married a slave. It was to determine the status of her mulatto children. J. R. Brackett, *The Negro in Maryland*, p. 34, f. n.

⁶ "And be it further enacted, that all issues of English, or other free born women, that have already married negroes, shall serve the master . . ." Sec. III. Act of 1663. Quoted by Williams, *History of the Negro Race in America*, Vol. 1, p. 240. See, also, Brackett, *The Negro in Maryland*, pp. 32-34.

⁷ J. S. Bassett, *Slavery and Servitude in the Colony of North Carolina*, pp. 58-59.

⁸ *Ibid.*, p. 58.

⁹ *Ibid.*, pp. 68-69.

¹⁰ E. R. Turner, *The Negro in Pennsylvania*, pp. 29-31.

the rarest exception there is no reason to believe.[11] Then, as now, such mixed unions roused an indignant protest from the decent members of the community.[12]

Such intermarriages as did take place in these early days, seem to have been invariably with the meanest classes of the whites.[13] The marriages were contrary to law and to public sentiment, and were entered into at the price of social ostracism and legal punishment. Williams,[14] speaking of the first statute establishing slavery in Maryland, says:

> Section two was called into being on account of the intermarriage of white women and slaves. Many of these women had been indentured as servants to pay their passage to this country, some had been sent as convicts, while still others had been apprenticed for a term of years. Some of them, however, were very worthy persons. . . .

Brackett[15] also speaks of marriages between these English serving-women and the slaves or free Negroes. Turner[16] speaks of two mixed marriages in Pittsburgh in 1788. In one case, the couple was said to occupy a respectable

---

[11] E. R. Turner, *The Negro in Pennsylvania*, pp. 194-95. Bassett, *Slavery and Servitude in the Colony of North Carolina*, pp. 69, 58-59.

[12] See, for e.g., Turner, *The Negro in Pennsylvania*, pp. 195-96. Also, E. I. McCormac, *White Servitude in Maryland*, p. 67.

[13] In North Carolina in 1727 "a white woman was indicted in the General Court because she had left her husband and was cohabiting with a Negro slave." Bassett, *Slavery and Servitude in the Colony of North Carolina*, p. 58. "Among the servants imported into the colony, there were often women of a very low type, who during their term of servitude intermarried with negro slaves." McCormac, *White Servitude in Maryland*, p. 67.

[14] *History of the Negro Race in America*, Vol. 1, p. 240.

[15] *The Negro in Maryland*, p. 196.

[16] *The Negro in Pennsylvania*, p. 194.

position.[17] Branagan[18] declares that such marriages were common in Philadelphia after the repeal in 1780 of the laws applying to the Negro. The grandmother of Benjamin Banneker[19] was an English felon transported to the colony of Delaware.[20] There seems to be absolutely no evidence of any marriages of a mixed sort in which the white contracting party was not of the lowest and usually of a vicious class.

But whatever little intermarriage may have taken place between the Negroes and the servant class of whites in early colonial times, it decreased to an almost absolute zero as the status of the Negro became fixed and better understood. The spirit of fellowship that at first existed between the slaves and the indentured servants, imported criminals, paupers, and prostitutes gradually gave place to the feeling of bitter hatred that, throughout the days of slavery, characterized the relations of the "poor whites" and the Ne-

[17] "Cette famille est une des plus respectables de cette ville." Brissat de Warville, *Nouveau Voyage,* pp. 33, 34. Quoted by Turner, *The Negro in Pennsylvania,* p. 195, f. n.

[18] "I solemnly declare, I have seen more white women married to, and deluded through the arts of seduction by negroes in one year in Philadelphia, than for the eight years I was visiting. [In the West Indies and the Southern States.]" "There are many, very many blacks, who . . . begin to feel themselves consequential, . . . will not be satisfied unless they get white women for wives, and are likewise exceedingly impertinent to white persons in low circumstances." "I know a black man who seduced a young white girl . . . who soon after married him, and died with a broken heart; on her death he said he would not disgrace himself to have a negro wife, and acted accordingly, for he soon after married another white woman." "There are perhaps hundreds of white women thus fascinated by black men in this city, and there are thousands of black children by them at present." Branagan, *Serious Remonstrances,* pp. 70-71, 73, 74, 75. Quoted by Turner, *The Negro in Pennsylvania,* p. 195, f. n.

[19] See page 190 below.

[20] J. W. Cromwell, *The Negro in American History,* pp. 86-97.

groes. In the slave states, there was no intermarriage, except rarely among the creoles of Louisiana.[21] In the North, there was very little. Where such marriages were not forbidden by law, they were forbidden by the decent elements of the white community. Turner's summary of the situation in Pennsylvania is, in general, characteristic of the entire non-slave holding parts of the country. He says:[22]

> After a while a strong feeling was aroused, so that in 1821 a petition was sent to the Legislature, asking that mixed marriages be declared void, and that it be made a penal act for a negro to marry a white man's daughter. In 1834 such a marriage provoked a riot at Columbia; while in 1838 the subject caused a vehement outburst in the Constitutional Convention then assembled. Three years later a bill to prevent intermarriage was passed in the House, but lost in the Senate. From time to time thereafter petitions were sent to the Legislature, but no action was taken; the obnoxious marriages continuing to be reported, and even being encouraged by some extreme advocates of race equality. Nevertheless what the law left undone was largely accomplished by public sentiment and private action. As time went on marriages of white people with negroes came to be considered increasingly odious, and so became far less frequent. When a case occurred, it was usually followed by swift action and dire vengeance. The fact that a white man was living with a negro wife was one of the causes of the terrible riot in Philadelphia in 1849.

In the period just preceding the Civil War, the emotional tension in the North and the preaching of amalgamation of

[21] F. L. Olmsted, *A Journey in the Seaboard Slave-States*, p. 636, quotes a resident as saying that ". . . White men, sometimes, married a rich colored girl; but he never knew of a black man to marry a white girl." Olmsted adds: "I subsequently heard of one such case."

[22] *The Negro in Pennsylvania*, pp. 195-96.

Nature of Race Intermixture in United States 133

the races by Phillips and others brought about a few intermarriages. One of the wives [23] of Frederick Douglass, for example, was a white woman. But the total number of such unions was so small as to be negligible.

In the period since the Civil War, mixed marriages have been very infrequent. Baker [24] gives one hundred and seventy-one as the number of mixed marriages in Boston for the six-year period ending in 1905. This is about the same average that has obtained for half a century.[25] Hoffman [26] found sixty-five such marriages to have taken place in Connecticut in the eleven-year period ending in 1893. For the same period fifty-eight such marriages were reported from Rhode Island. In Michigan, for the twenty-year period ending in 1893, he found a total of one hundred and eleven mixed marriages.[27] In Bermuda for the twelve-year period

---

[23] The second.

[24] Ray Stannard Baker, *Following the Color Line*, p. 172.

[25] The following table gives the number of mixed marriages by five year periods from 1855 to 1887.

	Total	Average per year
1855—59	50	10
1862—66	45	9
1867—71	88	17.6
1873—77	172	34.4
1878—82	121	24.2
1883—87	124	24.8
1890	24	24

[26] F. L. Hoffman, *Race Traits and Tendencies*, pp. 199 ff.

[27] Hoffman seems to have included in his figures cases of open concubinage as well as conventional and lawful unions. According to the statement presented to the Michigan Legislature in 1915 less than 40 mixed marriages have been legalized in the state in the past 30 years. The committee however were endeavoring to make a case against the proposed law to prohibit intermarriage and gave expression to a number of errors of fact. Hoffman is probably the better authority. *Report of Committee on Equitable Legislation*, "Treatise on Proposed Changes in the Law of Marriage."

from 1872 to 1883, there were one hundred and nine mixed marriages; for the following twelve-year period from 1884 to 1895, there were but fifty-eight.

In twenty-eight states the intermarriage of the races is forbidden by law,[28] in most cases under severe penalty.[29] In other states, the sentiment against such unions is sufficiently strong to make the question a regular subject of legislative debate.[30] That they are not forbidden in all the states is not that they are approved, but that the number of Negroes is so small and the number of such unions so few, that they constitute no menace sufficient to force protective legislative enactment. The Massachusetts attitude as described by Stone, is fairly typical of the more northern states where the Negro is not a grave and immediate problem.[31]

> For a period of 138 years Massachusetts prohibited intermarriage between whites and Negroes or mulattoes. The statute of Queen Anne of 1705 may be said originally to have been tinctured by the religious objection to a union between Christians and pagans. But it was several times reënacted long after such influences had ceased to exist. It was finally repealed in 1843. By such action Massachusetts did not by any means intend to declare in favour of racial intermarriage. The real significance of the repeal was that, whether consciously or unconsciously, the numerical insignificance of the Negro population had finally brought possibly a majority of the whites to a point from which they were able to view with entire indifference any pos-

[28] The constitutions of six of the states prohibit such marriages.
[29] E. A. Jenks, "The Legal Status of Negro-White Amalgamation in the United States." *American Journal of Sociology*, Vol. 21, pp. 666-78.
[30] In 1913 bills aimed at prohibiting Negro-white intermarriages were introduced in ten of the twenty states then permitting such unions. Jenks, *American Journal of Sociology*, Vol. 21, p. 666.
[31] A. F. Stone, *Studies in the American Race Problem*, pp. 60-61.

sible consequences of a formal reversal of the ancient policy of the state.

The large majority of the mixed marriages are of Negro or mulatto men and white women. In one hundred and fifty-eight of the one hundred and seventy-one cases reported by Baker, the groom was a Negro and the woman white.[32] In thirteen cases the groom was a white man. Of the fifty-eight mixed marriages in Rhode Island fifty-one were white females and seven were white males. Of the one hundred and eleven cases in Michigan ninety-three were white women and eighteen were white men.[33] [34] Stone[35] comments on the Boston situation as follows:

> . . . As a matter of fact, for the past five years, of all the Negro marriages in Massachusetts, an average of about 10 per cent have been mixed. Moreover, in these cases the white party is a woman, very infrequently a man. Of the 52 mixed marriages in 37 towns and cities of the state in 1900, 43 were between white women and Negro men. . . .
>
> During the five years from 1900 to 1904 there were 143 marriages between Negroes and whites in the city

[33]

Year	Groom Negro Bride white	Groom white Bride Negro	Total mixed marriages
1900	32	3	35
1901	30	1	31
1902	25	4	29
1903	27	2	29
1904	27	1	28
1905	17	2	19

[32] Baker, *Following the Color Line*, p. 172.

[33] Hoffman, *Race Traits and Tendencies*, p. 119.

[34] It is interesting in this connection to note that of the 18 white men married to Negroes 6 married black females and 12 mulatto females; of the 93 white women married to Negroes 47 were married to black males and 46 to mulatto males.

[35] Stone, *Studies in the American Race Problem*, pp. 62-63.

of Boston, and 907 in which both parties were Negroes. In other words, with a Negro population of 11,591 there were 1,050 marriages. Of these, 143, or 13.6 per cent, if my calculation is correct, married white persons. Of these mixed marriages 133 were cases of white women marrying Negro men, while only 10 white men married Negro women. With the white women in this instance representing 93 per cent of her race's participation in such alliances, it is safe to dogmatize as to the processes of race intermixture. And my investigations thus far lead me to believe that the same conditions exist in Chicago, Philadelphia, and New York.

The mixed marriages as a rule are of the lower classes of the whites. The woman in most of the unions are recent immigrants and often, no doubt, contract the alliances without realizing the social consequences.[36] Hoffman made a careful investigation of thirty-seven such mixed unions.[37] Eight were of white men living with Negro women, twenty-nine of white women living with Negro men.

Of the eight white men, four were legally married and four were not. Three of the number were criminals or criminal suspects. The others were outcasts: one was a saloon keeper, one had deserted a white wife and family, two others were of good families but were themselves of bad reputation.

Of the twenty-nine white women, nineteen were lawfully married to their Negro husbands, while ten were living in

[36] "... The few white women who have given birth to mulattoes have always been regarded as monsters; and without exception, they have belonged to the most impoverished and degraded caste of whites, by whom they are scrupulously avoided as creatures who have sunk to the level of the beasts of the field." P. A. Bruce, *The Plantation Negro as a Freeman*, p. 55.

[37] Hoffman, *Race Traits and Tendencies*, pp. 204-06.

Nature of Race Intermixture in United States 137

open concubinage. Five of these latter were of foreign birth. Eight of the number were prostitutes,[38] one was insane, and one was the daughter of respectable parents. Of the nineteen who were lawfully married, four were prostitutes, two were guilty of bigamy, four were either divorced or had deserted husbands, five were apparently of respectable parentage and contented with their husbands. Of the four others, Hoffman was able to obtain no information.

Of the twenty-nine Negro men, one was an industrious barber of good character, five were of fair repute, nine were idlers, loafers, or drunkards, and eleven were proved criminal. The character of the remaining three was not determined.

Hoffman concludes this phase of his study as follows:[39]

> Comment on these cases is hardly necessary. They tend to prove that as a rule neither good white men nor good white women marry colored persons, and that good colored men and women do not marry white persons. The number of cases is so small, however, that a definite conclusion as to the character of persons intermarrying is hardly warranted. However, it would seem that if such marriages were a success, even to a limited extent, some evidence would be found in a collection of thirty-six cases. It is my own opinion, based on personal observation in the cities of the South, that the individuals of both races who intermarry or live in concubinage are vastly inferior to the average types of the white and colored races in the United States; also, that the class of white men who have intercourse with colored women are, as a rule, of an inferior type.

[38] It is perhaps not generally understood to what extent sexually satiated prostitutes seek Negro men in their search for new stimulation. The same thing is true of many debauched white men.

[39] *Race Traits and Tendencies,* p. 206.

The great majority of the mixed marriages occur in the larger cities. Of the fifty-eight reported from Rhode Island, for example, fifty-two were from Providence.[40]

These mixed marriages are very frequently marriages of mulattoes, usually very light-colored mulattoes, with the poorer and lower class of white women. Not infrequently, it would seem these unions take place without the girl realizing that she is marrying a Negro. Cases where such facts are made the grounds for divorce proceedings, appear from time to time in the daily press. So uniform is it that the groom is of some importance and the bride a woman of the lower class, that some predict a final solution of the problem of the Negro in America by a fusion of the upper class Negroes with the lower class whites.[41]

> For this reason the idea, unpopular, to be sure, but still indicated by the facts, that the races in America are amalgamating is not unwelcome to many thinkers. . . .
>
> That simply goes to show that we are now part way along in the process, which I do not hesitate to say will be accomplished in time. The black race is to be absorbed.
>
> In fact, the thing will not be so repellant in a few hundred years as it is now. As it is, those who say the relation between whites and blacks is a symptom of mental defect on the part of the whites fail entirely to consider that times without number the scions of our best southern families have shown signs of such degeneracy.
>
> Is it not more reasonable to expect that as time goes on the more cultured blacks will more or less naturally intermingle with the least cultured whites in the

---

[40] Hoffman, *Race Traits and Tendencies*, p. 199.

[41] G. B. Foster, as quoted in the daily press. See, for e.g., the *Chicago Tribune*, 11-9-1914. See, also, DuBois, note 134, p. 164 below.

south until eventually the whole process will have been completed and our race will have absorbed the other? Surely, there is every reason to believe that that condition will result.

However this may be, it is evident that the origin of the mulatto group and its subsequent growth have been brought about, only in a very minor degree, through the conventional marriage relation. Such marriages as do take place are almost exclusively Northern Negroes, frequently light-colored mulattoes, with women of the lower classes and especially with European immigrant girls.[42] The desire of the Negro in this respect is, when he becomes wealthy, frequently taken advantage of by white adventuresses of questionable virtue. A certain prize fighter of national reputation is a case in point.[43]

The Concubinage of Colored Women by White Men

Another source of the increase of the mulatto group has been the concubinage of colored women by white men. This form of sex relation was fairly common in certain sections during the period of slavery. The relation, where it existed, approached often more nearly a form of polygamy than that of an indiscriminate sex relation. To what extent the relationship existed during the slavery days or even at the present time, it is not possible to say. The custom varied in different sections and in the same section at different

[42] ". . . In the majority of intermarriages the white women belong to the lower walks of life. They are German, Irish, or other foreign women, respectable, but ignorant. . . ." Baker, *Following the Color Line*, p. 172.

[43] There is here no intention to put in question the sincere devotion and pure romantic love that doubtless led to the marriage unions between such men as Frederick Douglass, President Scarborough of Wilberforce, Ira Aldridge, the actor, and other prominent mulattoes and their white wives. See note 4, p. 316.

times. No doubt there were isolated instances of the sort everywhere, throughout the whole period that the Negro has been in the country. That it was a uniform custom of the slave-owning class, there is no reason to believe: that it was common in certain regions, there is no reason to doubt.[44]

The form of this sex relation was exclusively of white men and Negro women. In general, it seems not to have been a promiscuous relation between the master class and the female slaves, but a relation between some favorite slave girl and a young man of the family.[45] It was not in any sense a forced relation on the part of the Negress; on the contrary, it was a relation to which the girl of the upper classes of the Negroes aspired as the highest honor and privilege which she could attain. To the girl it was, in the great majority of cases, a matter of being honored by a white man.[46]

When a child or children resulted from the association, they not infrequently received their freedom—generally along with that of the mother—and occasionally, at least, received an education and a start in life. To escape the restrictions placed upon the free Negro in many of the Southern States, these natural children, and other faithful slaves whom the master might wish to free, were frequently taken into free territory and there given their freedom.[47]

[44] See pages 92-93 above.
[45] See note 25, p. 176 below.
[46] J. S. Bassett quotes a physician whom he considers trustworthy and who was raised on a rice plantation near Wilmington, North Carolina, as saying that "... Among themselves the slaves were immoral, but, generally speaking, there were no illicit relations between them and the white men. The white boys were sometimes intimate with the housemaids...." *Slavery in the State of North Carolina*, p. 86.
[47] "At this time [about 1850] says Mr. Brown: 'Cincinnati was full of women, without husbands, and their children. These were sent by the planters of Louisiana, Mississippi, and some from Tennessee, who

The highest development of the system of concubinage seems not to have been between the slave-holding families and their slaves, but between the free mulatto women and the non-slave-holding men. In its fullest development, the system flourished where there were the largest number of free Negro women of mixed ancestry and of some degree of culture and refinement. In Charleston, in Mobile, and especially in New Orleans, the system reached a stage little short of a socially sanctioned institution. Olmsted's description of the system in New Orleans shortly before the war gives a picture of concubinage at its point of highest development.[48]

> I refer to a class composed of the illegitimate offspring of white men and colored women (mulattos or quadroons), who, from habits of early life, the advantages of education, and the use of wealth, are too much superior to the negroes, in general, to associate with them, and are not allowed by law, or the popular prejudice, to marry white people. The girls are frequently sent to Paris to be educated, and are very accomplished. They are generally pretty, and often handsome. I have rarely, if ever, met more beautiful women, than one or two of them, that I saw by chance, in the streets.

had got fortunes and had found that white women could live in those states, and in consequence, they had sent their slave wives and children to Cincinnati and set them free.'" Booker T. Washington, *The Story of the Negro*, Vol. 1, p. 227. The Mr. Brown quoted was a free Negro or mulatto. This would seem to indicate that the scarcity of white women was the determining factor in the intermixture. Wilberforce, Ohio, is said to have a settlement of this sort. "The thing that gives a peculiar and interesting character to many of these ante-bellum Negro settlements is that they were made by Southern slave-holders who desired to free their slaves and were not able to do so under the restrictions that were imposed upon emancipation in the Southern states. Many of the colored people in these settlements were the natural children of their master. . . ." *Ibid.*, Vol. 1, pp. 234-35.

[48] *A Journey in the Seaboard Slave States*, pp. 594-97.

They are much better formed, and have a much more graceful and elegant carriage than Americans in general, while they seem to have commonly inherited or acquired much of the taste and skill, in the selection and arrangement, and the way of wearing dresses and ornaments, that is the especial distinction of the women of Paris. Their beauty and attractiveness being their fortune, they cultivate and cherish with diligence every charm or accomplishment they are possessed of.

Of course, men are attracted by them, associate with them, are captivated, and become attached to them, and, not being able to marry them legally, and with the usual forms and securities for constancy, make such arrangements "as can be agreed upon." When a man makes a declaration of love to a girl of this class, she will admit or deny, as the case may be, her happiness in receiving it; but, supposing she is favorably disposed, she will usually refer the applicant to her mother. The mother inquires, like a Countess of Kew, into the circumstances of the suitor; ascertains whether he is able to maintain a family, and, if satisfied with him, in these and other respects, requires from him security that he will support her daughter in a style suitable to the habits she has been bred to, and that, if he should ever leave her, he will give her a certain sum for her future support, and a certain additional sum for each of the children she shall then have.

The wealth, thus secured, will, of course, vary—as in society with higher assumptions of morality—with the value of the lady in the market; that is, with her attractiveness, and the number and value of other suitors she may have, or may reasonably expect. Of course, I do not mean that love has nothing at all to do with it; but love is sedulously restrained, and held firmly in hand, until the road of competency is seen to be clear, with less humbug than our English custom requires about it. Everything being satisfactorily arranged, a tenement in a certain quarter of the town is usually hired, and the couple move into it and go to housekeeping—living as if they were married. The woman is not, of course, to be wholly deprived of the society of others—her former acquaintances are continued, and she sustains her relations as daughter, sister, and friend. Of course, too, her husband (she calls him so—why shouldn't she?) will be likely to continue, also, more or less in, and form a part of, this kind of society. There are parties and balls—*bals masqués*—and all the movements and customs of other fashionable society, which they can enjoy in it, if they wish. The women of this sort are represented to be exceedingly affectionate in disposition, and constant beyond reproach.

During all the time a man sustains this relation, he will commonly be moving, also, in reputable society on the other side of the town; not improbably, eventually he marries, and has a family establishment elsewhere. Before doing this, he may separate from his *placée* (so she is termed). If so, he pays her according to agreement, and as much more, perhaps, as his affection for her, or his sense of the cruelty of the proceeding, may lead him to; and she has the world before her again, in the position of a widow. Many men continue, for a long time, to support both establishments—particularly, if their legal marriage is one *de convenance*. But many others form so strong attachments, that the relation is never discontinued, but becomes, indeed, that of marriage, except that it is not legalized or solemnized. These men leave their estate, at death, to their children, to whom they may have previously given every advantage of education they could command. What becomes of the boys, I am not informed; the girls, sometimes, are removed to other countries, where their color does not prevent their living reputable lives; but, of course, mainly continue in the same society and are fated to a life similar to that of their mothers.

The extent to which concubinage prevails at the present time, it is not possible to determine. There is no unanimity

144 *The Mulatto in the United States*

in the opinions expressed and no wide investigation on the basis of which an estimate can be made. The relation shocks the conventional, middle-class sex ethics of the community and the pronouncements so frequently met with on the subject are seldom anything more than an offhand expression of passion and prejudice. That the relative importance of this particular form of race intermixture is generally grossly exaggerated seems certain, but how numerous the cases of concubinage actually are, it is wholly impossible to say.

Unlawful Polygamy

Aside from a very little lawful intermarriage and a larger, but wholly indeterminable, amount of unlawful, subsurface polygamy; there is, and seems always to have been, a much larger number of sexual irregularities between the races which are wholly casual in their nature.[49] It is this casual meeting and temporary association of individuals, a relation which approaches more nearly a form of prostitution than a form of polygamy, that is now, and seems always to have been, the characteristic form of intermixture that has existed between the races in America. It is not confined to any one section of the country [50] nor to any one

---

[49] It is this third and numerically more important element that is overlooked by Mr. DuBois when he asserts that the mulatto is the product of "a system of concubinage of colored women in slavery days, together with some intermarriage." See *The Negro American Family*, p. 47. Also, see the article in *Inter-Racial Problems, The Negro* and elsewhere.

[50] The *Independent*, Vol. 55, p. 454, says, speaking editorially: "None of the intermixture is the fruit of marriage. It has been nearly all produced in the South, and is all the fruit of white fathers and darker mothers." Here is exaggeration almost to the point of misstatement. It is not "all the fruit of white fathers and darker mothers:" some of it is the fruit of marriage. It has been "nearly all produced in the South" only in the sense that nearly all of the race has been in the

social class in the community.⁵¹ It goes on everywhere where class differences exist and where the vicious elements have an opportunity to associate.

Russell⁵² studying the free Negroes in Virginia concludes that they were in large measure the result of illicit relations between the masters and the slave women. Turner⁵³ concludes his study of the matter in Pennsylvania by freeing the master class from the charge of debauching the slave women. Bassett seems to doubt that the master class was an important element in production of the bastard race. Speaking of the laws enacted in regard to bastardy in 1715 and 1741 which provided extra terms of service for the servant who became a mother of a bastard child, he says:⁵⁴

> It is also evident that the sin of the servant would be an advantage to the master, since he would thereby

South. Relatively the intermixture of the races has been greater in the Northern and Border States than in the South.

[51] The *New York Age*, the best of the Negro papers, in an unmannerly editorial replying to a coarse but on the whole truthful and accurate statement concerning the morals of Negro women, asserts that it is "the Southern Aristocrat" who is responsible for the mulattoes. Issue 9-2-1915.

[52] ". . . Illegal marriages and of associations of whites with free negroes was so disreputable and disgraceful that they were entered into by the vilest white persons at the price of chastisement by privately organized bands of white persons supported by community sentiment. The free mulatto class . . . was of course the result of illegal relations of white persons with negroes; but excepting those born of mulatto parents, most persons of the class were not born of free negro or free white mothers, but of slave mothers and were set free because of their kinship to their master and owner." J. H. Russell, *The Free Negro in Virginia*, p. 127.

[53] "It must be said that the stigma of illicit intercourse in Pennsylvania would not generally seem to rest upon the masters, but rather upon servants, outcasts, and the lowlier class of whites." *The Negro in Pennsylvania*, p. 31.

[54] *Slavery and Servitude in the Colony of North Carolina*, pp. 83-84.

secure her services for a longer period. We have not the least evidence that such a thing did happen, yet it is possible that a master might for that reason have compassed the sin of his serving-woman.

Whatever may have been the extent to which the master-class was involved—and there is no doubt that some portion of the bastard race was the offspring of temporary associations of white masters and slave women—there seems to be no evidence of a reliable sort to indicate that all, or even the major part of the mulatto group, was of this origin.[55] Concubinage certainly involved economically prosperous individuals of the white race and the choicer individuals from among the darker groups; the casual intermixture was characteristic of the undeniably common people of both races.

In the colonial days, one group of the mulatto population owed its origin to illicit intercourse between slave women and white servants.

The first introduction of the white indentured servants into the colonies is not known,[56] but by 1619, when the first Negroes came, they constituted a distinct class in the community life. The system was a colonial modification of the

[55] There is, of course, no scientific credence to be given to the stories of so many mixed-bloods that they are descendants of some prominent man. The making of genealogies is not confined exclusively to the newly-rich class of the whites. It is not meant to question, however, that certain eminent men may have been fathers of mulattoes. Benjamin Franklin was openly accused of keeping Negro paramours and seems to have made no attempt to deny it. "What is sauce for the goose is sauce for the gander." (1764.) "An humble attempt at scurrility." (1765), etc. Franklin, however, was not a member of the aristocratic class. His actions are rather an evidence of the part that the middle and lower class had to do with the production of the mulattoes. Thomas Jefferson has also been accused of being the father of mulatto children and he certainly was of the aristocratic class.

[56] J. C. Ballagh, *White Servitude in the Colony of Virginia*, p. 27, f. n.

European apprenticeship system then in vogue.[57] In general, this indentured servant class may be divided into three divisions on the basis of the cause of their immigration to America.[58] Many were free, poor people, anxious to go to America but unable to pay their way, who pledged their service for a term of years to gain passage. There were also a goodly number of persons, generally children, kidnapped in the streets of English cities and sold into servitude in the colonies. The third class were transported felons, dissolute individuals, vagabonds, prisoners of war and various others whom the government was anxious to get out of the country.[59] So many of this latter class were sent, that in 1663, they were present in sufficient numbers to imperil the government.[60] The importation was stopped in 1671, England diverting the stream for a time to the West Indies; but it was begun again in 1717 and continued, in spite of protests, to the time of the Revolution. It was not effectively stopped before 1788.[61] From 1664 to 1671, the average importation into Virginia alone was fifteen hundred a year.[62] It is estimated that from 1717 to the Revolution there were some fifty thousand criminals sent to the colonies.[63]

This white indentured servitude was just reaching its height in Virginia at the time the first Negroes were brought into the colony.[64] The number of Negroes increased slowly

[57] McCormac, *White Servitude in Maryland*, Chapter 1.
[58] Ballagh, *White Servitude in the Colony of Virginia*, p. 33. Bassett, *Slavery and Servitude in the Colony of North Carolina*, pp. 75-77.
[59] *Ibid.*, p. 30.
[60] Ballagh, *White Servitude in the Colony of Virginia*, pp. 36-37.
[61] *Ibid.*, pp. 37-38.
[62] *Ibid.*, p. 41.
[63] H. P. Fairbanks, *Immigration*, p. 48. See, also, McCormac, *White Servitude in Maryland*, pp. 93 ff.
[64] Ballagh, *White Servitude in the Colony of Virginia*, p. 91.

at first,[65] there being only thirty in the colony in 1650. In 1671 there were about two thousand slaves and six thousand white servants in Virginia. Twelve years later, the latter had nearly doubled, while the blacks had increased to about three thousand. The Negroes, however, proved their superiority as a servile labor class and from about 1685 on white servitude began to give way to black slavery. In Maryland, the white servants were numerous [66] and of the same general type as those of Virginia. Brackett [67] states that the English jails were in part emptied into the colonies and adds that many of the indentured class were adventurers and good-for-nothings. Elsewhere the situation was similar,[68] though in the other colonies the white servants did not form so high a percentage of the total population.[69]

It was these servants with whom the Negroes came into closest contact. Many of them, of course, were highly respectable persons,[70] but among them were "disorderly persons," [71] deported convicts, prostitutes, and the like, in great numbers. They courted the Negroes as agreeable companions.[72] The social condition of the black and white

---

[65] See p. 107 f. above.

[66] See McCormac, *White Servitude in Maryland*, Chapter 3, "Number and Economic Importance."

[67] Brackett, *The Negro in Maryland*, p. 118.

[68] Ballagh, *White Servitude in the Colony of Virginia*, pp. 92-93.

[69] Maryland, Pennsylvania and Virginia were the three chief colonies importing white servants.

[70] ". . . In many instances they were people of much worth who had met with misfortune, or who having been poor in the first place had taken advantage of this opportunity to make their fortunes in the New World. . . ." Bassett, *Slavery and Servitude in the Colony of North Carolina*, p. 80.

[71] Williams, *History of the Negro Race in America*, Vol. 1, p. 121.

[72] See Bassett, *Slavery in the State of North Carolina*, p. 22, for illuminating side-light on the consequences of the association of the Negroes and the low-class whites.

servants was at first much the same; they "were bound together by a fellowship of toil."[73] The relatively great number of the vicious whites in certain regions [74] made it inevitable that there should be much illicit relations between the races. The first case of intermixture of which there is any record is that of a white servant and a Negro woman.[75] "During the first half to three-quarters of a century there was an indiscriminate mingling and marrying."[76] Williams adds: [77]

> The contact of these two elements—of slaves and convicts—was neither prudent nor healthy. The halfbreed population increased and so did the free negroes. The negroes suffered from the touch of moral contagion of this effete matter driven out of European society.

There was a provision in the Maryland law of 1692 that any white man who married with or had a child by a Negro

[73] Williams, *History of the Negro Race in America*, Vol. 1, p. 121.

[74] The population of the present territory of Baltimore and Hartford in 1752 was given as follows:

Free whites	over	11,000
White servants	nearly	1,000
Convicts	5,000 to	6,000
Mulatto slaves		116
Negro slaves		4,027
Free mulattoes		196
Free Negroes		8

Brackett, *The Negro in Maryland*, pp. 175-76.

[75] This was the case of Hugh Davis. He was publicly flogged September 17, 1630, "before an assembly of negroes and others" for "defiling himself with a negro." "It was required that he confess as much the following Sabbath." Williams, *History of the Negro*, Vol. 1, p. 121, quoting Henning. See, also, Ballagh, *White Servitude in the Colony of Virginia*, pp. 72-73.

[76] Brackett, *The Negro in Maryland*, p. 121.

[77] *History of the Negro Race in America*, Vol. 1, p. 247.

woman should be put to service for a period of seven years.[78] In Pennsylvania, a white servant was indicted for sexual offence with a Negress in 1677.[79] In 1722, the Assembly was petitioned for relief from the practice of white people cohabiting with Negroes. A whole tract of land in Sussex County was known as "Mulatto Hall." The mulattoes, who were numerous, were the offspring of Negroes and low-class whites.[80]

In the earlier days, the association between the Negro slaves and the bonded servants was close, and this sympathetic relation held in some cases as between the free Negroes and the freed white servants. The poor whites in many cases tried to screen the fugitive slaves,[81] and the free Negro was not always improved by freedom.[82] "It was thought that a rather large proportion of the free colored females, particularly free mulattoes, were unchaste."[83] In Maryland, there was a special legal enactment to cover the case of free Negro women having children of white men.[84] Bassett[85] says of the early Negro slaves that "They were in the lowest moral condition . . .

[78] Brackett, *The Negro in Maryland,* p. 33.
[79] Turner, *The Negro in Pennsylvania,* pp. 29-30.
[80] *Ibid.,* pp. 30-31.
[81] Bassett, *Slavery and Servitude in the Colony of North Carolina,* p. 34.
[82] "The women grew unchaste, the men dishonest, until in many minds the term 'free negro' became a synonym of all that was worthless and despicable." David Dodge [O. W. Blacknall], "The Free Negroes of North Carolina." *Atlantic Monthly,* Vol. 57, p. 26.
[83] Russell, *The Free Negro in Virginia,* p. 137. He adds: "However this may have been, there is ample documentary evidence to show that in the 19th century there was a large class of the free colored population the members of which were respectable and observant of decency and regularity in their family relation."
[84] Brackett, *The Negro in Maryland,* pp. 33, 195.
[85] *Slavery and Servitude in the Colony of North Carolina,* p. 30.

Nature of Race Intermixture in United States 151

They were bestial, given to the worst venereal diseases and they had little or no regard for the marriage bond." Brickwell, who was a physician, says that the white men of the colony suffered a great deal from a malignant kind of venereal disease which they took from the slaves.[86] The looseness of the marriage tie among the free blacks was notorious.[87] Strenuous measures were necessary to maintain order among the assemblages of the blacks and whites.[88]

As the Negroes increased in numbers, however, distinctions were made between the blacks and the whites. The heavier work was put upon the Negroes "and the servant class as more intelligent was reserved for the lighter tasks."[89] The Negresses were frequently employed in the field work with the men. Many of the servants were taken into the master's house. "Women-servants were commonly employed as domestics."[90]

The servants, as a class, came quickly to exaggerate the difference. They worked with the Negro but did not live with him. The feeling of fellowship that at first existed between the white servants and the black slaves gradually gave place to social estrangement.[91] "Yet, in spite of the strong social antipathies, there was some illicit relations

---

[86] *Ibid.*, pp. 30, 59. It is probable that they contracted this disease from the Indian rather than from the Negro slaves. If from the Negroes, they had received it from the Indians.

[87] Brackett, *The Negro in Maryland*, p. 189.

[88] ". . . Friends were still troubled by the racing of horses and the meeting of negroes . . . Great crowds of idle whites and blacks, they said, drank and behaved riotously there—until, in 1747, horse racing was forbidden, also, and the constables of the neighborhood ordered to disperse all crowds of slaves, at the time of the yearly meetings, if necessary by whipping and by the assistance of a posse." *Ibid.*, p. 102.

[89] Ballagh, *White Servitude in the Colony of Virginia*, p. 69.

[90] *Ibid.*, p. 69.

[91] Russell, *The Free Negro in Virginia*, pp. 124-27.

between shameless white persons and Negroes."⁹² Williams,⁹³ speaking of Maryland, says that the Negro slaves who were at first courted by the convicts and other lowly whites, at length came to be treated worse by them than by the opulent and intelligent slave dealers.

This attitude of superiority and the disposition to keep free from all association with the Negro, which was at all times true of many individuals and which later came to be a marked characteristic of the whole poor white class, is thus stated by Ballagh:⁹⁴

> The natural pride of the free man sustained this feeling, together with the strong race prejudice that has ever separated the Englishman from an inferior and dependent race. . . . These sentiments were effective with the better class of servants in keeping them aloof from association with such inferiors. With convicts and the lower classes, where such considerations were not always sufficient, the law. . . . Freemen and servants alike were subjected to severe penalties for intercourse with negroes, mulattoes and Indians, and intermarriage with them or with infidels was prohibited by many statutes prescribing the punishment both for the offender and the minister who performed the ceremony. The limitation of the servants, marriages upon the master's consent was a sufficient safe-guard in their case, and but little responsibility may be regarded as attaching to them for the growth of the mulatto class. As was natural between two dependent classes whose conditions were different and widely in favor of one class, race prejudice and pride were at their strongest and developed jealousies which did not exist between master and his dependent or the freedman and the slave. A disposition on the part of the servants to keep them-

⁹² Russell, *The Free Negro in Virginia*, p. 124.
⁹³ *History of the Negro Race in America*, Vol. 1, p. 247.
⁹⁴ *White Servitude in the Colony of Virginia*, pp. 71-73.

selves free from all association with negroes was perceptible.

Another body of the mulattoes were children of white servant women by slave and free Negro men. There seems to have been a considerable number of these mulattoes in Virginia toward the end of the seventeenth century.[95] By the law of Virginia, these children were bound out by the church wardens until the age of thirty. The master was required to provide some degree of education for the apprentices.[96] The servant woman guilty of having a mulatto child was sold for five years as a punishment.[97] These mulatto children of white women account, in small part, for the large number of free mulattoes in Virginia in the middle and latter part of the seventeenth century.[98]

In Maryland from 1692, there were penalties for white women allowing themselves to be with child by colored persons and for colored men guilty of the act.[99] The same penalty was provided for slaves and free colored persons.[100] Says McCormac:[101]

> While this law [1681] very effectually protected the servant from evil designs of an avaricious master, it did not prevent lewd conduct on the part of the servant. Mingling of the races continued during the 18th

[95] *Ibid.*, pp. 72-74.
[96] Russell, *The Free Negro in Virginia*, pp. 40 ff., 138.
[97] "Where the offence occurred, then, it was more likely to do so in the case of a free person than of a servant, . . ." Ballagh, *White Servitude in the Colony of Virginia*, p. 73.
[98] W. H. Thomas, *The American Negro*, p. 6.
[99] Brackett, *The Negro in Maryland*, p. 196.
[100] *Ibid.*, p. 191. "There were not a few cases of such offspring." In 1790 there is a case of a sale of a white woman and her mulatto child as servants. There are other cases in 1793 and 1794. See, also, p. 140 f. n.
[101] McCormac, *White Servitude in Maryland*, pp. 69-70.

century, in spite of all laws against it. Preventing the marriage of white servants with slaves only led to a greater social evil, which caused a reaction of public sentiment against the servant. Masters and society in general were burdened with the care of illegitimate mulatto children. . . .

In Pennsylvania, especially in the neighborhood of Philadelphia, a mulatto population grew up, some of which were slave and some were free, according to the condition of the mother. Says Turner:[102]

> . . . The child of a slave was not necessarily a slave if one of the parents was free. The line of servile descent lay through the mother. Accordingly the child of a slave mother and a free father was a slave, of a free mother and a slave father a servant for a term of years only. The result of the application of this doctrine to the offspring of a negro and a white person was that the mulattoes were divided into two classes. Some were servants for a term of years; the others formed a third class of slaves.

The act of 1725-1726 recognized this. The law enumerated four classes of Negro servants. "Fourthly, all mulatto children who were not slaves for life, were to be bound out until they were thirty-one years of age."[103] Bassett,[104] in enumerating the sources of the free Negro population, says:

> Another [source] was the children of white women by negro men. There is evidence that not a few such people were in the government. Taken all together, there was a considerable number of free negroes among the people by the close of the Colonial period.

[102] *The Negro in Pennsylvania*, pp. 24-25.
[103] *Ibid.*, pp. 91-92.
[104] *Slavery and Servitude in the Colony of North Carolina*, p. 67.

Nature of Race Intermixture in United States 155

Delaware in 1721 passed an act punishing adultery and fornication. It provided that in case of children of a white woman by a slave, the County Court bound them out until they were thirty-one years of age.[105] The number of mulattoes born to white women was nowhere large but that the number was considerable there is no reason to doubt.

There appears also to have been some intermixture between the low-class white women and the Indian men.[106] The Indians were never under the social ban to the same extent as the Negro. The distinction between mulattoes, *mustees*, and half-breed Indians was not always clearly made; the term mulatto was frequently used to include all three.[107] It may well be that in some of the cases mentioned of white women having mulatto children, the offspring were really half-breed Indians.

Intermarriage with Indians

The Negro has everywhere and at all times mixed freely with the Indian. The barriers to social equality were less between them than between either and the white. There was some ground of sympathy between them and there were no laws forbidding intermixture.[108] In many of the colonies, the first slaves were Indians.[109] The captives in battle

[105] Williams, *History of the Negro Race in America*, Vol. 1, p. 250.

[106] Brackett, *The Negro in Maryland*, p. 117, mentions such a case. ". . . At about the same time, a Pocomok Indian was imprisoned for rape of an English woman. . . . As it was found that the woman had willingly erred, the Indian was merely whipped, according to English law, and advised by the court to be more circumspect."

[107] Russell, *The Free Negro in Virginia*, p. 130. See, also, Bassett, *Slavery in the State of North Carolina*, p. 90. He here quotes a correspondent as saying that "many of them [mulattoes] were descended from Indian and . . ."

[108] Russell, *The Free Negro in Virginia*, pp. 41, 127 ff.

[109] Bassett, *Slavery and Servitude in the Colony of North Carolina*,

were enslaved,[110] and not a few were kidnapped along the unsettled coasts and sold into slavery among the more settled colonies.[111] How many Indian slaves there were, it is impossible to say; they were classed with the blacks and no difference was made between them and other slaves.[112] They were not particularly adapted to slavery,[113] and as the Negroes increased, they gradually disappeared.[114] They were thrown into close association with the Negroes, intermarried readily with them, and were gradually absorbed by and disappeared into the growing body of blacks.[115]

pp. 71-74. B. C. Steiner, *A History of Slavery in Connecticut*, pp. 9 ff. "Indian Slavery."

[110] Massachusetts sold the captives in King William's war into slavery. Virginia made slaves for life of those Indians taken in war but hesitated to do so with those offered for sale by other Indians. Steiner, *A History of Slavery in Connecticut*, p. 9. Brackett, *The Negro in Maryland*, p. 19. Bassett, *Slavery and Servitude in the Colony of North Carolina*, pp. 72 ff.

[111] The first slaves in North Carolina were of this sort. *Ibid.*, p. 71.

[112] H. S. Cooley, *A Study of Slavery in New Jersey*, pp. 11-13.

[113] "At first some masters enslaved Indian women to increase their slave-progeny. This cross was not adapted to slavery, because those of Indian blood knew the country and were better able to escape. Consequently a law was passed in most states forbidding the enslavement of the children of Indian mothers. For this reason many Negro men took Indian wives so that their children might be born free. ..." J. F. Gould, "The Negro Finding Himself," Speech before the Boston Business League, A Negro Organization. Quoted in the *Boston Reliance*, a Negro newspaper. It is not meant for humor.

[114] Massachusetts in 1712 and Connecticut in 1716 forbade the importation of Indian slaves on the ground that they were fierce and caused trouble. Bassett, *Slavery and Servitude in the Colony of North Carolina*, p. 73.

[115] *Ibid.*, p. 72. Dodge, *Atlantic Monthly*, Vol. 57, pp. 29-30. ". . . . many, if not the larger part of the free negroes whose freedom dates further back than this century show traits in mind and body that are unmistakably Indian. . . ." The Indians seem to have been more used as concubines than were the Negresses and consequently more of them set free because they had borne half-breed children. This was especially

Nature of Race Intermixture in United States 157

The reservations set apart in the seventeenth and eighteenth centuries in many cases became the common home for Indians and free Negroes.[116] [117] As the Negroes frequently outnumbered the Indians, these settlements generally lost all but a tradition of Indian ancestry.[118] Runaway slaves frequently sought refuge among the Indians. In some cases, they were harbored[119] and taken into the tribe. In

---

true of the French settlements. Both the French and the English feel less repugnance toward the Indian than toward the Negro. H. A. Trexler, *Slavery in Missouri*, p. 80. See, also, note 118, p. 157 below.

[116] John Fisk, *The Discovery of America*, Vol. 2, pp. 427 ff., has an excellent brief description of Indian slavery.

[117] A petition in 1843 in regard to the Pamunkey reservation in King Williams County stated "that all but a small remnant of the old Indian tribe was extinct, and that in its place were free mulattoes, . . . 'They are so mingled with the negro race as to have obliterated all striking features of Indian extraction. It is the general resort of free negroes from all parts of the country.'" Russell, *The Free Negro in Virginia*, p. 129. White persons in the vicinity of the reservation of the Nottaways and kindred tribes affirmed, in 1821, that the wives and husbands of the Indians were free Negroes and "that they had neither prudence nor economy." *Ibid.*, p. 129. Of the inhabitants of the Gingaskin reservation it was said in 1787 "that those who were not entirely black had 'at least half black blood in them.' The place was called Indian Town, but many of the squaws had negroes for husbands, and the Indian braves lived with black wives." *Ibid.*, p. 128.

[118] Bureau of American Ethnology. *Handbook of the American Indians*, Part 1, p. 914. "There is no doubt that many of the broken coast tribes have been completely absorbed into the negro race." See, also, p. 81 above.

[119] "In treaties made with the governor of Maryland with various Indians, in 1661 and 1663, there is the stipulation that the Indians are to return any runaway 'Englishmen.' Later the neighboring Indians were encouraged to seize runaways by the reward of a blanket or its value. Treaties with them forbade their harboring servants and slaves, who were to be given over to the nearest English plantation. The backwoods offered a near retreat for runaways. As a certain tribe of Indians had evidently been regardless of the rights of the good people of Maryland in their servants and slaves, the Governor and Council decided, in

158   *The Mulatto in the United States*

other cases, they simply became the slaves of the Indians among whom they sought refuge.[120] The Cherokees and the Creeks were large slave holders and for the most part mixed on terms of equality with their black slaves. The Seminoles at a later date owned large numbers of slaves with whom they had intermixed. There seem also to have been in their tribe many runaways who were not classed as slaves.

Intermixture During Slavery and at Present

The illicit relations between the Negroes and the low-class whites, which in some regions at least characterized the racial situation during a considerable portion of the colonial period, very greatly decreased as the institution of slavery developed. On the one hand, the general and bitter hatred that existed everywhere in the slave states between the "poor white class" and the slaves tended to keep the races apart and to keep intermixture at a minimum.[121]

1722, to send to these a messenger with a treaty of peace and friendship, and the promise of a reward of two blankets and a gun to every Indian who should return a slave. These allurements were evidently unavailing, for three years later it was decided to send again, to invite the chiefs to Annapolis. . . ." Brackett, *The Negro in Maryland*, pp. 74-75.

[120] Bassett, *Slavery and Servitude in the Colony of North Carolina*, p. 57, quotes Brikell, *Natural History of North Carolina*, p. 273, as saying that "The Indians . . . had a natural and irreconcilable hatred for the negroes and delighted in torturing them. When they would meet runaways in the woods they would attack them vigorously, either killing them or driving them back to the whites."

[121] This was by no means always the case between the free Negroes and the poor whites. See Bassett, *Slavery in the State of North Carolina*, p. 43. Dodge, *Atlantic Monthly*, Vol. 59, p. 29, says: ". . . Hardly a neighborhood was free from low white women who married or cohabited with free negroes. Well can I recollect the many times when, with the inconsiderate curiosity of a child, I hurriedly climbed the front

Nature of Race Intermixture in United States 159

On the other hand, whatever may have been the extent of the irregular relationships between the slave-holding class and their female slaves, the slave system as a working and developed institution regulated strictly the conduct of the slaves and thereby restricted, in a measure, irregular relations between them and the general white population.[122] Miss Frances A. Kemble, who spent some time in Georgia about 1850, naïvely testifies to this fact.[123]

> I observed, among the numerous groups that we passed or met, a much larger proportion of mulattoes than at the rice-island: upon asking Mr. .... why this was so, he said that there no white person could land without his or the overseer's permission, whereas on St. Simon's which is a large island containing several plantations belonging to different owners, of course the number of whites, both residing on and visiting the place, was much greater, and the opportunity for intercourse between the blacks and whites much more frequent.[124]

gate-post to get a good look at a shriveled old woman trudging down the lane, who, when young, I was told, had had her free-negro lover bled, and drank some of his blood, so that she might swear she had Negro blood in her."

[122] Bruce, *The Plantation Negro as a Freeman*, p. 17, gives a good statement of the restraining effects of slavery on the Negro.

[123] *Residence on a Georgian Plantation*, p. 162.

[124] In another place, speaking of a certain mulatto woman, Miss Kemble says: "This woman was a mulatto daughter of a slave called Sophy, by a white man of the name of Walker, who visited the plantation," p. 190. Of another mulatto she says: "The woman's father had been a white man who was employed for some purpose on the estate," p. 194. It was of course to the master's interest to prevent intermixture so far as he was able to do so. "If a woman had children she was rendered less desirable as a slave. . . ." Frequently slave women were offered for sale for no other reason than that they had children. Cooley, *A Study of Slavery in New Jersey*, p. 55. However, this was not always the case. Brickell, *Natural History of North Carolina*, p. 272,

160   *The Mulatto in the United States*

In the cities and towns of the South, however, there was no such degree of restraint exercised over the slaves as was the case on the plantations. Opportunities for association with others than the master class were greatly increased. A much larger per cent of the slaves were house servants. The number of free Negroes and free mulattoes was larger. The better opportunity for association resulted in a greatly increased amount of intermixture in the cities.[125] Here there was a casual mixture totally different in kind from the more or less permanent or regular association that frequently existed between the slave owner and a favorite Negress. It was in general the vicious elements of the whites which were responsible for the mulattoes in the cities; on the plantations, generally speaking, the Negro woman was screened as far as possible from association with this class of whites.

The disorganization resulting from the breakdown of the master and slave relationship, brought with it an enormous increase of racial intermixture. The restraint under which the slaves had been held shielded them from general association with the vicious whites. As they realized the fact of their freedom, they wandered in great numbers to the towns and cities [126] where they gave themselves up to a pro-

---

says that "a fruitful woman amongst them being very much valued by the planters and a numerous issue esteemed the greatest riches in the country." Quoted by Bassett, *Slavery and Servitude in the Colony of North Carolina*, pp. 57-58.

[125] "The slave-holders of the Southern states . . . are benevolently doing their best, in one way at least, to raise and improve the degraded race, and the bastard population which forms so ominous an element in the social safety of their cities . . ." Kemble, *Residence on a Georgian Plantation*, p. 14. That it was essentially a city phenomenon in the South is correct: that it was the slave-holding class which was responsible, wholly or chiefly, is notoriously undemonstrable.

[126] Steiner, *A History of Slavery in Connecticut*, p. 80, comments upon this tendency of the manumitted slaves of Connecticut and attributes

longed celebration which was frequently characterized by a more or less promiscuous sexual intercourse among the Negroes themselves and between their women and the vicious white elements of the cities.[127]

Wherever the Union armies went in the South, they were besieged by an army of Negro women. Says Thomas, a severe and unsympathetic but on the whole a frank and accurate critic of his own race:[128]

> ... It may have been the outcroppings of gratitude to Federal victors, or reckless abandon to lust, but the inciting cause is immaterial, so long as the shameful fact is true, that, wherever our armies were quartered in the South the negro women flocked to their camps for infamous riot with the white soldiery. All occupied cities, suburban rendezvous, and rural bivouacs, bore witness to the mad havoc daily wrought in black womanhood by our citizen soldiery. We have personal knowledge of many Federal officers of high station, and some of strong prejudices against the race, who openly kept negro mistresses in their army quarters; nor do we doubt that the present lax morality everywhere observable among negro womenkind is largely due to the licentious freedom which the war engendered among them. Slavery had its blighting evils, but also its wholesome restraints.[129]

At the present time, the intermixture of the races seems to be going on more rapidly than at any time in the past.[130]

it to "their gregarious tendencies." See, also, J. R. Brackett, *Notes on the Progress of the Colored People Since the War*, p. 25.

[127] F. A. Bancroft, *The Negro in Politics*, pp. 14 ff.

[128] *The American Negro*, p. 14.

[129] It is a significant fact that venereal diseases were practically unknown in the South outside of a few cities before the War and the Negroes were generally free from them. Following the wake of the Union armies they rapidly spread throughout the whole black population of the South. See, however, p. 151 above.

[130] Sir Harry H. Johnston, *The Negro in the New World*, p. 98, points

As has been previously pointed out, some of this increase is due to legal intermarriage between the races, and some to a more or less ordered but unlawful concubinage of mulatto and Negro girls by white men. Relations of a more vicious sort, however, are responsible for the large per cent;[131] and these take two forms. On the one hand, there is a debauching by white men of the lighter-colored mulatto girls whom they, of course, do not marry. In their turn, the mulatto men debauch, but refuse to marry, the black girls.[132]

It is necessary to remember that the amount of intermixture is, in general, proportional to the opportunity for contact. Granting numerous individual exceptions, the general statement holds true that the women of a lower race everywhere are honored by the attention of the men of a superior caste. It is not only true of the Negro, but is true of every race or class within a race, which is culturally inferior and recognizes itself as inferior.

In summarizing, we may say that the intermixture of the races everywhere has gone on to the extent of the white man's wishes. The Negro woman never has objected to,

out a similar fact in regard to Brazil. "After emancipation the movement toward a fusion of the races between the ex-slave and the descendants of his Luso-Brazilian masters went on more rapidly even than during the three centuries of mild servitude."

[131] The great majority of the mixed-blood race is of course the result of marriage between the mulattoes themselves.

[132] Said a Negro Y. M. C. A. Secretary, speaking before a mixed audience at the Frederick Douglass Center in Chicago: ". . . No colored girl who comes to Chicago has been in the city forty-eight hours without being besieged by the colored men and boys of the city whose one effort and desire is to work her downfall. We talk of the way in which the white men wrong our girls but it is our men and boys who least respect and honor them." The black girl is flattered by these attentions, especially when they come from mulatto men just as the mulatto girl is flattered by the attention of white men.

and has generally courted, the relationship. It was never at any time a matter of compulsion; on the contrary it was a matter of being honored by a man of a superior race. Speaking generally, the amount of intermixture is limited only by the self-respect of the white man and the compelling strength of the community sentiment.

Intermixture went on rapidly during the colonial days especially where the Negro was in contact with the indentured servant class, and in regions where there was a scarcity of white women. There was a large intermixture between the Indians and the Negroes wherever these two races were in contact. Occasionally the Negro men found white wives or formed extra-matrimonial alliances with the white women of the servant class. As the status of the slave became better defined and a social difference was made, the friendly relation between the Negroes and the white servants gave place to a feeling of hatred between the Negro and the poor white class. This, together with the more strict discipline over the slaves, generally prevented much intermixture of these classes during the period that slavery existed as a national institution.

Mixture of the races probably went on more slowly during the period that slavery existed as a national institution, than in the period before or the period since. Such relations as existed between the master class and the slave women were generally a kind of sub-surface polygamy and were rather a process of further whitening the mixed-blood race than a mixture of the whites and blacks. This was during the slavery period, and the same thing is true to-day where concubinage exists, the relation being generally one between a mulatto woman and a white man; seldom a relation between a white man and a Negro woman.[133]

[133] W. Laird Clowes, *Black America*, pp. 142-43, points out that "the

The amount of racial intermixture, being conditioned by the opportunity for association of the races and especially for association of the lower classes, has, in general, been greatest where the Negro has been least numerous as compared to the white race. Consequently the intermixture always has been greater in the cities and towns than in the rural districts, and relatively greater in the North than in the South. Since the freedom of the Negroes and their immigration to the towns and cities, intermixture of the races in the South has increased. It is in the urban situation that the Negro girls and women come into contact most frequently with dissolute white men. It is there, too, that the opportunity to conceal the relationship makes the control of the situation by the prevailing public sentiment less effective than in the rural situation.

Finally, such intermixture of the races as now goes on, outside a very little intermarriage, is, for the most part, between the vicious elements of both races. Under the slave regime, especially as it took place outside the cities, it was often a relation between a better class of white men than is now usually the case and the choicest and usually the lightest-colored Negro girls. At the present time, there is a disposition on the part of the better-class whites and a growing sentiment among the Negro middle-class to avoid such relationships. There is, however, much intermixture between certain classes of whites and mulatto girls [134] and between mulatto men and Negro girls. It seems to be on

chief sinners—if sinners they can be called in such connection—are the coloured, as distinct from the pure negro, women of the South."

[134] Mr. DuBois has pointed out that the process of intermixture goes on between the mulatto girls and the lower grade of whites. ". . . in many an instance a prudent negro mother finds it wise to send her good-looking yellow daughter to some institution to save her from the temptation of association with the lowest grade of white boys in the

the whole, though not exclusively, a casual association of the lower classes of the whites and frequently the lower classes of both races.

neighborhood." Quoted by Raymond Patterson, *The Negro and His Needs,* p. 35.

It is interesting to compare this with the situation in Chile where, it is said, that "very few prostitutes can make a living" because the half-breed girls "are so easy." E. A. Ross, *South of Panama,* pp. 222-26.

CHAPTER VII

THE GROWTH OF THE MULATTO CLASS

THE first Negroes introduced into the English Colonies in America were probably not introduced as slaves.[1] White servitude was the rule before the Negro came. He was brought into more or less intimate contact with these white indentured servants, and probably little difference was at first made between his status and theirs. It was the first contact in any appreciable numbers of the North European peoples with the African races. Aside from whatever natural antipathy may have existed between people so widely different in physical appearance, there was no sentiment of hostility toward the black man, no traditional prejudice, and no customary caste feeling of superiority.[2] Such feeling as did exist was probably not so much a matter of race as it was a matter of religion.[3] The Negroes were "heathen" and the distinction was between Christians and Barbarians rather than between people of white and

---

[1] "Beyond all question the first negroes brought in were not introduced as freemen. The only question is whether, upon entering the colony, they became servants or slaves. . . ." J. H. Russell, *The Free Negro in Virginia*, p. 23. See, also, p. 19.

[2] *Ibid.*, p. 137.
H. S. Cooley, *A Study of Slavery in New Jersey*, p. 57.
Edward Ingle, *The Negro in the District of Columbia*, p. 43.
David Dodge, "The Free Negroes of North Carolina," *Atlantic Monthly*, Vol. 57, p. 24, gives 1830 as the date, and reaction against abolitionism the cause, of change in race prejudice.

[3] J. R. Brackett, *The Negro in Maryland*, pp. 30 ff.

people of black skin.

The early colonial conception of slavery was very different from that which came to prevail at a later time. The system was new, imperfect, immature; there existed no crystallized body of doctrine as to the slaves' condition or status. Nor was there any strong body of sentiment opposed to the institution. The seventeenth century idea of a slave was that of a servant for life. It was for the most part a domestic institution as opposed to an industrial one. The slaves were recognized as persons not, as in the later conception, things. In most cases, they lived in close relation to the family of the master and neither in law nor in custom were they regarded in any way as very different from other servants and apprentices. They were laborers and probably not considered, nor treated very differently from other laborers. The very strangeness of the Africans and their physical, cultural, and temperamental differences from the settlers may have given them a status unlike that of other persons in the colonies. Their number was very small, however, and it was, in general, a generation after their first introduction before black slavery was recognized by law. It had existed as a well-established and well-understood custom long before it anywhere received legal sanction.

But gradually the Negroes acquired or were assigned a separate and inferior status. From the status of servants, they acquired the status of servants for life, or slaves, and finally that of servants in perpetuity. As white servitude declined, the status of servant or slave came to be associated with color; and slavery became the presumptive status of all Negroes. Moreover, the early conception of a slave as a person serving for life, gave place to the conception of a slave as a thing rather than as a person. "Gradually," says Turner,[4] "the very best negroes had come to be regarded as of an alien race, and as an outcast and degraded people with whom no intimate association was possible." Color prejudice grew up as the characteristics of the Negroes became better known and increased in strength with the increase in numbers of the blacks.[5] Where the numbers remained small, the prejudice remained very largely a simple, organic, repulsive reaction against the strange and the ugly. As long as the numbers remained so small as to constitute no immediate menace, the outward expression of the race prejudice remained in abeyance. Where the slaves were more numerous and better known, the sentiments and attitudes were more definitely organized and the Negro, as such, was assigned a separate and lower economic and social status as the only conceivable working relation that could exist between two groups at the opposite extremes of human culture.

This race, ever more and more separated from the white group by the action of the whites, was in no sense a homogeneous group.[6] Its members were much alike as to color and other physical characteristics, but in temperament[7] and in talent they differed much as other men differ. As their domestication progressed, they rapidly became a less

[4] E. R. Turner, *The Negro in Pennsylvania*, p. 199.

[5] *Ibid.*, p. 143. See, also, J. C. Ballagh, *White Servitude in the Colony of Virginia*, pp. 97 ff.; and G. W. Williams, *History of the Negro Race in America*, Vol. 1, p. 142.

[6] There were among the slaves, representatives of many African tribes as well as Australian Blacks, natives of Oceania and New Guinea. Well over one-half of the slaves, however, were Negroes from the West African Coast. See C. H. Otken, *Ills of the South*, pp. 203 ff. for an attempt to identify and evaluate the different tribal elements.

[7] The very considerable number of Indians and later of Indian-Negro intermixtures among the slaves did much to increase the temperamental differences.

and less homogeneous group. This natural differentiation within the group, due to the different rate at which individuals were able to accommodate themselves to civilized manners and customs, was being constantly increased by the addition of new arrivals from Africa.[8]

But aside from differences in native talent and the length of the period of domestication of the Negroes brought to America, there were other forces at work tending to bring about a differentiation within the Negro group. Such things as climate, occupations, types of people in the different regions or colonies, afforded the black man unequal opportunities for assimilating the white man's culture. Diversity in customs, sentiments, racial heredity, and religious belief made differences in his treatment. The differences in climate and consequently in occupations in various sections of the country, made a difference in his work. The wide variety of conditions naturally produced a great difference in the rate at which the Negroes acquired the outward forms of English culture.

The relative numbers of the Negroes and whites varied widely in various sections of the country. In most of the northern sections the proportionate number of Negroes was never large.[9] As a result, they came more into contact with the white people and consequently their opportunity to assimilate the white man's culture was superior to the opportunity of those Negroes whose lot fell in sections of the country where the proportion of Negroes to whites was greater. The negative side of the proposition is of equal importance. Where the number of Negroes was small, they

---

[8] J. S. Bassett, *Slavery and Servitude in the Colony of North Carolina*, pp. 56-57.

[9] "For the most part, only one or two negroes were owned by any person." B. C. Steiner, *A History of Slavery in Connecticut*, p. 21.

170   *The Mulatto in the United States*

had not the same opportunity to associate with one another and so did not have the opportunity to develop and perpetuate their African traditions and culture. The Negroes more rapidly in some sections than in others, therefore, simply because of differences in numbers, threw off the language and traditions of Africa and took on the language and customs of their masters.

Another differentiating factor among the slaves, was the lack of uniformity among the slaveholders themselves. While as a class the slaveholders represented the educational, moral, economic, intellectual, and social aristocracy; and stood for all that was best in American life, they were by no means all of the same high type. The slave in the household of a wealthy, educated, and refined gentleman had a vastly better opportunity than did the slave in the household of the ignorant and the vicious.[10] In some cases, at least, the slaves were given some education, taught the religion of their masters and had some opportunity for association with the white people.[11] In other cases they were denied these things or had no opportunity to secure them.

Again, some slaves early received their freedom. This was the case in all parts of the country. At a later period, it was especially the case in the North where slavery was not the profitable economic institution that it proved to be in other parts of the country. The actual number freed

[10] Frances A. Kemble, *Journal of a Residence on a Georgian Plantation*, p. 24. Ballagh, *White Servitude in the Colony of Virginia*, pp. 97 ff.

[11] Susan D. Smedes, *A Southern Planter*, p. 40. Speaking of Lunsford Lane, J. S. Bassett, *The Anti-Slavery Leaders in North Carolina*, pp. 61-62, says that "His parents . . . had been kept in the town for family service, and thus their offspring had opportunities beyond the other negroes. Lunsford early learned to read and write . . . Many men of political prominence visited his master's house, and from waiting on these he acquired much general information. . . ."

was, of course, greater in the South. There grew up, therefore, a body of free Negroes who, though their condition on the whole seems often not to have been superior to that of the slaves,[12] were free to follow their own inclinations as to employment, the accumulation of property, associations, and the like.

A still more profound difference was that between the condition of the town and plantation slaves. In the former situation, they were brought into continual contact and association with various members of the opposite race.[13] The plantation Negroes, on the other hand, were isolated

[12] "... Except for natural procreation, the principal additions or recruits to this class [free Negroes] throughout this period were the result of illegitimacy. There was no tendency to attribute to a few negroes and mulattoes of such low origin any higher social standing than that occupied by more than 99 per cent of their race and color...." Russell, *The Free Negro in Virginia*, p. 126. However, "... before the time of the active propagation of the antislavery doctrines, there existed little if any prejudice against the education of free colored persons." *Ibid.*, p. 137. See, also, pp. 51, 76.

"... before 1780 a negro even if free was far from being as free as a white man...." Turner, *The Negro in Pennsylvania*, p. 113. See, also, p. 127.

"... Free negroes were despised rather than hated, ... and though some gained and held a place of comparative comfort and security, the mass came under the obloquy attached to slavery without participation in the benefits enjoyed by the average bondsman." E. Ingle, *Southern Sidelights*, p. 285. See, also, p. 279. See, also, Williams, *History of the Negro Race in America*, Vol. 1, pp. 315, 286; Cooley, *A Study of Slavery in New Jersey*, pp. 45 ff.; Steiner, *A History of Slavery in Connecticut*, p. 23, f. n.; J. S. Bassett, *Slavery in the State of North Carolina*, pp. 34 ff.; Bassett, *Slavery and Servitude in the Colony of North Carolina*, pp. 66 ff.

[13] These slaves "who thus came under the religious influence of their masters and mistresses" were most likely the ones first converted to Christianity. See Bassett, *Slavery and Servitude in the Colony of North Carolina*, pp. 48-50. See, also, E. Ingle, *The Negro in the District of Columbia*, p. 19.

from the cultured race and in continual association with other Negroes. They did not get into touch with the whites. They retained, therefore, the language, the customs, and the traditions of their African home, for years and generations after the more fortunately situated Negroes had cast them off.

> . . . The house servants in Charleston or Savannah, in close personal and confidential touch with the master and mistress, and with opportunities to acquire a certain degree of book-learning, and much more valuable culture in morality and refinement, were quite different from the workers in the rice-fields or among the canes, many of whom were steeped in the superstition of barbarism and clung to African gibberish fifty years after they had passed from the decks of the slaver.[14]

In the back country the contact was more intimate than on the larger plantations and, while not so varied, was frequently more effective even than the city life.

> In North Carolina, and elsewhere, no doubt, it was noticeable that slavery, . . . was of a milder type in the western counties. Here the farms were small. Slave-owners had but few slaves. With these they mingled freely. They worked with them in the fields, plowing side by side. The slave cabins were in the same yard with the master's humble home. Slave children and, indeed, slave families were directly under the eye of the master, and better still, of the mistress. . . .[15]

Finally, and possibly of greatest importance, was the occupational differentiation among the members of the Ne-

[14] Ingle, *Southern Sidelights*, p. 264. See, also, P. A. Bruce, *The Plantation Negro as a Freeman*, p. 74.

[15] Bassett, *Slavery in the State of North Carolina*, p. 8. See, also, Dodge, *Atlantic Monthly*, Vol. 57, p. 21.

gro group. Some were house and body servants, some were mechanics, some were laborers and field hands. The first had the opportunity of intimate daily association with the master's family.[16]

The second had not only that association, but the education and training necessary to make of them efficient workmen.

> . . . But the superior slave class, and the one that represented all that was best in Negro development, was the mechanics who were in most cases conspicuous for their ability and achievements, for slavery included among its mechanical industries every form of handicraft, and as the ability to acquire a mechanical art carries with it a fair degree of intelligence, it is not surprising that negro artisans, who were carefully selected for their special lines of work, should have developed characters superior to their less fortunate fellows.[17]

The third class came little into contact with the whites.[18] On the plantation, they might never see the master and seldom any white man from one year's end to another. On the larger plantations and in Jamaica, it was even possible for the slaves to see little more of the white man than did their ancestors in Africa. On these larger plantations, the institution was a more strictly economic one in contrast to the more patriarchal type it assumed in the back country and on the smaller plantations.

[16] "I should tell you that Aleck's parents and kindred have always been about the house of the overseer, and in daily habits of intercourse with him and his wife; and wherever this is the case the effect of involuntary education is evident in the improved intelligence of the degraded race." Kemble, *Residence on a Georgian Plantation*, p. 24. See, also, W. H. Thomas, *The American Negro*, p. 15.

[17] *Ibid.*, pp. 15-16. See, also, p. 67.

[18] *Ibid.*, p. 15.

For these reasons and perhaps for others—because of superior natural talent, superior advantages, superior education and training, because of their freedom—there was a separation within the Negro group that dates from the beginning of the Negroes' American life. Some of the classes thus formed were isolated geographically and socially and found their chief or only associations with others of their kind. Other more fortunate classes had the advantage of association and contact with the cultured race.

In the ranks of the favored classes, there was a preponderance of mulattoes. From their first appearance, and increasingly as the system developed and the control of economic forces allowed a body of trained house servants to grow, the mulattoes formed the house and body servants. When not all could be employed in house work, they were most frequently the ones chosen to learn the trades. They were the ones employed in skilled work. In any case, they came into more close, constant, and intimate association with the white people. This was more especially the case as the institution became older and the number of slaves increased to where a more complete division of labor was possible. There are a number of circumstances each sufficient to account in part for the excess of mulattoes in the favored classes.

In the first place, it was generally believed throughout the slavery period that the mulattoes were superior in intelligence to the black slaves.[19] In spite of their inferior bodily strength, they commanded a higher price in the slave market.[20] Because of this belief—the truth or falsity of the belief is not here in question—they were most often chosen

[19] Kemble, *Residence on a Georgian Plantation*, p. 240.
[20] Ray Stannard Baker, *Following the Color Line*, p. 164.

The Growth of the Mulatto Class 175

for the tasks that required an exercise of skill and intelligence.[21] Thomas [22] says that "the Negroes coarse in speech and crude in action were assigned to labor in the fields and forest. . . ." After speaking of the class of domestic servants he adds:

> . . . Another equally intelligent, but more self-reliant class, was the slaves employed in portage in commercial centers, together with many others engaged in occupations which required little supervision, but a fair degree of personal intelligence and practical judgment to perform rightly.

Because of the presumption of the mulattoes' superior intelligence the industrial as opposed to the common labor classes were, so far as the number of mulattoes allowed a choice to be made, mulatto classes.

In the early days some few, at least, of the mulattoes were children of white women.[23] Where this was the case the child had the advantage of a white mother's care and training and this, even of the type of white woman who gave birth to a mulatto child, was doubtless superior to the training that could be given a child by the Negro mother. Consequently the child, other things equal, would be somewhat superior to the child of a black mother. More-

---

[21] "The fact that the majority of those entrusted with responsibility and of those who succeeded best in acquiring knowledge, both of letters and of industrial arts, during slavery were mulattoes, and the fact that the majority of those of the present who have made creditable attainments are of mixed blood, go to prove that a mixture of white blood has had much to do in the matter of higher ambition, mental force, and efficiency of the talented few. . . ." C. H. McCord, *The American Negro as a Defective, Dependent and Delinquent*, p. 50.

[22] *The American Negro*, pp. 15, 16.

[23] See pp. 152 ff. above.

over, as the status of the child followed that of the mother, it would, in most cases, ultimately become a free man or woman with whatever advantages went with the status. Such ancestry, consequently, tended to increase the percentage of mulattoes in the free Negro group.

In some cases, there existed a paternal or other blood relationship between the mulatto slave and the master. How numerous such cases were, it is wholly impossible to say;[24] but where such relationships existed, the individual was doubtless favored over other individuals of the servile class.[25] He was likely to receive his freedom, generally with that of his mother and often with some property for a start in life.[26] But whether or not such individuals went to swell the ranks of the free Negro group, they were, by heredity[27]

---

[24] See p. 139 above.

[25] "Indeed it was notorious that freemen sold their own mulatto children born in Virginia." J. P. Dunn, *Indiana*, p. 223. This was probably more notorious than accurate. There were doubtless such cases but the stories that the slave-owning class made this a practice are no longer a part of the mental furnishings of any one of standard development. ". . . Everywhere there were usually a number of prosperous free negroes. Most of them were mulattoes, not a few of them were set free by their fathers and thus they fell easily into the life around them. This mulatto class was partly due to the easy sexual relations between the races. A white man who kept a negro mistress ordinarily lost no standing in society on account of it. The habit, though not common, was not unusual. Often the mistress was a slave, and thus there were frequent emancipations either by gift or by purchase of liberty, till the stricter spirit of the laws after 1831 checked it." Bassett, *Slavery in the State of North Carolina*, pp. 45-46.

[26] See Booker T. Washington, *Story of the Negro*, Vol. 1, pp. 227 ff.

[27] So far as a sex relation exists anywhere between a master and a subject race it is always the choicest females who are so honored. The statement in the text, therefore, refers to the colored side of the mulattoes' ancestry. There is no implication of or denial of fundamental racial superiority. Their mothers were the choicest individuals of their race.

The Growth of the Mulatto Class

and training, the best specimens of the race and raised the percentage of mulattoes in the favored classes.

But the most important reason that the mulatto was chosen in preference to the Negro for any employment that brought him into association with the master family was the fact that he was a better looking animal.[28] He made a better appearance.[29] For this reason he was selected as the house and body servant. This favored class of domestic servants "were usually bright and intelligent negroes who, through contact and sympathetic supervision, acquired in many instances a training in manners and methods of incomparable grace and efficiency." [30]

The Negroes everywhere made distinctions among themselves.[31] The free Negroes recognized the difference between themselves and the slaves. The town Negroes considered themselves superior to the country Negroes. In the same way, the house servants held themselves superior to the field hands. The basis on which the distinctions were most usually made was that of color. The free Negroes were very frequently mulattoes.[32] The house servants also were fre-

---

[28] Sir Harry H. Johnston, "Racial Problems and the Congress of Races," *Contemporary Review*, Vol. 100, p. 154.

[29] "She was quite indifferent to the public opinion that required only fine-looking, thoroughly trained servants about the establishment of a gentleman." Smedes, *A Southern Planter*, p. 65.

[30] Thomas, *The American Negro*, p. 15. ". . . The mulattoes were employed in towns. . . . I have seen great plantations with not one of them —all black." Bassett, *Slavery in the State of North Carolina*, p. 90, quoting a correspondent, apparently with approval.

[31] The various opprobrious epithets applied to members of the race, and to the opposite race as well, have always been most widely used by the Negroes themselves. "Crackers," "twisters," "niggers," "burr-heads," "mule-niggers," "polka dots" and the like, if not invented by Negroes were and are more often used by them than by the opposite race. See The *Chicago Defender*, Editorial "So Say We," 10-9-1915.

[32] In 1860, for e.g., 2,554 of the 3,441 free Negroes were mulattoes.

quently of mixed-blood and the same was true to a greater extent of the town Negroes than of the plantation Negroes and lower-class slaves. The mulatto slaves held themselves superior to the black slaves and claimed privileges on account of color. The white man considered the mulatto superior to the black man and the mulatto, taking over the white man's way of thinking, claimed membership in the superior ranks on account of his relative absence of color.

> The mulatto woman, Sally, accosted me again today and begged that she might be put to some other than field labor. Supposing she felt herself unequal to it, I asked her some questions, but the principal reason she urged for her promotion to some less laborious kind of work was, that hoeing in the field was so hard to her on "*account of her color*" and she therefore petitions to be allowed to learn a trade. I was much puzzled at this reason for her petition, but was presently made to understand that, being a mulatto, she considered field labor a degradation; her white bastardy appearing to her a title to consideration in my eyes. The degradation of these people is very complete, for they have accepted the contempt of their masters to that degree that they profess, and really seem to feel it for themselves, and the faintest admixture of white blood in their black veins appears at once, by common consent of their own race, to raise them in the scale of humanity. I had not much sympathy for this petition.[33]

While the distinctions among the members of the race on the basis of color were everywhere made, the "color line" was most carefully and rigidly drawn where there existed

In New Orleans 7,357 of the 9,084 free Negroes were mixed-bloods. Elsewhere the proportion was usually not so high but was everywhere marked. See notes 46, 47, p. 116 above.

[33] Kemble, *Residence on a Georgian Plantation*, p. 194.

the largest body of free Negroes. Evans says:[34]

> I was told by an intelligent light-coloured woman whom I met in Alabama, who was married to a well-to-do mulatto there, and who came from Charleston, South Carolina, that in her early days in that city she had no black associates, and that between the light-coloured and black there was a gulf fixed similar to that separating the former from the whites. Later in life when she moved into Alabama she found there no such class distinctions between black and coloured. Her ancestors on both sides had been freed men for two generations, the family owned property, and had a recognized position in Charleston.

Fannie Jackson, a mulatto who is said to have been the first Negro woman to graduate from a reputable college, testifies to this spirit of superiority on the part of the mulattoes.[35]

> So I went out to service. Oh, the hue and cry there was, when I went out to live! Even my aunt spoke of it; she had a home to offer me; but the "slavish" element was so strong in me that *I make myself a servant.* Ah, how those things cut me then! But I knew I was right, and I kept straight on.

Frederick Douglass testifies to the same fact [36] as does Mr. DuBois,[37] Edward Blyden [38] and, naïvely or otherwise,

---

[34] Maurice S. Evans, *Black and White in the Southern States,* p. 93. See, also, Ray Stannard Baker, "The Tragedy of the Mulatto," The *American Magazine,* Vol. 65, p. 588.

[35] J. W. Cromwell, *The Negro in American History,* p. 213.

[36] *Life and Times,* p. 458.

[37] ". . . The thing that makes the mulatto especially useful is that, with the white man, he shares the pride of his white blood and is less likely than the black to submit to artificial distinctions of race where nature has bridged them. . ." *Crisis,* Editorial, 9-1913.

[38] E. W. Blyden, *Christianity, Islam and the Negro Race,* p. 18.

most of the other Negroes who have become articulate.[39] The white man always has considered the mulatto superior to the black Negro; and the mulatto, taking over the white man's way of thinking, considered himself superior and attributed the superiority to the fact of his mixed blood. He formed exclusive organizations and claimed superiority on the basis of color.

The Negroes in general accepted the assumption of superiority on the part of the mulattoes and, like the mulatto and the white man, attributed the observed superiority to the admixture of white blood.[40] Speaking of the boat songs of a certain river plantation group, Miss Kemble says:[41]

> One of their songs displeased me not a little, for it embodied the opinion that "twenty-six black girls not make mulatto yellow girl"; and I told them I did not like it they have omitted it since. This desperate tendency to despise and undervalue their own race and color, which is one of the very worst results of their abject condition, is intolerable to me.

The ideal of the Negro was thus the light-colored man. He envied him his color [42] and his superiority. Often he

[39] Thomas, *The American Negro*, pp. 186, 408, 407.

T. T. Fortune, "Place in American Life," in Washington, *The Negro Problem*, pp. 227, 226.

The *Boston Reliance*, 3-13-1915.

The *Kansas City Herald*, 2-13-1915.

The *Kentucky (Louisville) Reporter*, 1-23-1915.

The *Washington Sun*, 4-9-1915.

[40] Patience Pennington, *A Woman Rice Planter*, p. 235.

[41] *Residence on a Georgian Plantation*, p. 219. See, also, Pennington, *A Woman Rice Planter*, p. 387; and Blyden as quoted in the *Crisis*, 9-1913, pp. 229-30.

[42] Thomas, *The American Negro*, p. 67.

Blyden, *Christianity, Islam and the Negro Race*, pp. 24-25, 89.

Baker, *American Magazine*, Vol. 65, p. 589.

The Growth of the Mulatto Class

hated him for his ambition to escape from the race and align himself with the whites.[43]

Once started, the mulatto class tended to perpetuate itself. However much the Negro hated the exclusive mulatto, every black man was anxious to gain admission to the mulatto class. Admission, in the absence of mixed-blood, was most readily obtained by marriage into the group. Consequently, it was the almost universal desire of the Negro to marry light-colored women [44] and, to the extent of their importance, they were successful in doing so.[45] A roll of the Negroes who have married white women or light-colored mulattoes would include the great majority of the men who have gained any distinction either within or without the race.

Thus by association, education, and tradition, the mulattoes came to be superior men. They had white blood and because of their white blood they had superior advantages. The white man considered them superior and, as a consequence of this, they considered themselves superior.[46] This gave them a confidence in themselves that the black Negroes did not have. They felt more important. Among the Negro group they enjoyed a prestige because of their

[43] "The same feeling [caste feeling of white superiority] is frequently met with among sober-minded blacks, who, much to one's surprise sometimes, are found to resent the ambitious attempts of their fellows, generally mulattoes, to rise above their own race and align themselves with the whites." B. W. Smith, *The Color Line*, pp. 173-74. See, also, Monroe Work, "The Passing Tradition and the African Civilization," *The Journal of Negro History*, Vol. 1, Number 1, p. 35.

[44] Baker, *The American Magazine*, Vol. 65, p. 589.

[45] Bruce, *The Plantation Negro as a Freeman*, pp. 143-44.

[46] "In discussions of the race problem there is one factor of supreme importance which has been so far disregarded . . . to wit, the opinion or *idea* which a race has of itself and the influence exerted by this idea." A. Fouillée, "Race from the Sociological Standpoint," *Inter-Racial Problems*, pp. 24 ff.

mixed blood, and this reacted to further inflate the mulattoes' idea of themselves.[47] So, entirely aside from any question of racial superiority, the mulatto is and always has been the superior man.[48]

[47] See Raymond Patterson, *The Negro and His Needs*, p. 40.
[48] See, E. B. Reuter, "The Superiority of the Mulatto," *American Journal of Sociology*, Vol. 23, pp. 83-106.

CHAPTER VIII

THE LEADING MEN OF THE NEGRO RACE

IT has been pointed out frequently both by the friends and the critics of the race, that the Negro in America has not as yet produced an individual entitled to rank among the world's geniuses. Kelly Miller [1] has said that, judged by European standards, the race has produced no man of even secondary rank. Mr. DuBois would seem to agree that this is a fair statement of fact.[2] Indeed, it seems to be claimed nowhere by serious students that the race has produced any man whose achievements have not been surpassed by scores of men of a different racial extraction.

Whatever may be the amount of truth in this generally accepted belief—and there is no intention here to prove or disprove it, nor to affirm nor deny it—it is certainly true that the race has differentiated during its life in America. The difference separating the extremes within the race has become very great. Some individuals have, perhaps, not greatly advanced beyond the standards of life of their African ancestors; others have in all essential respects measured up to the best standards of modern civilized life. It is with these latter individuals, quite regardless of the degree of their absolute native ability, with whom we are here concerned. It is not a question of genius or even of emi-

[1] *Race Adjustment*, p. 188.
[2] W. E. B. DuBois, "The Advance Guard of the Race," The *Booklover's Magazine*, Vol. 2, p. 3.

nence; it is a question of relative superiority and of leadership. It is relative and not absolute superiority that determines the value of the individual in a social situation.

Quite aside, then, from all question of genius, the Negro race in America has produced a number of individuals who in spite of, or because of, their black blood have reached a level of achievement well above the average of either race. Judged by any fair standard there have been and are to-day Negroes who deserve to be ranked as exceptional men in that their accomplishments are well above the level of the accomplishments of other individuals of their group.[3] It is true that the number is not great. Compared with the great number of the race it must even be admitted that the number is pitifully small. But that there are successful men, men of ability and of talent, among the race is not to be denied. They are to be found in greater or lesser numbers in all the various lines of human endeavor: in industrial and commercial pursuits; in the learned professions; in literature, art, and music; wherever, in short, are to be found the men of other races.

When the existence of such prominent men is pointed out it is frequently asserted that they are not Negroes but mulattoes. "Although," says Ingalls,[4] "more than two hundred thousand enlisted in the Union armies, no full-blood negro holds a commission in the army or navy and in the militia their organization is distinct." "We . . . find," says Stone,[5] "that where the Negro participates to any extent in the administration of affairs . . . the race is almost invariably represented solely by its mulatto type." "Apparently, the mulatto as a whole is superior to the pure African

---

[3] DuBois, *Booklover's Magazine*, Vol. 2, p. 4.
[4] John J. Ingalls, "Always a Problem," *Chicago Tribune*, 5-28-1898.
[5] A. F. Stone, *Studies in the American Race Problem*, p. 27.

Negro," says Chancellor David Starr Jordan.[6] "Ninety per cent of all the leaders of the race are the offspring of the Caucasian," says Holm.[7] Belin says that "The so-called 'negroes,' who have in any way distinguished themselves above their fellows, are not full-blood negroes, but half-breeds."[8] "The recognized leaders of the race are almost invariably persons of mixed blood, and the qualities which have made them leaders are derived certainly in part and perhaps mainly from their white ancestry."[9]

Shufeldt[10] quotes Keane as saying that "No full-blood Negro ever has been distinguished as a man of science, a poet, or an artist, and the fundamental equality claimed for him by ignorant philanthropists is belied by the whole history of the race throughout the historic period." To the same point Dr. Carl Vogt[11] says that:

> As a proof in favor of the artistic and scientific capacity of the Negro, we find cited in nearly all the works the instance of Mr. Lille Geoffray of Martinique, an engineer and mathematician and corresponding member of the French Academy. The fact is that the mathematical performances of the above gentleman were of such a nature that, had he been born in Germany of white parents, he might, perhaps, have qualified as a mathematical teacher in a middle-class school, or engineer at a railway; but having been born in Mar-

[6] "Biological Effects of Race Movements," *Popular Science Monthly*, Vol. 87, pp. 267-70.

[7] J. J. Holm, *Race Assimilation or the Fading of the Leopard's Spots*, p. 279.

[8] H. E. Belin, "A Southern View of Slavery," *American Journal of Sociology*, Vol. 13, p. 518.

[9] *Encyclopædia Britannica*: Negro.

[10] R. W. Shufeldt, *The Negro: A Menace to American Civilization*, p. 43.

[11] *Lectures on Man*, pp. 192-93.

tinique of colored parents, he shone like a one-eyed man among the totally blind. M. Lille Geoffray, besides, was not a pure Negro, but a mulatto.

By other writers, all this is flatly contradicted. The equality of races is stoutly asserted and the superiority of the mulatto to the full-blooded Negro as stoutly denied. Mr. Washington on a number of occasions stated his belief in the equality of the Negro to the mulatto. The A. M. E. Church *Review* [12] says editorially that ". . . we colored people can never subscribe to the doctrine of the superiority of the mulatto over the black element in brain power." But of all those who have expressed their opinion, Mr. DuBois seems to be the most emphatic and the most extreme in his assertions on this subject. "If we study cases of ability and goodness and talent among the American Negroes, we shall," he says, "have difficulty in laying down any clear thesis as to effect of amalgamation. As a matter of historic fact the colored people of America have produced as many remarkable black men as mulattoes." [13]

The purpose here is not to evaluate the work done by these remarkable men. It is not intended to determine what place they do or should occupy as compared with successful white men in similar lines of endeavor. It is not even intended to show in how far they have risen above the average of their fellows. The purpose is merely to determine, on the basis of the most complete and representative lists of exceptional Negroes that have been compiled, in how far they are black men and in how far they are men of mixed blood. It is the assumption and the assertion that there are as many black men as mulattoes among the exceptional men of the race that we propose to submit to the test of

[12] October 1915, p. 133.
[13] DuBois, *Booklover's Magazine*, Vol. 2, p. 15.

cases that Mr. DuBois suggests.[14]

In all other countries where a mulatto group exists alongside of a group of unmixed blood, there seems to be a preponderance of mulattoes among the gifted individuals of the race. In Jamaica the educated and professional classes of the race are mulattoes.[15] In Haiti the ten per cent of mixed-bloods have constituted the ruling and professional classes since the massacre of the French.[16] In South Africa the mulattoes are "the intellectual aristocracy of the dark-skinned population." [17] In Brazil it is the mixed-bloods who have attained to a degree of civilization, while the purer-blooded natives and Negroes seem to have cast off, partially at least, the degree of civilization acquired under the regime of slavery.[18] Elsewhere, the same thing seems to be true.[19] The mixed-bloods in every racial situa-

[14] There is, of course, no intention of "proving" by such a method any "thesis as to the effect of amalgamation." The effect of amalgamation is a biological problem with which we are not here concerned. Moreover it is not susceptible of demonstration by the means that Mr. DuBois suggests. It is the final assertion, that among the exceptional men of the Negro race there are as many black as mulatto men, that we propose to examine.

[15] William Thorp, "How Jamaica Solves the Negro Problem," *World's Work,* Vol. 8, pp. 4908-13.

W. P. Livingstone, "The West Indian and American Negro," *North American Review,* Vol. 185, p. 647.

Stone, *Studies in the American Race Problem,* p. 27.

[16] H. V. H. Prichard, *Where Black Rules White,* pp. 80 ff.

Earl Finch, "The Effects of Racial Miscegenation," *Inter-Racial Problems,* p. 110.

[17] H. E. S. Freemantle, *The New Nation,* pp. 217-18. See, also, M. S. Evans, *Black and White in South East Africa,* pp. 289-90. Élisée Reclus, *Africa,* Vol. 4, p. 149.

[18] Jean Baptiste de Lacerda, "The *Metis* or Half-Breeds of Brazil," *Inter-Racial Problems,* pp. 380-82.

[19] Charles E. Woodruff, "Some Laws of Racial and Intellectual Development," *Journal of Race Development,* Vol. 3, p. 175.

Friedrich Ratzel, *The History of Mankind,* Vol. 1, p. 397.

tion seem to have risen, as a group, above the status of their darker kin, while the individuals of talent who have appeared—the individuals who have made some conspicuous success in life—are, with rare exception, men of mixed blood.

Historically the same thing seems to hold true. Of the names of Negroes coming down to us from the past, there is a preponderating majority of men of mixed blood and a scarcity, almost an entire absence, of men of unmixed Negro ancestry. Alexandre Dumas, by all odds the most gifted individual whom history shows to have possessed Negro blood, was probably a quadroon.[20] Alexander Pushkin, the Russian poet, had a trace of Negro blood.[21] It is sometimes said that Robert Browning had a trace of Negro blood, but there seems to be absolutely no basis for this tradition.[22] About the close of the eighteenth century, Abbé Grégoire published a volume [23] to prove the equality of the Negro intellect. This volume contained the biographies of fifteen Negroes [24] each one of whom, according to

[20] One grandmother was a Negress of San Domingo but whether of full-blood is not known. See *Encyclopædia Britannica.* Burr, *The Autobiography,* p. 155, speaking of Dumas' Memoirs, says: "His own figure is painted therein in crude, staring colors, as bright as life . . . a figure out of Balzac and the *Comedie Humaine.* Part Napoleonic soldier, part San Dominican negro, . . . ye gods of the drama, what an heredity! . . . he seems to us a savage tale-teller, seated at the campfire, holding his companions breathless. Alternately lazy and energetic, sensual and shrewd, he has all the undiluted primitive forces of huge vitality and huge laughter."

[21] One-sixteenth or less Negro blood. His maternal great-grandfather was a Negro but whether of full-blood is not certain.

[22] ". . . There is no ground for the statement that the family was partly of Jewish Origin." *Encyclopædia Britannica.*

[23] H. Grégoire, *An Enquiry Concerning the Intellectual and Moral Faculties, and Literature of Negroes; followed with an account of the Life and Works of Fifteen Negroes and Mulattoes, distinguished in Science, Literature and Arts.* Translated by D. B. Warden, 1810.

[24] Higiemonde or Higiemondo: an Indian painter "commonly named

Van Evrie, was a man of mixed blood.[25] François Dominique Toussaint, the guerilla chief of the Negro insurrectionists in Haiti, seems not to have been a full-blooded Negro.[26] Mr. Lille Geoffray of Martinique, engineer, mathematician and corresponding member of the French acad-

the negro," p. 171. Grégoire seems not certain that there was such a man or if there was that he was a Negro.

Annibal: an officer in the Russian artillery at the time of Peter the Great.

The Son of Annibal: a mulatto.

Anthony William Amo: born in Guinea, educated in England.

L'Islet Geoffray: a mulatto.

James Durham: mulatto slave, practiced medicine in New Orleans.

Thomas Fuller: mathematical prodigy. Apparently a Negro.

Othello: published "An Essay Against the Slavery of Negroes." "Othello" was a pseudonym. The race of the writer is not known. There seems to be no reason for calling him a Negro.

Benjamin Banneker: a mulatto.

Ottobah Cugoano: published his reflections of the slave trade and the slavery of Negroes.

James Eliza John Capitein: educated in Holland. Wrote some Latin verses.

William Francis: Jamaican Negro of the eighteenth century. Educated in England. Taught Latin and mathematics in Jamaica.

Olandad, or Gustavus Vassa: brought to England as a child; wrote memoirs.

Ignatius Sancho: an English butler. An edition of his letters was printed after his death.

Phyllis Wheatley Peters: apparently black.

[25] *White Supremacy and Negro Subordination*, p. 163. Van Evrie would seem to be in error here. Tradition has it that both Thomas Fuller and Mrs. Peters were full-blood Negroes. See p. 190 below.

[26] ". . . Judging from his pictures, you cannot but form the opinion that Toussaint was not a pure-blooded negro: the features, the shape of the head, the setting of the eyes are all so many strong reasons against such a supposition." Prichard, *Where Black Rules White*, p. 278. For a contrary opinion see the *Negro Year Book*, 1914-15, p. 75. C. V. Roman, *American Civilization and the Negro*, opposite p. 8, gives a picture of Toussaint and calls him a "full-blood." Either the picture or the caption is in error: the picture is not that of a full-blood Negro.

emy, was a mulatto.[27]

In America, even at an early date, a number of members of the race had risen to some prominence. The most noted of these was, perhaps, Phyllis Wheatley Peters. Born in Africa, about 1750, she was presumably a full-blooded Negro though there is absolutely nothing known concerning her ancestry. She was sold into slavery and in 1761 she was brought to America where she served in the household of Mrs. John Wheatley of Boston and from whom she received some slight instruction in English and Latin. She went to London with the son of her mistress. While there she published a small volume of poems upon which rests her claim to fame. She certainly was not a poet,[28] but her efforts were an evidence of the race's capacity for intellectual improvement.

Thomas Fuller,[29] a mathematical prodigy of the same period, seems also to have been a black man. He enjoyed considerable local fame because of his power to perform complicated mathematical calculations. He was unable to read or write and, as is usual with prodigies of this sort, seems to have been a mental defective.

Benjamin Banneker seems to have a decidedly better claim to prominence than either of the preceding. He is said to have constructed the first clock made in America; later he published an almanac.[30] Banneker was a free mulatto[31] of Maryland. He was a neighbor and friend of

[27] Vogt, *Lectures on Man*, pp. 192-93.
[28] B. G. Brawley, *The Negro in Literature and Art*, p. 13.
C. G. Woodson, *History of Negro Education*, p. 90.
[29] G. B. Williams, *History of the Negro Race in America*, Vol. 1, p. 399.
Woodson, *History of Negro Education*, pp. 87-88.
[30] Woodson, *History of Negro Education*, pp. 90-91, 62-63.
[31] Williams, *History of the Negro Race in America*, Vol. 1, pp. 385, 390. See p. 131 above.

Ellicott who acted for him in the capacity of a press agent. He seems to have received assistance from Ellicott, but the extent of his indebtedness is uncertain.

James Durham [32] of Philadelphia and later of New Orleans was born a slave in 1767. From his master, who was a physician, he learned to read and write and to compound simple medicines. When freed by his master, he built up a successful medical practice among the mulatto creoles in New Orleans. Durham was a mulatto.

Most of the prominent Negroes of the time were preachers. George Leile,[33] who preached in Georgia and later founded the first Negro Baptist colony in Jamaica, was a mulatto.

Andrew Bryan, the founder of the African Baptist church, was a man of mixed blood, as was John Chavis,[34] an itinerant preacher of the Methodist church. John Gloucester of Tennessee, founder of the African Presbyterian church in Philadelphia, was probably a black man. Henry Evans, an itinerant preacher of the Presbyterian church, seems also to have been a Negro of pure blood.[35] Lemuel Haynes, the first Negro Congregational minister, was a mulatto, as was Richard Allen, the founder of the Negro Methodist Church.

In the decade preceding the Civil War, owing to the fact that the emotional attitude of the people of the North magnified out of all focus the doings of any black man, it is

---

[32] *Negro Year Book* 1914-1915, p. 334.
J. A. Kenney, *The Negro in Medicine*, p. 6.
Woodson, *History of Negro Education*, pp. 88-89.
[33] Also known as George Sharp.
[34] J. S. Bassett, *Slavery and Servitude in the Colony of North Carolina*, p. 73, says Chavis was a full-blood Negro. This seems to be an error. See, also, the same writer's article in the *American Journal of Sociology*, Vol. 13, p. 826.
[35] Bassett, *Slavery and Servitude in the State of North Carolina*, p. 57.

somewhat surprising that there did not appear a group of prominent men of the race. The only one, however, who succeeded in rising above mediocrity was Frederick Douglass, an anti-slavery agitator and journalist. His father was a white man [36] and his mother a slave of unknown color, but with sufficient Indian intermixture to show prominently in the features as well as in the disposition of her noted son.[37]

During the entire period that slavery existed as a national institution, individuals frequently escaped from the border states into free territory. Especially during the latter years of the slave regime, there were a considerable number of these runaway slaves. An organized and elaborate system of criminal procedure grew up toward the end of the slave period and became known as the Underground Railroad. As was to be expected, the free Negroes and escaped slaves took some part in this outlawry. The Year Book [38] names the most notorious of these Negroes and gives sketches of their careers.[39] Of the fifteen, Harriet Tubman

[36] *New International Encyclopædia:* Frederick Douglass.
[37] Booker T. Washington, *The Story of the Negro,* Vol. 1, p. 132.
[38] *Negro Year Book,* 1914-1915, pp. 102-06.
[39]

William Wells Brown	mulatto
Frederick Douglass	mulatto
James Forten	mulatto
Mifflin Wistar Gibbs	mulatto
Mrs. F. E. W. Harper	mulatto
Lewis Hayden	mulatto
Lunsford Lane	mulatto
Robert Purvis	mulatto
Charles Lenox Remond	mulatto
J. B. Russwurm	mulatto
William Still	mulatto
Sojourner Truth	mulatto
Harriet Tubman	black
David Walker	mulatto
William Whipper	mulatto

seems to have been a black woman; the other fourteen were mulattoes.[40]

Since the Civil War, all lines of endeavor in America have been open to the Negro. In some cases he has met with prejudice and discrimination; in other cases his color has given him a prestige not enjoyed by his white competitor.[41] At the present time, there is no insuperable, external obstacle to the Negro's entrance to, and success in, any of the ordinary lines of human endeavor, as is evidenced by the fact that Negroes have entered all of them and that individuals of the race have achieved some degree of success in each of the different lines.

There have been compiled and published, from time to time, lists of these Negroes who have risen to prominence. It may be that these lists do not contain the names of all the successful Negroes. It may also be true that many of the names which appear are those of men who have shown no great talent or achieved no great renown. But it may be fairly assumed that they are, in most cases at least, men of some importance and prominence in their community and that they are leaders in a larger or smaller way within their racial group. If this be so, a determination of the ancestry of these men should be a fair index as to the percentage of mulattoes and full-blooded Negroes among the leaders and other prominent men of the race.

Mr. DuBois has compiled such a list,[42] illustrated by full page photographs of ten living [43] Negroes who represent

---

[40] J. S. Bassett, *Anti-Slavery Leaders of North Carolina*, p. 321, says Lane's parents were "of pure African descent." This is emphatically denied by Negroes who knew him personally.

[41] B. W. Smith, *The Color Line: A Brief in Behalf of the Unborn*, pp. 43-44.

[42] DuBois, *Booklover's Magazine*, Vol. 2, pp. 2-14.

[43] July, 1903.

the "Advance Guard of the Race." [44] To the list, the editors add a similar sketch and a similar photograph of Mr. DuBois. These men "measured by any fair standard of human accomplishment . . . are distinctly men of mark." [45] Regarding the racial ancestry of these men Mr. DuBois says: [46]

> . . . Of the men I have named, three are black, two are brown, two are half-white, and three are three-fourths white. . . . If we choose among these men the two of keenest intellect, one is black and the other brown; if we choose the three of strongest character, two are yellow and one is black. If we choose three according to their esthetic sensibility, one is black, one is yellow, and one three-fourths white.

Seven of the ten are admittedly mulatto, so may be passed without comment. Three are said to be "black." But by this term, it cannot be meant to assert that they are full-blood Negroes. The only three men in the list who could possibly be called "black" are Dunbar, the poet; Miller, the mathematician; and Woods, the electrician. Of these men Dunbar, according to all accounts, was a real Negro. Kelly Miller is a brown mulatto.[47] Granville T.

"Charles W. Chestnutt	Novelist	mulatto
Paul Laurence Dunbar	Poet	black
Francis J. Grimké	Clergyman	mulatto
Kelly Miller	Mathematician	black
Edward H. Morris	Lawyer	mulatto
Henry O. Tanner	Artist	mulatto
W. L. Taylor	Business man	mulatto
Booker T. Washington	Politician	mulatto
Daniel H. Williams	Surgeon	mulatto
Granville T. Woods	Electrician	Australian-Malay

[45] *Booklover's Magazine*, Vol. 2, p. 2.
[46] *Ibid.*, p. 15.
[47] W. I. Thomas, "Race Psychology," *American Journal of Sociology*, Vol. 17, p. 746, speaks of Miller as a "full-blooded black." The *At-*

Woods seems to have no drop of African blood. He is an Australian by birth [48] and by ancestry a mixture of Malay Indian and Australian Black.[49] Of these ten names, then, one is that of a Negro, one that of an Australian of mixed ancestry, and the remaining eight are mulattoes. If Mr. DuBois be included in the list, the count then stands one Negro to ten men of mixed blood.

In 1903, the Pott Publishing Company issued a small volume of essays by Negroes discussing different phases of the Negro problem in America.[50] Seven writers contributed to the volume.[51] Of these men, one was a black Negro and six were mulattoes. Of the six, two were men of about equal parts of white and black; while the other four were from three-fourths to fifteen-sixteenths white.

In one of the essays in the volume, Mr. DuBois again treats the subject of the Negro leaders under the caption

lantic Advocate calls him a "full-blooded colored man." He seems to consider himself a Negro and is generally so claimed by the race. As we are concerned here with social and not with biological facts we have placed Professor Miller in the full-blood group in spite of his mixed ancestry. See note 44, p. 194 above.

[48] Miller, *Race Adjustment*, p. 197, says that Woods was born in Ohio.

[49] "His mother's father was a Malay Indian, and his other grandparents were by birth full-blooded savage Australian aborigines born in the wilds back of Melbourne. . . . At the age of 16, Woods was brought by his parents to America. . . ." S. W. Balch, "Electrical Motor Regulation," *Cosmopolitan*, Vol. 18, p. 762.

[50] *The Negro Problem: A Series of Articles by Representative American Negroes of To-day.*

[51]

C. W. Chestnutt	mulatto
W. E. B. DuBois	mulatto
Paul L. Dunbar	black
T. Thomas Fortune	mulatto
H. T. Kealing	mulatto
Wilford H. Smith	mulatto
Booker T. Washington	mulatto

"The Talented Tenth" and finds twenty-one men and two women worthy of this title. Supplying the initials, supplementing the list with an indication of the ground on which their claim to greatness rests and an indication of their ancestry, we have:

Ira Aldridge	Negro actor	mulatto
Benjamin Banneker	Invented clock; published almanac	mulatto
B. K. Bruce	Reconstruction politician	mulatto
Alexander Crummell	Preacher	black
Paul Cuffe	In charge of the first load of Negroes sent to Liberia	mulatto and Indian
Frederick Douglass	Runaway slave; anti-slavery agitator; politician	mulatto and Indian
James Durham	Practiced medicine	mulatto
R. B. Elliott	Reconstruction politician	mulatto
H. H. Garnett	Preacher	mulatto[52]
R. T. Greener	Reconstruction politician	mulatto
Lemuel Haynes	Early Negro preacher	mulatto
John M. Langston	Reconstruction politician	mulatto
D. A. Payne	Bishop of the African Methodist Church	mulatto
J. W. C. Pennington	Underground Railroad operator	mulatto
Phyllis Wheatley Peters	Slave of John Wheatley; writer of verse	black
Robert Purvis	Agitator; Underground Railroad operator	mulatto
Charles L. Remond	Agitator; Underground Railroad operator	mulatto
J. B. Russwurm	A governor of Liberia	mulatto
McCune Smith	Physician and druggist	mulatto
Sojourner Truth	Underground Railroad agent	mulatto
David Walker	Agitator	mulatto
B. T. Washington	Principal Tuskegee Institute	mulatto
Bert Williams	Comedian	mulatto

Of the women named one was a mulatto and one was a black Negro. Of the twenty-one men, all were mulattoes.

[52] Sometimes mistakenly classed as a full-blood Negro.

The Leading Men of the Negro Race 197

Two of these men, Garnett and Crummell, are sometimes classed as full-blooded Negroes; but this seems to be contrary to the facts. Both men were the offspring of a mixed ancestry. The father of Crummell is said to have been an African chief. He married a free Negro woman of mixed blood. The son, however, is very dark in color and passes as a Negro of full-blood. He is accordingly listed with the full-bloods here.

The Negro Star Publishing Company [53] advertises for sale the pictures of "all the great men of the race." [54] Their complete list comprises the pictures of twelve persons. The single woman whose picture is included in the collection was a mulatto. Of the eleven photographs remaining, one is that of a black man—Dunbar,—one is that of a man—Toussaint—concerning whose racial ancestry there may be a reasonable doubt,[55] and nine are photographs of men who are obviously and admittedly mulattoes.[56]

Kelly Miller in a chapter on "Eminent Negroes" [57] names sixteen individuals. Presumably these persons are, in the

---

[53] Greenwood, Mississippi.
[54] See any issue of the *Negro Star,* for e.g., 1-14-1916. Letter from the General Manager under date of 1-25-1916.
[55] See p. 189 above.
[56]

Crispus Attucks	mulatto
W. E. B. DuBois	mulatto
Frederick Douglass	mulatto
Alexandre Dumas	mulatto
Paul Laurence Dunbar	black
Richard T. Greener	mulatto
John Mercer Langston	mulatto
S. Coleridge Taylor	mulatto
Henry O. Tanner	mulatto
François Dominique Toussaint	mulatto
Sojourner Truth	mulatto
Booker T. Washington	mulatto

[57] *Race Adjustment,* pp. 186-98.

198   *The Mulatto in the United States*

opinion of Mr. Miller, the best that the race in America has produced. "The names here presented," he says [58] "are at least respectable when measured by European standards. It is true that no one of them reaches the first, or even the second degree of luster in the galaxy of the world's greatness." But they are all individuals in whose accomplishments the race may well take pride. Of the names presented, one is that of a black woman, one that of a black man, and the remaining fourteen are names of men of mixed blood. The complete list follows:

Ira Aldridge	Actor	mulatto
Benjamin Banneker	Inventor	mulatto
Charles W. Chestnutt	Novelist	mulatto
Frederick Douglass	Politician	mulatto
W. E. B. DuBois	Writer	mulatto
Paul Laurence Dunbar	Poet	black
Lemuel Haynes	Minister	mulatto
Elijah T. McCoy	Inventor	mulatto
Phyllis Wheatley Peters	Poet	black
W. S. Scarborough	Teacher	mulatto
B. T. Tanner	Bishop	mulatto
Henry O. Tanner	Artist	mulatto
B. T. Washington	Educator	mulatto
Daniel H. Williams	Physician	mulatto
George H. Williams	Writer	mulatto
Granville T. Woods	Inventor	mulatto [59]

Cromwell [60] presents a slightly variant list. His intention, as stated in the preface to his volume, is the publication of a book which will give "the salient points in the history of the American Negro, the story of their most eminent men and women . . ." The twenty persons selected include

---

[58] *Race Adjustment,* p. 188.
[59] See note 49, p. 195 above.
[60] J. W. Cromwell, *The Negro in American History.*

The Leading Men of the Negro Race 199

three women and seventeen men. One of the women and three of the men were black. The sixteen remaining are names of mixed-blood individuals. His selection of the "most eminent men and women" of the race is as follows:

Benjamin Banneker	mulatto
Edward W. Blyden	mulatto [61]
Blanche Kelso Bruce	mulatto
George F. T. Cook	mulatto
John F. Cook, Jr.	mulatto
John F. Cook, Sr.	mulatto
Fanny M. Jackson Coppin	mulatto
Alexander Crummell	black [62]
Paul Cuffe	mulatto
Frederick Douglass	mulatto
Paul Laurence Dunbar	black
Robert Brown Elliott	mulatto
Henry Highland Garnett	mulatto [63]
John Mercer Langston	mulatto
Daniel Alexander Payne	mulatto
Phyllis Wheatley Peters	black
Joseph Charles Price	black [64]
Henry Osawa Tanner	mulatto
Sojourner Truth	mulatto
Booker T. Washington	mulatto

The California Eagle[65] advertises for sale the pictures of "the most Famous Men of the Colored Race, living and dead." Their picture features eight men, one of whom,—Dunbar—was black. The remaining seven are names of men

[61] Cromwell calls Blyden a full-blood Negro but this seems not to have been the case. He was a dark man of mixed ancestry.
[62] See p. 197 above.
[63] See note 52, p. 196 above.
[64] Cromwell calls Price a full-blood Negro. He was probably not a man of unmixed Negro blood. He passed, however, as a full-blood Negro and the race took great pride in claiming him as such. A good photograph appears on p. 212 of Cromwell's book.
[65] A Negro newspaper of Los Angeles, California.

of mixed blood.[66]

The Colored American Review[67] offers a similar list which is, in the opinion of the editors, "the largest and finest collection of 'Famous Negroes,' both past and present, in America and abroad."[68] Thirty-two names appear in the printed list. Of these, five are names of women, and twenty-seven are names of men. Of the five women, one is a pure-blooded Negress, and the remaining four are mulattoes. Of the twenty-seven names of men, three are of full-blooded Negroes and twenty-four are of mulattoes. The complete list and descriptions to which is here added an indication as to the purity of blood, is as follows:

Hon. Harry Boss	Lawyer and Legislator	mulatto
William Stanley Braithwaite	Poet and Critic	mulatto
Rev. W. W. Brown	Eminent Baptist Divine	mulatto
Harry T. Burleigh	Singer and Composer	mulatto
Anita Bush	Actress	mulatto
Bob Cole	Actor and Comedian	mulatto
Hon. James Curtis	Lawyer, Minister to Liberia	mulatto
Frederick Douglass	Statesman	mulatto
Howard P. Drew	Athlete, Runner	mulatto
W. E. B. DuBois	Educator and Author	mulatto
Alexandre Dumas	Author	mulatto
Paul Laurence Dunbar	Poet	black
James Reese Europe	Musician and Composer	mulatto
Mathews Henson	Explorer	mulatto
Ernest Hogan	Comedian	mulatto
J. Rosamond Johnson	Composer	mulatto
" Crispus Attucks		mulatto
Frederick Douglass		mulatto
W. E. B. DuBois		mulatto
Alexandre Dumas		mulatto
Paul Laurence Dunbar		black
H. O. Tanner		mulatto
Coleridge Taylor		mulatto
Booker T. Washington		mulatto

[67] A semi-monthly magazine, published in New York City.
[68] See, for e.g., the issue of March, 1916, p. 187.

The Leading Men of the Negro Race 201

James W. Johnson	Ex-U. S. Consul and Author	mulatto
Mme. Jones (Black Patti)	Singer	mulatto [69]
Hon. Wm. H. Lewis	Ex-U. S. Ass't. Dist. Atty.	mulatto
Sam Lucas	The Original Uncle Tom	mulatto
Kelly Miller	Philosopher and Author	black [70]
Robert Russa Moton	Educator	black
Phyllis Wheatley Peters	Famous Poet	black
Rev. Clayton Powell	Eminent Baptist Divine	mulatto
Henry Tanner	Artist	mulatto
Coleridge Taylor	Musician and Composer	mulatto
Major Taylor	Champion Bicycle Rider	mulatto [71]
Aida Walker	Actress and Dancer	mulatto
Mme. C. J. Walker	Hair Culturist, Lecturer	mulatto
George Walker	Actor and Composer	mulatto
Booker T. Washington	Educator	mulatto
Bert Williams	Comedian	mulatto

All the present Bishops of the A. M. E. Z. Church [72]
All the present Bishops of the A. M. E. Church

The Reverend J. A. Duncan, Pastor of the Ebenezer African Methodist Episcopalian Church of Stockton, California, in an article in *The California Eagle*, a Negro newspaper, under the title "Our Famous Colored Women," names fourteen women. One name is that of a full-blooded Negress. The thirteen names remaining are of women of mixed ancestry. The compilation is as follows:

Mrs. Ida Wells-Barnet	mulatto
Madam Flora B. Bergen	mulatto
Miss Hallie Quinn Brown	mulatto
Henrietta Vinton Davis	mulatto
Frances E. Harper	mulatto
Sissieretta Jones	mulatto [73]
Edmonia Lewis	mulatto

[69] Classed by some correspondents as a full-blood Negress.
[70] See note 47, p. 194 above.
[71] One correspondent called Taylor black. The consensus of opinion, however, was that he was a brown mulatto.
[72] See pages 276 ff. for an analysis of these groups.
[73] See note 70, p. 201.

202   *The Mulatto in the United States*

Phyllis Wheatley Peters	black
Madam Selika	mulatto
Mrs. Amanda Smith	mulatto
Fannie Church Terrell	mulatto
Sojourner Truth	mulatto
Ada Overton Walker	mulatto
Mrs. Booker T. Washington	mulatto [74]

At the beginning of the year 1916, Mr. DuBois issued a *Who's Who in Colored America*.[75] This publication contained the names of 139 individuals who, in the opinion of the editor, were the real intellectual and social aristocracy of the American Negro. The *Who's Who* contained the names of one hundred and thirty-one men and eight women. The list recorded the names of four men whom the Negroes themselves claim as "black" and for social purposes may be so considered, though two, and possibly three, of the four have been modified by an earlier admixture of white blood. Concerning three of the men, no information was obtained. They seem not to be well-known to the members of their race.[76] The remaining one hundred and twenty-four men are mulattoes. The eight women are all mulattoes. Of the one hundred and thirty-two mulattoes two are dark,[77] while about one-half approximate the white race in features, head-form, and skin coloration. Taking the list as a whole, there is present somewhat over four times as much white as Negro blood. The complete list follows:[78]

[74] The third wife of Booker T. Washington.
[75] The *Crisis Calendar* for 1916.
[76] See note 82, p. 207 below.
[77] That is, they are less than one-half white. One is three-fourths black. The exact amount of Negro blood in the other is not known, but is approximately three-fourths.
[78] The poetic designations are the work of the compiler; the present writer adds the ethnic information. The initials, wrongly given in a few cases, have been corrected.
It has been asserted that the list contains the names of fifteen full-

The Leading Men of the Negro Race

WHO'S WHO IN COLORED AMERICA [19]

Charles W. Anderson	Worthy Public Official	mulatto
C. E. Bentley	Pioneer in Dental Reform	mulatto
H. C. Bishop	Religious Organizer	mulatto
J. W. E. Bowen	Lecturer and Teacher	mulatto
R. H. Boyd	Captain of Industry	mulatto
W. Stanley Braithwaite	Poet and Interpreter of Literature	mulatto
B. G. Brawley	Author	mulatto
Miss H. Q. Brown	Elocutionist	mulatto
Mrs. B. K. Bruce	Astute and Gracious Leader	mulatto
John E. Bruce	Popular Writer	mulatto
Roscoe C. Bruce	Educational Leader	mulatto
I. T. Bryant	Church Officer	mulatto
W. H. Bulkley	Efficient Educator	mulatto
Harry T. Burleigh	Maker of Songs	mulatto
Miss Nannie H. Burroughs	Organizer of Women	mulatto
William H. Bush	Organist	mulatto
J. S. Caldwell	Bishop of the Church	mulatto
James L. Carr	Able Advocate	mulatto
W. J. Carter	Able Advocate	....
C. W. Chestnutt	Man of Letters	mulatto
George W. Cook	Financier	mulatto
Will Marion Cook	Musician	mulatto
L. J. Coppin	Bishop of the Church	mulatto
W. H. Crogman	Teacher and Kindly Gentleman	mulatto
Harry S. Cummings	Political Leader and Lawyer	mulatto
A. M. Curtis	Surgeon and Physician	mulatto
James L. Curtis	Minister to Liberia	mulatto
J. C. Dancey	Public Official	mulatto
Franklin Dennison	Lawyer and Leader	mulatto
R. N. Dett	Composer	mulatto
J. H. Douglass	Violinist	mulatto
W. E. Burghardt DuBois	Editor and Author	mulatto
James Reese Europe	Composer and Organizer of musicians	mulatto

blooded Negroes. Such assertion can be maintained only by adopting a very different definition of the term *full-blooded* from that used as the basis for this study. See *Crisis*, 12-1917, p. 77.

[19] The *Crisis Calendar*, 1916.

WHO'S WHO IN COLORED AMERICA—*Continued*

S. D. Ferguson	Venerable Bishop	mulatto
J. S. Flipper	Bishop of the Church	mulatto
T. Thomas Fortune	Founder of Negro Journalism	mulatto and Indian
S. C. Fuller	Pioneer in Psychiatry	mulatto
Henry W. Furniss	Able Diplomatist	mulatto
W. H. Goler	Educational Leader	mulatto
J. M. Gregory	Veteran Educator	mulatto
R. T. Greener	Pioneer Public Servant	mulatto
Archibald H. Grimké	Publicist and Writer	mulatto
F. J. Grimké	Preacher of the Word of God	mulatto
G. C. Hall	Deft Surgeon	mulatto
W. H. H. Hart	Able Advocate and Defender	mulatto
J. R. Hawkins	Church Leader	mulatto
Mason A. Hawkins	Educational Leader	mulatto
W. Ashbie Hawkins	Capable Lawyer	mulatto
Roland W. Hayes	Sweet Singer	mulatto
L. M. Hershaw	Civil Servant	mulatto
L. H. Holsey	Church Leader	mulatto
J. W. Hood	Venerable Prelate	mulatto
John Hope	Teacher of Youth	mulatto
W. A. Hunton	Apostle to Young Men	mulatto
John E. Hurst	Church Leader	mulatto
E. W. D. Isaacs	Preacher and Publisher	mulatto
J. T. Jenifer	Venerable Preacher	mulatto
Harvey Johnson	Venerable Preacher	mulatto
H. L. Johnson	Public Official	mulatto
J. A. Johnson	Apostle to Africa	mulatto
James W. Johnson	Writer and Poet	mulatto
Rosamond Johnson	Composer and Orchestra Leader	mulatto
R. E. Jones	Able Editor	mulatto
L. G. Jordan	Missionary	mulatto
Ernest E. Just	Student of Living Things	mulatto
H. T. Kealing	Teacher and Educator	mulatto
Lucy Laney	Protector of Women and Girls	mulatto
R. Augustus Lawson	Teacher of Music	mulatto
B. F. Lee	Bishop of the Church	mulatto
James Lewis	Public Official	mulatto
W. H. Lewis	Lawyer and Public Official	mulatto

The Leading Men of the Negro Race

WHO'S WHO IN COLORED AMERICA—Continued

W. Logan	Financial Officer	mulatto
John R. Lynch	Pioneer in Political Service	mulatto and Indian
E. McCoy	Skilled Inventor	mulatto
John R. Marshall	Military Pioneer	mulatto
Cassius Mason	Preacher of Righteousness	....
James C. Matthews	Political Leader and Jurist	mulatto
K. Miller	Author and Critic	black
John Mitchell	Editor and Business Man	mulatto
W. E. Mollison	Banker and Business Man	mulatto
I. T. Montgomery	Founder of a Town	mulatto
G. W. Moore	Religious Leader	mulatto
Lewis B. Moore	Teacher of Teachers	mulatto
J. E. Mooreland	Builder of Men's Clubs	mulatto
E. C. Morris	Baptist Leader	mulatto
E. H. Morris	Chosen Leader	mulatto
W. R. Morris	Able Advocate	mulatto
N. F. Mossell	Hospital Founder	mulatto
Lucy Moton	Teacher of Courtesy	mulatto
Robert R. Moten	Organizer	black
Daniel Murray	Bookman	mulatto
J. C. Napier	Public Official	mulatto
Father Oncles	Priest of the Church	mulatto
H. B. Parks	Bishop of the Church	mulatto
I. Garland Penn	Church Official	mulatto
C. H. Phillips	Bishop of the Church	mulatto
Henry L. Phillips	Practical Apostle	mulatto
P. B. S. Pinchback	Pioneer of Reconstruction	mulatto
R. C. Ransom	Orator and Editor	mulatto
J. B. Reeve	Honored Preacher	mulatto
H. A. Rucker	Efficient Public Official	mulatto
Mrs. J. St. P. Ruffin	Pioneer Club Woman	mulatto
W. S. Scarborough	Scholar in Letters	mulatto
E. J. Scott	Able Secretary	mulatto
I. B. Scott	Bishop of the Church	mulatto
William E. Scott	Artist in Colors	mulatto
C. T. Shaffer	Servant of the Church	mulatto
R. Smalls	Hero and Public Servant	mulatto
B. S. Smith	Lawyer and Public Officer	mulatto
C. S. Smith	Bishop of the Church	mulatto
H. C. Smith	Veteran Editor	mulatto

WHO'S WHO IN COLORED AMERICA—Continued

T. G. Steward	Chaplain and Writer	mulatto
B. T. Tanner	Venerable Prelate	mulatto
H. O. Tanner	Artist in Colors	mulatto
Mrs. Mary Church Terrell	Lecturer and Leader of Women	mulatto
R. H. Terrell	Judicial Officer	mulatto
W. Monroe Trotter	Intrepid Agitator	mulatto
W. V. Tunnell	Preacher and Teacher	mulatto
C. H. Turner	Student of Living Things	mulatto
E. Tyree	Bishop of the Church	black
G. W. Vass	Religious Leader	mulatto
W. T. Vernon	Public Official	black
Maggie B. Walker	Able Business Woman	mulatto
A. Walters	Bishop and Leader	mulatto
Wm. A. Warfield	Surgeon and Administrator	mulatto
Marcus F. Wheatland	Noted Physician	mulatto
Clarence C. White	Musician	mulatto
Fred White	Organist	mulatto
G. H. White	Congressman and Banker	mulatto and Indian
Bert Williams	Apostle of Laughter	mulatto
D. H. Williams	Master of Surgery	mulatto
E. C. Williams	Teacher of Youth	mulatto
W. T. B. Williams	Social Student	mulatto
Carter G. Woodson	Student of History	mulatto
J. W. Woodson	Able Lawyer	....
Monroe N. Work	Social Statistician	mulatto
R. R. Wright	Noted Educator	mulatto
R. R. Wright, Jr.	Editor and Student	mulatto
Charles Young	Military Expert and Brave Soldier	mulatto

Such a list, as the compiler himself says,[80] is necessarily largely a matter of personal opinion. In order to eliminate in so far as possible this personal equation, letters were sent to each of the persons in the foregoing list whose address it was possible to secure, asking each to name the twenty-five living Negroes who, in the opinion of the per-

[80] Letter from Mr. DuBois under date of 2-10-1916.

son addressed, were the foremost men of the race. The men addressed proved about thirty per cent courteous. Thirty-six lists were received, including in all two hundred and fifty separate names.[81] One hundred and forty-four names appeared but a single time in the whole series of lists submitted [82] and, inasmuch as they thus represent the opinion of a single individual,[83] they are dropped from further consideration here.[84] One hundred and six names remained. Of these, eight are dark men of Negro features, though probably not in every case full-blooded Negroes. Ninety-eight are admittedly mulattoes. The list of names, the number of times the individual was mentioned in the letters received, the vocation and ethnic composition follows:

THE FOREMOST AMERICAN NEGROES
in the opinion of
PROMINENT MEN OF THE RACE

81	R. R. Moton	Principal Tuskegee Institute	black
30	W. E. B. DuBois	Editor and writer	mulatto
26	Kelly Miller	Teacher and writer	black
23	William Henry Lewis	Lawyer and politician	mulatto
23	Daniel H. Williams	Physician and surgeon	mulatto
21	Emmett J. Scott	Secretary Tuskegee Institute	mulatto

[81] A number of lists contained twenty-four names: a dead-lock, apparently, between accuracy and modesty. A few lists contained names in excess of twenty-five.

[82] This is not to be taken as evidence that each man included his own name in the list submitted and got no other mention. In only six of the thirty-six lists submitted did the compiler include himself and in each such case his name appeared in other lists.

[83] One man submitted the Bishops and General Officers of his church as including all the foremost American Negroes. Another included Sam Langford, the prize fighter, among the twenty-five greatest men of the race. A number of other peculiarities of personal preference appeared.

[84] Of these 144 names 7 were of black men, 95 of mulattoes and 42 were of individuals whose racial ancestry was not determined.

THE FOREMOST AMERICAN NEGROES—*Continued*

18	R. H. Terrell	Justice Municipal Court, D. C.	mulatto
17	J. C. Napier	Former Registrar U. S. Treas.	mulatto
17	Alexander Walters	Bishop A. M. E. Zion Church	mulatto
16	Richard H. Boyd	Preacher and banker	mulatto
15	Charles W. Anderson	Former United States Internal Revenue Collector	mulatto
15	William S. Braithwaite	Poet	mulatto
15	W. S. Scarborough	President Wilberforce Univ.	mulatto
13	John Mitchell, Jr.	Editor	mulatto
13	William Pickens	Dean, Morgan College	Negro and Indian and possibly white
13	Henry O. Tanner	Painter	mulatto
13	Charles E. Young	Lieut. 9th U. S. Cavalry	mulatto
12	Charles W. Chestnutt	Novelist	mulatto
12	R. R. Wright, Jr.	Editor and preacher	mulatto
11	J. W. E. Bowen	Teacher	mulatto
11	R. T. Greener	Teacher and politician	mulatto
11	R. E. Jones	Editor	mulatto
11	John R. Lynch	Politician and writer	mulatto and Indian
11	E. C. Morris	Preacher	mulatto
10	Benjamin F. Lee	Bishop A. M. E. Church	mulatto
9	Harry T. Burleigh	Singer	mulatto
9	Archibald H. Grimké	Politician	mulatto
9	J. E. Moorland	International Secretary Y. M. C. A.	mulatto
9	Edward H. Morris	Lawyer	mulatto
8	John Hope	President Morehouse College	mulatto
8	James W. Johnson	Writer	mulatto
8	Isaiah T. Montgomery	Founder of Negro town	mulatto
8	William H. Trotter	Editor and agitator	mulatto
7	Charles Banks	Cashier Negro bank	black
7	Will Marion Cook	Musician	mulatto and Indian
7	Solomon C. Fuller	Physician	mulatto
7	T. Thomas Fortune	Editor	mulatto and Indian
7	Francis J. **Grimké**	Preacher	mulatto
7	George C. Hall	Physician	mulatto

The Leading Men of the Negro Race

THE FOREMOST AMERICAN NEGROES—Continued

7	I. Garland Penn	Preacher	mulatto
7	W. T. Vernon	Bishop A. M. E. Church	black
7	C. T. Williams	Preacher	mulatto
7	Bert Williams	Comedian	mulatto
6	E. E. Just	Teacher	mulatto
6	C. V. Roman	Physician	mulatto
6	T. G. Steward	Teacher	mulatto
5	Roscoe C. Bruce	Superintendent Negro schools of Washington, D. C.	mulatto
5	C. S. Smith	Bishop A. M. E. Church	mulatto
4	Ira T. Bryant	Secretary A. M. E. S. S. Union	mulatto
4	John E. Bush	Lodge official	mulatto
4	George W. Clinton	Bishop A. M. E. Zion Church	black
4	William Henry Crogman	Teacher	mulatto
4	J. C. Dancy	Former United States Recorder of Deeds	mulatto
4	F. A. Dennison	Lawyer	mulatto
4	John R. Hawkins	Teacher	mulatto and Indian
4	J. W. Hood	Bishop A. M. E. Zion Church	mulatto
4	George E. Haynes	Teacher	mulatto
4	John Hurst	Bishop A. M. E. Church	mulatto
4	H. T. Kealing	President Western Reserve University	mulatto
4	P. B. S. Pinchback	Reconstruction politician	mulatto
4	R. L. Smith	Business man	mulatto
4	C. G. Woodson	Teacher	mulatto
3	C. E. Bentley	Dentist	mulatto
3	R. E. Church, Jr.	Memphis, Tenn.	mulatto
3	Levi J. Coppin	Preacher	mulatto
3	B. J. Davis	Editor	mulatto
3	B. O. Davis	Lieut. 10th U. S. Cavalry	mulatto
3	J. Rosamond Johnson	Pianist	mulatto
3	L. G. Jordan	Preacher	mulatto
3	W. E. King	Editor	mulatto
3	Fred R. Moore	Editor	mulatto
3	N. F. Mossell	Physician	mulatto
3	H. H. Proctor	Preacher	mulatto
3	R. C. Ransom	Editor	mulatto
3	E. P. Roberts	Physician	mulatto

THE FOREMOST AMERICAN NEGROES—*Continued*

3	I. B. Scott	Preacher	mulatto
3	Charles Henry Turner	Teacher	mulatto
3	Ralph W. Tyler	Former Auditor U. S. Navy	mulatto
2	R. A. Carter	Bishop C. M. E. Church	mulatto
2	George W. Carver	Teacher	black
2	Nick Chiles	Editor	mulatto
2	George W. Cook	Teacher	mulatto
2	S. E. Courtney	Physician	mulatto
2	M. W. Dogan	President Wiley University	mulatto
2	J. E. Ford	Preacher	mulatto
2	S. W. Green	Lodge official	mulatto
2	Sutton E. Griggs	Preacher	mulatto
2	W. J. Hale	President of Industrial School	mulatto
2	Ferdinand Havis	Grocer	mulatto
2	A. F. Herndon	Barber and Insurance Agent	mulatto
2	W. A. Hunton	Intern. Sec'y Y. M. C. A.	mulatto
2	John T. Jenifer	Preacher	mulatto
2	C. F. Johnson	Physician	mulatto
2	H. T. Johnson	Editor	black
2	J. Albert Johnson	Bishop A. M. E. Church	mulatto
2	Scipio H. Jones	President Ark. Negro Business League	mulatto
2	Warren Logan	Treasurer, Tuskegee Institute	mulatto
2	Christopher Perry	Newspaper writer	mulatto
2	Benjamin T. Tanner	Bishop A. M. E. Church	mulatto
2	Evans Tyree	Bishop A. M. E. Church	black
2	J. Milton Waldron	Preacher	mulatto
2	W. A. Warfield	Physician	mulatto
2	George H. White	Reconstruction politician	mulatto
2	W. T. B. Williams	Teacher	mulatto
2	Monroe N. Work	Editor, *Negro Year Book*	mulatto
2	Nathan B. Young	President of Industrial School	mulatto

It will have been observed that in the foregoing lists there has been a frequent repetition of certain names. The names of Douglass, Washington and H. O. Tanner, for example, each appears eight times, that of Dunbar seven times, that of Phyllis Wheatley Peters six times and a number of other names appear two or more times each. Making correction for these duplications and omitting the list compiled by Grégoire as having nothing more than an antiquarian interest or value there remain the names of two hundred and forty-six individuals. Of this total, two hundred and twenty-two are the names of men and twenty-four the names of women. Of the twenty-four women two were black and twenty-two mulattoes. Of the two hundred and twenty-two men, the ancestry of three was not determined. Of the two hundred and nineteen remaining names fourteen are of men who are full-blooded or nearly full-blooded Negroes. Two hundred and five are names of mulattoes. Thus of the total of two hundred and forty-six persons considered, two hundred and twenty-seven are mulattoes, sixteen are black and three are unknown.

These data thrown into tabular form follow (p. 212):

Of the two hundred and forty-six persons so far considered, the ratio of mulattoes to Negroes of pure blood is slightly more than fourteen to one. Attention has been called to the fact that in a few cases there is a disagreement concerning the mixture of blood. In such cases, the individual is classed as black or mulatto according as the evidence seems to favor the one or the other. Where the weight of the evidence seems equal, the individual is placed in the full-blooded group. The number of questionable cases, however, is so small that error in their classification would not materially alter the general figures. If all the cases concerning which there is a reasonable doubt were to be classed as full-blooded Negroes, the ratio of mulattoes to full-bloods would still be approximately eleven to one. If all such questionable cases were thrown into the mulatto group, the ratio would be somewhat more seriously affected; it would then stand at twenty, or perhaps twenty-five, to

SUMMARY OF ETHNIC COMPOSITION

COMPILATIONS	MEN Black	Mulatto	Unknown	Total	WOMEN Black	Mulatto	Total	TOTALS Black	Mulatto	Total
Miscellaneous	3	12	0	15	1	0	1	4	12	16
Underground Railroad	0	12	0	12	1	2	3	1	14	15
"Advance Guard"	2	8	0	10	0	0	0	2	8	10
"The Negro Problem"	1	6	0	7	0	0	0	1	6	7
"The Talented Tenth"	1	20	0	21	1	1	2	2	21	23
The "Negro Star"	1	10	0	11	1	0	1	2	11	12
"Eminent Men"	1	14	0	15	1	0	1	2	14	16
"Negro in Am. Hist."	3	14	0	17	1	2	3	4	16	20
The "Calif. Eagle"	1	7	0	8	0	0	0	1	7	8
The "Col. Am. Rev."	3	24	0	27	1	4	5	4	28	32
"Famous Col. Women"	0	0	0	0	1	13	14	1	13	14
"Who's Who"	4	124	3	131	0	8	8	4	132	139
"Foremost Negroes"	8	98	0	106	0	0	0	8	98	106
Gross Totals	28	349	3	380	7	31	38	35	380	418
Repetitions	14	144	0	158	5	9	14	19	153	172
Corrected Totals	14	205	3	222	2	22	24	16	227	246

212   *The Mulatto in the United States*

one.

In the opinion of the Negroes themselves, these lists would seem to include all members of the race—and many others—who have made any success in life which would entitle them to mention outside purely racial or local circles. It includes some men of first-rate intellectual ability and a few men of exceptional talent; perhaps, a few men of eminence. But in the first stages, at least, of the evolution of a primitive folk, great men, as measured by the standards of a more advanced group, are of less importance and of less worth than is that larger and less conspicuous group of men and women who rise but slightly above the mass of their fellows. The exotic is interesting and important as an indication of the latent capacity and possibility of the group; he is not the power that moves and guides the group in its slow and tedious evolution. It is within the group of men, superior to the great mass yet not so far in advance of them as to form a divergent and hence a racially useless group, that the great majority of the individuals mentioned fall. The number of men, however, considering the method of their selection, is perhaps too small to justify any general conclusion. By increasing the number of cases, though this necessarily will involve men of a lesser degree of talent and of note, and will thereby tend to raise the proportion of blacks to mulattoes,[85] any errors due to sampling will be overcome. The tentative ratio of fourteen to one will therefore be allowed to stand until the examination of larger groups leads to its modification or verification.[86]

[85] The ratio of blacks to mulattoes in the general population is approximately five to one.

[86] The method of investigation pursued in this and the three following chapters was first to assemble as inclusive and exhaustive a list as possible of men reputed to be of Negro blood who had in some way distinguished themselves above their fellows. The fact that they were

mentioned in compilations of prominent Negro men and women, in books or articles by or about Negroes, in lists specially prepared for this study by Negroes of wide acquaintance among their race, in lists of officials or leaders in Negro organizations, in lists of men or women successful in business, professional or artistic endeavor, or individuals mentioned in the literature as men of importance, was taken as evidence of importance in the group. In this way it is believed there has been brought together a list of men and women which includes every person of any real importance whom the race has so far produced, and most, at least, of those who have in any way, even locally and in very minor degree, been important men among their fellows.

The problem was then to determine which of these persons were pure-blood Negroes and which were of mixed ancestry. This matter of color is perhaps the most tender point in the whole race question. Even in the books and articles that purport to be of a biographical nature the subject is seldom mentioned. Unless the man mentioned is strikingly black or is a blood relation of some prominent white man any reference to ancestry seldom appears. Another group of Negro writers—and the practice is followed by some white "students" of race matters—refers to every individual with a brown skin as a man of unmixed Negro blood. A certain group among the mulattoes themselves tends to claim as mixed-bloods all those individuals of enviable distinction and refers to others and especially to those of unsavory reputation as black Negroes. Unreliable as it generally is, all this reference to ancestry was collected, compared and verified. A second source of information was the printed photographs with which almost every book by a Negro writer is profusely embellished. Where the photographs seemed to be genuine and showed beyond question a man of mixed blood or where the photograph showed a man who was apparently a white man yet called Negro in the legend or the text the man was tentatively classed as a mulatto. Further information was secured either directly or by letter from both black and white men acquainted with the men in question. In one or more of these ways the original list was separated into three: those who are pure-blood Negroes or accepted as such, those who are notoriously and admittedly mulattoes, and those individuals whose racial ancestry was unknown or disputed. This third list was sub-divided according to sections of the country and according to occupations and professions. These lists were then submitted to reliable men in the section of the country represented who were engaged in the various occupations and professions. After further revision the remaining list of names was again submitted to Negro men of wide acquaintance among the race. The response to this final appeal gave little additional information and the letters accompanying the return of the manuscript were in almost every case characterized by such comments as the following quoted verbatim from this series of letters:

". . . In most cases I do not consider these men of any real note. You have included many Negroes who have not risen above mediocrity. . . ."

". . . In looking over your list I find so many of mediocre fame that, I am at a loss to divine to what use you intend to put the information. . . ."

". . . I am interested in the list of names which you present because among them are hardly any of the best known colored people in the United States or in American history. Perhaps you did not mean to use the best known Negroes as the basis of your inquiry."

". . . Your list is altogether beyond my knowledge. Of most of these people I have never heard. I fear that the few about whom I can be certain will be of very little service to you."

When this stage of the inquiry was reached the couple of hundred names remaining out of the original list of several thousand were, with half a dozen exceptions, dropped from further consideration. They were, in the opinion of the best informed men of the race, names of persons of absolutely no consequence one way or the other. In a few cases the names of these men were retained in order to give in complete form an original compilation.

The chapters in their final form were submitted in whole or in part to men of widest information on matters of racial interest for final verification.

CHAPTER IX

THE HISTORY AND BIOGRAPHY OF THE NEGRO

THREE attempts have been made by Negroes to write histories of the race.[1] These works differ very widely in method and to some extent deal with different periods. Two volumes by Williams cover the American period from 1619 to 1880. Brawley treats of the same period and brings the account down to the present. The volume of DuBois is for the most part an attempt to build a tradition and to supply "history" rather than an attempt to record and interpret facts. One chapter, however, deals with the Negro in America in a semi-historical way.

In Williams's narrative, mention is made of some one hundred and forty-five different men and women as being of Negro blood. This number includes several white persons erroneously classed as Negroes, a list of individuals who were members of the first conference of the African Methodist Episcopal church, slaves, Negro sailors, free Negroes, fugitive slaves, Negro criminals, and various other characters with no better claim to distinction. To consider such persons here, not only would cumber the ground with useless timber, but would have a tendency to obscure the essential facts. Where, therefore, it did not appear from the narrative or from other sources that these men displayed some degree of native ability, made some contribution to the life

[1] G. W. Williams, *History of the Negro Race in America;* W. E. B. DuBois, *The Negro;* and G. B. Brawley, *A Short History of the American Negro.*

The History and Biography of the Negro 217

of the period in which they lived, or were persons of note in their own day and circle, they have been eliminated from consideration.² After eliminating from the total those persons who have little or no better claim to eminence than would an equal number of individuals taken at hazard from the general Negro population, there still remained the names of seventy persons. Of this number, however, the names of sixteen have appeared one or more times in the lists given in the preceding chapter,³ and so are omitted here. The names remaining are as follows:

Granville S. Abbott	Preacher. Writer of verse	mulatto
John Adams	First Negro teacher in D. C.	mulatto
James Enoch Ambush	Founded Wesleyan Seminary	black⁴
Duke William Anderson	Baptist minister	mulatto
E. D. Basset	Former minister to Haiti	mulatto and Indian
Charlotte Beams	Early teacher of Negroes	mulatto
Maria Becraft	Early teacher of Negroes	mulatto
Henry Boyd	Inventor and manufacturer	mulatto
John M. Brown	Bishop A. M. E. Church	mulatto
R. H. Cain	Bishop A. M. E. Church	black⁵
Lott Carey	Baptist preacher	black⁶
Mary A. S. Carey	Teacher and speaker	mulatto
William H. Carney	Soldier in Civil War	mulatto⁷
Eliza Ann Cook	Started school for Negroes	mulatto
Alexander Cornish	Started school for Negroes	mulatto
Louisa Parke Costin	Started school for Negroes	mulatto
William Costin	Bank messenger	mulatto and Indian

² See, also, note 86, p. 213 above.

³ Of the sixteen names dropped for this reason one is that of a black man, one that of a black woman and fourteen are those of mulatto men.

⁴ One authority called Ambush a mixed-blood.

⁵ Several authorities called Cain a mulatto.

⁶ Two authorities called Carey a mulatto.

⁷ One authority called Carney a full-black. This was obviously an error.

218   *The Mulatto in the United States*

John Cuffe	Free Negro in Mass.	mulatto and Indian
Ann Dandridge	Mother of W. Costin	mulatto
John V. DeGrasse	Physician	mulatto
Louise DeMortie	Started an asylum for Negroes	mulatto
William F. Dickerson	Bishop A. M. E. Church	mulatto [8]
John H. Fleet	Started school for Negroes	mulatto
Miss Charlotte Forten	Mrs. F. H. Grimké	mulatto
Nicholas Franklin	Started school for Negroes	mulatto
Gabriel	Insurrectionist	mulatto
John P. Green	Mass. Legislature 1881	mulatto
Leonard Grimes	Baptist minister	mulatto
Mrs. Anna M. Hall	Started school for Negroes	mulatto
Alexander Hayes	Started school for Negroes	black
Bishop Loguen	Writer and preacher	mulatto
Benjamin M. McCoy	Preacher	mulatto
Charles H. Middleton	Started school for Negroes	mulatto
Charles L. Mitchell	Member Legislature of Mass.	mulatto
Lindsay Muse	Started a Sunday School, D. C.	mulatto
Charles Pierce	Preacher A. M. E. Church	mulatto
James Poindexter	Baptist preacher	mulatto
William Paul Quinn	Bishop A. M. E. Church	mulatto [9]
Thomas Wright Roberts	Bishop A. M. E. Church	mulatto
James Shorter	Started school for Negroes	mulatto
Benjamin Snow	Cause of the "Snow Riot" 1835	mulatto
Austin Stewart	Author	mulatto
Marshall W. Taylor	Preacher	mulatto-Indian
Alex S. Thomas	Photographer	mulatto
H. M. Turner	Bishop A. M. E. Church	mulatto
Nat Turner	Insurrectionist	mulatto
Denmark Vesey	Insurrectionist	mulatto
S. R. Ward	Author	mulatto
T. M. D. Ward	Bishop A. M. E. Church	mulatto [10]
A. W. Wayman	Bishop A. M. E. Church	black
Nelson Wells	Started school for Negroes	mulatto
Mary Wormley	Started school for Negroes	mulatto
William Wormley	Started school for Negroes	mulatto
Richard Wright	First A. M. E. Conference	mulatto

[8] One correspondent called Dickerson pure-black.
[9] Two correspondents called Quinn a full-blood Negro.
[10] Ward is quite dark. He was called full-blood by two authorities.

The fifty-four new names presented in this list are in ten cases names of women—all mulattoes—and in forty-four cases, names of men. Of the men, five are given as full-blooded Negroes. Of the total fifty-four persons, forty-nine are names of mixed-bloods, and five are names of black Negroes.

In the volume by Mr. DuBois, the names of sixteen American Negroes are mentioned. Two of these are names of women, and fourteen are names of men. Both the women and three of the men seem to have been full-blooded Negroes. Eleven of the men are known to have been of mixed blood. Of the total of sixteen, however, thirteen have been mentioned in one or more of the previous lists and are omitted here. The three names remaining are, in each case, names of mulattoes. They are:

James Barbadoes	Anti-slavery agitator	mulatto
J. C. Gibbs	Reconstruction Politician	mulatto
William Lambert	Underground Railroad agent	mulatto

Brawley mentions one hundred and twenty-four individuals in all of Negro descent. Twenty-four of these have been omitted from consideration as being names of men of very slight importance even in their own time and circle.[11] The names of sixty of these have appeared in preceding lists and so are omitted here.[12] Of the remaining forty names, thirty-one are of men and nine are of women. Of the nine names of women all are mulattoes. Of the men, twenty-six are names of mulattoes and five are of black men. Of the total list of names, thirty-five are of mulattoes and five are of black Negroes. The forty not previously mentioned are

[11] One—Madison Washington—seems to have been merely a literary character. See story by Frederick Douglass.

[12] Of the 60 names omitted for this reason, 6 are of black men, 3 of black women, 47 are mulatto men and 4 are mulatto women.

as follows:

C. C. Antoine	Reconstruction politician	mulatto
E. M. Bannister	Painter	mulatto
Thomas Bethune	Musical prodigy	black
Nellie Brown	Singer	mulatto
Richard L. Brown	Painter	mulatto
Eugene Burkins	Invented rapid-fire gun	mulatto
Anthony Burns	Well-known fugitive slave	mulatto
Cato	Insurrectionist	mulatto [13]
Melville Charlton	Organist	mulatto
James D. Corrothers	Newspaper writer	mulatto
A. K. Davis	Reconstruction politician	mulatto
Robert C. DeLarge	Reconstruction politician	mulatto
Oscar J. Dunn	Reconstruction politician	mulatto
Silas X. Floyd	Writer of folklore	mulatto
Thomas Garrett	Underground Railroad worker	mulatto
Monday Gell	Insurrectionist	black
Richard H. Gleaves	Reconstruction politician	mulatto [14]
Elizabeth T. Greenfield	Singer	mulatto
Mrs. E. A. Hackley	Singer	mulatto
Hazel Harrison	Pianist	mulatto
The Hyer Sisters	Singers	mulattoes
Elijah Johnson	Colonist to Liberia	mulatto
Absolom Jones	First Negro Episcopal Rector	black [15]
Thomy Lafon	Philanthropist	mulatto
Bertina Lee	Sculptor	mulatto
John McKee	Philanthropist	mulatto
J. E. Matzeliger	Inventor	mulatto
Alice Ruth Moore	Wife of Dunbar	mulatto
John Peters	Married Phyllis Wheatley	black
W. B. Purvis	Inventor	mulatto
Joseph H. Rainey	Reconstruction politician	mulatto
A. J. Ransier	Reconstruction politician	mulatto
James T. Rapier	Reconstruction politician	mulatto
Hiram R. Revels [16]	United States Senator	mulatto-Indian
William A. Sinclair	Writer	black

[13] Two correspondents called Cato black.
[14] One authority called Gleaves black.
[15] Three correspondents considered Jones a mulatto.
[16] Revels came from the Croatan Indian group. See pp. 81, 85 above.

The History and Biography of the Negro 221

A. O. Stafford	Principal of Negro School	mulatto
Roy W. Tibbs	Pianist	mulatto
Meta Vaux Warrick	Mrs. Fuller, Sculptor	mulatto [17]
Felix Wier	Violinist	mulatto

Among the books dealing with the Negro in America are a number of volumes of a semi-biographical and personal sort written by Negroes. In and of themselves these volumes are, in general, of very slight value or importance. But they do each serve the purpose of bringing together a group of men who, in the opinion of the compiler, are among the important men of the race. Here, as elsewhere in the writing of Negroes, there is seldom a reference made to the ethnic composition of the biographer's subject. But as the volumes of the sort generally contain numerous photographic reproductions, it is often possible to form from them a fairly accurate judgment concerning the racial ancestry of the men discussed. A summary of some of these books will throw additional light upon the present problem.

The volume by Gibson and Crogman [18] contains biographical sketches of a large number of men and women of Negro blood. In nearly one hundred cases, the sketches are accompanied by photographs of the men and women.[19]

---

[17] See W. F. O'Donnell, "Meta Vaux Warrick. Sculptor of Horrors." The *World To-day*, Vol. 13, pp. 1139-45. Miss Warrick claims to be descended from an African princess.

[18] J. W. Gibson and W. H. Crogman, *The Colored American*. The fact that a book is referred to is not to be taken as an endorsement of the work. The volume of Gibson and Crogman, for example, is absolutely devoid of any merit.

[19] It is not to be assumed here or elsewhere that a judgment as to a man's ethnic ancestry rests solely upon the interpretation of a printed photograph. Unless the evidence of racial intermixture is so strikingly obvious as to preclude the possibility of error other sources of information have been resorted to. Where positive evidence could not be obtained or where the evidence obtained was conflicting the man has

222 The Mulatto in the United States

Sixty-four of the photographs are of men, and thirty-three are of women. Of the men, one photograph is that of a black man and four others are of men who are black, though possibly not pure-blooded Negroes. The remaining fifty-nine are photographs of mulattoes. Of the women, two photographs are of dark individuals who for present purposes are classed as black though purity of blood is not a certainty in either case. Thirty-two of the men and sixteen of the women have been previously mentioned, so are dropped from the list.[20] Forty-nine names remain. Of these, thirty-two are of men, three of which are of black men and twenty-nine of mulattoes. Of the seventeen names of women, two are of Negroes and fifteen are of mulattoes. The list of names, omitting those which have appeared previously, is as follows:

J. W. Adams	mulatto
Rev. W. G. Alexander	mulatto
Dr. J. B. Banks	mulatto
Miss Ella D. Barrier	mulatto
Henry Black	mulatto
Rev. E. R. Carter	mulatto
A. C. Cornell	mulatto
Mrs. W. M. Coshburn	mulatto
Walter M. Coshburn	mulatto
Prof. W. H. Council	black
William Custalo	mulatto
J. H. Darden	mulatto
Mrs. L. A. Davis	mulatto
Louis Earnest	black
Miss Hattie Gibbs	mulatto
Nora A. Gordon	mulatto

been classed as a full-blood Negro or as a mulatto depending upon whether the bulk of the evidence favored the presumption of pure or mixed blood. Special attention is called to such cases.

[20] Two of the names dropped for this reason are of black Negroes; the other names, twenty-eight of men and fourteen of women, are those of persons of mixed blood.

E. Hansberry	mulatto
Prof. W. E. Holmes	mulatto
Mrs. Emma T. Hort	mulatto
Hon. S. J. Jenkins	mulatto
James Kelly	mulatto
Horace King	mulatto
W. W. King	mulatto
M. N. King	mulatto
J. T. King	mulatto
G. H. King	mulatto
M. J. Lehman	mulatto
Rev. W. W. Lucas	mulatto
Rev. Leigh B. Maxwell	black
Prof. J. L. Murray	mulatto
Rev. Cyrus Myers	mulatto
Rev. M. W. D. Norman	mulatto
Miss Ida Platt	mulatto
Mrs. Mary Rice Phelps	black
B. F. Powell	mulatto
Mrs. M. A. Robinson	mulatto
Rev. D. J. Sanders	mulatto
Dr. B. E. Scruggs	mulatto
Huston Singleton	mulatto
Albretta Moore Smith	mulatto
Charity Still	black
D. A. Straker	mulatto
Lillian J. B. Thomas	mulatto
Mrs. Margaret Washington	mulatto
Rev. W. B. West	mulatto
Miss Emma Rose Williams	mulatto
Mrs. D. H. Williams	mulatto
Mrs. Fannie Barrier Williams	mulatto
Mrs. Sylvanie F. Williams	mulatto

M. W. Gibbs [21] in the preface to his volume [22] says:

I have aimed to give an added interest to the narrative by embellishing its pages with portraits of men who have gained distinction in various fields, . . .

[21] Gibbs was a mulatto.
[22] *Shadow and Light.*

He gives in all the photographs of thirty men. Of these, one is that of a full-blooded Negro.[23] Three are men concerning whose racial ancestry there may be a reasonable doubt.[24] The remaining twenty-six are beyond all question men with a considerable proportion of white intermixture and frequently with only a trace of Negro blood. Nineteen of the names have appeared in preceding groups.[25] The remaining eleven are as follows:

Joseph A. Booker	black
William Calvin Chase	mulatto
W. B. Derrick	black
A. Bishop Grant	mulatto
John Green	mulatto
William H. Hunt	mulatto
I. G. Ish	mulatto
Chester W. Keatts	mulatto
James B. Parker	mulatto
William A. Pledger	mulatto
J. P. Robinson	black

Dr. D. W. Culp, a mulatto physician of Palatka, Florida, compiled and published in 1902 a volume of essays [26] by one hundred American Negroes. The volume is chiefly notable for the fact that it contains full page photographs of each of the one hundred contributors. Of the book and the writers the compiler himself says: [27]

[23] Paul Laurence Dunbar.

[24] Rev. J. A. Booker, Bishop W. B. Derrick and Rev. J. P. Robinson. The latter may be a man of unmixed Negro blood; the two former are probably men of mixed blood. All three are dark as to color and have the characteristic rough features of the African though in no case of an extreme sort.

[25] Of the nineteen names omitted for this reason, one is that of a full-blood Negro and eighteen are names of mulattoes.

[26] *Twentieth Century Negro Literature or Cyclopedia of Thought by One Hundred of America's Greatest Negroes.*

[27] Preface, pp. 6, 10.

The History and Biography of the Negro 225

This is the only book in which there is such a magnificent array of Negro talent. Other books of a biographical character are objected to, by intelligent people who have read them, on the ground that they contain too few sketches of scholarly Negroes, and too many of Negroes of ordinary ability. . . . But it is not to be understood that the one hundred men and women mentioned in this book are the only Negro scholars in this country. So far from this, there are hundreds of other Negroes who are as scholarly, as prominent and as active in the work of uplifting their race as the one hundred herein given. . . .

The writers of this book are one hundred of the most scholarly and prominent Negroes in America.

Of the one hundred contributors to the volume, twelve are women and eighty-eight are men. The women are in each case mulattoes. Of the eighty-eight men, seventy-six are clearly and obviously men of mixed blood. Of the twelve remaining, all are "black" men though probably not more than four are men of unmixed Negro blood. Omitting twenty-seven men and three women whose names have appeared in earlier pages,[28] the list is as follows:

J. H. Anderson	Minister, Wilkesbarre, Pa.	mulatto
S. G. Atkins	President Industrial School	mulatto
H. E. Baker	Clerk in U. S. Patent Office	mulatto
J. D. Bibb	Teacher, Atlanta, Ga.	mulatto
E. L. Blackshear	President Industrial School	mulatto
Mrs. Ariel Bowen	Atlanta, Ga.	mulatto
Mrs. Rosa D. Bowser	Teacher, Richmond, Va.	mulatto
E. M. Brawley	Baptist preacher	mulatto
Geo. F. Braggs, Jr.	Rector Episcopal Church	mulatto
W. H. Brooks	Baptist preacher	mulatto
S. N. Brown	Preacher	mulatto
Henry R. Butler	Physician	mulatto
W. D. Chappelle	Preacher, A. M. E. Church	mulatto

[28] Of the 30 names omitted for this reason, 5 are of full-blood Negroes, 22 of men of mixed blood and 3 of women of mixed blood.

J. M. Cox	President of College	mulatto
J. W. Cromwell	Washington, D. C.	mulatto
D. W. Davis	Baptist preacher	black
I. D. Davis	Presbyterian preacher	mulatto
Mrs. Paul Laurence Dunbar	Washington, D. C.	mulatto
L. B. Ellerson	Preacher, Jacksonville, Fla.	mulatto
J. R. Francis	Physician and Surgeon	mulatto
A. U. Frierson	Teacher, Biddle University	black
J. W. Gilbert	Teacher, Paine College	mulatto
M. W. Gilbert	Baptist preacher	mulatto
G. A. Goodwin	Teacher, Atlanta Baptist College	mulatto
N. W. Harllee	Teacher, Dallas, Texas	mulatto
W. H. Heard	Preacher, Atlanta, Ga.	mulatto
J. T. Hewin	Lawyer, Richmond, Va.	mulatto
Andrew F. Hilyer	Washington, D. C.	mulatto
H. A. Hunt	Teacher, Biddle University	mulatto
Miss Lena T. Jackson	Teacher, Nashville	mulatto
J. Q. Johnson	Preacher	mulatto
J. W. Johnson	Teacher, Jacksonville, Fla.	mulatto
J. H. Jones	Teacher	mulatto
T. W. Jones	Business man, Chicago	mulatto
D. J. Jordan	Teacher, Morris Brown College	black[20]
S. Kerr	Rector Episcopal Church	mulatto
George L. Knox	Editor	mulatto
W. I. Lewis	Newspaper reporter	mulatto
Mrs. Warren Logan	Tuskegee Institute	mulatto
R. S. Lovinggood	President of College	mulatto
Mrs. Lena Mason	Hannibal, Mo.	mulatto
M. C. B. Mason	Preacher	black
G. M. McClellan	Teacher, Louisville, Ky.	mulatto
J. H. Morgan	Preacher, Bordentown, N. J.	mulatto
G. W. Murray	Lawyer, Providence, S. C.	mulatto
D. W. Olney	Dentist, Washington, D. C.	mulatto
W. E. Partee	Preacher, Richmond, Va.	mulatto
B. H. Peterson	Teacher, Tuskegee Institute	mulatto
Mrs. Pettey	Newbern, N. C.	mulatto
J. R. Porter	Atlanta, Ga.	mulatto
I. L. Purcell	Lawyer, Pensacola, Fla.	mulatto
A. St. George Richardson	President of College	mulatto
G. T. Robinson	Attorney, Nashville, Tenn.	black

[20] Opinion is divided as to whether he should be called a Negro or a mulatto. He is a brown skinned man.

R. G. Robinson	Principal LaGrange Academy	mulatto
Mrs. M. E. C. Smith	Teacher, Jacksonville, Fla.	mulatto
R. S. Smith	Lawyer, Washington, D. C.	mulatto
Prof. J. H. Smythe	President of Reformatory	mulatto
Mrs. Rosetta D. Sprague	Washington, D. C.	mulatto
James Storum	Teacher, Washington, D. C.	mulatto
Mary B. Talbert	Buffalo, N. Y.	mulatto
T. W. Talley	Teacher, Tuskegee Institute	mulatto
R. W. Thompson	Editor	mulatto
T. de S. Tucker	Teacher, Baltimore, Md.	mulatto
W. N. Wallace	Editor	mulatto
O. M. Waller	Rector Episcopal Church	mulatto
H. L. Walker	Teacher, Augusta, Ga.	mulatto
J. W. Whitaker	Tuskegee Institute	mulatto
J. R. Wilder	Physician and Surgeon	mulatto
J. B. L. Williams	Pastor M. E. Church	mulatto
R. P. Wyche	Pastor Presbyterian Church	mulatto

Of the seventy new names given above, sixty are names of men and ten are names of women. Of the men, five are black and fifty-five mulatto, while of the ten women all are mulattoes.

Mrs. Williams [30] gives a list of sixty of the presumably best known members of the Negro race. Thirty-nine of these are men and twenty-one are women. Six of the men, while possibly not full-blooded Negroes, may be fairly classed as "black." Twenty of the men and eight of the women are clearly mulattoes. The remaining thirteen men and thirteen women, while doubtless mulattoes, have all the characteristic features of the Caucasian race. So of the total list of thirty-nine men, not above six can be said to be real Negro and thirty-three, at least, are mulattoes. Of the twenty-one women, all are clearly mixed-bloods. Omitting the names of twenty-two men and fourteen women which have appeared before,[31] the list is as follows:

[30] Fannie Barrier Williams, *A New Negro for a New Century*.

[31] Of the thirty-six names omitted for this reason twenty-two are of

Dr. A. R. Abbott	mulatto
Lieut. John H. Alexander	mulatto
Louis B. Anderson	mulatto
H. E. Archer	mulatto
Mrs. Henrietta M. Archer	mulatto
Ferdinand L. Barnett	mulatto
Mrs. Anna J. Cooper	mulatto
E. J. Cooper	black
J. Webb Curtis	mulatto
Mrs. S. J. Evans	mulatto
John R. Francis	mulatto
John B. Frence	mulatto
General Maximo Gomez	mulatto
Mrs. Hart	mulatto
Mary C. Jackson	mulatto
Miss Lutie A. Lytle	mulatto
William M. Martin	mulatto
Alexander Miles	mulatto
J. Frank McKinley	mulatto
Ida Gray Nelson	mulatto
J. F. Wheaton	mulatto
Edward Wilson	mulatto
N. B. Wood	mulatto
James H. Young	mulatto

Of the twenty-four new names in Mrs. Williams's list, seventeen are of men and seven of women. One of the men is black or nearly so. Sixteen of the men and all of the women are mulattoes. Of the twenty-four new names one is that of a black Negro and twenty-three are names of mulattoes.

Mr. DuBois, in a volume on the *Philadelphia Negro*,[32] mentions seventeen men of Negro blood. Eight of the number, all mulattoes, have appeared in the foregoing lists. Of the remaining nine names, four are of mulattoes. These are:

men and fourteen of women. Of the twenty-two names of men, five are those of full-blood Negroes and seventeen of mulattoes. All of the fourteen women are mulattoes.

[32] W. E. B. DuBois, *The Philadelphia Negro*.

The History and Biography of the Negro 229

Robert Adger	Furniture business	mulatto
Peter Augustin	Caterer	mulatto
Henry Minton	Caterer	mulatto
Stephen Smith	Lumber business	mulatto

Of the five remaining, there is nothing recorded or even known.[33] Of the whole list of seventeen, then, at least twelve were mulattoes and six were of unknown parentage.

In Booker T. Washington's *Life of Frederick Douglass*, a total of sixty-nine Negroes are mentioned. Seven of these, fugitive slaves and the like, are dropped from consideration.[34] Of the sixty-two names remaining, fifty-seven are men and five are women. Of the men, two are black and fifty-five are mulattoes. The five women are all mulattoes. Thirty-three of these names have been listed previously.[35] The names of those not heretofore mentioned are:

Grandmother Bailey	Grandmother of Fred Douglass	mulatto
Anthony Barrier	Father of Fannie B. Williams U. G. R. R. agent	mulatto-Indian
Amon C. Beaman	Anti-slavery Agitator	mulatto
Hugh M. Browne	Founded school	mulatto
Anthony Burns	Fugitive slave	mulatto [36]
Peter H. Clark	Teacher	mulatto
Thomas Coppin	Agitator	mulatto
William Crafts	Fugitive slave	mulatto
Mrs. William Crafts	Fugitive slave	mulatto
J. Howard Day	Anti-slavery agitator	mulatto

[33] Robert Bogle, Henry Jones and Prosser were caterers. Thomas Shirley contributed to start a Negro school. The fifth man, Juan, was a murderer.

[34] Booker T. Washington calls Lucretia Mott a Negro. This seems to be an error. She was apparently a white woman.

[35] Of the total thirty-three names omitted from the list on this account, twenty-nine are names of men and four are names of women. Each of the four women and twenty-eight of the twenty-nine men are of mixed blood.

[36] One correspondent called Burns a full-blood Negro.

Martin R. Delaney	Anti-slavery agitator	mulatto
Thomas L. Dorsey	New York Caterer	mulatto
Charles R. Douglass	Son of Fred Douglass	mulatto
H. Ford Douglass	Anti-slavery agitator	mulatto
Lewis H. Douglass	Son of Fred Douglass	mulatto
George T. Downing	Delegate to President	mulatto
Thomas Downing	U. G. R. R. Agent	mulatto
John F. Ganes	Teacher	mulatto
Primus Hall	Ante-bellum teacher	mulatto
William Hollowell	Friend of Douglass	mulatto
John Jones	Delegate to President	mulatto
Benjamin Lundy	Anti-slavery agitator	mulatto
William E. Mathews	Visited President Johnson	mulatto
Stephen J. Myres	U. G. R. R. Agent	mulatto
Charles M. Ray	Anti-slavery agitator	mulatto
William Rich	U. G. R. R. Agent	mulatto
A. W. Ross	Delegate to President	mulatto
G. L. Ruffin	Teacher, Massachusetts	mulatto
Theodore S. Wright	Anti-slavery agitator	black

Of the twenty-nine names here presented, twenty-seven are of men and two of women. Of the men, one is a full-blooded Negro, and twenty-six are mulattoes. The two women named are mulattoes. Of the total twenty-nine names, one is that of a full-blooded Negro and the remaining twenty-eight are of mulattoes.

In Oscar Garrison Villard's *Life of John Brown*, the names of thirty Negroes are mentioned.[37] Some dozen of these are names of boys, or slaves, or Negro neighbors of Brown who, being mentioned only incidentally in the narrative, are here left out of consideration. Of the remaining eighteen names, two are of women and sixteen of men. Of the names of men, one is that of a black man and fifteen are of mulattoes. Of the two names of women, one is that of a black woman and one of a woman of mixed blood. Ten of the individuals have been previously mentioned and

[37] Villard is of course a white man but his volume is included here because of the group of Negroes not elsewhere mentioned.

The History and Biography of the Negro 231

their names are omitted here.[38] The names of persons not previously mentioned are as follows:

Osborn Perry Anderson	One of the "Men at Arms"	mulatto [39]
James M. Bell	Friend of John Brown	mulatto
John Anthony Copeland	One of the "Men at Arms"	mulatto
Newby Dangerfield	One of the "Men at Arms"	mulatto [40]
Jim Daniels	Slave in Kansas	mulatto
Shields Green	One of the "Men at Arms"	black [41]
James E. O'Harra	United States Congress	mulatto
Lewis S. Leary	One of the "Men at Arms"	mulatto

Of the eight new names here presented, one is that of a black man and seven are names of men of mixed blood.

In the volume by Carter Godwin Woodson on Negro education,[42] are mentioned the names of one hundred and fifty individuals as Negroes who had some part either as teachers or as students in the eduation of the Negro before the Civil War. One of these individuals was an East Indian who seems to have had no admixture of Negro blood.[43] He is here dropped from further consideration as are also the names of some half a dozen who are simply mentioned as slaves, and a goodly number of other persons of such minor importance that they were unknown outside their own family group. After these eliminations one hundred and seven names remained. Of these, eighty-eight were men and nineteen were women. Of the men, seventy-nine were mulattoes

---

[38] These ten names include one black woman, one mulatto woman and eight mulatto men.

[39] Also known as Perry Anderson Osborn. He had a habit of reversing his name.

[40] Or perhaps Dangerfield Newby. His father was a white man by the name of Newby.

[41] Of John Brown's "Men at Arms" sixteen were white men and five were Negroes. Green was the only Negro of full blood.

[42] *The Education of the Negro Prior to 1861.*

[43] William Appo, musician.

and nine were black men. Eighteen of the women were mulattoes and one seems to have been a woman of pure blood. Sixty of the one hundred and seven names have appeared in preceding lists.[44] The forty-seven not previously mentioned are listed as follows:

John C. Anderson	Musician	mulatto
B. W. Arnett	Teacher in Pennsylvania	mulatto
A. T. Augusta	Physician	mulatto
George Bell	Built Negro school in D. C.	mulatto
James T. Bradford	Caterer, Baltimore	mulatto
F. L. Cardozo	Studied in white school	mulatto
T. Morris Chester	Student at Pittsburg	mulatto
Daniel Coker	Teacher in Baltimore	mulatto
J. C. Corbin	Teacher in Kentucky	mulatto
Martha Costin	Teacher in D. C.	mulatto
Garrison Draper	Lawyer in Maryland	mulatto
Charles Henry Green	Slave who learned to read	mulatto
Robert Harlan	Taught by master's family	mulatto
Josiah Henson	Fugitive slave. Preacher	black
George Horton	Slave. Preacher. Illiterate	mulatto
William L. Jackson	Musician	mulatto
John Thomas Johnson	Teacher, Pittsburg	black
John S. Leary	North Carolina Legislature	mulatto
Samuel Lowry	Early preacher in Tenn.	black
Martha Martin and sister	Educated slaves	mulattoes
Mary E. Miles	Teacher in Mass. and Pa.	mulatto
S. T. Mitchell	Once President of Wilberforce	mulatto
J. Morris	Student in Charleston	mulatto
Robert Morris	Early Politician, Mass.	mulatto
William Nell	"Embellished Negro History"[45]	mulatto
Gowan Pamphlet	Preacher in Virginia about 1800	black
John Prout	Teacher in D. C.	mulatto
Charles L. Reason	Teacher of Negroes	mulatto
Sarah Redmond	Negro school girl	mulatto

[44] Of the 60 omitted for this reason 52 were men and 8 were women. Of the men 3 were black and 49 were of mixed blood. Of the women, one was black and the remaining 7 were mulattoes.

[45] Woodson, *Education of the Negro*, p. 281.

Fannie Richards	Teacher in Detroit	mulatto
D. R. Roberts	Preacher, Chicago	mulatto
B. K. Sampson	Teacher, Avery College	mulatto
Mary Ann Shadd (Carey)	Teacher in Canada	**mulatto**
Thomas Sidney	Helped build school house	black
John Baptist Snowden	Preacher	black
T. McCants Stewart	Studied in Charleston	mulatto
Mother of Mary C. Terrell	Learned French and English	mulatto
Father of R. H. Terrell	Learned to read when a slave	mulatto
Julian Troumontaine	Teacher, Savannah	mulatto
George B. Vachon	Teacher, Avery College	mulatto
T. P. White	Reconstruction politician	mulatto
W. J. White	Taught by white mother	mulatto
Ann Woodson	Taught by mistress	mulatto
Emma J. Woodson	Teacher, Avery College	mulatto
James Wormley	Student in D. C.	mulatto
Mary Wormley	Teacher, D. C.	mulatto

In Daniels's [46] study of the Boston Negroes [47] are mentioned some men and women of the Negro race of more or less prominence in and about Boston in the early days. This number is exclusive of some dozen or score of individuals who are simply mentioned as slaves, of children and of obscure individuals who do not appear from the text or other sources of information to be persons of any note or prominence in the community. Of the one hundred and forty-eight considered, one hundred and twenty-five are names of men and twenty-three are names of women. Of the men, fourteen appear to have been black or at least considered so by people who recall them. One hundred and eleven are known to have been men of mixed blood. Of the women, one was black and twenty-two were mulattoes. Of the one hundred and forty-eight individuals whose ancestry was traced, fifteen were black or nearly so and one hundred and

---

[46] Daniels is a white man but his book is included here because of the large number of New England Negroes whom he mentions.
[47] John Daniels, *In Freedom's Birthplace*.

thirty-three were individuals of mixed blood. Forty of the names appear in preceding lists and are omitted here.[48] The names of those individuals who have not been mentioned heretofore are:

Mrs. Agnes Adams	Organizer of Negro women	mulatto
Isaac B. Allen	Served on Governor's Council	black [49]
Macon B. Allen	First Negro admitted to the bar	mulatto
J. H. Allston	Member Common Council, Boston	mulatto
Philip J. Allston	Member Negro Business League	mulatto
E. H. Armistead	Member Common Council, Boston	mulatto
William O. Armstrong	Member of Congress	mulatto
Powhattan Bagnall	Minister	mulatto
J. B. Bailey	Taught boxing in Boston	mulatto
Gertrude M. Baker	Teacher in Cambridge	mulatto
Walden Banks	Member Common Council, Boston	mulatto
Jehial C. Beaman	Pastor A. M. E. Z. Church	mulatto
Edgar P. Benjamin	Lawyer, Boston	mulatto
Paul C. Brooks	Member Common Council, Boston	mulatto
E. E. Brown	Deputy Tax Collector, Boston	mulatto
W. W. Bryant	First Negro official in Boston	black
Seymour Burr	Soldier in the Revolution	mulatto
Mrs. Olivia Ward Bush	Negro Club woman, Boston	mulatto
Jacqueline Carroll	Teacher, Boston	mulatto
Julius B. Chappelle	Member Mass. Legislature	mulatto
J. Milton Clark	Member Common Council, Cambridge	mulatto [50]
Jonas Clark	Abolitionist, Boston	black
Bob Cole	Comedian	mulatto
Robert F. Coursey	Property owner, Boston	mulatto

[48] Of the 40 omitted, 7 were women and 33 men. Of the women, one was black and six were mulattoes. Of the men, 2 were black and 31 were mulattoes.
[49] This is not concurred in by all the authorities.
[50] He and his brother were called "The White Slaves."

W. Alexander Cox	Member Negro Business League	black
Joshua Crawford	Lawyer. Politician	mulatto [51]
W. E. Crum	Minister to Liberia	mulatto
William Crowdy	"Prophet"	black
Thomas Dalton	Merchant	mulatto
Louise DeMortie	Teacher, New Orleans	mulatto
Mark DeMortie	Abolitionist	mulatto
Theodore Drury	Opera Producer	mulatto
Rev. Henry Duckery	Office holder, Boston	mulatto
William Dupree	Federal appointee	mulatto
Hosea Easton	Abolitionist	mulatto
Joshua Easton	Mass. anti-slavery society	mulatto
Eliza Gardner	Organizer of Negro women	mulatto
C. N. Garland	Physician, Boston	mulatto
Nelson Gaskins	Member Common Council, Boston	mulatto
Julius B. Goddard	Office holder, Washington	black [52]
George F. Grant	Dentist, Boston	mulatto
Marjorie Groves	Teacher, Boston	mulatto
Charles H. Hall	Member Common Council, Boston	mulatto
Charles E. Harris	House of Representatives, 1894-95	mulatto
Gilbert C. Harris	Wig manufacturer, Boston	mulatto
William A. Hazel	Draftsman and architect, Boston	mulatto
Robert Hemmings	Painter in Paris	mulatto
John T. Hilton	Abolitionist, Boston	mulatto
M. Hamilton Hodges	Singer in Australia	mulatto [53]
A. H. Hunt	Physician	mulatto
Billy Johnson	Comedian	mulatto
W. C. Lane	Physician. Office holder	mulatto
George Latimer	Fugitive slave	mulatto
Andrew E. Lattimore	House of Representatives	mulatto
Joseph Lee	Innkeeper, Boston	mulatto
J. H. Lewis	Tailor, Boston	mulatto

[51] One correspondent considered Crawford a full-blood Negro.
[52] Questioned by one authority.
[53] Hodges is a dark mulatto, not a full-blood Negro as is frequently asserted.

236   *The Mulatto in the United States*

William C. Lovett	Officer Negro Business League	mulatto
George W. Lowther	House of Representatives, 1883	mulatto
Geo. Reginald Margetson	Poet	mulatto
Napoleon B. Marshall	Deputy Tax Collector	mulatto
John Sella Martin	Minister, Boston	mulatto
W. Clarence Matthews	Athletic director	mulatto
Cornelius McKane	Physician, Boston	black
Mrs. Nellie B. Mitchell	Music teacher	mulatto
Clement G. Morgan	Lawyer. Alderman	black
William G. Nell	Father of William C. Nell	mulatto
Osborn A. Newton	Member Common Council	mulatto
Dr. Thomas W. Patrick	Pharmacist, Boston	mulatto
Rev. Thomas Paul	Early abolitionist	mulatto
"Dr." Peters	Husband of Phyllis Wheatley	black
Don T. Pinheiro	Dentist. West Indian	mulatto
Coffin Pitts	Old clothes dealer	black
"Elder" Plummer	Minister, Boston	mulatto [54]
James W. Pope	Member Common Council, Boston	mulatto
John T. Raymond	Minister in Boston	mulatto
Theodore H. Raymond	Director Y. M. C. A.	mulatto
William L. Reed	Deputy tax collector	mulatto
Dr. Isaac L. Roberts	Physician, Boston	mulatto [55]
David R. Robinson	Member Common Council, Boston	mulatto
David Rock	Lawyer. Physician	mulatto
Stanley Ruffin	Member Common Council, Boston	mulatto
John E. Scarlett	Member Gen. Colored Association	mulatto
Rev. M. A. N. Shaw	Minister. West Indian	mulatto [56]
S. William Simms	Janitor. Common Council, Boston	mulatto
Blanche V. Smith	Teacher in Boston	mulatto
Eleanor A. Smith	Teacher in Boston	mulatto
Mrs. Hannah G. Smith	Organizer of Negro women	mulatto

[54] One correspondent called Plummer a black man.
[55] One authority called Roberts a full-blood.
[56] Called by one authority "pure-Negro." He is a dark brown man but seems to be of mixed ancestry.

Harriet Smith	Teacher in Boston	mulatto
Joshua B. Smith	Caterer. Abolitionist	mulatto
Mary E. Smith	Teacher in Boston	mulatto
William Stevenson	Member Common Council, Boston	mulatto
James Still	Leader following war	mulatto
H. Gordon Street	Editor, Boston	mulatto
Julian Stubbs	Office holder, Washington, D. C.	mulatto
Robert T. Teamoh	House of Representatives, 1916	mulatto
James M. Trotter	Father of politician	mulatto
Dihdwo Twe	Liberian student in Boston	black
Walker	Comedian	mulatto
Edwin G. Walker	Legislature. Son of David Walker	mulatto
Walter F. Walder	In Liberia	mulatto
Mrs. S. I. N. Washington	Daughter of G. T. Downing	mulatto
Charles W. M. Williams	Clerk of Juvenile Court, Boston	black
James G. Wolff	Clerk under district attorney	mulatto
James H. Wolff	Head of Massachusetts G. A. R.	mulatto
E. I. Wright	Physician	mulatto
Mrs. Minnie T. Wright	Organizer of Negro women	mulatto
Butler R. Wilson	Attorney	mulatto
Iola D. Yates	Teacher	mulatto

Of the one hundred and eight new names here presented, twelve are names of men who are generally considered to be full-blood Negroes. The remaining ninety-six names are in all cases names of mulattoes. Sixteen of these are of mulatto women and eighty are names of mulatto men.

Booker T. Washington prepared a most elaborate compilation of the sort that we are considering in this chapter. In the two volumes of the work,[57] are mentioned nearly four hundred individuals who have made a success in life somewhat above the average of their fellows. In most cases the

[57] *The Story of the Negro.*

success is not great; it can only be called success, in fact, when it is measured by the low level of efficiency that prevails generally in the black group. But even the small degree of relative success makes these persons exceptional men within the race, and this is the matter of importance here. Dropping from the count some score of individuals, in most cases slaves, criminals, children and the like concerning whom there is absolutely nothing known and who do not appear from the text or from other sources to have been in any way important persons, there remain three hundred and fifty-one individuals. Of these, three hundred and eleven are names of men and forty are of women. Of the men, twenty-nine seem to have been black or nearly so and two hundred and eighty-two are known to have been men of mixed blood. Of the forty women, six passed as black and thirty-four were mulattoes. Of the total three hundred and fifty-one individuals, thirty-five passed as black and three hundred and sixteen were persons of mixed ancestry. Omitting the names of persons who have been mentioned in preceding lists [58] we have the following names:

Lewis Adams	Teacher, Tuskegee Institute	mulatto
A. R. Abbott	Physician	mulatto
William G. Allen	Published "National Watchman"	mulatto
Ernest Attwell	Business Agent, Tuskegee	mulatto
Joseph S. Attwell	Preacher	mulatto
L. K. Attwood	Bank President, Jackson, Miss.	mulatto
Maria L. Baldwin	Teacher, Cambridge, Mass.	mulatto
John J. Benson	Farmer, Alabama	mulatto
William E. Benson	Real Estate dealer, Alabama	mulatto
E. C. Berry	Hotel keeper, Athens, Ohio	mulatto
Jesse Binga	Real Estate Dealer, Chicago	mulatto

[58] One hundred and seventy names are thus omitted—151 men and 19 women. Of the men 14 were black and 137 were mulattoes; of the women one was black and 18 were mulattoes.

James Bond	Berea College trustee	mulatto
B. Boyd	Physician, Nashville	mulatto
Jack Bowler	Insurrectionist 1800	black
Fellow Bragg	Free Negro tailor, N. C.	mulatto
A. M. Brown	Physician, Alabama	mulatto
Rev. William W. Brown	Organized True Reformers	mulatto
Henry E. Brown	Director Y. M. C. A.	black [59]
J. H. Bugg	Physician, Savannah	mulatto
W. P. Burrell	Secretary of True Reformers	mulatto
George L. Burroughs	U. G. R. R. Agent, Illinois	mulatto
L. L. Burwell	Physician, Selma, Alabama	mulatto
Hon. J. E. Bush	Lodge official	mulatto
Bishop J. B. Campbell	Made donation to Wilberforce	mulatto [60]
Richard Carroll	Founded home for orphans	mulatto
Paul Chretien	Father of free Negro in La.	mulatto
Elijah Cook	Undertaker, Montgomery, Ala.	black
Bishop Elias Cottrell	Founded industrial school	mulatto
Henry K. Craft	Tuskegee Institute	mulatto
Samuel Crowther	First native Bishop to Africa	black
Boston Crummell	Father of Alexander. "African Prince"	black
W. D. Crum	Collector of Customs, Charleston	mulatto
Bishop Curtis	54 Mass. Regiment in Civil War	mulatto
Austin Dabney	Soldier in Revolution	mulatto
Sam Dailey	Donated land to reform school	black
William Howard Day	Published "The Alienated American"	mulatto
Jennie Dean	Established industrial school	black [61]
George de Baptiste	U. G. R. R. Agent, Michigan	mulatto
Juan de Valladelid	Negro Count, Seville, 1474	mulatto
John H. Deveaux	Collector of Customs, Savannah	mulatto
Rev. Moses Dickson	Founder of Fraternal Order	mulatto [62]
Dr. Sadie Dillon	First woman doctor in Alabama	mulatto
C. N. Dorsette	First Doctor in Montgomery	mulatto

[59] Disputed by one authority.
[60] One authority called Campbell "a pure Negro."
[61] One correspondent said "dark mulatto."
[62] One authority considered Dickson a pure Negro.

Vice-President Dossen	Liberian embassy	black
Charles R. Douglass	Son of Frederick Douglass	mulatto
Dubuclet	Physician and musician, France	mulatto
Alexander Dunlop	Northern political agitator	mulatto
E. F. Eggleston	Preacher, Baltimore	mulatto
Matilda A. Evans	Physician, Orangeburg, S. C.	black [63]
W. R. Fields	Undertaker, Savannah	mulatto
John S. Gaines	Cincinnati	mulatto
G. W. Gibson	Ex-President of Liberia	mulatto
Henry Gordon	Donation to Wilberforce	mulatto
Sarah Gordon	Wife of Henry Gordon	mulatto
Rev. William Gray	Organized Savings and Loan Co.	mulatto
Benjamin T. Green	Mound Bayou	mulatto
William E. Gross	Caterer, New York	mulatto
George C. Hall	Physician, Chicago	mulatto
Prince Hall	"Master" first Masonic Lodge	mulatto
R. M. Hall	Physician, Baltimore	mulatto
Fenton Harper	Married Francis Ellen Watkins	mulatto
T. N. Harris	Physician, Mobile	mulatto
Jare Haralson	United States Congress	black
T. S. Hawkins	Physician	mulatto
Matt Henson	With Peary	mulatto
E. M. Hewlett	Lawyer and politician, D. C.	mulatto
L. P. Hill	Founded industrial school	mulatto
Mrs. L. Hill	Wife of L. P. Hill	mulatto
Richard Holloway	Free Negro of Charleston	mulatto
J. T. Holly	Bishop of Haiti	black
Harry Hosier	Methodist preacher	black
A. Hubbard	Toronto Board of Trade	mulatto-Indian
John Hyman	United States Congress	mulatto
Deal Jackson	Farmer, Albany, Georgia	black
Jennie Jackson	First Jubilee Singer	black [64]
John Jasper	Illiterate preacher, Va.	black
Cordelia A. Jennings	Teacher in Philadelphia	mulatto
Mrs. Mary F. Jennings	Teacher	mulatto
Rev. O. C. Jenkins	Courtland, Va.	mulatto
L. E. Johnson	Y. M. C. A., Washington, D. C.	mulatto

[63] Or nearly so.
[64] The authorities about equally divided.

The History and Biography of the Negro 241

Sol. C. Johnson	Editor Savannah "Tribune"	black
J. G. Jones	Early settler in Chicago	mulatto
Wiley Jones	Business man, Pine Bluff, Ark.	mulatto
J. A. Kenney	Physician, Tuskegee	mulatto
Lambert family	Seven musicians	mulattoes
Bishop Isaac Lane	Founded Lane College	mulatto
Matthew Leary	Father of politician	mulatto
Matthew Leary, Jr.	Reconstruction politician	mulatto
Jefferson Long	U. S. Congress from Georgia	mulatto
S. L. Lugrade	Stock holder, Boley Bank	mulatto
U. G. Mason	Physician, Alabama	mulatto
Victoria E. Matthews	New York	mulatto
Owen McCarty	Runaway slave, 1773	mulatto
Sam McCord	Farmer in Alabama	mulatto
E. H. McKissack	Treasurer of Odd Fellows, Miss.	mulatto
John Merrick	Founder Mutual and Provident Association, N. C.	mulatto
Thomas H. Miller	U. S. Congress, S. C.	mulatto
Ben Montgomery	Slave of Joseph Davis	mulatto
Thornton Montgomery	Slave of Joseph Davis	mulatto
Albert Morris	Free Negro tailor, N. C.	mulatto
Freeman Morris	Free Negro tailor, N. C.	mulatto
Francis J. Moultry	Caterer, Yonkers, N. Y.	mulatto
George A. Myers	Barber, Cleveland, Ohio	mulatto
Charles E. Nash	Politician. Reconstructionist	mulatto
Owen T. B. Nickens	Teacher in Ohio, 1820	mulatto
Peter Ogden	First Negro Odd Fellow	mulatto
Keebe Ossie	On last ship load of slaves	Mandingo
Joseph E. Otis	Northern Political Agitator	mulatto
Dinah Pace	Founded Industrial School	mulatto
C. W. Perry	Business man, Boley, Oklahoma	mulatto
I. Garland Penn	Physician	mulatto
John Peterson	Principal first Negro Normal	mulatto
Napoleon Pinchback	Brother of P. B. S. Pinchback	mulatto
L. M. Pollard	Bank director, Savannah	mulatto
Maggie Porter	Mrs. Cole, Detroit. Singer	black [65]
Joseph C. Price	President Livingston College	black
Charles B. Purvis	Teacher, Howard University	mulatto
Charlotte Ray	First Negro woman lawyer	mulatto
S. C. Redmond	Physician, Jackson, Miss.	mulatto

[65] One correspondent called Mrs. Cole "Pure Negro."

L. S. Reed	Organized Union Benefit Assoc.	mulatto
Frank Reid	Farmer near Tuskegee	mulatto
Dow Reid	Farmer near Tuskegee	mulatto
John S. Rock	Lawyer, Boston, about 1865	mulatto
Mrs. U. A. Ridley	Brookline, Mass.	mulatto
H. K. Rischer	Baker, Jackson, Miss.	mulatto
A. W. Ross	Northern political agitator	mulatto
David Ruggles	U. G. R. R. Agent	mulatto
James S. Russell	Teacher, Lawrenceville, Va.	mulatto
Thomas Rutling	Jubilee Singer	mulatto
Peter Salem	Soldier in battle of Bunker Hill	mulatto
George M. Sampson	Teacher, Tallahassee, Fla.	mulatto
Benjamin Sampson	Teacher, Wilberforce, Ohio	mulatto
James D. Sampson	Published *The Colored Citizen*	mulatto
Thomas Sanderson	Associated with Prince Hall	mulatto
J. M. Sanifer	Farmer, Alabama	mulatto
Walter Scott	Officer Negro Bank, Savannah	mulatto
Victor Sejour	Writer of verse, Paris	mulatto
Pixley Isaka Seme	Student at Columbia, 1907	Zulu
Mrs. Mary E. Shaw	Gave money to Tuskegee	mulatto
Ella Sheppard	Mrs. G. W. Moore. Singer	mulatto
Mr. Sheppard	Father of singer	mulatto
W. H. Sheppard	Missionary to Africa	mulatto
Mrs. J. A. Shorter	Wife of Bishop Shorter	mulatto
Alfred Smith	Successful cotton grower of Okla.	mulatto
Charles H. Smiley	Early caterer, Chicago	mulatto
James McCune Smith	Early physician	mulatto
John H. Smythe	Minister to Liberia	mulatto
John C. Stanley	"Barber Jack." Free Negro	mulatto
John Stanley	Son of John C. Stanley	mulatto
Alexander Stanley	Son of John C. Stanley	mulatto
Charles Stanley	Son of John C. Stanley	mulatto
W. E. Sterrs	Physician, Decatur, Alabama	mulatto
Carrie Steele	Founded orphanage in Atlanta	mulatto
F. A. Stewart	Physician, Nashville	mulatto
Peter Still	Fugitive slave. Brother of William Still	mulatto
John St. Pierre	Father of Mrs. Josephine Ruffin	mulatto-Indian
St. Benedict, The Moor	Palermo, Sicily	mulatto

The History and Biography of the Negro 243

D. C. Suggs	Teacher in Georgia	mulatto
R. R. Taylor	Teacher, Tuskegee	mulatto
James C. Thomas	Undertaker. "Richest Negro in N. Y."	mulatto
Mrs. Lucy Thurman	W. C. T. U. Worker	mulatto
John S. Trower	Caterer, Philadephia	mulatto
Victor H. Tulane	Grocer, Philadelphia	mulatto
Benjamin S. Turner	U. S. Congress, Alabama	mulatto
Denmark Vesey	Insurrectionist, 1822	mulatto
Josiah T. Wall	U. S. Congress, Florida	mulatto
O. S. B. Wall	Captain in Civil War	mulatto
S. R. Ward	Editor "Imperial Citizen," 1848	mulatto
J. H. N. Waring	Teacher, Baltimore	mulatto
Westons	Wealthy family, Charleston, S. C.	mulattoes
Heber E. Wharton	Teacher, Baltimore	mulatto
George Washington Williams	Minister to Haiti, 1888	mulatto
Henry Work	Father of Monroe Work	mulatto
Elizabeth E. Wright	Founder of Voorhees Ind. School	black

Of the one hundred and eighty new names presented in this list, one hundred and fifty-seven are of men and twenty-three are of women. One hundred and forty-two of the men and eighteen of the women are of mixed blood. Fifteen of the men and five of the women are Negroes who seem to be of pure blood.

The analysis of this semi-biographical and semi-historical material has given in all the names of six hundred and twenty-seven individuals not mentioned in the preceding chapter, who have made a more or less conspicuous success in life as measured by the standards of the Negro race. Five hundred and twenty-two of the names are of men and one hundred and five are names of women. Of the five hundred and twenty-two names of men mentioned four hundred and sixty-five are of mulattoes and fifty-seven are names of black Negroes. The names of the one hundred and five women divide into ninety-eight mulattoes and seven black women. Of the total six hundred and twenty-seven names, sixty-four are names of black Negroes and five hundred and sixty-three are names of individuals of a mixed ancestry (see p. 245).

Of the six hundred and twenty-seven persons considered in this chapter, the ratio of mulattoes to Negroes of pure blood is approximately nine to one. In a few cases, there was not full agreement among men acquainted with the person in question as to whether he should be classed as a man of pure or of mixed blood. Attention has been called to these cases as they appeared in the text. The rule followed in such cases was to class the man as a pure-blood Negro unless the evidence to the contrary seemed conclusive. It is believed, therefore, that any errors of classification that may appear tend to make the ratio of mulattoes to Negroes of pure blood appear somewhat smaller than is actually the case. However, any error in classification of a single man or even a dozen or a score out of a list of over six hundred would not materially alter the ratio. Should the twenty odd individuals in the full-blood group concerning whose purity of blood there has been question raised, be placed in the mixed-blood group the ratio of mulattoes to full-bloods would stand slightly over thirteen to one. Should, on the other hand, the dozen individuals in the mulatto group who by some correspondents were called full-blooded be placed in the full-blooded group the ratio of mulattoes to full-bloods would be slightly over eight to one. Any considerable variation from the findings of nine mulattoes to one full-blood Negro in the books analyzed, would imply a shifting from the definition of mulatto accepted for the purpose of this study.[66]

[66] A Negro with sufficient admixture of white blood to readily distinguish him from Negroes of pure blood. See p. 11 above.

SUMMARY OF ETHNIC COMPOSITION

BOOKS	MEN Black	MEN Mulatto	MEN Total	WOMEN Black	WOMEN Mulatto	WOMEN Total	TOTALS Black	TOTALS Mulatto	TOTALS Total
Williams: Hist. of the Negro	5	39	44	0	10	10	5	49	54
DuBois: The Negro	0	3	3	0	0	0	0	3	3
Brawley: Hist. of the Am. Negro	5	26	31	0	9	9	5	35	40
Gibson & Crogman: The Col. Am.	3	29	32	2	15	17	5	44	49
Gibbs: Shadow and Light	3	8	11	0	0	0	3	8	11
Culp: 20th Cent. Negro Lit.	5	55	60	0	10	10	5	65	70
Williams: New Negro for a N. C.	1	16	17	0	7	7	1	23	24
DuBois: Philadelphia Negro	0	4	4	0	0	0	0	4	4
Washington: Frederick Douglass	1	26	27	0	2	2	1	28	29
Villard: John Brown	1	7	8	0	0	0	1	7	8
Woodson: Negro Education	6	30	36	0	11	11	6	41	47
Daniels: Freedom's Birthplace	12	80	92	0	16	16	12	96	108
Washington: Story of the Negro	15	142	157	5	18	23	20	160	180
Totals	57	465	522	7	98	105	64	563	627

CHAPTER X

THE NEGRO AND THE MULATTO IN PROFESSIONAL AND ARTISTIC PURSUITS

THE various lists given in the preceding chapters probably include the great majority of the Negroes who have shown noteworthy ability, or made any very exceptional success in life. But as these lists were for the most part of a general nature, that is, groupings of men and women from various lines of human endeavor, it may be worth while to consider the relative success the black Negro and the mulatto have had in some of the specific lines of endeavor. For this purpose we will consider: I. the Army and Navy, II. Politics, III. Inventions, IV. Medicine and Dentistry, V. Law, VI. Education, VII. the Ministry, VIII. Literature, IX. Editors and Newspaper men, X. Artists, XI. the Stage, XII. Composers and Musicians, and XIII. Business men.

The Negroes have played a part, albeit no very conspicuous one, in every war in which the United States has been involved. In the Revolutionary War, Negroes, both slave and free, were found on both sides. Crispus Attucks, a Boston man of mixed Indian, Negro, and white blood, is said to have been the first man killed in the so-called Boston Massacre. In the second war with Great Britain, and especially in the Battle of New Orleans, Negro soldiers were engaged in considerable numbers.[1] In the Civil War, espe-

---

[1] *Negro Year Book*, 1914-1915, pp. 154-55.

The Negro and the Mulatto in Pursuits 247

cially during the latter stages, large numbers of Negro soldiers were enlisted in the Union armies.[2] While the Confederacy consistently refused to allow slaves to be employed as soldiers and in some cases refused to accept the proffered assistance of free Negroes,[3] the Southern armies nevertheless employed a considerable number of Negroes, both slave and free, as laborers, and a few free Negroes seem to have been enrolled as soldiers.[4]

The Negro Year Book[5] mentions three men as having gained some distinction in the Civil War: A. T. Augusta, Surgeon in the Seventeenth Regiment United States Volunteers; A. W. Abbott, Army Surgeon; and H. M. Turner, an Army Chaplain. All three men were mulattoes.

Three Negroes have been graduated from the United States Military Academy at West Point.[6] They were in each case mulattoes.

In the United States Army, there are eleven Negro officers.[7] They are in every case mulattoes.

Lt. Col. A. Allensworth, (retired) Chaplain, 24th Infantry	mulatto
Major W. T. Anderson, (retired) Chaplain, 9th Cavalry	mulatto

[2] The soldiers seem to have been about equally divided between Negroes and mulattoes. The 55th Regiment of Volunteer Infantry, for example, had a total of 980 enlisted men. Four hundred and thirty were mulattoes and 550 were apparently pure black. The black men were probably two or three times as numerous as the mulattoes in the general population. See Burt G. Wilder, "The Brain of the American Negro," *Proceedings of the First National Negro Conference*, p. 49.

[3] The color of these free Negroes, according to General Butler, was "about that of Vice-President Hamlin, or the late Mr. Daniel Webster." See J. P. Ficklen, *The History of Reconstruction in Louisiana*, p. 121.

[4] *Negro Year Book*, 1914–1915, pp. 157-59.

[5] *Ibid.*, p. 159.

[6]

Henry O. Flipper	mulatto
John H. Alexander	mulatto
Charles Young	mulatto

[7] *Ibid.*, p. 161.

Lieutenant Louis A. Carter, Chaplain, 10th Cavalry	mulatto
Lieutenant B. O. Davis, 10th Cavalry	mulatto
Lieutenant J. E. Green, 25th Infantry	mulatto
Lieutenant W. W. Gladden, Chaplain, 24th Infantry	mulatto
Major John R. Lynch, (retired) Paymaster	Indian and mulatto
Captain G. W. Prioleau, Chaplain, 9th Cavalry	mulatto
Lieutenant O. J. W. Scott, Chaplain, 25th Infantry	mulatto
Captain T. G. Steward, (retired) Chaplain, 25th Infantry	mulatto
Major Charles Young, 9th Cavalry	mulatto

From all other sources of information were obtained facts in regard to twenty-six other men who hold, or have held, military positions of some importance in the regular army or in the National Guard, or have particularly distinguished themselves by deeds of valor. Of these men, three were dark men; though in no case is it certain that they were Negroes of full blood. The other twenty-three were in all cases mulattoes.[8]

In the military affairs of the nation, it would thus appear that the race, so far at least as offices and honors go, is represented almost exclusively by its lighter-colored members. Of the forty-four men mentioned in this section, forty-one at least are men of mixed blood. Nine of these men have been previously mentioned in other connections. Thirty-two of the remaining thirty-five men are mulattoes. Throwing into tabular form this information concerning the ethnic ancestry of these members of the race who have distinguished themselves in a military way we have the following:

[8] In military affairs Toussaint is, of course, the one conspicuous example of military ability among the members of the race so far. He was probably not a full-blood Negro though he was identified with and led the blacks as opposed to the mulatto faction. The National heroes of Cuba—Gomez and Maceo—are said to have both been men of some intermixture of Negro blood. The same thing seems to be true of Panco Villa. None of these men, however, excepting Toussaint, displayed any particular ability as military leaders.

The Negro and the Mulatto in Pursuits

	Black	Mulatto	Total
Soldiers in the Revolutionary War	0	1	1
Soldiers in the Civil War	0	3	3
Graduates of West Point	0	3	3
Officers of the U. S. Army	0	11	11
Other Noted Soldiers	3	23	26
Totals	3	41	44
Names Repeated	0	9	9
Corrected totals	3	32	35

In the Navy, so far as officers go, the Negroes are not represented.

The Negro has played no very conspicuous or important part in the political life of America. For the most part, he has been barred from participation in politics. Prior to the Civil War, speaking generally, he took no part in the political life of the country. The emancipation of the Negro and the Reconstruction following, brought into prominence a number of Negroes who passed into oblivion with the passing of the Reconstruction regime and the restoration of law and order in the southern states.[9] Since this period, politics—except in a very limited and mostly local way—has all but ceased to be a field of endeavor open to men of the race.

Furthermore, the part that the Negro has taken in the political life of the country has not reflected to his credit. Bruce [10] says:

[9] "In considering who and what are representative Negroes there are circumstances which compel one to question what is a representative man of the colored race. Some men are born great, some achieve greatness and others lived during the Reconstruction period. . . ." Paul Laurence Dunbar, "Representative American Negroes," *The Negro Problem*, p. 189.

[10] P. A. Bruce, *The Plantation Negro as a Freeman*, p. 72.

... Those who have obtained seats in the Legislature, have won no special reputation for practical capacity by an intelligent devotion to business; and as they are generally silent members or wandering and irrelevant when they have risen to their feet, they have exercised no marked influence on the enactment of laws, except by the votes they have cast. Indeed, the majority have not been at all superior to the mass of their race in force of character or intellect; many, in fact, have been inferior, and their election to a position of so much responsibility can only be explained on the ground of accident. The prominence of the office they occupy only brings out into the broadest contrast their incompetence to represent the interests of their own people, much less advance the general prosperity of a commonwealth.

All this is probably true and exactly the same thing is true of the country's white politicians.

But we are not here concerned with an evaluation of the Negroes as politicians further than to point out that they are not to be taken as representing in any true sense what Mr. DuBois has called the "Advance Guard of the Race,"[11] any more than the white politicians are to be taken as representing the highest degree of the honesty, intelligence, and public spirit of the white community. The Negro politicians are, however, a conspicuous group and, as such, have been selected here for analysis into their black and mixed elements.

The race has been represented in the National Senate by two members—Hiram R. Revels and Blanche K. Bruce. The former was a Croatan Indian and the latter a mulatto.

In the National House of Representatives, there have been twenty members of the Negro race, not more than three

[11] W. E. B. DuBois, *Booklover's Magazine*, Vol. 2, pp. 2-14.

The Negro and the Mulatto in Pursuits

of whom were Negroes of even approximately full blood. *The Negro Year Book* lists them as follows:[12]

Richard H. Cain	S. C.	43rd and 45th Congress..	4 years	black
H. P. Cheatham	N. C.	52nd and 53rd Congress.	4 years	mulatto
R. C. Delarge	S. C.	42nd Congress	2 years	mulatto
R. B. Elliott	S. C.	42nd Congress	2 years	mulatto
J. Haralson	Ala.	44th Congress	2 years	black
John Hyman	N. C.	44th Congress	2 years	mulatto
J. M. Langston	Va.	51st Congress	2 years	mulatto
Jefferson Long	Ga.	41st Congress	2 years	mulatto
John R. Lynch	Miss.	42nd, 44th & 47th Cong.	6 years	mulatto
T. H. Miller	S. C.	51st Congress	2 years	mulatto
G. W. Murray	S. C.	53rd and 54th Congress.	4 years	black [13]
Charles E. Nash	La.	44th Congress	2 years	mulatto
J. E. O'Harra	N. C.	48th and 49th Congress..	4 years	mulatto
J. H. Rainey	S. C.	44th to 48th Congress	10 years	mulatto
A. J. Ransier	S. C.	43rd Congress	2 years	mulatto
James T. Rapier	Ala.	43rd Congress	2 years	mulatto
Robert Smalls	S. C.	44th, 45th & 47th Cong..	6 years	mulatto
B. S. Turner	Ala.	42nd Congress	2 years	mulatto
Josiah T. Wall	Fla.	42nd, 43rd & 44th Cong.	6 years	mulatto
George H. White	N. C.	55th and 56th Congress.	4 years	mulatto

In 1869, Ebenezer Don Carlos Bassett,[14] a man of mixed mulatto and Indian parentage, was appointed Resident Minister and Consul General to Haiti. He was the first Negro given an appointment by the Federal government. He held the position for eight years.

During the Reconstruction regime in the South, several

[12] 1914-1915, p. 151.

[13] Shufeldt, not always reliable, is authority for the statement that Murray was a black man. Murray had a rather unsavory reputation having divorced his Negro wife and married a white woman. He was later convicted of forgery and sentenced to a three-year term in the penitentiary. "Every line of his cannon-ball head was modeled on African lines. His complexion is that of the ace of spades, and his features are of the pronounced negro type...." R. W. Shufeldt, *The Negro a Menace to American Civilization*, p. 189.

[14] *Negro Year Book*, 1914-1915, p. 152.

Negroes attained the position of Lieutenant Governors. These men were as follows:[15]

Louisiana
C. C. Antoine	mulatto
Oscar J. Dunn	mulatto
P. B. S. Pinchback	mulatto

South Carolina
R. H. Gleaves	mulatto
Alonzo J. Ransier	mulatto

Mississippi
Alexander K. Davis[16]	mulatto

John R. Lynch[17] in a recent volume[18] on the part played by the Negro in the Reconstruction of the South, mentions nineteen men prominent during the period. Four of these men seem to have been black, and fifteen to have been men of mixed blood. The list follows:

Roscoe Bruce	Son of Ex Senator Bruce	mulatto
Rev. Noah Buchanan	Republican Convention of Miss. 1869	black
T. W. Cardoza	Candidate for office, Miss. 1873	mulatto
H. C. Carter	Proposed candidate for Lieut. Gov., Miss.	mulatto
A. K. Davis	Candidate for Lieut. Gov. of Miss. 1873	mulatto
Frederick Douglass	Politician	mulatto
Robert Gleed	State Senator of Miss.	black
Sam Henry	Pres. of Republican Club	mulatto
James Hill	Candidate for Sec. of State of Miss.	mulatto
H. P. Jacobs	Baptist preacher and politician	mulatto
James Lynch	Methodist preacher. Political candidate	mulatto
William McCary	Signed bond for J. R. Lynch in 1869	mulatto
I. T. Montgomery	Boliver County, Miss.	mulatto

[15] G. W. Williams, *History of the Negro Race in America*, p. 585.

[16] Davis was a candidate in 1873 but was not elected. Mr. Williams is not the only Negro who lists him among the Negro Lieutenant Governors. See B. T. Washington, *Frederick Douglass*, pp. 279-80.

[17] See pages 205, 208 above.

[18] *The Facts of Reconstruction.*

The Negro and the Mulatto in Pursuits   253

P. B. S. Pinchback	Lieutenant Governor of Miss.	mulatto
H. R. Revels	United States Senator	Croatan Indian
David Singleton	Signed a bond for Lynch in 1869	mulatto
T. W. Stringer	State Senator, Mississippi	mulatto
J. M. P. Williams	Baptist preacher. Political candidate	black
J. M. Wilson	Member of Legislature, Mississippi	black

The Negro Year Book names four Negroes now holding federal offices.[19] These men are all mulattoes. They are:

Charles W. Anderson	mulatto
Collector of Internal Revenue, New York City	
James A. Cobb	mulatto
Assistant District Attorney for the District of Columbia	
Charles Cottrell	mulatto
Collector of Customs, Honolulu, H. I.	
Robert H. Terrell	mulatto
Judge of Municipal Court, Washington, D. C.	

The Negro Year Book names two Negroes in the diplomatic service of the United States.[20] One of these men is a Negro of pure blood and the other is a mulatto. They are:

George W. Buckner	mulatto
Minister Resident and Consul General, Liberia	
Richard W. Bundy	black
Secretary of Legation, Liberia	

The Negro Year Book names eight Negroes in the consular service of the United States.[21] Two of these men are Negroes of pure blood and six are mulattoes. The list is as follows:

James G. Carter	mulatto
Consul at Tamatave, Madagascar	
William H. Hunt	mulatto
Consul at Saint-Étienne, France	

[19] *Negro Year Book*, 1914-1915, p. 152.
[20] *Ibid.*, p. 153.
[21] *Ibid.*, p. 153.

George H. Jackson   mulatto
   Consul at Cognac, France
James W. Johnson   mulatto
   Consul at Corinto, Nicaragua
Lemuel W. Livington   black
   Consul at Cape Haitien, Haiti
Christopher H. Payne   mulatto
   Consul at St. Thomas, West Indies
Herbert R. Wright   black
   Consul at Puerto Cabello, Venezuela
William J. Yerb   mulatto
   Consul at Sierra Leone, West Africa

The Negro Year Book names the following as the more important political positions held by Negroes during the presidential administration of William Howard Taft:[22]

J. N. W. Alexander   mulatto
   Register of Land Office, Montgomery, Alabama
G. W. Buckner   mulatto
   U. S. Minister and Consul General to Liberia
John E. Bush   mulatto
   Receiver of Public Moneys, Little Rock, Arkansas
Henry W. Furniss   mulatto
   Envoy Extraordinary and Minister Plenipotentiary, Port au
      Prince, Haiti
George H. Jackson   mulatto
   United States Consul to Cognac, France
James W. Johnson   mulatto
   United States Consul at Corinto, Nicaragua
Joseph Lee   mulatto
   Collector of Internal Revenue for Florida
William H. Lewis   mulatto
   Assistant Attorney General
Whitfield McKinley   mulatto
   Collector of Customs, Port of Georgetown, D. C.
Fred R. Moore   mulatto
   United States Minister and Consul General to Liberia
James C. Napier   mulatto
   Register of the Treasury

[22] *Negro Year Book*, 1914-1915, p. 27.

Robert Smalls mulatto
  Collector of Customs at Beaufort, S. C.
R. H. Terrell mulatto
  Municipal Court of Washington, D. C.
Ralph W. Tyler Indian and mulatto
  Auditor of the Navy

In addition to the foregoing lists, an additional list of men, not heretofore mentioned, was compiled from all the available sources of information. It included, so far as it was possible to obtain them, the names of all men who are mentioned in the literature as having held elective or appointive offices, or as otherwise having distinguished themselves by political ability, or gained political prominence. After eliminating from the list thus compiled, the names of all men who have a better claim to distinction than the political one and who were consequently placed in other categories, one hundred and fifty-two names remained. Of these, one hundred and thirty-seven were mulattoes; and fifteen, so far as the evidence goes, seem to have been full-blooded Negroes. In tabular form, the facts stand as follows:

	Black	Mulatto	Total
United States Senators	0	2	2
United States Representatives	3	17	20
Resident Minister to Haiti	0	1	1
Lieutenant Governors [23]	0	6	6
Reconstructionists	4	15	19
Federal Officials	0	4	4
In Diplomatic Service	1	1	2
In Consular Service	2	6	8
Holders of Political Positions	0	14	14
Miscellaneous	15	137	152
Totals	25	203	228
Names repeated	3	48	51
Corrected totals	22	155	177

[23] See note 16, p. 252 above.

It would appear from these facts that in the political life of the country—as measured by the relative amount of office holding—that the man of mixed blood is somewhat over seven times as successful as the full-blooded Negro. This, too, is on the principle of classifying as full-bloods, all Negroes where there seems to be any reason to doubt the fact of a mixed ancestry.

The number of inventions by members of the Negro race is very small.[24] Scarcely half a dozen names are required to enumerate the whole list that the most liberal-minded would class as important.[25] The patent office makes no record of the race of the patentees, so that it is not possible to know the Negro inventors with any certainty or completeness. A list of alleged Negro inventors was furnished to the Paris Exposition in 1900.[26] The list contains two hundred and one separate names but in almost every case there is absolutely no information available concerning the men themselves. In all, information was obtained in regard to twenty-seven of the inventors listed. Of these four are said to be black and twenty-three are admittedly mulatto. The men whose ancestry it was possible to trace, with the invention on which they received a patent, follows:

[24] Harry E. Baker, a mulatto clerk in the United States Patent Office, claims to have verified 800 patents granted to Negroes. He estimates that 400 others, unverified, have been granted. His plan of discovery and verification has been to circularize the patent attorneys, newspapers, "conspicuous citizens of both races," etc., on the subject. "The answers to this inquiry cover a wide range of guess work, many mere rumors and a large number of definite facts. These are all put through the test of comparison with the official record of the patent office. . . ." But even at the highest estimate that Mr. Baker claims for his race the number of inventors is pitifully small. H. E. Baker, *The Colored Inventor*.

[25] *Negro Year Book*, 1914-1915, names sixteen, pp. 284 ff.

[26] Reprinted in D. W. Culp's *Twentieth Century Negro Literature*.

The Negro and the Mulatto in Pursuits 257

L. C. Bailey	Folding bed	mulatto
L. W. Benjamin	Broom moistener	mulatto
Miss M. E. Benjamin	Gong and Signal chairs	mulatto
L. Blue	Hand corn shelling device	mulatto
Henry Brown	Receptacle for storing papers	mulatto
Eugene Burkins	Rapid-fire gun	mulatto
M. A. Cherry	Velocipede	mulatto
J. S. Coolidge	Harness attachment	mulatto
W. R. Davis	Library table	black
J. H. Dickinson	Piano player devices	mulatto
T. H. Edmonds	Separating screens	mulatto
D. A. Fisher	Joiner's clamp	mulatto
A. F. Hilyer	Registers	mulatto
W. A. Lavalette	Early printing device, about 1879	mulatto
F. J. Loudin	Sash fastener	mulatto
J. E. Matzeliger	Machine for attaching soles to shoes	mulatto
E. McCoy	Lubricators	mulatto
G. W. Murray	Attachments for agricultural implements	mulatto
L. Nance	Game apparatus	black
O'Connor	Alarm for boilers	black
W. B. Purvis	Paper bag machines	mulatto
E. P. Ray	Dentist's Chair device	mulatto
H. H. Reynolds	Safety gate for bridges	mulatto
E. H Sutton	Cotton Cultivator	black
G. T. Woods	Electrical appliances	Australian[27]
James Wormley	Life saving apparatus	mulatto
P. B. Williams	Electrical railway track switch	mulatto

In his pamphlet,[28] Mr. Baker names twelve additional Negro inventors. Concerning four of these, no information was obtained. The eight remaining, all of whom are mulattoes, are as follows:

Benjamin Banneker	Clock. Published almanac	mulatto
W. Douglass	Harvesting machine attachments	mulatto
Shelby Davidson	Tabulating device	mulatto

[27] See note 49, p. 195.
[28] *The Colored Inventor.*

James Doyle	A mechanical server	mulatto
James Forton	Device for managing sails	mulatto
R. Pelham	Tabulating device	mulatto
C. V. Richey	Register for telephone calls	mulatto
Lyates Woods	Electrical appliances	Australian

The *Negro Year Book* [29] gives practically the same list. The only additional name is that of a free Negro of Maryland, Henry Blair, who secured patents for a corn harvester in 1834 and again in 1836. There is nothing stated and presumably nothing known concerning his color. The fact, however, that he was free at least gives the presumption that he was a man of mixed blood.

During the past eighteen months, the Negro journals and papers have mentioned thirteen additional patents granted to Negroes.[30] Ten of these men are mulattoes, one a man of unmixed blood and two, while probably not full-blood, are very nearly so.

Of the forty-eight inventors, then, of whom it was possible to secure information—and the number seems to include most of the important as well as most of the recent ones—forty-one are men of mixed blood and seven are either full black or nearly so. Nine of these men, however, have been mentioned in other connections. Of the thirty-nine new names, seven are of black Negroes and thirty-two of mulattoes—a ratio of nearly five to one.[31] The collected information falls into the following tabulation:

[29] 1914-1915. See pp. 282 ff.

[30] For the eighteen months ending June, 1916. There may of course have been others that escaped notice.

[31] It is quite probable that if data were available concerning any large number of the Negro inventors of lesser note that this ratio of about one black man to five mulattoes would be maintained or the proportion of black men might even be increased. Minor inventions are very frequently if not generally the work of men in daily contact with the machines they use and for which they invent improvements.

	Black	Mulatto	Total
Twentieth Century Negro Literature	4	23	27
The Colored Inventor	0	8	8
Miscellaneous	3	10	13
Totals	7	41	48
Names repeated	0	9	9
Corrected totals	7	32	39

The medical profession, more perhaps than any other in which Negroes are found, is made up of trained men. At least a certain minimum of training is required that a man be licensed to practice. The medical degree, even from the least reputable institutions, stands for something in the way of training. It is not an honorary degree, and legal provisions prevent the practice of medicine by men wholly untrained.

The census of 1910 gave 3,777 as the number of Negro physicians in the United States. Of these a few have attained something more than local reputation. *The Negro Year Book* [32] mentions three of those who have "achieved national reputation": Daniel H. Williams of Chicago, George C. Hall of Chicago, and A. M. Curtis of Washington, D. C. All of these men are light-colored mulattoes.

Dr. Kenney gives brief sketches of some sixty-eight Negro physicians.[33] While he distinctly states that there are hundreds of others "just as worthy and whose accomplishments are as brilliant as those selected," the list nevertheless contains most, at least, of the better-known Negro physicians. The list is as follows:

A. W. Abbott	Washington, D. C.	mulatto
W. G. Alexander	Orange, N. J.	mulatto

[32] 1914-1915, p. 334.
[33] John A. Kenney, *The Negro in Medicine*.

A. T. Augusta	Virginia	mulatto
B. R Bluitt	Dallas, Texas	mulatto [34]
Robert F. Boyd	Nashville, Tenn.	mulatto
Roscoe C. Brown	Richmond, Va.	mulatto
L. L. Burwell	Selma, Ala.	mulatto
H. R. Butler	Atlanta, Ga.	mulatto
George E. Cannon	Jersey City, N. J.	mulatto
Simeon L. Carson	Washington, D. C.	mulatto
Rebecca J. Cole	Washington, D. C.	mulatto
S. E. Courtney	Boston, Mass.	mulatto
A. M. Curtis	Washington, D. C.	mulatto
U. G. Dailey	Chicago, Ill.	mulatto
John W. Darden	Opelika, Ala.	mulatto [35]
John DeGrasse	New York City	mulatto
C. N. Dorsett	Montgomery, Ala.	mulatto
A. W. Dumas	Natchez, Miss.	mulatto
Chas. B. Dunbar	New York and Liberia	mulatto
James Durham	New Orleans, La.	mulatto
John C. Ferguson	Virginia	mulatto
Joseph Ferguson	Richmond, Va.	mulatto
Joseph J. France	Portsmouth, Va.	mulatto [36]
S. C. Fuller	Westborough, Mass.	mulatto
H. F. Gamble	Charleston, W. Va.	mulatto
C. N. Garland	Boston, Mass.	mulatto
E. E. Green	Macon, Ga.	mulatto
George C. Hall	Chicago, Ill.	mulatto
John B. Hall	Boston, Mass.	mulatto
R. T. Hamilton	Dallas, Texas	mulatto
F. S. Hargrave	Wilson, N. C.	mulatto
W. H. Higgins	Providence, R. I.	mulatto
J. Seth Hills	Jacksonville, Fla.	mulatto
E. C. Howard	Philadelphia, Pa.	mulatto
John E. Hunter	Lexington, Ky.	mulatto
A. B. Jackson	Philadelphia, Pa.	mulatto
Peter A. Johnson	New York City	black
A. D. Jones	Atlanta, Ga.	mulatto
Miles B. Jones	Richmond, Va.	black

[34] Called black by one authority.

[35] Darden is a dark brown man. One authority considers him a full-blood Negro.

[36] One authority writes that France is a "dark man but probably not pure Negro."

The Negro and the Mulatto in Pursuits 261

John W. Jones	Winston Salem, N. C.	mulatto [37]
John A. Kenney	Tuskegee, Ala.	mulatto
J. R. Levy	Florence, S. C.	mulatto [38]
A. C. McClennon	Charleston, S. C.	mulatto
David K. McDonough	New York City	mulatto
A. M. Moore	Durham, N. C.	mulatto
N. F. Mossell	Philadelphia, Pa.	mulatto
John S. Outlaw	Los Angeles, Calif.	mulatto
Loring B. Palmer	Atlanta, Ga.	mulatto
W. F. Penn	Atlanta, Ga.	mulatto
C. B. Purvis	Washington, D. C.	mulatto
Rapier	Washington, D. C.	mulatto
Peter Williams Ray	New York City	mulatto
E. P. Roberts	New York City	mulatto
C. V. Roman	Nashville, Tenn.	mulatto
David Rosell	New York City	mulatto
Chas. H. Shepard	Durham, N. C.	mulatto
T. H. Slater	Atlanta, Ga.	black
James McCune Smith	New York City	mulatto
Willis E. Sterrs	Montgomery, Ala.	mulatto
F. A. Stewart	Nashville, Tenn.	mulatto
Tucker.	Washington, D. C.	mulatto
A. M. Townsend	Nashville, Tenn.	mulatto
John W. Walker	Asheville, N. C.	mulatto
L. P. Walton	Atlanta, Ga.	mulatto
W. A. Warfield	Washington, D. C.	mulatto
Daniel H. Williams	Chicago, Ill.	mulatto
James H. Wilson	Philadelphia, Pa.	black
A. A. Wych	Charlotte, N. C.	mulatto

Of the sixty-eight names here presented, four are of full-blooded Negroes. The remaining sixty-four seem in all cases to be men of mixed blood. In five of these cases, the men are dark in color and one correspondent called each of them a full-blooded Negro. This, however, was not concurred in, in any case, by the other authorities consulted. Consequently, they have been classed as men of mixed blood and attention called to the dissenting opinion. The list

---

[37] Called full-blood by one authority.
[38] A dark mulatto, sometimes called full-blood.

contains twenty-two names which have been mentioned in other connections. Omitting these, the list then stands: four Negroes of full-blood and forty-two mulattoes. Five of the latter number are brown or dark mulattoes.

Dr. Kenny's list seems to be the most elaborate and accurate of any single discussion of the Negro physicians. From various other sources, however, a considerably more extensive list was compiled. While it does not, perhaps, contain the names of so many men of first-rate ability and perhaps contains more names of men of second-rate ability, it is nevertheless made up of physicians of sufficient note or promise to gain mention in the literature dealing with the Negro, or in the publications of the race. The men included seem in all cases to be of some prominence within the profession and, consequently, leaders of some importance among the people.

This compilation from miscellaneous sources includes the names of two hundred eight physicians not previously mentioned. Two hundred of these are men and eight are women. Of the men eleven are black or nearly so, while one hundred and eighty-nine are undoubtedly of mixed blood. Of the women, one is classed as black and seven are classed as mulattoes. Of the eleven men recorded as black it would not be safe to assert that more than one-half are men of unmixed Negro blood; but to all intent and purpose, twelve of the entire list are Negroes of full blood.

There seems to have been made no special study which brings together a representative list of successful Negro dentists, and no separate list is here presented. Several of the men discussed in the volume by Dr. Kenney are dentists, or practice dentistry in connection with their medical practice. The same thing is true of many of the men in the list compiled from miscellaneous sources.

The Negro and the Mulatto in Pursuits

Omitting names of men which have been previously mentioned in other connections, there remains a total of two hundred and fifty-four physicians and dentists who, if not in all cases the most prominent men in the professions, are at least representative men and, in all cases, men of some note in the professional circles of the Negro group. Of these men sixteen are either very dark mulattoes or full-blood Negroes, while two hundred and thirty-eight are persons of mixed blood. Among the leaders of these professions, then, the ratio of mulattoes to Negroes of full blood appears to be approximately fifteen to one. The lists summarize as follows:

	MEN			WOMEN			
	Black	Mul.	Total.	Black	Mul.	Total	Totals
Kenney: N. in Medicine	4	64	68	0	0	0	68
Miscellaneous	11	189	200	1	7	8	208
Totals	15	253	268	1	7	8	276
Names repeated	0	22	22	0	0	0	22
Corrected totals	15	231	246	1	7	8	254

There seems to have been published no list of the prominent Negro lawyers. As a practitioner no Negro lawyer has made anything more than a minor and local reputation. The exceptions that might be made to this statement would be in the case of men previously listed among the politicians. Many of these men are lawyers by profession, in some cases by training, but their reputation in few, if any, cases rests upon their legal learning or successful practice. Their prominence is rather due to the conspicuous political offices they have held.

Reference to the book and magazine literature and an examination of some thousand of Negro newspapers and magazines extending over a period of eighteen months, resulted in a compilation of names of Negro lawyers of some note who have not been mentioned previously. Classing as mulattoes only those who are conspicuously and unmistakably so, and as full-bloods, all black men as well as those where there could exist any reasonable doubt concerning the mixture of blood, it was found that the ratio of mulattoes to Negroes of pure blood was nine to one. Of the ninety-nine men in the list, ten were classed as black and eighty-nine as mulattoes. Of the latter group, four at least have some Indian as well as white blood in their ethnic composition.

The teachers, more than any other professional group among the American Negroes, are representative of all that is best and most promising in the race. They are the men, somewhat superior in training and education, who are in intimate daily contact with the best minds among the youth of the race and by precept and example, endeavor to improve the intellectual and moral status of the race. The Negro teachers are, in general, persons of importance in the Negro group and enjoy a prestige which, aside from their professional influence, makes them leaders among the people. It is, moreover, comparatively easy to select from the great number of teachers the men and women who are most prominent and presumably most influential in matters concerning the welfare of the race.

Of the fifty-seven educational institutions listed in *The Negro Year Book* [39] under the head of *Universities and Colleges*, twenty-six at least have white men as presidents. Of the remaining thirty-one, the presidents of twenty-six are mulattoes; the presidents of three are black men. Whether the remaining two have white men, mulattoes, or black men as presidents was not determined. This list of Universi-

[39] 1914-1915, pp. 246-47.

ties and Colleges excluding the institutions with white men at their heads is as follows:

Allen University Columbia, S. C.	W. W. Beckett	mulatto
Arkansas Baptist College Little Rock, Ark.	Joseph A. Booker	black
Bennett College Greensboro, N. C.	J. E. Wallace	mulatto
Biddle University Charlotte, N. C.	H. L. McCrorey	mulatto
Campbell College Jackson, Miss.	W. T. Vernon	black
Central City College Macon, Ga.	William E. Holmes	mulatto
Central Texas College Waco, Texas	J. W. Strong	mulatto
Conroe College Conroe, Texas	David Abner	mulatto
Edward Waters College Jacksonville, Fla.	John A. Grigg	mulatto
Guadaloupe College Seguin, Texas	D. J. Hull	....
Houston College Houston, Texas	F. W. Gross	black
Jackson College Jackson, Miss.	Z. T. Hubert	mulatto
Kittrell College Kittrell, N. C.	C. G. O'Kelley	mulatto
Lampton College Alexandria, La.	M. M. Ponton	mulatto
Lane College Jackson, Tenn.	J. F. Lane	mulatto
Livingstone College Salisbury, N. C.	W. H. Goler	mulatto
Miles Memorial College Birmingham, Ala.	G. A. Payne	mulatto
Morehouse College Atlanta, Ga.	John Hope	mulatto
Morris Brown University Atlanta, Ga.	W. A. Fountain	mulatto

Payne University Selma, Ala.	H. E. Archer	mulatto
Philander-Smith College Little Rock, Ark.	J. M. Cox	mulatto
Roger Williams University Nashville, Tenn.	A. M. Townsend	mulatto
Samuel Huston College Austin, Texas	R. S. Lovingood	mulatto
Selma University Selma, Ala.	M. W. Gilbert	mulatto
Shorter College Argenta, Ark.	O. L. Moody	....
State University Louisville, Ky.	W. T. Amiger	mulatto
Va. Theol. Sem. & College Lynchburg, Va.	R. C. Woods	mulatto
University of West Tenn. Memphis, Tenn.	M. V. Lynk	mulatto
Western University Quindaro, Kansas	H. T. Kealing	mulatto
Wilberforce University Wilberforce, Ohio	W. S. Scarborough	mulatto
Wiley University Marshall, Texas	M. W. Dogan	mulatto

A number of these men have been mentioned in previous lists. Omitting these and the two whose ethnic composition is unknown, the new names are in sixteen cases of mulattoes and in one case that of a full-blooded Negro.

In the sixteen institutions for women,[40] the president or principal in all cases except two seems to be a white man or woman. Miss M. M. Bethune, a dark mulatto, is at the head of the Daytona Training School for Girls at Daytona, Florida. Miss Nannie H. Burroughs, a mulatto woman, is at the head of the National Training School for Women and Girls at Washington, D. C. The former institution enrolls about three hundred pupils; the latter, about one hundred.[41]

[40] *Negro Year Book*, 1914-1915, p. 248.
[41] *Ibid.*, p. 248.

The Negro and the Mulatto in Pursuits 267

The various schools of theology are for the most part conducted by white men. So far as known, those not conducted by white men are under the direction of mulattoes. In general, these schools of theology are in connection with one of the universities or colleges just listed.[42]

What is true of the theological schools and the institutions for women, is equally true of the professional schools of law,[43] medicine,[44] dentistry,[45] and pharmacy.[46] They are generally departments of the universities or colleges and, if not in charge of white men, seem in every case to be under the direction of men of mixed blood. It would seem that in no case is a black man in administrative charge of one of these schools.

The State Agricultural and Mechanical Colleges, on the other hand, are for the most part under the presidency of men of the Negro race. Of the seventeen such schools listed in *The Negro Year Book*,[47] one has a white president,[48] one a Negro president, and fourteen have mulatto presidents. Omitting the institution under the presidency of a white man, the list is as follows:

Agricultural and Industrial State Normal School Nashville, Tenn.	W. J. Hale	mulatto
Agr. and Mechan. College for the Colored Race Greensboro, N. C.	James B. Dudley	mulatto
Agricultural and Mechanical College for Negroes Normal, Ala.	W. S. Buchanan	mulatto

[42] *Ibid.*, pp. 248-49.
[43] *Ibid.*, p. 250.
[44] *Ibid.*, p. 250.
[45] *Ibid.*, p. 250.
[46] *Ibid.*, pp. 250-51.
[47] Issue for 1914-1915, pp. 251-52.
[48] Hampton Normal and Agricultural Institute, Hampton, Va.

Alcorn Agr. and Mechanical College Alcorn, Miss.	J. A. Martin	mulatto
Branch Normal College Pine Bluff, Ark.	F. T. Venegar	black
Colored Agricultural and Normal University Langston, Okla.	Inman E. Page	mulatto
Colored Normal, Industrial and Mechanical College Orangeburg, S. C.	R. S. Wilkinson	mulatto
Fla. Agr. and Mechan. College for Negroes Tallahassee, Fla.	Nathan B. Young	mulatto
Ga. St. Ind. College Savannah, Ga.	Richard R. Wright	Mandingo
Ky. Normal and Industrial Institute for Colored Frankfort, Ky.	G. P. Russell	mulatto
La. Agr. and Mechanical College Baton Rouge, La.	J. S. Clark	mulatto
Lincoln Institute Jefferson City, Mo.	B. F. Allen	mulatto
Md. Normal and Agricultural Institute Sandy Springs, Md.	G. H. C. Williams	mulatto
Prairie View State Normal and Industrial College Prairie View, Texas	E. L. Blackshear	mulatto
State College for Colored Students Dover, Del.	W. C. Jason	mulatto
West. Va. Colored Institute Institute, West Va.	Byrd Prillerman	mulatto

Three men in the above list have been previously mentioned in other connections. Omitting these, there is mentioned in this group thirteen new names, one of which is that of a pure-blooded Negro and twelve are names of men of mixed blood.

It may be objected, however, that, inasmuch as an administrative position in a college or a university is a political position, the presidents and principals of schools are not fairly representative of the educational leadership. In a sense, this is true. There exists everywhere among the rank and file of the race and among a large percentage of the more enlightened classes, a prejudice against admitting mulatto superiority and a conscious policy of advancing black men to conspicuous figure-head positions simply because of their color. Consequently, it may be well to look at the intellectual part of the teaching force as represented by the faculty membership.

Tuskegee Institute, as the largest and best known of the Negro schools, may be taken as an example. The present principal is a black man.[49] The school has a teaching force of approximately two hundred. Of this number, nine, none of whom are in high positions,[50] are Negroes who generally pass as full-bloods.[51] One hundred and eighty-four are persons of mixed blood.[52] Of the nine full-blooded Negroes, one is a woman and eight are men. Of the one hundred and

[49] R. R. Moton.
[50] "... Indeed, I saw no one in high position at Tuskegee who would not, with a very small lightening of hue, have been taken without question for a white man...." William Archer, *Thro Afro-America*, p. 108.
[51] G. W. Carver, Agriculture
John H. Palmer, Registrar
J. L. Whiting, Teacher of Mathematics
F. L. West, Shoemaking
R. S. Pompey, Assistant in Dairy Husbandry
W. A. Tate, Swine Raising
John W. Goiens, Clerk
Willie M. Hendley, Matron
W. M. Rakestraw, Negro Conference Agent
[52] This analysis is on the basis of the faculty listed in the *Annual Catalogue* for 1909-1910.

eighty-four mulattoes, one hundred and sixteen are men and sixty-eight are women.

From various miscellaneous sources, there was made a compilation of Negro teachers in various schools and colleges who are mentioned in the race literature as men of prominence and influence in the affairs of the race. After removing from this compilation the names of individuals included in other lists, there remained two hundred and sixty-three names. Again calling all black who are not obviously and noticeably of mixed blood and classifying the remainder as mulattoes there were found to be twenty-two black and two hundred and forty-one persons of mixed blood. Of those classified as black, six are men and sixteen are women. Of those classified as mulattoes one hundred and eighty-four are men and fifty-seven are women.

The thing that is true in respect to the teachers in the schools and colleges, is true also of the student body. According to *The Negro Year Book*,[53] the degree of Doctor of Philosophy has been conferred upon eleven Negroes by reputable Universities.[54] In all cases, with possibly one exception, the recipients were men of mixed blood. The list is as follows:

T. Nelson Baker	Yale 1903	black
Edward A. Bonchet	Yale 1876	mulatto
William L. Bulkley	Syracuse 1893	mulatto
J. R. L. Diggs	Ill. Wesleyan 1906	mulatto
W. E. B. DuBois	Harvard 1895	mulatto
George E. Haynes	Columbia 1912	mulatto
Lewis B. Moore	Pennsylvania 1896	mulatto
Pezavia O'Connell	Pennsylvania 1898	mulatto
C. H. Turner	Chicago 1907	mulatto
C. G. Woodson	Harvard 1912	mulatto
R. R. Wright, Jr.	Pennsylvania 1911	mulatto

[53] 1914-1915, p. 231.

[54] E. V. Just, a light mulatto, received the Ph.D. degree from the University of Chicago in 1916.

The Negro and the Mulatto in Pursuits 271

It has been pointed out already that the college graduates are for the most part individuals of mixed blood. Of the one hundred and fifty-seven pictured in certain copies of *The Crisis* examined, not above one-seventh can be classed as black even when all who are not conspicuously of mixed blood are placed in that category.

In Chicago, the Negroes for the most part are segregated within the boundaries of one high school district.[55] Consequently, most of the Negro high school students in the city attend the one school and constitute about twenty per cent of its total enrollment. Enquiry concerning the relative number of mulattoes and pure-blooded Negroes enrolled, disclosed the startling fact that every Negro student in attendance was of the mixed-blood class.[56]

To obtain further information along this line, letters were addressed to administrative officers or teachers in the principal Negro schools bearing the name of college or university. Information was received in regard to twenty-five of the leading schools. Generally the information was accompanied by the request that the name of the individual furnishing the information be not divulged. In most cases, the figures are based on estimation rather than on actual count. A tabulation of the data received gives the following:

BLACK AND MULATTO STUDENTS IN LEADING NEGRO SCHOOLS

	Enrolled	Mulatto	Black
Arkansas Baptist College Little Rock, Ark.	350	315	35
Atlanta University Atlanta, Ga.	430	409	21
Benedict College Columbia, S. C.	700	694	6

[55] Wendell Phillips.
[56] The date of this inquiry was 10-3-1916.

BLACK AND MULATTO STUDENTS IN LEADING NEGRO SCHOOLS
(*Continued*)

	Enrolled	Mulatto	Black
Chaflin University Orangeburg, S. C.	413	241	172
Ingleside Seminary Burkeville, Va.	126	93	33
Knoxville College Knoxville, Tenn.	400	300	100
Lane College Jackson, Tenn.	300	260	40
Lincoln University Lincoln Univ., Pa.	216	156	60
Livingstone College Salisbury, N. C.	289	231	58
Montgomery Industrial School Montgomery, Ala.	340	300	40
Morgan College Baltimore, Md.	312	312	0
National Training School for Women and Girls Washington, D. C.	100	67	33
Paine University Augusta, Ga.	219	182	37
Rust University Holly Springs, Miss.	260	234	26
Scotia Seminary Concord, N. C.	287	275	12
Selma University Selma, Ala.	483	323	160
Shaw University Raleigh, N. C.	485	395	90
Spelman Seminary Atlanta, Ga.	703	503	200
Straight University New Orleans, La.	555	421	134
Swift Memorial College Rogersville, Tenn.	205	137	68

BLACK AND MULATTO STUDENTS IN LEADING NEGRO SCHOOLS
(*Continued*)

	Enrolled	Mulatto	Black
Talladega College	71	67	4
Talladega, Ala.			
Tillosten College	250	190	60
Austin, Texas			
Walden University	765	695	70
Nashville, Tenn.			
Wilberforce University	450	394	56
Wilberforce, Ohio			
Wiley University	463	373	90
Marshall, Texas			
	9,172	7,567	1,605

The number of mulattoes to black Negroes in the student body of these schools stands thus, according to the information submitted, in the approximate ratio of five to one. This tabulation, however, can be taken as giving only an indication of the facts. In only two cases are the figures based on an actual inquiry. One of these investigations showed the entire student body to be mulatto; the other showed only six students out of a total of seven hundred who did not know of any mixture of blood. An accurate statement in the case of many of the other schools would reduce the number reported as full-blooded almost, if not quite, to the vanishing point and probably would reduce materially the proportion in the case of all. But the ratios as given may perhaps be taken as indicating the approximate numbers who are dark in color—say three-fourths or more Negro blood—and those who are so obviously of mixed blood as to permit of no question.

Throwing the data in regard to the teachers and school officials who are not elsewhere mentioned into tabular form we have the following:

	MEN			WOMEN			
	Black	Mul.	Total	Black	Mul.	Total	Totals
College Presidents	3	26	29	0	0	0	29
Women Principals	0	0	0	0	2	2	2
Pres. Agr. & Ind. Col.	1	15	16	0	0	0	16
Tuskegee Institute	8	116	124	1	68	69	193
Doctors of Philosophy	1	11	12	0	0	0	12
Miscellaneous	16	184	200	6	57	63	263
Totals	29	352	381	7	127	134	515
Names repeated	2	13	15	0	0	0	15
Corrected totals	27	339	366	7	127	134	500

The Negro preachers on the average are not a particularly superior class of men. As a rule, they are uneducated and frequently are profoundly ignorant.[57] Morally they are perhaps inferior to any other group of professional men among the Negroes.[58] But aside from training, or native ability, or character, they are a conspicuous and influential group. The ignorant and immoral preacher, just as the one of character and training, is a leader among his people. The church, through its preachers, does more perhaps than any other institution except the lodge, to modify and direct the thinking and the acting of the race. The preacher, then, regardless of his training or character, must be taken as representing leadership among the Negroes.

[57] Not one in ten has so much as a high-school education according to a writer in the *New York Age*. See issue of 10-7-1915. Daniels, speaking of the Boston Negro preachers, says that "most of them are ignorant and incompetent floaters and hangers-on . . ." John Daniels, *In Freedom's Birthplace*, p. 248.

[58] Daniels considers that over 25 per cent of the Boston preachers "are patently lax in their morals, and the majority is not free from more or less suspicion." *Ibid.*, p. 248. See, also, Archer, *Thro Afro-America*, p. 139, and C. H. Brough, "Work of the Commission of Southern Universities on the Race Question," *Atlantic Congress*, 1913, p. 362.

The Negro and the Mulatto in Pursuits 275

Many of the Negroes who gained prominence prior to the emancipation did so through their preaching. *The Negro Year Book* [59] gives a list with brief biographical sketches of these "noted Negro preachers" prior to the Civil War. The list contains the names of sixteen men and one woman. Tradition has it that five of these men were full-blooded Negroes; the evidence seems fairly conclusive that twelve of the number were men of mixed blood. Fifteen of the seventeen have been previously mentioned in other connections. The two additional men are Jack, or Uncle Jack, and Joseph Willis. Jack was an itinerant preacher in Virginia. "He was a full-blooded African and was licensed to preach in the Baptist Church." [60] Willis was a free Negro in South Carolina. He "organized the first Baptist Church west of the Mississippi." [61] He was, probably, a mulatto.

Among the present-day Negro clergy, the Bishops and the general officers of the principal religious denominations may perhaps be taken as typical of the Negro preacher at his best.

The Negro Year Book [62] gives the Bishops of the Colored Methodist Episcopal Church as follows:

R. A. Carter	Atlanta, Ga.	mulatto
N. C. Cleaves	Jackson, Tenn.	mulatto
Elias Cottrell	Holly Springs, Miss.	mulatto
L. H. Holsey	Atlanta, Ga.	mulatto
M. F. Jamison	Leigh, Tex.	mulatto
Isaac Lane	Jackson, Tenn.	mulatto
C. H. Phillips	Nashville, Tenn.	mulatto
G. W. Stewart	Birmingham, Ala.	mulatto
R. S. Williams	Augusta, Ga.	mulatto

[59] Issue for 1914–1915, pp. 170–76.
[60] *Negro Year Book*, 1914–1915, p. 174.
[61] *Ibid.*, p. 174.
[62] *Ibid.*, p. 179.

276 *The Mulatto in the United States*

The General Officers of the Colored Methodist Episcopal Church are given as follows: [63]

J. A. Bray	Birmingham, Ala.	mulatto
William Burrows	Memphis, Tenn.	....
A. R. Calhoun	Pine Bluff, Ark.	mulatto [64]
John W. Gilbert	Birmingham, Ala.	mulatto
J. A. Hamlett	Jackson, Tenn.	mulatto
J. C. Martin	Jackson, Tenn.	mulatto
J. H. Moore	Pine Bluff, Tenn.	mulatto
L. E. Rosser	Jackson, Tenn.	....
J. C. Stanton	Pittsobo, N. Car.	mulatto
J. R. Starks	Sedalia, Mo.	mulatto
R. S. Stout	Pine Bluff, Ark.	mulatto

The Bishops of the African Methodist Episcopal Church are as follows: [65]

W. D. Chappelle	Columbia, S. C.	mulatto
James M. Conner	Little Rock, Ark.	black [66]
L. J. Coppin	Philadelphia, Pa.	mulatto
J. S. Flipper	Atlanta, Ga.	mulatto
W. H. Heard	Philadelphia, Pa.	mulatto
John Hurst	Baltimore, Md.	mulatto
J. Albert Johnson	Philadelphia, Pa.	mulatto
Joshua M. Jones	Wilberforce, Ohio	mulatto
B. F. Lee	Wilberforce, Ohio	mulatto
H. B. Parks	Chicago, Ill.	mulatto and Indian
C. T. Shaffer	Chicago, Ill.	mulatto
C. S. Smith	Detroit, Mich.	mulatto
B. T. Tanner	Philadelphia, Pa.	mulatto
H. M. Turner	Atlanta, Ga.	mulatto
Evans Tyree	Nashville, Tenn.	black [67]

The list of general officers of the African Methodist Episcopal Church is as follows: [68]

[63] *Negro Year Book,* 1914-1915, p. 179.
[64] One correspondent called Calhoun a full-blood Negro.
[65] *Negro Year Book,* 1914-1915, p. 180.
[66] Conner is himself authority for this classification.
[67] Generally so considered.
[68] *Negro Year Book,* 1914-1915, p. 180.

The Negro and the Mulatto in Pursuits

G. W. Allen	Nashville, Tenn.	mulatto
Ira T. Bryant	Nashville, Tenn.	mulatto
J. C. Caldwell	Nashville, Tenn.	black [69]
J. R. Hawkins	Washington, D. C.	mulatto
A. S. Jackson	Waco, Texas	mulatto
J. T. Janifer	Chicago, Ill.	mulatto
J. I. Lowe	Philadelphia, Pa.	black
J. Frank McDonald	Kansas City, Mo.	mulatto
J. W. Rankin	New York City	mulatto [70]
R. C. Ransom	Philadelphia, Pa.	mulatto
B. F. Watson	Washington, D. C.	mulatto
R. R. Wright, Jr.	Philadelphia, Pa.	mulatto

The Bishops of the African Methodist Episcopal Zion Church are as follows: [71]

J. W. Alstor	Montgomery, Ala.	mulatto
G. L. Blackwell	Philadelphia, Pa.	mulatto [72]
J. S. Caldwell	Philadelphia, Pa.	mulatto
G. W. Clinton	Charlotte, N. C.	black
C. R. Harris	Salisbury, N. C.	mulatto
J. W. Hood	Fayetteville, N. C.	mulatto
Alexander Walters	New York City	mulatto
A. J. Warner	Charlotte, N. C.	black

Below are listed the general officers of the African Methodist Episcopal Zion Church: [73]

S. G. Atkins	Winston-Salem, N. C.	mulatto
Frank K. Bird [74]	Charlotte, N. C.	mulatto
Aaron Brown	Pensacola, Fla.	mulatto [75]
G. C. Clement	Charlotte, N. C.	mulatto

[69] This may be open to question. See photograph in *A. M. E. Church Review*, Jan. 1916, p. 182.

[70] All authorities agree in calling Rankin a mulatto. His photographs show a man of rather typical Negro features. See, for example, the *A. M. E. Church Review*, Jan. 1916, p. 177.

[71] *Negro Year Book*, 1914-1915, p. 181.

[72] One authority called Blackwell a full-blooded Negro.

[73] *Negro Year Book*, 1914-1915, p. 181.

[74] Deceased.

[75] A dark man.

278   *The Mulatto in the United States*

J. C. Dancy	Philadelphia, Pa.	mulatto
W. H. Goler	Salisbury, N. C.	mulatto
J. S. Jackson	Birmingham, Ala.	mulatto
L. W. Kyles	Mobile, Ala.	mulatto
M. D. Lee	Rock Hill, S. C.	mulatto [76]
John F. Moreland	Charlotte, N. C.	mulatto
T. W. Wallace	East St. Louis, Ill.	mulatto
J. W. Wood	Philadelphia, Pa.	mulatto

The only Bishop of the Methodist Episcopal Church is Isaac B. Scott [77] of Monrovia, Liberia. Scott is a mulatto.

The general officers of the Methodist Episcopal Church are as follows: [78]

J. N. C. Coggins	Topeka, Kan.	mulatto
M. S. Davage	New Orleans, La.	mulatto
Samuel D. Ferguson	Cape Palmas, West Africa	mulatto
C. C. Jacobs	Sumter, S. C.	mulatto
E. M. Jones	Montgomery, Ala.	mulatto
Robert E. Jones	New Orleans, La.	mulatto
W. W. Lucas	Atlanta, Ga.	mulatto
George W. Moore	Nashville, Tenn.	mulatto
I. G. Penn	Cincinnati, O.	mulatto
I. L. Thomas	Baltimore, Md.	mulatto
S. N. Vass	Raleigh, N. C.	mulatto
J. P. Wragg	Atlanta, Ga.	mulatto

The officers of the National Baptist Convention are as follows: [79]

S. W. Bacote	Kansas City, Mo.	mulatto
R. H. Boyd	Nashville, Tenn.	mulatto
Miss N. H. Burroughs	Washington, D. C.	mulatto
A. A. Cosey	Mound Bayou, Miss.	mulatto
S. E. Griggs	Memphis, Tenn.	mulatto
R. B. Hudson	Selma, Ala.	mulatto
E. W. D. Isaac	Nashville, Tenn.	mulatto

[76] One authority considered Lee a full-blood Negro.
[77] *Negro Year Book*, 1914-1915, p. 182.
[78] *Ibid.*, pp. 182-83.
[79] *Ibid.*, p. 182.

The Negro and the Mulatto in Pursuits

L. G. Jordan	Philadelphia, Pa.	mulatto
Robert Mitchell	Bowling Green, Ky.	mulatto
E. C. Morris	Helena, Ark.	mulatto
W. G. Parks	Philadelphia, Pa.	mulatto
A. J. Stokes	Montgomery, Ala.	mulatto

The list of officers of the New England Baptist Convention is as follows: [80]

W. A. Harrod, Cor. Sec'y	Connecticut	mulatto
W. Bishop Johnson, President	Washington, D. C.	mulatto
W. P. Lawrence, Vice-President	New Jersey	mulatto
Holland Powell, Rec. Sec.	New York City	mulatto
Robert D. Wynn, Treasurer	New Jersey	mulatto

A summary of the preachers and church officials thus far mentioned follows:

	Black	Mulatto	Unknown	Total
Noted early preachers	5	12	0	17
Bishops C. M. E. Church	0	9	0	9
Gen. Officers C. M. E. Church	0	9	2	11
Bishops A. M. Church	2	13	0	15
Gen. Officers A. M. E. Church	2	10	0	12
Bishops A. M. E. Z. Church	2	6	0	8
Gen. Officers A. M. E. Z. Church	0	12	0	12
Bishops M. E. Church	0	1	0	1
Gen. Officers M. E. Church	0	12	0	12
Officers Nat. Bap. Conv.	0	12	0	12
Officers New Eng. Bap. Conv.	0	5	0	5
Totals	11	101	2	114
Names repeated	6	51	0	57
Corrected totals	5	50	2	57

The two Negro officers [81] of the Episcopal Workers Among the Colored People are both mulattoes.[82] The Ne-

---

[80] *Ibid.*, p. 182.
[81] *Ibid.*, p. 182.
[82] H. B. Delaney, President, and G. F. Bragg, Secretary.

gro members of the Executive Committee of the International Sunday School Association already have appeared in other connections in the previous lists. The six Negro priests in the Catholic Church [83] so far as known are mulattoes. Father Augustus Tolton of Chicago, the first Negro Priest in the United States,[84] was a dark man of mixed blood. Father Raphard [85] of Philadelphia, the one Negro Priest in the Greek Catholic Church,[86] is a dark man, but not a full-blooded Negro. The Oblates of Providence,[87] a Catholic Sisterhood, was founded by Father Joubert, a Sulpician Priest, in 1829. The four young women who composed its original membership were mulattoes.[88] The founders, under the direction of Father Rousselon, of the Congregation of the Sisters of the Holy Family, were four "free women of color." All seem to have been mulattoes.[89] The Knights of Peter Klaver was founded by three white men and four Negroes. Three of the Negroes were mulattoes, the other of unknown ancestry. Among the International Secretaries of the Y. M. C. A. are six Negroes.[90] Four of these are known to be mulattoes and two are unknown.

Among these minor organizations of a religious or semi-religious sort, then, there is mentioned but one man of presumably pure Negro blood though there are several who are unknown.

A summary of the organizations previously mentioned is as follows:

[83] *Negro Year Book*, 1914-1915, p. 182.
[84] Died 1913.
[85] Rev. Robert Morgan.
[86] *Negro Year Book*, 1914-1915, pp. 183-84.
[87] *Ibid.*, p. 184.
[88] *Catholic Encyclopædia.*
[89] *Ibid.*
[90] *Negro Year Book*, 1914-1915, p. 187.

	Black	Mulatto	Unknown
Officers, Episcopal Workers among the C. P.	0	2	0
Afro-American Presbyterian Council	0	1	3
N. Members, Intern. S. S. Association	1	2	0
Negro Priests, Catholic Church	0	3	3
Negro Priest, Greek Catholic Church	0	1	0
Charter Members, Oblates of Providence	0	4	0
Charter Members, Sisters of the H. Family	0	4	0
Knights of Peter Claver	0	3	1
Y.M.C.A. International Secretaries	0	4	2
Totals	1	24	9

The foregoing lists of church bishops and other officials and functionaries would seem to be a fairly comprehensive and representative representation of the leadership among the various churches and church organizations. A suggestion as to the racial ancestry of the rank and file of the Negro ministry is given by the photographs in the books, magazines, and papers of the race. No class among the Negroes advertise themselves with more persistency and shamelessness than do the preachers. Almost every issue of almost every Negro publication has from one to a dozen or twenty photographic reproductions of preachers who have delivered, or are about to deliver, some masterpiece of pulpit oratory. The current publications of the race, therefore, furnished a rather rich assortment of Negro divines. A compilation of Negro preachers from these current publications and from the literature generally was made and classified as in preceding cases. The tabulation included in all four hundred and ninety-five names. Of these eight were of women and four hundred and eighty-seven were of men. Eighty-six of the men and three of the women were dark Negroes though not in all cases full-blooded. Four hundred and one of the men and five of the women were mulattoes.

This study has brought together the names of six hundred and forty-three members of the Negro ministry. Six hundred and thirty-five of them are men. Ninety-eight of these are of men who are, or for social purposes may be considered to be, full-blooded Negroes. Five hundred and twenty-six are men who are obviously of mixed blood. There are eight women, of whom three are black and five are mulattoes. Nine of the individuals listed are of unknown ancestry. The ratio of mulattoes to blacks among the educated and the better known members of the Negro ministry thus stands between five and six to one. When the names previously mentioned are removed there remain the names of five hundred and eighty persons. Ninety-five of these are considered as full-bloods and four hundred and eighty-five are known to be mulattoes. The ratio here stands slightly over five to one.

In literature, the Negro has as yet produced little, if anything, of permanent value. Much has been attempted and in many lines, but little, if any, first-class work has appeared so far.

In poetry and fiction, with rare exceptions, the Negroes who have published works have been men ashamed of their own race and who have assimilated but imperfectly the white man's civilization. The works have been imitations of the white man, an attempt to give artistic expression to a life that the writers did not share and but imperfectly understood. Ashamed of the black man, and frequently unacquainted with him, the Negro writers have been unable, or unwilling, to give expression to real Negro life. The effort has been made to present the Negro as a white man with a colored skin.[91] In fiction, as in life, the effort to make a white man of a Negro has failed. As a result of the failure on the part of the writers to understand either the Negroes or the white people, the Negro in literature has been a creation that is like neither the one nor the other. Aside from the slight work of Paul Laurence Dunbar, a frank interpretation of Negro life and Negro character by a Negro who knows his people and is not ashamed of them is yet to be written.

In other forms of writing, the Negro has been handicapped by a lack of training. Few Negroes are trained men. A dozen names include all the men of the race who have received a first-class university training. Even the number of college graduates is very small, and most of these are from so-called colleges or universities which are generally not prepared either in equipment or faculty to give a first-class high school training. The graduates of the best of these "Universities" at most are trained in two years of college work. Consequently little is to be expected of the Negro in a scholarly way—the surprise is that there has been anything. Of real scientific study by Negroes, there has been almost nothing; of first-class historical study, very little. On the Negro question, to the discussion of which the Negroes have contributed more in volume than to any other question, no Negro as yet has been able to give an unbiased, objective statement.

The only attempt worthy of any serious consideration, by a member of the race, to evaluate the writing of Negroes is that of G. B. Brawley. In a small volume published in

[91] The Negroes in fiction seem always to be mixed-bloods, octoroons or near-white, and only the rough and despicable and pitiable characters are black.

284   *The Mulatto in the United States*

1910,[92] he says [93] that he has attempted

> ... to test in the light of critical principles the literature so far produced by the Negro people of America, and to review their achievement in every department of the fine arts. Much that has been written on the Negro Problem, while it may have some value in the search for truth, is, from the standpoint of polite literature, absolutely worthless; so that comparatively little of the writing on this large subject has been considered.

He discusses the work of five writers of the race who have more or less claim to consideration as writers of literature. Two of these, Phyllis Wheatley Peters and Paul Laurence Dunbar, were pure-blooded Negroes. The other three: C. W. Chestnutt, W. E. B. DuBois and W. S. Braithwaite, are men of mixed blood. All of these persons have been mentioned in other connections in this or the preceding chapters.

These persons, according to Mr. Brawley, compose the list of Negroes who have produced anything in the way of literature. In a further chapter [94] on "Other Writers," whilst making no claim that they have produced any literature, he mentions nineteen other writers with more or less claim to note. Three of these seem to be white persons,[95] two to be black or nearly so, and fourteen to be persons of mixed blood. All these persons, with the exception of Inez C. Parker, an imitator of Dunbar, and Mrs. A. E. Johnson, the author of a Sunday School book, have been included in one or more of the preceding lists. Both these women seem to be mulattoes.

In this connection, perhaps, should be mentioned *The Jour-*

---
[92] *The Negro in Literature and Art.*
[93] Preface.
[94] Chapter VII, pp. 35-38.
[95] William C. Frost, H. B. Frissell and Lidia Marie Childs.

nal of Negro History, the first issue of which appeared in January, 1916. It is almost exclusively the work of white men and women and mulattoes. The Executive council and list of associate editors as announced in the first issue included the names of eleven Negroes, ten of whom are mulattoes. Omitting the names of white persons connected with the publication and also the names of Negroes included in other compilations, four names remain. These men are:

J. A. Bigham	Atlanta	mulatto
Walter Dyson	Washington	mulatto
A. D. Jackson	Chicago	mulatto
G. C. Wilkinson	Washington	mulatto

In a pamphlet reprinted from the Fourteenth Report of the Atlanta Conference, under the title *Negro Literature*, are mentioned some sixty-five names exclusive of the white persons included apparently by mistake. Forty-three of these names have been mentioned in other connections. Of the names remaining, twelve are of mulattoes and ten are names or pseudonyms of individuals concerning whom there is nothing known. Of the total number, five seem to have been black.[96] The others so far as known were mulattoes.

A further compilation of the names of Negro writers mentioned in the literature includes almost every Negro who has risen to any prominence.[97] But in relatively few cases does their best claim to distinction rest upon their published works. They have in most cases, therefore, been included in other divisions of this chapter or in the preceding chapters. There still remain, however, the names of forty-nine

---

[96] Wheatley, Dunbar, Sinclair, Miller and Crummell.

[97] "... A list of 2,200 negro authors was once compiled by the Library of Congress and investigation showed that with very few exceptions these Negro authors came from the mixed stock." C. A. Ellwood, *Sociology and Modern Social Problems*, p. 206.

individuals who have published works of more or less importance and who are not elsewhere mentioned. Adding to these the two mentioned by Brawley, four men on the Editorial Staff of *The Journal of Negro History* and twelve from the pamphlet on *Negro Literature*, we have a total of sixty-seven names of individuals whose reputations rest wholly or in part on their ability as literary artists, and who have not been mentioned elsewhere in these chapters. Fifty-nine of these are names of men, and eight are names of women. All the women are mulattoes. Four of the men are full-blooded Negroes, while the remaining fifty-five are mulattoes. Of the total sixty-seven, four are pure Negroes and sixty-three are of mixed ancestry—a ratio of nearly sixteen to one.

In the field of Negro journalism, new ventures are made almost every week and old ventures fail with almost equal frequency. Most of the journals have a short and not very prosperous existence. Of the thousands of such ventures since John B. Russwurm started *The Journal of Freedom* in 1827, there was, in 1914, a total of four hundred and fifty being published.[98]

A list was made of the more important of these journals and their editors taken as representing one phase of leadership. A goodly number of these men are editors only incidentally and have been mentioned in other connections. Eighty-eight, however, have not been included elsewhere. Of this list, seven—all mulattoes—are women. Eighty-one are men, twelve of whom are black men and sixty-nine, mulattoes. Of the eighty-eight, seventy-six are mulattoes and twelve are black—a ratio of something over six to one.

In the field of artistic and semi-artistic endeavor, the Negro is almost unrepresented. The few individuals who

[98] *Negro Year Book*, 1914-1915, p. 373.

have made success already have been mentioned in other connections. H. O. Tanner in painting and Meta Vaux Warrick [99] in sculpture are the most conspicuous examples of artistic success. Both these persons are of mixed blood; Tanner is light and Miss Warrick dark. E. M. Bannister, a New England mulatto, was perhaps the first Negro to succeed as an artist. Brawley [100] mentions William A. Harper, a mulatto of Chicago, as among the more promising of the younger painters. As sculptors of success or promise should be mentioned Edmonia Lewis and Bertina Lee. Both are mulattoes. In addition to these six names mentioned by Brawley as worthy of serious consideration, mention was made in the literature of five other painters of some note who have not been mentioned elsewhere. In each of these cases, the individuals are mulatto men. Five of the six names mentioned by Brawley have been mentioned elsewhere.

On the stage, in competition with the performers of the white race and playing before audiences of white people, very few Negroes have been able to make even a tolerable success. Whether due to a peculiarly difficult apprenticeship through which the Negro with stage ambitions must pass [101] or to a relative absence from the race of any histrionic ability of a high order,[102] the number of Negro stage celebrities is very small. The drama has had no considerable following among the race, and the productions depending upon race patronage for support generally have not been of a high order of merit. Brawley [103] names Ira

---

[99] Mrs. S. C. Fuller.

[100] *The Negro in Literature and Art*, p. 44.

[101] Brawley, *The Negro in Literature and Art*, p. 39.

[102] P. A. Bruce, "Race Segregation in the United States," *The Hibbert Journal*, Vol. 13, p. 877.

[103] *The Negro in Literature and Art*, pp. 39 ff.

Aldridge as the one Negro who succeeded in the legitimate drama. Aldridge was a mulatto. In musical comedy, he names Bert A. Williams and Aida Overton Walker as the most successful. Both are mulattoes.

From various other sources, a compilation was made of the more popular Negro players.[104] Excluding names previously mentioned, the list contained the names of one hundred and thirteen men and women with more or less claim to distinction. Fifty-nine of these names were of women, and fifty-four were of men. Four of the women and four of the men are dark-colored Negroes of approximately full blood. Fifty-five of the women and fifty of the men are obviously mulattoes, in a large per cent of cases very light-colored mulattoes. Of the total number, one hundred and thirteen, one hundred and five are mulattoes and eight are Negroes of pure or nearly pure blood, a ratio somewhat over thirteen to one. Most of the more talented and better-known Negro actors have been mentioned in other compilations, and so are excluded from this summary. They are in every case persons of mixed blood. To include them in the summary would slightly raise the proportion of mulattoes.

Several Negroes have been more or less justly famed for their ability as orators. Brawley [105] names Frederick Douglass, J. C. Price, and Booker T. Washington as the most conspicuous. Price was a black man; the other two were mulattoes. Oratory, however, is an abdominal rather than cerebral exercise, so there seemed no reason for making a special category to include men gifted in this way. Such men, in case they seemed to be of some consequence,

---

[104] A few readers not elsewhere mentioned are included in this compilation.

[105] *The Negro in Literature and Art*, pp. 41-42.

The Negro and the Mulatto in Pursuits 289

have been placed in other lists.

The plantation melodies were the Negro's first efforts in a musical way and his reputation for music rests for the most part upon this crude, primitive music. These melodies seem to be distinctly an American product—the African had no music—and largely a product of the latter days of slavery. They express in a simple way the joys and sorrows of an untutored people. It was in the rendition of this music that the Negro excelled. The words are of unknown origin and of no literary value, generally without sense. The plantation melodies were very close to wordless music.

Later the Negroes adopted and sometimes adapted the simple church hymns; they sometimes excel in the production of this sort of music. A relatively small and untrained congregation frequently is able to produce effective church music. The "coon songs" so far as composition was concerned were largely the work of white men. In "rag time" the Negro had a minor part though the assertion that it is a racial product has about the same claim to credence as has the claim that it is music.

However the Negro already has done something in a musical way. "There are scattered indications," says Kelly Miller,[106] "that the Negro possesses ambition and capacity for high-grade classical music." A few vocalists have appeared whose reputation rests upon something more than the prestige of color.[107] A small number have a musical education, several are successful writers of popular songs, while others have made some reputation as performers. But on the whole, it must be recognized that the Negro in music

[106] *Race Adjustment*, p. 241.

[107] There is a popular myth more or less current in both the races that the Negro is a natural musician and the audience finds in the most barbarous performance by Negro talent the thing for which their prepossessions call.

Aldridge rather than a reality.[108]

No critical study apparently has been made of the Negro musicians, and no compilation of any considerable number of the leading ones. Johnson [109] names seven composers, performers, or teachers of music. Brawley mentions twenty-four [110] who have made some success in a musical way. Elsewhere throughout the literature, other individuals of talent or promise are mentioned. From the various sources, a compilation was made without an attempt on the part of the present writer to evaluate the compositions, the vocal power, or the technical skill of the persons mentioned. The miscellaneous list thus secured included in all, exclusive of those mentioned elsewhere in this study, the names of one hundred and seventy-one musicians and composers. One hundred and ten of these are names of men and sixty-one are names of women. Of the men one hundred were mulattoes and ten were black men. Of the women, three were found to be black and fifty-eight to be mulattoes. Of the one hundred and seventy-one, one hundred and fifty-eight are mulattoes and thirteen are Negroes of full blood. This is on the basis of classing as full-blooded all individuals who are approximately so. This is a ratio of slightly over twelve to one.

A recapitulation of the various lists of men and women whose ethnic composition has been analyzed in this chapter shows a total of 2,129 names. Of these, 1,844 are names of men and 285 are names of women. The 1,844 men divide

[108] No account is here taken of the indecent songs as they are for the most part unwritten. For their number and variety and for the extent to which they are generally known by the children as well as by the men of the race, as well as for their minutely detailed vulgarity and lascivious indecency they are perhaps not equaled by the lewd literature of any people.

[109] James W. Johnson, "The Negro of To-day in Music," *Charities*, Vol. 15, pp. 58-59.

[110] *The Negro in Literature and Art*, pp. 53 ff.

THE RELATIVE SUCCESS OF THE NEGRO AND MULATTO IN SELECTED FIELDS OF ENDEAVOR

	Men			Women			Totals		
	Black	Mulatto	Total	Black	Mulatto	Total	Black	Mulatto	Total
Army and Navy	3	32	35	0	0	0	3	32	35
Politics	22	155	177	0	0	0	22	155	177
Invention	7	32	39	0	0	0	7	32	39
Medicine & Dentistry	15	231	246	1	7	8	16	238	254
Law	10	89	99	0	0	0	10	89	99
Education	27	339	366	7	127	134	34	466	500
Ministry	92	480	572	3	5	8	95	485	580
Literature	4	55	59	0	8	8	4	63	67
Newspapers	12	69	81	0	7	7	12	76	88
Art	0	6	6	0	0	0	0	6	6
Stage	4	50	54	4	55	59	8	105	113
Music	10	100	110	3	58	61	13	158	171
Totals	206	1638	1844	18	267	285	224	1905	2129

into 206 Negroes of pure or nearly pure blood and 1,638 of mixed blood. The 285 women divided into 18 pure and 267 of mixed blood. The total number of black Negroes is 224; the total number of mulattoes is 1,905. The ratio of mulattoes to Negroes of full blood is slightly more than eight and one-half to one. The relationship existing in the different groups is best shown in the tabulation (see p. 291).

CHAPTER XI

THE NEGRO AND THE MULATTO IN BUSINESS AND INDUSTRY

IN the business and economic world, the Negro has not as yet been able to enter into successful competition with other more energetic and commercially-minded peoples. The half-century since the Emancipation has seen the race crowded out, little by little, from many of the occupations in which it formerly held a virtual monopoly.

There are, however, numerous instances of Negroes who have made a success in a larger or smaller way in the business life of the community. Where the Negro has been sufficiently isolated from competition with other peoples, individuals have been able to build up successful business enterprises. In general, this has been by building up a business within the race, though there are numerous instances of successful business enterprises that do not depend entirely upon race patronage. In fact, the United States Census figures seem to bear out the statement [1] that there is little possibility of a Negro business man making a living solely from the patronage of the race. Two-thirds of his patronage must be white in order for him to succeed. The accuracy of such a generalization varies with the section of the country and the nature of the business enterprise.

Booker T. Washington has brought together a large group of inconspicuous Negroes who have made some de-

[1] *The Colored People of Chicago: An Investigation Made for the Juvenile Protective Association,* 1913.

gree of success in the business or industrial world.² The group includes farmers, grocers, barbers, and men of that general type. The men mentioned, then, are, for the most part, of no particular individual concern, but as a whole they represent what is best and most prosperous among the Negro middle-class group. To attempt to find the racial ancestry of many of these men would require an amount of work out of all proportion to the significance of the findings. No attempt has been made, therefore, to make the information concerning this group of men complete. Considerably over half the number, including all the more conspicuous ones, have been determined and the findings given for what they may be worth. There is no reason to believe that the relative ratios of blacks and mulattoes would be materially altered, if the data were brought to completeness.

The total list of men and women mentioned in the volume contains the names of some persons previously mentioned in other connections and a larger number, including nearly all of any real importance, will appear in a later and more representative list.³ The list of names, therefore, is not reproduced here, but a summary is given showing the distribution into mulattoes and full-blooded Negroes of those not elsewhere mentioned. This list includes the names of twenty-three women and one hundred and thirty-five men. Of the men, eleven seem to be black and one hundred and twenty-four are mulattoes. Twenty-two of the women are mulattoes and one seems to be a full-blooded Negress. Of the one hundred and fifty-eight individuals, twelve are classed as black and one hundred and forty-six are mulattoes. The ratio of mulattoes to blacks in this list is slightly

² *The Negro in Business.*
³ Pages 298 ff. below.

over twelve to one.

Of the successful business enterprises carried on by Negroes, the most conspicuous, perhaps, are the Negro banks. These institutions in most cases are small but their presidents form, if not the best, at least the most conspicuous, class of successful men in the Negro business world. They are the business aristocracy. For this reason, the group of Negro bankers has been selected for analysis into the black and mixed elements for the light that it may give in determining the relative success of these elements in the economic and commercial life of the community.

The Negro Year Book [4] gives the list of Negro banks and, where known, their presidents. The total list includes the names of fifty-eight separate institutions. In seven cases, the president of the institution is not given. Of the fifty-one presidents named, the ancestry of twelve was not determined. Of the thirty-nine institutions whose presidents are known, four seem to be black men and thirty-five mulattoes, a ratio of about nine to one. Seventeen of the fifty-one have been mentioned in other connections. Of the seventeen previously mentioned, all are mulattoes. The list of banks, omitting those whose presidents have been mentioned in other connections, is taken from the *Year Book*. There is here added information, where the facts are known, in regard to the ethnic composition of the presidents of the institutions.

Alabama Penny Saving and Loan Company Birmingham, Ala.	J. O. Diffay	mulatto
Alabama Savings Bank Selma, Ala.	Henry A. Boyd	mulatto
American Bank Chicago, Ill.	Wm. D. Neighbors	mulatto

[4] Issue of 1914-1915, pp. 311-13.

Anderson Tucker and Company, Bankers Jacksonville, Fla.	C. H. Anderson	black
Anniston Penny Savings Bank Anniston, Ala.	T. J. Jackson	mulatto
Atlanta State Savings Bank Atlanta, Ga.	J. O. Ross	mulatto
Bank Boley and Trust Company Boley, Okla.	Johnson	mulatto
Bank of Mound Bayou Mound Bayou, Miss.	J. W. Frances	mulatto
Brickhouse Savings Bank Hare Valley, Va.	B. T. Coard, Jr.	....
Crown Savings Bank Newport News, Va.	E. C. Brown	mulatto
Delta Penny Savings Bank Indianola, Miss.	W. A. Attaway	mulatto
Dime Bank Kinston, N. C.	T. B. Holloway	....
Enterprise Savings Bank Springfield, Ill.	John M. Mosby	....
Farmers' and Citizens' Savings Bank Palestine, Texas	E. M. Griggs	black
Farmers' and Mechanics' Bank Tyler, Texas	W. A. Redwine	....
Forsyth Savings and Trust Company Winston-Salem, N. C.	J. S. Hill	....
Fraternal Bank and Trust Company Fort Worth, Texas	W. H. McDonald, Cashier	....
Fraternal Savings Bank and Trust Company Memphis, Tenn.	J. J. Scott	mulatto
Houston Savings Bank Salisbury, Md.	Melvin J. Chisum	mulatto
Industrial Savings Bank Washington, D. C.	John W. Lewis	mulatto
Isaac Smith Trust Company Newbern, N. C.	Isaac H. Smith	black

Mechanics' Investment Co. Savannah,. Ga	A. L. Tucker	mulatto
Montgomery Penny Savings Bank Montgomery, Ala.	N. H. Alexander	mulatto
Mutual Aid and Banking Company Newbern, N. C.	J. P. Stanley	mulatto
Mutual Savings Bank Portsmouth, Va.	J. F. Riddick	....
Nickel Savings Bank Richmond, Va.	R. F. Taniel	....
Orgen Savings Bank Houston, Texas	F. L. Lights	black
Penny Savings Bank Columbus, Miss.	W. L. Mitchell	....
People's Bank and Trust Company Muskogee, Okla.	L. A. Bell	mulatto
People's Dime Savings Bank and Trust Co. Staunton, Va.	Samuel Lindsay	....
People's Savings Bank and Trust Company Nashville, Tenn.	J. M. Townsend	mulatto
Solvent Savings Bank and Trust Company Memphis, Tenn.	J. M. Sanford	mulatto
Sons and Daughters of Peace Penny, Nickel & Dime Savings Bank Newport News, Va.	S. A. Howell	....
Southern One Cent Savings Bank Waynesboro, Va.	D. W. Baker	....

This list includes the names of thirty-four men not heretofore mentioned. In twelve cases, the ancestry of these men was not determined. In the twenty-two remaining cases, four are names of men of full blood and eighteen are names of mulattoes.

Of the various organizations of Negro business men, the

298 The Mulatto in the United States

largest is the National Negro Business League. This organization was founded in 1900 and, with its subsidiary state organizations, numbers among its members almost every Negro of business or of professional importance anywhere in the country. The life members of the organization form the most representative list of successful and leading Negroes anywhere available. The officers elected for 1914-1915, the Executive Committee and the list of Life Members as given in the Report of the Fifteenth Annual Convention of the League have been arranged in alphabetical order and are here reproduced. To the lists as given in the report, is here added the fact of mixed or pure blood in all cases where the facts could be obtained.

The officers elected for 1914-1915 were as follows:

Booker T. Washington Tuskegee, Ala.	President	mulatto
Charles Banks Mound Bayou, Miss.	First Vice-President	black
J. E. Bush Little Rock, Ark.	Second Vice-President	mulatto
John M. Wright Topeka, Kansas	Third Vice-President	mulatto
P. J. Allston Boston, Mass.	Fourth Vice-President	mulatto
Charles H. Brooks Philadelphia, Pa.	Fifth Vice-President	mulatto
Emmett J. Scott Tuskegee, Alabama	Secretary	mulatto
Charles H. Anderson Jacksonville, Fla.	Treasurer	mulatto
F. H. Gilbert Brooklyn, N. Y.	Registrar	mulatto
R. C. Houston Fort Worth, Texas	Assistant Registrar	mulatto
William H. Davis Washington, D. C.	Official Stenographer	mulatto
E. A. Robinson Kansas City, Mo.	Sergeant at Arms	mulatto

Negro and Mulatto in Business and Industry

The executive committee was given as follows:

W. T. Andrews	Sumpter, S. C.	mulatto
J. B. Bell	Houston, Texas	mulatto
S. E. Courtney	Boston, Mass.	mulatto
S. G. Elbert	Wilmington, Del.	mulatto
T. J. Elliott	Muskogee, Okla.	mulatto and Indian
W. C. Gordon	St. Louis, Mo.	mulatto
George C. Hall	Chicago, Ill.	mulatto
T. H. Hayes	Memphis, Tenn.	mulatto
Algernon B. Jackson	Philadelphia, Pa.	mulatto
J. C. Jackson	Lexington, Ky.	mulatto
R. E. Jones	New Orleans, La.	mulatto
Scipio A. Jones	Little Rock, Ark.	mulatto
J. C. Napier, Chairman	Nashville, Tenn.	mulatto
Logan H. Stewart	Evansville, Ind.	mulatto

The list of life members was given as follows:

Cyrus Field Adams	Chicago, Ill.	mulatto
M. S. Alexander	Millard, La.	black
William Alexander	Little Rock, Ark.	mulatto
Phillip J. Allston	Boston, Mass.	mulatto
Charles W. Anderson	New York City	mulatto
W. T. Andrews	Sumter, S. C.	mulatto
W. A. Attaway	Greenville, Miss.	mulatto
Henry Avant	Helena, Ark.	mulatto
W. H. Ballard	Lexington, Ky.	mulatto
Charles Banks	Mound Bayou, Miss.	black
Mrs. Charles Banks	Mound Bayou, Miss.	mulatto
Charles T. Bass	Sullivan, Ind.	mulatto
Mme. I. B. Beale	West Newton, Mass.	mulatto
J. B. Bell	Houston, Texas	mulatto
E. C. Berry	Athens, Ohio	mulatto
Jesse Binga	Chicago, Ill.	mulatto
J. H. Blodgett	Jacksonville, Fla.	mulatto
James A. Bond	Williamsburg, Ky.	mulatto
Theophilus Bond	Madison, Ark.	mulatto
Eugene P. Booze	Mound Bayou, Miss.	mulatto
J. W. E. Bowen	Atlanta, Ga.	mulatto
H. A. Boyd	Nashville, Tenn.	mulatto
R. F. Boyd	Nashville, Tenn.	mulatto

R. H. Boyd	Nashville, Tenn.	mulatto
Charles H. Brooks	Philadelphia, Pa.	mulatto
W. H. Brooks	New York City	mulatto [a]
D. H. Brown	St. Augustine, Fla.	mulatto
Ira T. Bryant	Nashville, Tenn.	mulatto
Nannie H. Burroughs	Louisville, Ky.	mulatto
W. M. Burroughs	Memphis, Tenn.	....
Chester E. Bush	Little Rock, Ark.	mulatto
Mrs. Cora E. Bush	Little Rock, Ark.	mulatto
J. E. Bush	Little Rock, Ark.	mulatto
J. A. Cabaniss	Washington, D. C.	mulatto
R. C. Calhoun	Eatonville, Fla.	mulatto
T. J. Calloway	Washington, D. C.	mulatto
Richard Carroll	Columbia, S. C.	mulatto
James G. Carter	Tamatave, Madagascar	mulatto
H. M. Charles	New Orleans, La.	mulatto
R. R. Church	Memphis, Tenn.	mulatto
George W. Clinton	Charlotte, N. C.	black
J. A. Cobb	Washington, D. C.	mulatto
Walter L. Cohen	New Orleans, La.	mulatto
N. W. Collier	Jacksonville, Fla.	mulatto
Bishop E. Cottrell	Holly Springs, Miss.	mulatto
Samuel E. Courtney	Boston, Mass.	mulatto
John Covington	Houston, Texas	black
A. C. Cowan	Brooklyn, N. Y.	mulatto
W. Alexander Cox	Cambridge, Mass.	mulatto
W. W. Cox	Indianola, Miss.	mulatto
Mrs. Belle Davis	Indianapolis, Ind.	mulatto
Charles T. Davis	Council Bluffs, Iowa	mulatto
George W. Davis	Muskogee, Okla.	mulatto
Wm. H. Davis	Washington, D. C.	mulatto
A. C. Dungee	Montgomery, Ala.	mulatto
S. G. Elbert	Wilmington, Del.	mulatto
Mrs. S. G. Elbert	Wilmington, Del.	mulatto
T. J. Elliott	Muskogee, Okla.	mulatto [b]
J. Emanuel	New York City	black
Wm. P. Evans	Laurinburg, N. C.	mulatto
C. E. Ford	Buffalo, N. Y.	mulatto
G. W. Franklin	Chattanooga, Tenn.	black
S. A. Furniss	Indianapolis, Ind.	mulatto

[a] One authority calls Brooks a full-blood.
[b] A mixture of white, Negro and Creek Indian.

James E. Garner	New York City	mulatto
J. H. Garner	Columbia, S. C.	mulatto
George A. Gates	Nashville, Tenn.	.... [7]
Mifflin W. Gibbs	Little Rock, Ark.	mulatto
F. H. Gilbert	Brooklyn, N. Y.	mulatto
C. W. Gilliam	Okolona, Miss.	mulatto
W. L. Girideau	Jacksonville, Fla.	mulatto
James H. Gordon	Brooklyn, N. Y.	mulatto
W. C. Gordon	St. Louis, Mo.	mulatto
A. A. Graham	Pheobus, Va.	mulatto
Bishop Abraham Grant	Kansas City, Kan.	mulatto
F. A. Gray	Greenwood, Miss.	....
Miss Mary A. Gray	Paris, Ill.	mulatto
C. A. Groves	Edwardsville, Kan.	mulatto
J. G. Groves	Edwardsville, Kan.	mulatto
Walter P. Hall	Philadelphia, Pa.	mulatto
J. A. Hamlin	Raleigh, N. C.	mulatto
James R. Hamm	Boston, Mass.	mulatto
Mrs. Carol V. Harris	Chicago, Ill.	mulatto
Gilbert C. Harris	Boston, Mass.	mulatto
J. H. Harris	England, Ark.	mulatto
Henry A. Hatcher	Waterbury, Conn.	....
Allen Hatter	Little Rock, Ark.	mulatto
John R. Hawkins	Washington, D. C.	mulatto
Thomas H. Hayes	Memphis, Tenn.	mulatto
Wm. V. Hewitt	Muskogee, Okla.	....
John A. Hibbler	Little Rock, Ark.	mulatto
George Hoagland	Bloomington, Ill.	mulatto
W. H. Holtzclaw	Utica, Miss.	mulatto
A. C. Howard	New York City	mulatto
Alexander S. Howard	Washington, D. C.	mulatto
P. W. Howard	Jackson, Miss.	mulatto
S. P. Hurst	Clarksdale, Miss.	mulatto
G. M. Howell	Atlanta, Ga.	mulatto
J. C. Jackson	Lexington, Ky.	mulatto
E. B. Jefferson	Nashville, Tenn.	mulatto
A. N. Johnson	Nashville, Tenn.	mulatto
C. F. Johnson	Mobile, Ala.	mulatto
W. H. Johnson	Baynesville, Va.	mulatto
W. I. Johnson	Richmond, Va.	mulatto
E. P. Jones	Vicksburg, Miss.	mulatto

[7] One authority says that Gates is a white man.

Miss Hazel K. Jones	Little Rock, Ark.	mulatto
R. E. Jones	New Orleans, La.	mulatto
Scipio A. Jones	Little Rock, Ark.	mulatto
T. W. Jones	Topeka, Kansas	mulatto
L. G. Jordan	Louisville, Ky.	mulatto
Mrs. Mary Josenberger	Fort Smith, Ark.	mulatto
C. W. Keatts	Little Rock, Ark.	mulatto
W. A. Kennedy	Boley, Okla.	....
Willis A. Kersey	Indianapolis, Ind.	mulatto
H. W. Keys	Nashville, Tenn.	mulatto
H. H. King	Yazoo City, Miss.	mulatto
D. L. Knight	Louisville, Ky.	black [a]
J. A. Lankford	Jacksonville, Fla.	mulatto
J. R. Levy	Florence, S. C.	mulatto
A. L. Lewis	Jacksonville, Fla.	mulatto
J. H. Lewis	Boston, Mass.	mulatto
M. N. Lewis	Newport News, Va.	mulatto
Warren Logan	Tuskegee, Ala.	mulatto
W. L. Majors	St. Louis, Mo.	mulatto
M. C. B. Mason	Cincinnati, Ohio	black
U. G. Mason	Birmingham, Ala.	mulatto
Anthony McCarthy	New York City	mulatto
J. B. McCulloch	Muskogee, Okla.	mulatto
E. E. McDaniel	S. McAlester, Okla.	mulatto
J. D. McDuffy	Ocala, Fla.	mulatto
D. C. McGilbray	Boynton, Okla.	....
E. H. McKissack	Holly Springs, Miss.	mulatto
Moses McKissack	Nashville, Tenn.	....
Kelly Miller	Washington, D. C.	black
T. J. Minton	Philadelphia, Pa.	mulatto
I. T. Montgomery	Mound Bayou, Miss.	mulatto [b]
B. J. Morgan	Indianapolis, Ind.	mulatto
T. Clay Moore	Nashville, Tenn.	mulatto
E. C. Morris	Helena, Ark.	mulatto
R. R. Moton	Hampton, Va.	black
W. O. Murphy	Atlanta, Ga.	mulatto
J. C. Napier	Nashville, Tenn.	mulatto
Mrs. J. C. Napier	Nashville, Tenn.	mulatto
W. D. Neighbors	Chicago, Ill.	mulatto
Dave Nelson	Scotts, Ark.	mulatto

[a] Or nearly so.
[b] Often incorrectly called a full-blood Negro.

Negro and Mulatto in Business and Industry

F. M. Nesbitt	Memphis, Tenn.	....
Charles Nunn	Haughville, Ind.	black
Berry O'Kelly	Method, N. C.	mulatto
R. C. Owens	Los Angeles, Cal.	mulatto
Mrs. R. C. Owens	Los Angeles, Cal.	mulatto
Inman E. Page	Langston, Okla.	mulatto [10]
Thomas F. Parks	Louisville, Ky.	mulatto
C. H. Parrish	Louisville, Ky.	mulatto [11]
Fred D. Patterson	Greenfield, Ohio	mulatto
Spenser Patterson	St. Denis, Md.	mulatto
F. A. Payton, Jr.	New York City	mulatto
A. C. Perdue	Muskogee, Okla.	mulatto
E. S. Peters	Mobile, Ala.	mulatto
James T. Peterson	Mobile, Ala.	mulatto
W. R. Pettiford	Birmingham, Ala.	mulatto
L. M. Porter	Little Rock, Ark.	mulatto
Wm. M. Porter	Cincinnati, Ohio	mulatto
Troy Porter	Paris, Ill.	mulatto
Harry T. Pratt	Baltimore, Md.	mulatto
S. D. Redmond	Jackson, Miss.	mulatto
Mrs. Leila Walker Robinson	New York City	mulatto
W. E. Roberson	New Orleans, La.	mulatto
Wade C. Rollins	Prairie View, Texas	mulatto
J. O. Ross	Atlanta, Ga.	mulatto
P. C. Roundtree	Little Rock, Ark.	mulatto
H. A. Rucker	Atlanta, Ga.	mulatto
Mrs. Daisy Saffell	Shelbyville, Tenn.	mulatto
J. S. Sanford	Memphis, Tenn.	mulatto
M. P. Saunders	Brooklyn, N. Y.	mulatto
G. W. F. Sawner	Chandler, Okla.	mulatto
Mrs. Lena Sawner	Chandler, Okla.	mulatto
E. J. Sawyer	Bennettsville, S. C.	mulatto
W. A. Scott	Edwards, Miss.	mulatto
Scott, Wilkerson and Scott	Memphis, Tenn.	mulattoes
S. R. Scottron	Brooklyn, N. Y.	mulatto
T. J. Searcy	Memphis, Tenn.	....
G. W. Shadwell	Guthrie, Okla.	mulatto
H. C. Shepherd	Memphis, Tenn.	....
W. H. Sims	Muskogee, Okla.	mulatto
Alfred Smith	Oklahoma City, Okla.	mulatto

[10] One authority called Page a full-blood Negro.
[11] One authority considered Parrish a full-blood Negro.

Isaac H. Smith	New Bern, N. C.	black
R. L. Smith	Paris, Texas	mulatto
Wilford H. Smith	New York City	mulatto
C. C. Spaulding	Durham, S. C.	mulatto
J. B. Stephenson	Olive Branch, Miss.	....
J. M. Strauther	Greenville, Miss.	black
C. T. Taliaferro	Perry, Okla.	mulatto
H. A. Tandy	Lexington, Ky.	mulatto
Hilliard Taylor	Boley, Okla.	mulatto
Preston Taylor	Nashville, Tenn.	mulatto
Holmes Terrs	Holly Springs, Miss.	mulatto
Watt Terry	Brockton, Mass.	mulatto
James C. Thomas	New York City	mulatto
J. W. Thomas	Bennettsville, S. C.	black [12]
E. G. Tidrington	Indianapolis, Ind.	mulatto
John S. Trower	Germantown, Pa.	mulatto
E. D. Tucker	England, Ark.	....
Mrs. Pope Turnbo	St. Louis, Mo.	mulatto
M. W. Turner	Indianapolis, Ind.	mulatto
N. T. Velar	E. Pittsburg, Pa.	mulatto
W. T. Vernon	Washington, D. C.	black
Mrs. C. J. Walker	Indianapolis, Ind.	mulatto [13]
A. G. Wallace	Okmulgee, Okla.	mulatto
E. E. Ward	Columbus, Ohio	mulatto
B. T. Washington	Tuskegee, Ala.	mulatto
J. W. Washington	Marlin, Texas	mulatto
John L. Webb	Yazoo City, Miss.	mulatto
John W. Wells	Chicago, Ill.	....
Matthew Welmon	Brooklyn, N. Y.	....
R. W. Westberry	Sumter, S. C.	black
C. P. Williams	Chicago, Ill.	....
G. G. Williams	Philadelphia, Pa.	mulatto
J. A. Williams	Tampa, Fla.	black
J. S. Williams	Shreveport, La.	mulatto
S. Laing Williams	Chicago, Ill.	mulatto
E. D. Willis	Lexington, Ky.	mulatto
T. J. Wilson	Memphis, Tenn.	mulatto
T. J. Wilson, Jr.	New York City	mulatto
B. L. Windham	Birmingham, Ala.	mulatto
T. C. Windham	Birmingham, Ala.	mulatto

[12] Probably.

[13] One correspondent called Mrs. Walker full-blood.

L. Winter	Nashville, Tenn.	mulatto
S. W. Wood	Lonewa, La.	mulatto
John M. Wright	Topeka, Kan.	mulatto
John T. Writt	Pittsburg, Pa.	mulatto
Mrs. M. L. Young	Edwards, Miss.	mulatto

The list contains a total of two hundred and thirty-five separate names. Of these, eighteen are of women and two hundred and seventeen are of men. The eighteen women seem in every case to be mulattoes. Of the men, seventeen seem to be of pure blood, while in sixteen cases the facts were not discovered. In one hundred and eighty-four cases, the men are known to be mulattoes. Of the total two hundred and thirty-five, sixteen are not known, seventeen are black, and two hundred and two are mulattoes. The ratio of mulattoes to full-blooded Negroes stand approximately at twelve to one.

From all other sources, an additional compilation was made of successful business men. This list was independent of particular business connections. It contained real estate men, undertakers, farmers, merchants, and men in dozens of other lines of business. The criterion for selection was the known or alleged special success in an economic way. The list secured on this basis represents, naturally, a much more mixed group than either of the preceding. It includes, on the one hand, some of the most wealthy and highly successful Negroes in the country and, on the other, a goodly number whose success is only nominal. It is, however, believed to be a representative list of successful American Negro business men.

This compilation contained a total of three hundred and eighty-nine names. Twenty-eight of these were names of women and three hundred and sixty-one were names of men. The women were in every case mulattoes. Three hundred and six of the men were beyond question of mixed blood. Fifty-five were either full-blooded Negroes or very dark mulattoes. Of the total three hundred and eighty-nine, fifty-five were classed as full-blooded Negroes and three hundred and thirty-four as Negroes of mixed blood. The ratio of mulattoes to full-blooded Negroes stood, in this compilation, in the approximate ratio of six to one.

The analyses of the compilations of men and women successful in business and industry show, in each case, similar results, though with considerable variation between the different lists. Washington's *Negro in Business* contains the names of two hundred and twenty-six persons whose racial ancestry in one hundred and fifty-eight cases was determined. Twelve of these were classed as black and one hundred and forty-six were classed as mulattoes—a ratio of slightly over twelve to one. The thirty-nine bank presidents were in four cases classed as black and in thirty-five cases as mulattoes—a ratio of nearly nine to one. The two hundred and nineteen of the total two hundred and thirty-five officers and life-members of the National Negro Business League were found to be in seventeen cases black and in two hundred and two cases individuals of mixed blood—a ratio of approximately twelve to one. The list compiled from the miscellaneous sources contained the names of three hundred and eighty-nine persons, fifty-five of whom were found to be black and three hundred and thirty-four to be of mixed blood. This gives a ratio of slightly over six to one. The total number of names in the four compilations is eight hundred and twelve. Eighty-seven are classed as black and seven hundred and twenty-five as mulattoes, giving a ratio of something over eight to one.

The first three of these lists contain names elsewhere mentioned and in a few cases the same name is mentioned in more than one of the compilations. By removing all duplicates and all names of men who have been mentioned in other connections, the number of names is considerably reduced though the ratios found to obtain between the mulattoes and full-bloods is not materially altered. The ninety-eight names in Washington's *Negro in Business* not elsewhere mentioned are in seven cases names of black men and in ninety-one cases the names of mulattoes—a ratio of nearly thirteen to one. The twenty-two bank presidents not elsewhere mentioned are four black and eighteen mixed-bloods—a ratio of four and one-half to one. The one hundred and twenty-four names appearing exclusively in the list of life members of the National Negro Business League are in eight cases of black men and in one hundred and sixteen cases names of mulattoes—a ratio of fourteen and one-half to one. The list compiled from the miscellaneous sources contains no names elsewhere mentioned. In the four lists, there is a total of six hundred and thirty-three names not found in any other compilation. Seventy-four of these are of men who are classed as Negro, and five hundred and fifty-nine are classed as mixed-bloods. This is a ratio of somewhat under eight to one. It is thus seen that by removing from the lists the names of men of sufficient importance to be mentioned in more than one connection we have reduced slightly the ratio of mulattoes to Negroes of pure blood. A tabulation of the names appearing exclusively in these four lists follows:

	MEN			WOMEN			TOTALS		
	Black	Mul.	Total	Black	Mul.	Total	Black	Mul.	Totals
Negro in Business	6	70	76	1	21	22	7	91	98
Banks	4	18	22	0	0	0	4	18	22
N. N. B. League	8	101	109	0	15	15	8	116	124
Miscellaneous	55	306	361	0	28	28	55	334	389
Totals	73	495	568	1	64	65	74	559	633

There still remain a number of influential and important men and women of the Negro race who do not fall naturally into any of the preceding groups. There are individuals whose influence among their own people is shown by the positions to which they have been advanced in the various lodges and other strictly racial organizations. There are a considerable number of individuals who have gained some notoriety and exercise some influence on the thinking and acting of the members of the race through professional agitation. Other important and leading persons are engaged in Young Women's Christian Association and Young Men's Christian Association work and various other sorts of uplift work among the Negroes. There are prominent club women, church and social workers, professional and scientific men, newspaper men other than editors, farm demonstration agents, and various other successful and influential men and women who have not been heretofore mentioned.

These individuals were brought together in a final compilation of a more or less miscellaneous nature. The total number of names in this list was six hundred and thirty-five. Analysis of this list showed the names of five hundred men and one hundred and thirty-five women. Sixty-four of the men and five of the women were classed as black; though, here as elsewhere, this category contained the names of men who are by no means pure-blood Negroes. Four hundred and thirty-six of the men and one hundred and thirty of the women who were obviously and unmistakably of mixed-blood origin were classed as mulattoes. The classification of the six hundred and thirty-five names thus showed sixty-nine to be names of Negroes and five hundred and sixty-six to be names of mulattoes. This is a ratio of something over eight to one.

A combination of this list of names with the lists of busi-

Negro and Mulatto in Business and Industry 309

ness men previously tabulated, gives a total of 1268 names of men and women considered in this chapter and not elsewhere included. Of these, 1068 are names of men and 200 are names of women. The men classify as 137 black and 931 mulatto; the women, as 6 black and 194 mulatto. The total 1268 divide into 143 black and 1125 mulattoes—a ratio of nearly eight to one. Throwing the data into tabular form we have the following:

	Men			Women			Totals		
	Black	Mul.	Total	Black	Mul.	Total	Black	Mul.	Totals
Business men	73	495	568	1	64	65	74	559	633
Not classified	64	436	500	5	130	135	69	566	635
Totals	137	931	1068	6	194	200	143	1125	1268

The inquiry into the relative status of the mulattoes and the full-blooded Negroes in the United States has taken into consideration a total of 4267 men and women. Summaries showing the sex of the persons considered, as well as their distribution into mulattoes and Negroes of full-blood, have been given in connection with the various compilations. Recapitulations of these summaries have been given at the close of the chapters. Bringing together in a single table the partial findings separately arrived at, we have the following:

	Men			Women			Totals		
	Black	Mul.	Total	Black	Mul.	Total	Black	Mul.	Totals
Chapter VIII	14	205	219	2	22	24	16	227	243
Chapter IX	57	465	522	7	98	105	64	563	627
Chapter X	206	1638	1844	18	267	285	224	1905	2129
Chapter XI	137	931	1068	6	194	200	143	1125	1268
Totals	414	3239	3653	33	581	614	447	3820	4267

We are now in possession of a sufficient amount of detailed and verified data to express something more than mere opinion concerning the relative success of the Negro of pure and the Negro of mixed blood. The list of 4267 Negroes before us includes every member of the race who has made any marked success in life; it includes every member of the race mentioned in the histories as an individual of importance; it includes the men who are, in the opinion of some thirty-odd of the best informed Negroes in the country, the foremost living members of the race; it includes the names of those men and women who are, or have been, considered of enough importance to have received mention in the biographical and intimately personal accounts with which the literature of the Negroes abounds; it includes the names of those men who have attained any high civil or political position, or have made any particular reputation, either national or local, either within or without the race, in any professional or artistic pursuit; it includes the men who have made any particular success in business or industral lines; it includes, in short, as nearly complete and exhaustive a compilation as could be made of that relatively small group of Negroes who have risen superior to their fellows. It is believed that no Negro of first-class importance has failed to be included in some one of the various lists or summaries. It is believed that in very few cases individuals have been included whose accomplishments do not entitle them to some special mention when the criterion is, as here, unusual success within the Negro group. But granting that there may have been some few individuals omitted who should have been included and some few individuals included who should have been excluded—granting, that is, a reasonable margin of error—the list here brought together and analyzed contains the names of the members of the race who because of education, opportunity, special talent, superior native ability, exceptional industry or for other reason have made a noteworthy success in business, professional, artistic, or other lines of human endeavor and so have become the exceptional and the important men of the race. The list is composed of that group of men and women who compose the intellectual, social, and economic aristocracy of the Negro world.

In the analysis of this group of exceptional Negroes, effort was made to follow the same line of demarcation adopted by the Bureau of the Federal Census. In the group of full-blooded Negroes, were placed those who so consider themselves or are so considered by other Negroes who know them, as well as those individuals of undoubtedly pure Negro ancestry. In the group of mulattoes, were placed those individuals who claim to be mulattoes or who so pass in the communities in which they live, as well as those whose color and features show clearly and unmistakably that they are of a mixed racial origin. No individuals were placed in the mulatto group where the evidence of mixed ancestry did not appear to be conclusive. Many questionable and border-line cases were placed with and counted as Negroes of full blood. Consequently, in the full-blooded group, there are doubtless many individuals of mixed blood; probably a goodly percentage of them are in some degree of mixed ancestry; possibly there are in this so-called full-blooded group more individuals of mixed than of pure blood. A stricter definition of the terms *full-blooded* and *mixed-blood* would decrease the number classed as full-blooded and increase the mixed-blood group by an equal number. But in almost every case, the persons placed in the full-blooded group are dark-skinned individuals, of say three-fourths or more Negro blood, who consider themselves and pass among their fellows as Negroes of pure blood and, inasmuch as we are concerned with social conditions rather than with biological facts, there is no essential fallacy in so classing them.

Classified on this basis of distinction, 447 names fall into the full-blooded group and 3820 names fall into the group of mulattoes. The 614 women included in the total are in 33 cases classed as Negroes of full blood and in 581 cases as mulattoes. The ratio of mulattoes to black women thus stands at seventeen and six-tenths to one. The 3653 men are in 414 cases classed as Negroes of full blood and in 3239 cases as mulattoes. The ratio of mulattoes to black men thus stands at seven and eight-tenths to one.

The higher percentage of mulattoes among the list of women than among the list of men is due on the one hand to its being a smaller group and so representing a higher average of ability and, on the other hand, to the fact that many of the women owe their prominence to the fact that they are the wives of Negroes of importance. To the extent that the latter is the case, the preponderance of mulatto women is indicative of the tendency of marriage selection among the Negro males rather than of intellectual superiority among mulatto females. They are selected by the men because of their relative absence of color and owe their prominence to the fact of that selection.

In many of the lists, a very much higher ratio than eight and one-half to one was found to prevail. In a few large lists, generally of a miscellaneous sort, the ratio was somewhat lower. The rise above, or the fall below, this ratio of eight and one-half to one, it will have been noticed, depended in every compilation of any size upon the degree of importance and real distinction of the men whose names composed the list. The ratio of blacks to mulattoes, for example, in the compilation of doctors and dentists was approximately fifteen to one; while in the compilation of preachers, the ratio was approximately five to one. In the one case, membership in the profession implies at least a minimum of training and native ability; in the other case, membership in the profession implies the minimum of training and ability. The ratio of eight and one-half to one is thus the ratio prevailing between the mulattoes and blacks in a list of about four thousand of the most prominent individuals of the race. If the list be reduced in size by the elimination from it of the less important persons, the ratio of mulattoes to Negroes of pure blood would be correspondingly raised. By lowering the standard so as to include a yet larger number of persons in the compilation, the relative number of mulattoes to full-blooded Negroes would be correspondingly decreased. The ratio of eight and one-half to one, therefore, is the ratio prevailing when a standard is used, which draws the line between the mass of the race and the four thousand who are the race's foremost men.

The ratio of mulattoes to Negroes of full blood among the four thousand leaders of the race is eight and one-half to one. The ratio of blacks to mulattoes in the general Negro population, on the basis of the same definition of the terms, is approximately four to one. If the standard be raised so as to exclude the individuals of the lower degrees of ability and success, the proportion of mulattoes to Negroes of full blood will very greatly exceed the ratio of thirty-four to one. If the definition of full-blooded Negro be made to exclude those mixed-blood individuals of brown skin who pass as full-blooded Negroes, there will be a further increase, perhaps about a doubling, in the ratio of mulattoes to full-blooded Negroes among the leading men of the race. Stated in another way, the relative chances of a black child and a mulatto child, chosen at random from the members of the race, attaining to a position among the elite of the race are from thirty-four to fifty, or perhaps a hundred times as great in the case of the child of mixed blood. The relative chances of the mulatto child over the black child depend upon the standard of success called for and the degree of accuracy with which the terms *full-blooded* and *mixed-blood* are defined. On the basis accepted for the purposes of this study, the chances of the mulatto child developing into a leader of the race are thirty-four times as great as are the chances of a black child.

We have arrived then at the facts in regard to the assertion and the assumption which it was the purpose of this section to investigate. This assumption was that the Negro people in America have produced as many superior individuals of pure Negro blood as superior individuals of mixed blood.[14] The investigation has shown that the assertion is unsupported by the slightest basis of fact. Not even by accepting the loosest possible definition of terms, can it be made to appear that the full-blooded group even approaches within a measurable distance of the mixed-blood group in the production of men even slightly superior to the racial average. The full-blooded Negro group has not produced as many superior men as has the mulatto group. According to the strictness or the looseness of the definition of full-blooded Negro that is used, and the high or low degree of superiority that is accepted as the test, the twenty per cent of mixed-bloods among the American Negroes have produced eighty-five per cent or upwards of the race's superior men.

[14] See p. 186 above.

CHAPTER XII

THE RÔLE OF THE MULATTO IN THE INTER-RACIAL SITUATION

THE rôle that a mixed-blood race plays in an interracial situation in which it is placed is dependent for the most part on facts and forces outside the race itself and over which its members are able to exercise little or no control. Their ambition is much the same everywhere; their opportunity to realize their ambition varies with different social situations. The part they play in a social situation is dependent upon the attitude of the dominant group which, in turn, is largely dependent upon the exigencies of the general social situation.

The desire of the mixed-blood man is always and everywhere to be a white man; to be classed with and become a part of the superior race. The ideal—the center of gravity—of the hybrid group is outside itself. The ideal of beauty, of success, of all that is good and desirable is typified by the superior race. The ambition of the man of mixed-blood is to be identified with the superior group; to share its life, its work, and its civilization. Certain mixed-blood groups, as groups, have been able partly to realize this ambition. In individual and exceptional cases, persons of mixed-blood are able in most urban communities to escape from their group and pass as members of the advanced race. Everywhere, were it possible, the mixed-blood group would break with their darker relatives, hide their relationship to them, and, through marital relations, obliterate from their offspring the physical characteristics which mark them as members of a backward and despised race. Where this may not be, where an intolerable racial consciousness on the part of the superior race assigns individuals of all degrees of intermixture and of all stages of cultural advancement to the status of the backward race, the individuals of mixed ancestry tend to form a separate caste and to approach as near as may be to an equality with the superior group.

There would seem to be no exception to this among groups of mixed-bloods anywhere. The Eurasians despise the Indian, separate themselves from him and endeavor to approach, in habits, customs, and manner of life, the dominant British group.[1] They bitterly resent a special racial designation which sets them off from the English; they claim to be "European" and demand that they be so classed and recognized.[2] Among the Eskimos of the Greenland West Coast, the native's social standing is fixed according to his degree of approximation to the characteristic features of his Danish superiors.[3] The lighter the individual's color, the more eligible he is as a matrimonial possibility. The upper strata of Jamaica's "coloured" population separate themselves from the other mulattoes, call themselves "white," advocate intermarriage and, opportunity presenting, practice it.[4] The *metis* of Brazil draw a more or less rigid social

---

[1] Mary Helen Lee, *The Eurasian: A Social Problem*, pp. 12-13.
[2] J. Smith, *Ten Years in Burma*, p. 117. Lee, *The Eurasian*, p. 14.
[3] See p. 32 f. above.
[4] Davenport shows that among the hybrid population of Jamaica and Bermuda there is a marriage selection against the dark males. They have less opportunity to become husbands of light-colored women than do light-colored males and hence they have a smaller chance of becoming fathers. This selection, he thinks, must have a real effect, in successive generations, in causing the hybrids to become lighter. C. B. Davenport, *Heredity of Skin Color*, pp. 27 ff. See, also, William Thorp,

color line against the more highly colored groups and endeavor to form such matrimonial unions as will, they hope, bring their offspring yet closer to the white type.[5] The Spanish half-breeds everywhere show a similar tendency. "Every one wishes to be reckoned as a white man."[6] The mixed-breed Indians in the United States tend to intermarry among themselves and not with the full-bloods.[7] In the United States almost every Negro of prominence from Frederick Douglass to Jack Johnson has married a white woman or a light-colored mulatto.[8]

There is no intention here to criticize the mulattoes or

"How Jamaica Solves the Negro Problem," *World's Work*, Vol. 8, p. 4912; and Charles K. Needham, "A Comparison of Some Conditions in Jamaica with those in the United States," *Journal of Race Development*, Vol. 4, pp. 189-203.

[5] Jean Baptiste de Lacerda, "The *Metis* or Half Breeds of Brazil," *Inter-Racial Problems*, p. 382.

[6] James Bryce, *South America*, p. 460. E. A. Ross, *South of Panama*, p. 168.

[7] About four-fifths of the 88,030 persons of mixed Indian and white blood are one-half or more than one-half white. *Indian Population in the United States and Alaska*, United States Census, 1910, Supplement 1915, p. 35.

[8] ". . . Whereas we do not put our individual stamp of approval on Johnson marrying a white woman . . . but we still point to the many notable cases of black men who have married white women and the multitude of prominent colored individuals who barely miss committing the heinous crime by invariably marrying the near-white women of their race. What is so commonly practiced by the higher ups in every community should not be so highly censurable in Mr. Johnson's action simply because his matrimonial fitness largely looms up to the colored woman from a standpoint of financial healthiness of purse." C. A. Stokes, *Kansas City Sun*, a Negro paper, 4-3-1915. See, also, W. H. Thomas, *The American Negro*, p. 408; Maurice S. Evans, *Black and White in the Southern States*, p. 33; R. W. Shufeldt, *The Negro: A Menace to American Civilization*, p. 196; Ray Stannard Baker, "The Tragedy of the Mulatto," *American Magazine*, Vol. 65, pp. 582-98; Bert Williams as quoted in the *Chicago Defender*, 12-26-1914.

other men of mixed blood; quite the contrary. To recognize their desire to be white, their ambition to associate themselves through marriage or otherwise with the white race, is but to recognize their ability to appreciate the superior culture of the white group.[9] An opposite tendency on their part would go far towards establishing the thesis of the congenital inability of the lower group to assimilate white civilization. It would show a deliberate preference on their part for the inferior in the presence of the superior.

In contrast to the social ambition of the mixed-blood group, racial antipathy on the part of the dominant group is everywhere present.[10] Actual social equality between divergent racial groups in a population is found nowhere. Whether it be right or wrong, natural or artificial, this caste feeling exists and is always a factor in the racial situation. The way in which it manifests itself, varies with the people in contact and the conditions of their association. It may find its expression in a good-natured tolerance of the shortcomings of an inferior group; it may show itself as contempt for a weak and backward race; it may show itself as disgust at the strange manners and customs of a degraded people; it may be expressed as an intense and bitter hatred for the opposite race; it may take any one of a great number of forms; but it is nowhere wholly absent. In general, the wider the difference in physical and cultural traits between the two races in contact, the more intense and

[9] "The fact that it is always the lighter race that puts the taboo on the colored, and that the latter is everywhere eager to mix with the whites, is only an evidence of the general trend of choice towards the higher efficiency of the white race." U. G. Weatherly, "A World-Wide Color Line," *Popular Science Monthly*, Vol. 79, pp. 474-86.

[10] B. L. Putnam Weale, "The Conflict of Color," *World's Work*, Vol. 19, pp. 12327-29.

bitter is the antipathetic feeling between them.[11] It is more intense between the North Europeans and the blacks than between any other two races. It is usually, though not always, less marked between the Mediterranean races and the primitive peoples of America than between any other culture and nature peoples who have come into contact with each other.[12] The number of members of the lower race in the social situation is also a factor conditioning the feeling that their presence arouses. A few individuals of a divergent type may excite interest and curiosity; they may even enjoy a prestige simply by virtue of their unlikeness. But if present in greater numbers and especially if their presence is felt to constitute a menace to the superior culture, the feeling against them may rise to a pitch of fanatical barbarism. Political conditions may be such as to compel the disavowal of this race prejudice, business reasons may counsel its concealment, individual isolation from racial contact may even prevent its rising above the threshold of consciousness; but consciously or subconsciously it is an ever-present and active force wherever two races are in contact.

It is the desire for social equality on the part of the mixed-blood group in conflict with the caste feeling of superiority on the part of the dominant group which furnishes the key to an understanding of the place that the mixed-blood man occupies and the rôle which he plays in different racial situations. These are the factors which are always present and operating wherever a mixed-blood

[11] James Bryce, *The Relation of Advanced and Backward Races*, pp. 18-19.
[12] However, the Castilian Spaniards in Spanish America gave an exhibition of caste feeling and of contempt for inferior peoples perhaps nowhere else equaled in colonial history.

race has appeared between two groups distinct in appearance and divergent in culture, occupying the same territory in anything like equal numbers.

It is the conflict of these two factors which determines the rôle of the mulatto or other hybrid population. As a consequence of the variability of the factors among different racial groups and of their intensification, modification or disguisement in conformity to the peculiar needs of the particular situation, the mixed-blood populations are found to play quite different rôles in different inter-racial situations. They may be allowed to identify themselves with, and to become an integral part of, the culturally superior group or race. They may occupy a place apart, form an outcast group with a social status inferior to that of either of the parent races. They may be a connecting link between the white and the colored elements in the population. They may be used as a buffer between the extreme racial types in the community. They may identify themselves with, and become the leaders of, the lower race of the population. There may also be various combinations of these rôles and numerous transitional stages from one to another.

Where the hybrid race has been granted the opportunity, it has identified itself with the advanced group. The mixed-blood race of white, Indian, and Negro ancestry in Brazil affords perhaps the best illustration of this tendency.

The social advance of the *metis* began during the regime of slavery. "As they were more active and intelligent than the blacks, they soon made their way into the homes and were occupied in domestic service. Many of them won the esteem of their masters and those about them. Some of them, giving proof of real intelligence and devotion to their employers, were, from a feeling of gratitude, emancipated by the latter and were given the rudiments of an artistic education. . . ." [13] Many of those who were freed continued to live under the same roof with their former masters and their advance continued "in accordance with the laws of intellectual selection." [14]

At the time of the Emancipation,[15] the separation that already existed between the *metis* on the one hand and the Negroes and Indians on the other began to widen.[16] The *metis*, who were already found for the most part in the towns, became more exclusively an urban population. The class differences that had been accentuated for political purposes among the lower classes [17] gave them a profound "contempt for productive employments." They imitated the classes above them, ceased to labor, and formed a pseudo-leisure class.[18]

The Negroes from the moment of their emancipation became enamored of the leisure life. Neither they nor the Indians would longer engage in laborious occupations with any degree of regularity.[19] The Negroes began to withdraw from the centers of civilization and to find more congenial associates among the Indians of the interior with

[13] Lacerda, *Inter-Racial Problems*, p. 379. See, also, Sir Harry H. Johnston, *The Negro in the New World*, p. 99.

[14] Lacerda, *Inter-Racial Problems*, p. 379.

[15] 1888.

[16] The importation of slaves continued in Brazil to almost the date of emancipation. Over sixty thousand were imported in 1848. T. C. Dawson, *The South American Republics*, Part 1, p. 457.

[17] A. G. Keller, *Colonization*, p. 313.

[18] "But the mestizo runs to oratory and politics; not to labor." W. H. Koebel, *The South Americans*, p 97.

[19] ". . . the efforts which have been made in Brazil to attract the Indian or the mixed Indian and Negro population to the mines have not. . . . on account of the indolent nature of the colored inhabitants." Sir Charles W. Dilke, "Forced and Indentured Labor in South America." *Nationalities and Subject Races*, p. 106.

"The negro, no longer a slave but a free and occasionally a some-

whom they readily intermixed and into whose ranks they tended to disappear.[20]

At the time of the Revolution and the establishment of Brazilian independence, the mixed-blood group was sufficiently numerous and powerful to compel a recognition of social equality [21] and secure an equal place in the affairs of the government.[22] Consequently, the mixed-bloods came into closer contact with the culture group, while the gap between the mixed-bloods and the Negro-Indian group widened.[23] At the present time, the *metis* are sloughing off more and more the customs and habits of the colored races and conforming more closely to the manners of life of the white group. By marriage selection, they endeavor to make their children more like the Portuguese and less like the members of the lower groups. Economic and professional success, or the achievement of political position admits them to the lighter grades of Brazilian society. Poverty, atavism, or failure may throw individual members into

---

what arrogant person, works only when he feels inclined." Koebel, *The South Americans*, pp. 92-93.

". . . owing to the large proportion of negro blood among the working classes and the luxurious vegetation by means of which life can be at least supported with a minimum of effort, the people are inclined to be indolent. . . ." The *South American Year Book*, 1915, p. 216.

[20] Lacerda, *Inter-Racial Problems*, p. 381. Johnston, *The Negro in the New World*, p. 100 f. n.

It is to be remembered that conditions differ very radically in North and South Brazil. The great bulk of the Negro population is in the tropical regions of the North. Between the North and South Brazil "There is very little in common save the language." Koebel, *The South Americans*, p. 9. "So mixed is the blood of the lower classes that it is very difficult to tell who or what many people are, . . ." *South American Year Book*, p. 216.

[21] All races and classes are recognized by the constitution as equal.

[22] Lacerda, *Inter-Racial Problems*, p. 381.

[23] *Ibid.*, p. 382.

the lower groups between which and the mixed-blood group there is coming to exist the same impassable barrier which in the United States, Jamaica, and South Africa exists between the whites and the mulattoes.

> Of course in general mode of life, social customs, etc., the educated coloured people of Brazil are scarcely distinguishable from the Portuguese middle or upper classes, according to their means and social status. The peasants, however, away from the towns lead a more African existence, and except that the house or hut may be a little superior to the average negro home in Africa, manners and customs in domesticity are little changed from the standard of the Gold Coast or Dahomey—not a very low standard, by the by.[24]

The mixed-bloods are, therefore, for all essential purposes, a part of the advanced group, and tend to become more and more so. They have considerable influence in the governmental affairs of the country. All offices and honors are open to them. In the solution of the racial problem, so far as the above is true, they simply have no part. They have left the race, escaped from it, and by every means in their power endeavor to conceal and obliterate their former connection with and relationship to the primitive group.[25]

[24] Johnston, *The Negro in the New World*, p. 105.
[25] The idea that the Brazilian Negro is being absorbed into the white race and transformed into a white man without essentially changing the physical type of the population is hardly to be taken seriously. It represents a "hope and the belief" rather than a rational judgment. Mr. Roosevelt says that the men and women "with whom I closely associated were in the great majority of cases pure white, save in the comparatively rare instances where they had a dash of Indian blood"; that the men and women of high social position are as unmixed as the corresponding classes in Paris or Rome, and that they will continue to

> ... He is now a "Homem Brazileiro," and the word negro, even when applied to one of pure negro race, has come to be used only as a term of abuse, which may be made still further offensive by supplementing it with the words "de Africa." This has come to be one of the most offensive terms one can apply to a Brazilian citizen, even though he be of unmixed negro descent. If you must discriminate as to colour in conversation, you speak of a "preto." [26]

Under other conditions, the bastard race may be the connecting link which holds together the divergent racial and cultural elements in a population. This seems to be the rôle of the mixed-blood group where they are a numerically important part of the population, and where there is a relatively weak sense of nationality on the part of the white group. Stated in other words, it is their rôle in those interracial situations where there is a more or less rapid amalgamation in process between the divergent elements of the

---

be pure white; that the classes immediately below have absorbed and will continue to receive a small amount of Negro blood while in "the ordinary people" the absorption of Negro blood will be "large enough to make a slight difference in the type." And finally he quotes a Brazilian "statesman" to the effect that the Negro is disappearing by absorption into the white race and "his blood will remain as an appreciable, but in no way a dominant, element in perhaps a third of our people, while the remaining two-thirds will be pure whites." When it is remembered that an eighth and frequently a sixteenth or even less of Negro blood in a Negro-White cross is sufficient to "make a slight difference in the type" it is readily seen that, even if there should be no further increase in Negro blood, the population of the country will need to be increased by from one hundred and fifty to two hundred million white persons in order that the present ten million Negroes and mulattoes may be absorbed into the lower third of the population without producing more than a slight change in the type. The utterances of Mr. Roosevelt are often taken seriously. See T. R. Roosevelt, "Brazil and the Negro," *Outlook*, Vol. 106, pp. 409-11.

[26] Johnston, *The Negro in the New World*, p. 100.

population. It is the part played by the mixed-blood group in Cuba, in many parts of Spanish America, and in certain regions of Brazil.

In Cuba, the mulatto occupies much the position of a connecting link between the pure-bred Spaniard on the one hand and the full-blood Negro on the other. There is no sharp break between the whites and the mulattoes, nor between the mulattoes and the Negroes. The different shades of the hybrid group serve to connect the opposing cultural and physical types. They grade almost imperceptibly into the whites above them and into the blacks below them. The color line, in the sense in which that phrase is understood in the United States, Jamaica, and South Africa, is neither hard nor fast [27] and the mulatto is free to associate and to intermarry with the members of the white group.[28] In proportion to his success in life and his approximation to the Spanish cast of countenance, he is able to get himself accepted into the less exclusive grades of white or near-white society.[29] All this does not imply any lack of prejudice or caste feeling on the part of the Spaniards. Caste feeling does not center at any one point; it is diffused throughout the population.[30] Color is a badge of inferi-

[27] "Yet the Negro is losing ground, politically and socially, and unless he is content with his present status of farmer, laborer, petty tradesman, minor employee, and domestic servant, there will arise a 'colour question' here as in the United States." Johnston, *The Negro in the New World*, p. 60.

[28] The one thing that makes the relations of the races more friendlly in Cuba than in the United States is that there their desire to mix with the whites is granted. R. L. Bullard, "How Cubans Differ from Us." *North American Review*, Vol. 186, pp. 416-21. Note particularly p. 417.

[29] R. L. Bullard, "The Cuban Negro," *North American Review*, Vol. 184, p. 624.

[30] *Ibid.*, p. 628.

ority.[31] The men at the top are white; the men at the bottom are black.[32] Every man between is envious of the colors lighter than himself and contemptuous of those more highly colored.

The racial situation on the mainland is not markedly different. The mixed-blood race stands, industrially, politically and socially, between the white on the one hand and native on the other. Except where Negro blood is present, there is generally no sharp breach between the mixed-blood group and the white race and no definite breach between the mixed-blood group and the mother race. The mixed-bloods envy the white and endeavor to marry into the white or near-white society. In proportion to the difference in their social status, they despise the Indian and the Negro. The mixed-blood group, however, ranges in appearance from the near-white to the near-Indian type and so forms a physiological tie between the mixed-white and white group and the Negro and Indian group.

In general, the rôle of the mixed-blood individuals in Spanish America seems to be that of a connecting link between the extremes of the population. It is their part to mix with the whites and the blacks and to serve as a tie between the two. Racial amalgamation goes on between the whites and the mixed-bloods, and between the mixed-bloods and the Natives. The hybrid population is increased by both unions as well as by mixture among themselves, and the population approaches more and more to that of an exclusively hybrid one.[33]

[31] Bullard, *North American Review*, Vol. 184, p. 629.

[32] Many of the Negroes are no further advanced than those in the Congo. William Inglis, "The Future of Cuba," the *North American Review*, Vol. 183, pp. 1037-40. Note especially p. 1039.

[33] In some of the more advanced states it seems already to have reached this stage. Chile has, more than most South American coun-

The final outcome of these racial arrangements is dependent simply upon the relative numbers of the racial groups in the population. Where the hybrid is the numerically dominant group, as in Mexico,[34] it represents the probable future type [35] of the country's population.[36] Where the white group is the more numerous and especially where it is being constantly reinforced by immigration, as is the case of Southern Brazil, the hybrid group tends to approximate more and more the white type,[37] and a single color line to separate the mixed-white group from the mixed-Indian and black groups. Where the native group predominates and where there is no appreciable immigration and no effective caste feeling on the part of the mixed or superior groups to save them from a further infusion of native blood, the population is gradually reverting, in appearance and civilization, to the Indian type. The racial problem in the Spanish American countries finds its expression in periodical revolutions and a more or less chronic state of

tries, been able to draw the line between the whites and the various grades of pure- and mixed-blood natives below them. Keller, *Colonization*, p. 317. Bryce says "there are no longer any pure Indians" and that most of the aristocracy have remained pure white. *South America*, p. 232. See, also, p. 478.

[34] Seventy-five per cent mixed; 15 per cent Indian; 10 per cent European descent.

[35] If one may speak of a "type" in a hybrid population.

[36] Sir Charles Bruce, "The Modern Conscience in Relation to the Treatment of Dependent Peoples and Communities," *Inter-Racial Problems*, pp. 291-92. James Bryce, "Migration of the Races of Men," *Contemporary Review*, Vol. 62, p. 130. J. H. Van Evrie, *White Supremacy and Negro Subordination*, pp. 157-58. Friedrich Ratzel, *History of Mankind*, Vol. 2, p. 27.

[37] Lacerda, *Inter-Racial Problems*, p. 378. Luis Cabera, "The Mexican Revolution—Its Causes, Purposes and Results," *Annals of the American Academy of Political and Social Science*, Supplement, Jan. 1917, pp. 4-5.

guerilla warfare.

Where there exists a strong sense of nationality or of racial pride on the part of each of the two parent races in the situation, the mixed-blood individuals usually are without a respected position in the society of either. Each race having a civilization in which it believes and which it considers the superior of any other, there is no natural place for the half-castes except within the ranks of one or the other of the parent races. There is no middle ground. If they are rejected by both races or refuse to cast their lot with one and are rejected by the other, they are simply outcasts. They may form or be formed into a special caste, but it is a caste with an inferior social status within one or the other of the parent races, and not a class intermediate between the parent groups. The Eurasians are perhaps the best present-day example of a group rejected by both the races of which their ancestry is composed.

In the Asiatic situation, the colored races have their own civilization to which they hold with a tenacity at least equal to that which the white man shows for his. The difference in culture is not merely a matter of degree; it is a difference in kind. It is not that one is so much higher than the other, as is the case where the Negro and most of the lower races are in contact with the whites, as that they are different civilizations. To depart from one is not to approach the other; it is simply to decline in that civilization.

In this situation, the mixed-blood individuals must be either Europeans or Orientals. They cannot occupy a status above the one race and below the other. The civilizations are not so serially arranged. The hybrids cannot be part one and part the other. They may occupy an inferior status in either group, but this is not an indication that they, for that reason, stand nearer to the other. They cannot break connections with the white group without discarding European civilization; to go over to the colored group would be to accept the civilization of the Indians. But to the Orientals, the Eurasians are as much outcast as they are to the Europeans; they can no more be Hindus than they can be Englishmen. They must give up one civilization or the other, and content themselves as best they may with the status assigned them by the group with which they elect to be identified. The older Portuguese Eurasians have for the most part reverted to the Indian civilization and accepted a special status therein. The English Eurasians or "Indo-Europeans" have endeavored to be English [38] and have received some recognition from the British rulers, though they are nowhere accepted by the Europeans on terms of social equality. They occupy subordinate clerical positions in the government service and are almost wholly dependent upon the English patronage for the means of existence.

The Eurasian occupies an unenviable position. He is too proud to mix with the natives, who will, indeed, have none of him, and the European shuns him. He is a sort of social neutral stratum, regarded as foreign and looked upon with suspicion by the brown race, and looked down on with contempt by the white. Popularly supposed to inherit all the vices and none of the virtues of his parents, there is little ever said in his favor. I fear you cannot call the Eurasian trustworthy or truthful as a class, though of course there are many honorable exceptions. Certain it is he seldom rises to high employ, and is chiefly engaged in clerkly duties, for he has an unconquerable aversion to physical work or energy of any sort. The Eurasian

[38] ". . . they cling to their connection with the ruling class with a pride and persistency that is almost pathetic." Herbert Compton, *Indian Life in Town and Country*, p. 210.

society is one apart and unique, and its etiquette and manners are often a fine burlesque on those of the white race, with which its members are proud to claim connection. Their womenfolk affect gaudy colours, and a Eurasian ball will display as many rainbow tints as a mulatto one. . . ." [39]

They are a sensitive, generally discontented, and troublesome element in the community.[40] Their presence creates the most difficult of the minor problems in India. They stand in the presence of two civilizations and two race groups, but they are members of neither. They are compelled to remain a special group accepted by neither race and despised by both.[41] They are neither a connecting link between the races nor a harmonizing group between the extreme racial types. They are no more the spokesman or representative of the Hindus, than they are of the English. They are simply outcasts from both races with no natural rôle or dignified social status in the Indo-European situation.

Elsewhere in the East, the Oriental-European half-breed has developed much the same type of mind. He has no part to play in the inter-racial situation; he is himself a problem.[42] "The East seems to me to teach emphatically that the crossing of different races is always and everywhere a bad thing." [43]

[39] Compton, *Indian Life in Town and Country*, pp. 208-9.

[40] At the time of the Sepoy mutiny the Eurasians cast their lot with the Europeans and for a time a certain solidarity was established between them but the friendly feeling scarcely outlasted the time of danger.

[41] Élisée Reclus, *Asia*, Vol. 3, p. 389.

[42] See James A. LeRoy, *The Americans in the Philippines*, pp. 26, 65, 68 ff. Charles E. Woodruff, "Some Laws of Racial and Intellectual Development," *Journal of Race Development*, Vol. 3, p. 175.

[43] President Eliot, *Chautauquan*, Vol. 70, p. 285. See, also, Wu Ting-

Under certain other conditions, the presence of the mulatto population is utilized to lessen the friction between the pure-blooded races. The natural tendency of its members to form a separate parasitic caste when denied social equality with the dominant race is seized upon and fostered, and a caste developed in the community separate from either the white or the black, and standing between the two. In this position, they lessen the amount of contact between the extreme types of the population and so may lessen the clash between the races. They are used as a buffer between the pure-blooded groups.

It is in about this rôle that the mulatto seems to figure in the racial situation in the British colony of Jamaica. The group of ruling whites is very small,[44] but here, as elsewhere, the English have refused to debase their civilization by compromising with the colored element in the formation of their national institutions. The civilization is distinctively English. But the governmental policy, dictated by the home office, has been devised with a view towards harmony between the races.[45]

The mulattoes are not a numerically important part of the Negro population, but the white rulers have realized their possibilities for harm as dissatisfied agitators among the blacks. They also have realized the possibilities of the group as a harmonizing factor in the racial situation. As a consequence, they have utilized the mixed-bloods as a means of control of the lower and more numerous group,

Fang, "China," *Inter-Racial Problems*, pp. 128-29, and Moh. Sourour Bey, "Egypt," *Inter-Racial Problems*, p. 170.

[44] About 2 per cent. See p. 66 above.

[45] That English opinion, not local opinion, must be the ultimate judge of local affairs is the conscious policy of British Colonial rule. See Gilbert Murray, "Empire and Subject Races," *Nationalities and Subject Races*, pp. 7-8.

and as a means of lessening the friction between the extreme types of the population on the Island.

By catering to the mulattoes' desire for special recognition and by fostering their caste feeling of superiority to the blacks,[46] the English have built up a middle-class group between the white aristocracy and the black peasantry. This group includes the educated and professional classes of the Negro group and the more successful colored individuals in all lines of human endeavor.[47] The mulattoes belong to the intermediate class by right of birth.[48] Black men occasionally gain admittance if endowed with special natural ability, or if they have been exceptionally successful in the accumulation of property.[49]

This mulatto class has been separated in sentiments and

[46] The pride of the Jamaican in his white blood is shared by the other mixed-bloods of the Islands. "The Native Bermudians (brown) consider themselves much superior to the (black) Jamaicans." See Florence H. Doneilson, Appendix B (a) in Davenport, *Heredity of Skin Color*, p. 105.

[47] Earl Finch, "The Effects of Racial Miscegenation," *Inter-Racial Problems*, p. 111.

[48] "There is a considerable element of the Jamaica population which is known as 'sambo,' an element with about one-fourth of white blood; this Caucasian or Semitic mixture shows itself plainly in their color or their features, and they should, strictly speaking, be classed as 'coloured.' But very few members of this section of the people have so classified themselves in the census . . . the term coloured, having by custom come to be applied to persons of a distinctly brown or clear complexion." H. G. de Lisser, *Twentieth Century Jamaica*, p. 44. Quoted by Charles K. Needham, "A Comparison of Some Conditions in Jamaica with those in the United States," *Journal of Race Development*, Vol. 4, p. 192.

[49] *Ibid.*, pp. 191-92. Catering still further to the mulattoes' desire to be white certain members of the mulatto group of less than one-fourth Negro blood are allowed to designate themselves "whites by law." Membership in the latter group is conditioned by the whiteness of skin. They are the social aristocracy of the mulatto group though by no means necessarily the men of superior ability.

interests from the black group [50] by a deliberate and thorough-going application of the "divide and rule" policy.[51] By a judicious distribution of petty political offices and honors,[52] the whites secure their loyalty and coöperation in the affairs of government in spite of the rigid color line which they draw against them in social affairs. Any Negro who shows ability or talent for leadership is diplomatically separated from the black group and his loyalty to the government and to the ruling whites assured by a political or other honor proportional to his danger as a disgruntled agitator among the blacks. Such political honor or the accumulation of a considerable amount of property will allow him entrance to "colored" society and, if the honor or the fortune be sufficient, assure him a mulatto wife.[53] The larger the fortune, the whiter the wife.

In this way the black race is separated from its natural leaders and remains a black and happy, a contented and helpless mass.[54] The mulatto, dependent upon the white aristocracy for his political position and business opportunities and flattered by a racial designation that separates him from the peasantry and implies his superiority to it,

[50] J. A. Froude, *The English in the West Indies*, pp. 24-25.

[51] See Sir Henry Cotton, *Nationalities and Subject Races*, pp. 46-47, and Lala Lajpat Rai, "The Present Condition in India," *Nationalities and Subject Races*, pp. 32, 39. The discussion here is in regard to the Indian policy.

Compare the "divide and rule" policy of Spain's early colonial policy. H. C. Morris, *The History of Colonization*, Vol. 1, pp. 252-53.

[52] ". . . 'colored' men occupy most of the subordinate, and some of the higher positions in the public service." W. P. Livingstone, "The West Indian and American Negro: A Contrast," *North American Review*, Vol. 185, p. 647. See, also, Johnston, *The Negro in the New World*, pp. 280, 268.

[53] Thorp, *World's Work*, Vol. 8, pp. 4912-13.

[54] *Encyclopædia Britannica:* Jamaica; Thorp, *World's Work*, Vol. 8, p. 4910; Froude, *English in the West Indies*, p. 50.

maintains that obsequious and respectful attitude of mind toward his superiors which is a universal characteristic of the dependent and the unfree.[55] Harmony between the races is maintained at the price of a helpless peasantry and an intellectually prostituted middle-class group.[56]

This temporizing policy adopted in Jamaica is in strong contrast to that followed where the group of the white race in actual daily contact with the Negroes has been allowed to dictate the relationship of the races.[57] In all

[55] The mulattoes are not in all cases satisfied with the arrangement. Davenport quotes "An olive-skinned man" as saying: " 'I've often said I'd change the British flag for the American flag any day. In America they are prejudiced against *all* colored people. You may be a millionaire, but if you're colored you can't marry into white families or associate with them. Here with the English, if you are colored and have money you are all right, they associate with you; but if you haven't money you are nowhere. The English aren't as honest as the American, for they (English) hate the color just the same and only accept it for the money. . . .' " *Heredity of Skin Color*, Appendix B (b), p. 106. See, also, Livingston, *North American Review*, Vol. 185, pp. 646-47.

[56] H. E. Jordan, "Biological Status and Social Worth of the Mulatto," *Popular Science Monthly*, Vol. 82, p. 573, stresses the absence of political contention, Jamaica not being a self-governing colony, in accounting for the difference in the race problem in Jamaica and the United States. ". . . But perhaps the perfect adjustment between the races in Jamaica and the elimination of any 'problem' of this kind finds its explanation in a more rational and a more consistent political treatment made possible by the absence of any constitutional prescription. We may well suspect that the inconsistency of according to the negro legal (constitutional) equality and withholding it practically (politically and socially) has had a morally harmful effect upon both black and white. To stultify oneself as between one's theory and practice is always subversive of high moral tone. . . ."

[57] It is also very different from the German native policy. The Germans, believing that an educated native of any shade of color is necessarily a rascal, have avoided the complications produced by a semi-educated native population by conforming their native educational policy to the industrial needs of the situation. Keller, *Colonization*, p. 589.

these cases, the mulattoes are definitely excluded from social equality with the whites and forced to find their associates either with the colored group or among others of their own kind. No special provision has been made for them and they are dependent upon their own exertions—favored by the prestige their color gives them—for their success in life. No self-governing, North European group ever has been willing to compromise its civilization by admitting the lower race to an equal hand in the affairs of government. The more numerous the individuals in the colored group and the more their presence endangers civilized standards, the more unyielding has been the policy of exclusion.

In the self-governing colonies of South Africa, no effort is made to follow a policy toward the mulattoes that will insure harmony between the races.[58] An impassable color line is drawn by the whites between the races. The white man recognizes no difference between the various grades of Negroes and Negro intermixtures below him in the social scale.[59] Consequently, the mixed-bloods cannot form a buffer between the races as in Jamaica. Intermarriage does not occur and the refusal of the whites to recognize the mixed-bloods as being on a higher social plane than the natives, prevents them from being either a physiological or a social connecting link between the races.

The mulattoes, superior here as elsewhere, to the black element of their ancestry, resent the refusal of the white man to recognize their superiority and grant them special privileges and a special status.[60] They are a discontented and troublesome element in the community.[61] They cannot

[58] H. E. S. Freemantle, *The New Nation*, pp. 217-18.
[59] James Bryce, *Impressions of South Africa*, p. 375.
[60] M. S. Evans, *Black and White in South East Africa*, p. 289.
[61] Freemantle, *The New Nation*, pp. 319-20.

break with the white group and identify themselves with the black without discarding all the essential elements of white civilization.⁶² Their situation is, in many respects, like that of the Eurasians. Both groups stand between races having a strong sense of racial integrity and race pride. Both groups have to choose between the civilizations. The South African mulattoes can no more stand as part-native and part-white, than the Eurasians can be part-Hindu and part-European.

The South African mulattoes, then, are without a part to play in the racial situation. Numerically they are an insignificant part of the native population. The numbers, the organization, and the better developed sense of national pride and racial integrity among the natives prevent the mulattoes from enjoying great prestige among the black group. Their importance in the native group depends upon their worth rather than on the whiteness of their skin. Consequently, the mulattoes are slow to go over to the native population and identify themselves with the native group. They play no dignified rôle in the racial situation.⁶³

It remains to note in somewhat more detail the rôle that the mulatto has played and now plays in the racial situation in the United States. This falls more or less naturally into three pretty distinct parts: I. his rôle under the

---

⁶² The mulatto of course has no desire to do so. His contempt for the native is as great as is that of the white man. The prejudice between different groups for example, is so great that there are in Natal separate schools for natives, natives of St. Helena, Indians, Natal half-breeds and Mauritians. See M. S. Evans, *Black and White in the Southern States*, p. 262.

⁶³ For a discussion of the so-called Ethiopian movement see Freemantle, *The New Nation*, pp. 184-85; "The South African Natives," Ch. 4, *Report of the South African Native Races Committee; Current Literature*, Vol. 39, pp. 63-64.

slavery and reconstruction regimes; II. the present day "intellectuals" or "radicals," and III. the present day "conservatives" or "middle-class" group. A consideration of these stages in the mulattoes' rôle in the United States will be the task of the following chapter.

CHAPTER XIII

THE RÔLE OF THE MULATTO IN THE UNITED STATES

BETWEEN the Negro and the white American there always has been absolute social separation on the basis of color. At the time of their first contact on American soil, the two races differed in language, customs, and habits of life; in moral, mental, and religious development, as well as in ethnic origin, historical tradition, and physical appearance. A black skin, therefore, very quickly came to signify an inferior culture and, only a little later, came to be the badge of a servile condition. Between these races, there could be no social equality; there was not even a possibility of a harmonious working relation except on the basis of superiority and subordination.

When individuals of mixed ancestry presently appeared, there was manifested no disposition to treat them as essentially different from the Negro. Their physical appearance, though markedly different from that of the pure-blooded race, was sufficiently marked to set them off as a peculiar people. In large part, they were the offspring of a class of whites whose degraded status was not markedly superior to the status of the Negro; when such was not the case, the bastard origin of the mulattoes shocked the conventional moral sense of the community and militated against a community recognition of them as socially superior to the Negroes of full blood. This attitude presently found formal expression in the legislative enactments which assigned the mulatto to the status of the mother.

But the individual mulatto was, or what amounted to the same thing was believed to be, intellectually superior to the full-blooded Negro. Consequently, the occupational differentiation within the race everywhere operated to his advantage. The favored classes among the slaves, as the numbers of the mulattoes increased, came more and more to be light-colored classes. The trained mechanics and the trusted servants were drawn from the most intelligent; these were always assumed to be the mulattoes. Moreover, the mulattoes made a better appearance than the black Negro and were less offensive in close association, and so gravitated to those house and personal duties which brought them into personal association with the master class. The plantation slaves and the rough laborers in the cities and the towns were the black men. The division was, of course, not everywhere equally marked and it was seldom a sharp and complete separation. There were many full-blooded blacks among the favored classes and there were mulattoes in considerable numbers among the lower classes of slaves, but the tendency was toward a more and more complete separation of the colors. Manumission further widened the breach that existed in bondage. The free Negro group at all times contained a preponderance of mulattoes; in some places it was, to all intent and purpose, a mulatto group. Such education of the Negro as existed before the war was almost entirely mulatto education;[1] it was limited to the free Negroes and to certain favored individuals and groups among the slaves. All things tended to make the mulatto a superior man and to make the superior groups among

[1] A failure to recognize this fact is a glaring defect in the most important recent study of this subject by a mulatto. See C. G. Woodson, *The Education of the Negro Prior to 1861.*

the Negro race, mulatto groups.

On their side, the mulattoes were not slow to recognize their superiority and to exaggerate it. The lack of sympathy, for example, between the house servants—largely mulatto—and the field hands—mostly black men—was throughout the slavery period a characteristic feature of the institution.[2] As freemen, the mulattoes formed separate societies, where they existed in numbers sufficient to permit it, and held themselves aloof from the slaves and the black men. In the North, the free Negroes came to recognize the slavery of slaves, but claimed special recognition for themselves as free men.[3] During the slave regime, the free mulatto society of Charleston became an elaborately organized and highly exclusive institution. It still exists in much of its pristine glory.[4] In Louisiana and especially in Mobile and New Orleans, the free Latin-Negro creoles were so far separated in fact and in sympathy from the Negroes and the slaves, that they volunteered their services to the Confederacy at the outbreak of the Civil War. Elsewhere, though the break was generally not so obvious nor so wide, the same caste feeling separated the mulatto and the free Negro from the black man and the slave.

This potential mulatto class, however, received no special recognition from the dominant race. However, much as the mixed-bloods may have been favored as individuals

---

[2] E. Atkinson, "'The Negro a Beast,'" *North American Review*, Vol. 181, p. 209.

[3] W. E. B. DuBois, *Souls of Black Folk*, p. 49.

[4] "In places like Charleston they had (and still have to some extent) an exclusive society of their own which looked down on the black Negro with a prejudice equal to that of the white man." Ray Stannard Baker, "The Tragedy of the Mulatto," *American Magazine*, Vol. 65, p. 588. See, also, Maurice S. Evans, *Black and White in the Southern States*, p. 93.

while in bondage and helped as individual freemen, the dominant group everywhere refused to recognize mixture of blood as sufficient basis for special class recognition. The dominant group classed all Negroes, regardless of color, as members of the black race, and made divisions among them on other lines. Their classification was an economic and not an ethnic one; they, for example, separated the Negroes into slave and free, into house servants and plantation hands, and in various other ways according to the special situation. That these legal and industrial divisions corresponded largely to the division of the race into mixed-bloods and pure-bloods was, from the white man's point of view, incidental. He refused to countenance the mulatto group as a superior class in the community. The mulattoes, therefore, had only the pride of their white blood to sustain them as a separate and superior caste.

Throughout the slavery period, the mulattoes were usually not the leaders of the race; if indeed, one can speak of leaders before the Emancipation.[5] They were, in most cases, the superior individuals among the race;[6] they were hardly in a position to be leaders, they lacked the recognition of the dominant race. Those who were free were equally far from leadership. They were, for the most part, in the North and consequently they were generally without personal acquaintance with the real Negro and, in most cases, without any accurate knowledge of Southern life and conditions. They believed themselves to be superior to the black man and felt themselves to be inferior to the white man.[7]

[5] "... The great mass of the Negro people in the United States were dumb. In the plantation states, the black man was a chattel; in the Northern states, he was a good deal of an outlaw." Booker T. Washington, *Frederick Douglass*, p. 98.

[6] See p. 190 ff. above.

[7] J. R. Ficklin, *History of Reconstruction in Louisiana*, p. 127.

They formed, or tended to form, separate groups somewhere between the two and out of touch and sympathy with both. It was a matter of class separation on horizontal lines rather than a matter of leadership.

In the anti-slavery propaganda, the Negro or the Mulatto had little part.[8] He was the object about which the factions contended, but was, for the most part, not himself an actor in the drama. Certain Negroes were exploited by the abolitionists for campaign and demonstration purposes,[9] but so far as this was not the case, they were a quiescent and non-participating group in the national struggle. Baker [10] gives an accurate summary of the situation:

> In the antebellum slavery agitation Negroes played no consequential part; they were an inert lump of humanity possessing no power of inner direction; the leaders on both sides of the struggle that centered around the institution of slavery were white men. The Negroes did not even follow poor old John Brown. After the war the Negro continued to be an issue rather than a partaker in politics, and the conflict continued to be between groups of white men. . . . Even in Reconstruction times, and I am not forgetting exceptional Negroes like Bruce, Revels, Pinchback and others, the Negro was a partaker in the government solely by vir-

[8] A complete list of the Negroes who took any active or important part in the propaganda is given on page 192 above. Washington, *Frederick Douglass*, pp. 154-55, names twelve, all of whom are included in the list above.

[9] "William Lloyd Garrison was quick to discern that the cause needed this fugitive slave, more than any other man or thing, as an argument and an illustration of the further work of the anti-slavery society." Washington, *Frederick Douglass*, p. 72. He is speaking here of the anti-slavery people using Douglass as an exhibit. See, also, p. 144.

[10] Ray Stannard Baker, "Problems of Citizenship," *Annals of the American Academy of Political and Social Science*, Vol. 49, p. 93.

tue of the power of the North. As a class the Negroes were not self-directed, but were used by the Northern reconstructionists and certain political Southerners, who took most of the offices and nearly all the pilferings.

After the emancipation of the slaves, many Northern mulattoes presented themselves and were advanced by the abolitionists as the logical leaders of the newly freed race;[11] they assumed the rôle of spokesmen for the people of their color. The fact that they were members of the Negro race was accepted by themselves and by many of their Northern friends as evidence of sufficient qualification for the delicate and arduous task of leading and representing the liberated blacks.[12]

But aside from the caste feeling of superiority due to their white blood, their longer period of freedom, and their somewhat superior education, these Northern mulattoes were in other ways disqualified for any real leadership. The mulattoes and free Negroes were for the most part city men, while the Negroes were, and had always been, a rural population. The natural arrogance and naïve assumption of superiority which seem everywhere to be persistent traits of the city-bred men, served to widen the gulf that caste feeling made between the freedmen and their proposed leaders. They did not understand the country men. The gap was still further widened by their lack of knowledge of the South and the conditions prevailing there. Many of them had been associated directly or indirectly with the abolitionists who, though engaged for the better part of a generation in agitation, knew nothing about the Negro,[13]

[11] See Washington, *Frederick Douglass*, p. 270-71.

[12] Booker T. Washington, "Negro Disfranchisement and the Negro in Business," *Outlook*, Vol. 93, p. 311.

[13] Mr. Washington would include the whole North as well as the abo-

and but little about his condition. So, in addition to the prejudices and misconceptions common to their locality, the mulattoes were handicapped for any real leadership by the possession of a whole body of sentimental doctrine which when not false seldom had any relation to the objective facts. The abolitionists, and consequently their followers, saw everything in terms of their propaganda; their zealous devotion to their cause obscured their perception of reality. Facts were made to fit theory. They did not look upon the Negro as a primitive man whom slavery had been slowly raising to a higher cultural level; they looked upon him as an individual whom slavery had degraded to his present condition;[14] and attributed to him all the desirable traits of human nature. The Negro of their conception was an idealized abstraction; a glorified creature of the imagination and of the Uncle Tom's type of literature.[15] The refrain of the abolitionists that the Negro was "half a century ahead of the poor white man of the South," was accepted by their mulatto disciples as a fact. They rarely had anything more than a superficial comprehension of the meaning of the anti-slavery propaganda in which they took part; they were full of words, abstractions and misconcep-

litionists. ". . . the people of the North had . . . little knowledge of the Negro's character. . . ." *Frederick Douglass,* p. 248.

[14] "The Negro inherits a brain which work has cultivated for four generations, and added to it the skill of a practical hand. The white man inherits a brain sodden by the idleness of four generations, and he has improved his birthright by a life of soddenness. . . . Fairly considered, the only class ready for suffrage in the South is the Negro." Wendell Phillips, 1865. Quoted by F. A. Bancroft, *Negro in Politics,* p. 10.

[15] This idea persists among the Northern mulattoes even to-day. "I do not think it is claiming too much to say that 'Uncle Tom's Cabin' was a fair and truthful panorama of slavery; . . ." James W. Johnson, *The Autobiography of an Ex-colored Man,* p. 40.

tions, and, at the close of the war, they were dominated by the fixed determination to reverse the economic and social status of the two races in the South.

When these men went into the South after the war to become leaders of the newly-freed race, many of them for the first time came into contact with the real Negro. They had known an abstraction. The Negro and the conditions of his life were so unlike their expectations, and their own training was so pitifully inadequate that, in the crisis of their disillusionment in regard to the Negro's character and conditions, they were in general unable to accommodate themselves to the real conditions in such a way as to make them valuable men in the situation. The disillusionment brought a reaction in their sentiments and their attitudes toward him and toward themselves.[16] They became resentful toward the Negro.[17] They were unwilling or unable to

[16] "... We passed along until, finally we turned into a street ... and here I caught my first sight of colored people in large numbers. ... here I saw a street crowded with them. They filled the shops and thronged the sidewalks and lined the curb. I asked my companion if all the colored people in Atlanta lived in this street. He said they did not, ... The unkempt appearance, the shambling, slouching gait and loud talk and laughter of these people aroused in me a feeling of almost repulsion. ..." Johnson, *The Autobiography of an Ex-colored Man*, pp. 53-54.

[17] The most bitter arraignment of the Negro which at the same time keeps accurately to the facts is the volume of W. H. Thomas, *The American Negro*, a mulatto who went South after the War to be a leader of the race. As a disclosure of the mulattoes' sentiments and attitudes it is the most valuable single document in Negro literature. It states the things that others deny or endeavor to conceal. Said one of the most widely known mulattoes of the race in discussing the book: "Of course it's true; every word of it is true. But, damn it, we don't want those things told." The chief value of the document, however, is quite aside from the facts with which it deals. It lies in the treatment of the facts, in the naïve disclosure of the psychology of the disillusioned mulatto.

346   *The Mulatto in the United States*

put themselves on a social par with the freedman and to attempt to help him. They became more and more ashamed of their race and of the color which associated them with it.[18] Their contempt for the blacks, combined with their general ignorance of what to do or how to do it, made them for the most part men of no value in the situation. Instead of leaders, the mulattoes from the North tended to become agitators and so to become an additional race problem within the already difficult one of readjusting the relationships of the races.

The political reconstruction of the South gave a brief opportunity for the mulatto and Negro politicians.[19] In spite of the War and the Emancipation, the bulk of the Southern Negroes remained loyal to their Southern whites and willing to be led by them.[20] In order to insure the permanent supremacy of the Republican party in national politics, it was deemed necessary to use the newly-freed blacks.[21] But to do this, it was necessary to separate them

---

[18] The repulsive reaction of the Northern trained mulatto in contact for the first time with the real Negro has found its best expression to date in the book of Mr. DuBois, *The Souls of Black Folk*. This book is the outcome of the brief period of bitter exile which the author spent as a teacher in a Negro school in the South. Aside from the subject matter of which they treat these essays are an illuminating disclosure of the psychology of a timid and unpractical man, white in training, association, and thought and nearly white in appearance, with no real knowledge of his race and with only an academic sympathy for it, who is thrown for the first time among a body of blacks, classed with them, compelled to find his associates among them and who refuses, subconsciously, to accept the classification.

[19] These Negro politicians were very largely recruited from the free Negro class of the South.

[20] Mr. Washington says that the Negro would have followed the leadership of the Southern white "as willingly, if not more willingly, than that which he did accept." *Frederick Douglass*, p. 254.

[21] "As you once needed the muskets of the blacks, so now you need

in sympathy from their late masters. The first agency in the destruction of this loyalty was the Freedman's Bureau. To complete the work of alienating the sympathy of the Southern whites and blacks, and to anchor the black vote to the Republican party, was a task of the Reconstruction policy in general. To this end, every means known to venal politics—from simple theft to official murder—was employed without scruple or hesitation by a group of men debased beyond the power of common language to describe. Both races suffered from the policy.

In this period, the Negro and mulatto leaders were simply tools in the hands of the vandals. The independent part they had in the political life of the time was not an important nor a creditable one. A few men of ability appeared and also a few honest ones.[22] The majority of these men and all of any ability were mulattoes. The great mass of these Negro politicians, however, was not markedly superior to the rank and file of the newly enfranchised race,[23] and even the best were moved by no conceptions of unselfish public policy.[24] In nearly all cases, they were wholly un-

---

their votes." Charles Sumner, Speech in the Senate, *Works*, Vol. 11, p. 50.

[22] Washington, *Frederick Douglass*, pp. 278-80.

See, also, *Negro Year Book* for lists of these Negro politicians of Reconstruction days.

[23] "Beverly Nash, for many years the leader in the Senate and on the stump, had been a boot-black and a hotel porter." Bancroft, *The Negro in Politics*, p. 30. Nash was known as "a five thousand dollar man," that being the amount he always asked for his vote on important bills.

[24] "'. . . if the Negro knows enough to fight for his country, he knows enough to vote; if he knows enough to pay taxes to support the government, he knows enough to vote; if he knows as much when sober as an Irishman knows when he is drunk, he knows enough to vote.'" Frederick Douglass. Quoted by Washington, *Frederick Douglass*, pp. 258-59.

educated,[25] without responsibility,[26] and devoid of any sense of public or private honesty. They were, just as they were intended to be, simply a convenient means by which the white politicians could more easily rob and steal: the Negro was frequently allowed the questionable honor of holding a political position, while the white politician collected the plunder.[27]

The end of the Reconstruction Period marked an end of the Negro as a participant in the local political situation in the Southern States. The withdrawal of the Federal troops and the restoration of law and order, left them without a vocation or a support; they had no work or place in the life of the society. In large measure, they left the South at the close of the period. The Federal government, however, always has been liberal in the bestowal of political offices on the Negro politicians, and a few continued to exist throughout the South.

The reaccommodation of the races after the war and the Emancipation, and especially after the period of political reconstruction, took place in accordance with local conditions. The difference in different regions was, in the main, due to the presence of larger or smaller numbers of the unassimilated element in the body politic. In regions where the numbers were not great, they could be ignored; the

---

[25] In the South Carolina Legislature of 1873 for example, many of the members could neither read nor write. In Mississippi "the County supervisors were often black, only a few of whom could either read or write." Bancroft, *The Negro in Politics,* pp. 30, 39-40.

[26] In the South Carolina Senate 1868, "Only four of the Negro Senators were on the tax books; and they together paid only $2.10. Fifty-eight of the colored representatives paid no taxes." *Ibid.,* p. 22.

[27] "After a session or two of apprenticeship under white leaders, many of the Negro officials became adepts in the shameless practices of the time." *Ibid.,* pp. 29 ff.

greater percentage of Negroes in other regions colored the whole subsequent growth of the community life. At no time or place, however, were the Negroes able to exercise any marked influence on the course of events; they were nowhere able to modify the attitudes or even the overt acts of the dominant group. The policy or lack of policy was everywhere dictated by the white race. On the side of the Negroes, it was marked by their accommodation to a social policy which they were not able to control or modify. The policy has varied from time to time and from place to place, but it has done so without consulting the wishes of the Negroes. The single universal fact has been the consistent denial of social equality to members of the race.

In the South, the emancipation of the Negro was followed by a prolonged period of unfortunate doctrinaire experimentation which retarded a reaccommodation between the races that held any promise of permanence or mutual satisfaction. The first effect of the emancipation, once the Negroes realized its actuality, was a complete and profound economic, social, and moral disorganization of the Negro people. The white South was confronted with the problem of adjusting the relations of the races in conformity with the changed economic and legal conditions. There was no precedent to guide them. Nowhere had two such races ever arrived at mutually satisfactory working relations on any other basis than that of superiority and subordination. Slavery of the one by the other was the only adjustment that ever had worked.

The natural difficulty of the problem was made yet more difficult by the period of punishment visited on the South in the decade following the War. The promise of government grants of land and other property by the confiscation of the property of the white South and its redistribution among the late slaves, intensified the general economic disorganization resulting from the war and the emancipation of the slaves, and spread among the Negroes a general discontent with their condition and a disinclination to improve it by any real and continued effort.[28] The efforts to improve the Negroes' condition by means of a fashionable literary education, diverted some of the best energies of the race from the simpler and more important forms of education, produced a class of superficially educated men unfitted for any useful work among their people. The increase in the number of these, like the increase of the uneducated idle riff-raff, aggravated the friction between the races.[29] The efforts of the missionaries and others to bring about a revolution in the Negroes' character and in the inter-racial social life, inflamed their social ambitions and alienated the sympathy of the whites. The enfranchisement of the blacks prevented any normal division of opinion on matters of a public social nature. The paramount need of bending every effort toward the preservation of their civilization retarded progress toward a permanent and mutually satisfactory adjustment between the races.[30] The result of this period was the almost complete destruction of the mutually sympathetic feelings which so generally had characterized the relations of the races during the slave period.[31] As time went on, such friendlly association as survived the Reconstruction days—principally that between the older slaves and the

[28] W. L. Fleming, "Forty Acres and a Mule," *North American Review,* Vol. 182, pp. 721-37.

[29] McCord, *The American Negro as a Dependent, Defective and Delinquent,* p. 65.

[30] Bruce, "Race Segregation in the United States," *Hibbert Journal,* Vol. 13, p. 868.

[31] McCord, *The American Negro as a Dependent, Defective and Delinquent,* p. 18.

older slave masters—became less and less. The younger generation of both races had not the body of sentiment to withstand the crisis; those of a later generation lacked it altogether.[32] After a decade, the mechanics and skilled workmen in all industrial and domestic lines who had received their training under the slave regime, began to disappear or to become too old for further effective employment.[33] The new education had trained no younger ones to take their places. A decline in the Negroes' condition was inevitable; all through the period of political and social agitation and of classical education, the race lost ground. It was in the eighties that the Northern political, educational, and religious tutelage of the post-bellum period was coming to fruitage.[34]

In the meanwhile, however, there were other forces at work making for an adjustment of the races in accordance with the character of the two races and in response to the

[32] "The entire body of Negroes, under middle age, have not even a tradition among them of that kindly intercourse between the master and his bondsmen which did so much to smooth away the harsher features of slavery in its practical working. They cannot understand the feeling of loyalty which made their fathers the faithful protectors of the Southern white women and children when all the white men had been enrolled in the armies of the Confederacy." Bruce, *Hibbert Journal*, Vol. 13, p. 870. This loyalty of the slave to his former master is a thing that frequently does not fall within the comprehension of the present generation of mulattoes. Benjamin Brawley, one of the most capable of the present generation of mulattoes, discussing with considerable insight the recent fiction dealing with Negro characters, is unable to grasp the fact that a Negro of exceptional type should have preferred to remain with the old master. See, "The Negro in American Fiction," *Dial*, Vol. 60, pp. 445-50, especially the criticism of "Abraham's Freedom" (*Atlantic*, 9-1912), pp. 448-49.

[33] Booker T. Washington, *The Future of the American Negro*, Chapter 3.

[34] Sir Harry H. Johnston, *The Negro in the New World*, p. 403.

influences of the common environment. There was slowly growing up a body of industrious, law-abiding, and self-respecting Negroes, and with their increase in number, in wealth, and in self-respect, they were assuming a growing importance in the affairs of the race. Previous to the Emancipation, there was throughout the South a goodly number of property-owning free Negroes with a respected position in the life of the community. In the decades immediately following the emancipation of the Negroes, the Federal government distributed among them a considerable amount of property and, in addition to this Federal aid, there was the plunder which in many of the states came to the race during the period of Negro domination in political affairs.[35] After the war, and especially after the Reconstruction Period, a goodly number of Negroes had returned to their plantations,[36] or had settled down elsewhere and had begun to lead a frugal and industrious life, to educate their children and otherwise to make a common sense effort to improve their condition.[37] The conditions of life were absurdly easy.[38] Any industrious and sober man could, as the result of a few years' labor, become possessed of sufficient

[35] In only a few cases, however, were the Negro politicians sufficiently shrewd to save the fortunes accumulated through theft and corruption during the period of Negro domination.

[36] Nicholas Worth, *Autobiography*, p. 14.

[37] For the most part these were men who had received an industrial education under the slave regime. See Washington, "The Story of the Negro," *Outlook*, Vol. 93, p. 311.

[38] "It was easy to live in the South. The mild climate and fertile soil, the abundance of game in forest and stream, the bountiful supply of wild fruits, the accessibility of forests with firewood free to all, the openhanded generosity and universal carelessness of living made it possible for the average Negro to idle away at least half his time and yet live in tolerable comfort." G. S. Winston, "The Relations of the Whites to the Negroes." *Annals of the American Academy of Political and Social Science*, July, 1901.

land and other property to make him independent of the wage system. An honest, industrious, and useful Negro citizenship was the desire of the white South and every Negro who showed a disposition to improve his condition received the encouragement and assistance of the better class of white men.[39] In spite of all this, however, the growth of the middle-class was abnormally slow;[40] but there gradually emerged a body of men within the race possessed of a little property and of an ambition to accumulate more.

The two forces chiefly responsible for the rise of this racially independent middle-class, and a consequent new adjustment of the races, were the growth of the agricultural and industrial education for the Negro and the segregation of the Negro by the whites.[41] The whole movement to develop an industrially-educated, land-owning, law-abiding, and decent-living Negro group among the blacks, usually thought of in connection with the name of Booker T. Washington, was the result of an effort on the part of the white South and some of the saner leaders among the Negro people to make the Negro see and grasp his opportunity.[42] The movement was based on the wreck of the

[39] So general was the assistance of Southern white men to the ambitious and law-abiding Negro that Mr. Washington, himself the best representative of this growing middle-class, says that almost every successful man of the race can trace his success to the assistance of some white neighbor or friend. *The Story of the Negro*, Vol. 2, pp. 35 ff.

[40] *Ibid.*, Vol. 2, Chapter 2, "The Rise of the Negro Land-Owner," gives the most favorable statement of the case that can be made.

[41] These two main forces were, of course, assisted or modified by various minor factors operating locally.

[42] "A very weak argument often used against pushing industrial training for the Negro is that the Southern white man favors it, and therefore, it is not best for the Negro." Washington, *The Future of the American Negro*, p. 64.

earlier efforts to improve the condition of the Negroes. Classical education for the race was everywhere recognized to have failed.[43] The citizenship that had been given them had proved their detriment.[44] The campaign for social equality had been even more injurious to the Negroes and had proved even more of a failure.[45] The discussion of the Negroes' political status had served only to alienate the sympathy of the white man without resulting in any gain to the Negroes.[46] Antagonizing the white man, bewailing the fate of the Negroes, and blaming others for their pitiable condition, did not improve the situation.[47] The industrial movement was based on a recognition of the facts and a knowledge of the conditions. There was a frank recognition of the failure of the earlier program, an honest admission of the Negroes' defects of character,[48] an honest admission of the fact that the Negroes lacked not opportunity so much as energy and intelligence to take advantage of their opportunities; there was a recognition that coöperation between the races was necessary if the Negroes were to

---

[43] Just as the ideal of literary training for primitive people has everywhere failed to produce satisfactory results. "The defect of a primarily literary training lies in the fact that it distracts attention from the real intellectual needs of a race. . . . It ordinarily leads to a dangerous half-education implying a well-trained memory but an undeveloped judgment, together with an overweening self-confidence and vanity. . . ." Paul S. Reinsch, *Colonial Administration*, pp. 49-50.

[44] Washington, *The Future of the American Negro*, p. 65.

[45] Booker T. Washington, "Let Down Your Buckets Where You Are," Address delivered at the Cotton States Exposition in Atlanta, Georgia, September 18, 1895. Reprinted in Booker T. Washington, *Up From Slavery: Autobiography*, pp. 217-37.

[46] Hubert H. Bancroft, *The New Pacific*, pp. 606-7.

Evans, *Black and White in the Southern States*, pp. 205-6.

[47] See Edward Ingle, *The Negro in the District of Columbia*, p. 42.

[48] Evans, *Black and White in the Southern States*, pp. 204-5.

prove themselves desirable members of society.⁴⁹ It was a movement from within the race and the section of the counry affected.

Washington and Tuskegee were selected to symbolize the movement which has come to be the most important factor working for the development of the Negro. The movement helped to build up a self-respecting and useful group of successful farmers, mechanics, tradesmen, teachers, and the like who were not ashamed of their work or of their color.⁵⁰ It did, in a constructive and positive way, what the policy of segregation was doing in a negative way.⁵¹ The Negro began to buy land and to assume a fixed habitation. To the extent that he did so, he became an independent and self-respecting man and an asset to the community in which he lived.⁵² As this self-respecting class grew in numbers, wealth, and importance, it formed the nucleus about which the race could unite. It was the basis for a nationality. As the spirit of race pride and race consciousness and pride of accomplishment increased, there was an increasing tendency to race separation and consequently to the development of the bi-racial type of adjustment.

Meanwhile, and from a diametrically opposite direction, the policy of segregation operated to build up an independent Negro group. The segregation of the Negroes in many of the relations of life had, at the desire of the Negroes

[49] McCord, *The American Negro as a Defective, Dependent and Delinquent*, p. 125.

[50] The opponents of Mr. Washington deny that there is a "scintilla of evidence to show that the increase in these ventures and in property owning by Negroes is due solely or even mainly to the influence of industrial and agricultural education." V. P. Thomas, *The Crisis*, July, 1913, p. 145.

[51] Booker T. Washington, *The Story of the Negro*, Vol. 1, p. 31.

[52] See Evans, *Black and White in the Southern States*, p. 204.

themselves, taken place long before the Emancipation. With the freedom of the slaves came more voluntary segregation and, as the South began to recover from the financial effects of the War and the Reconstruction, came legal separation in more and more lines. With the disappearance of the older generation of slaves and slave-masters and the appearance of a newer generation containing many idle, insolent, and dangerously criminal Negroes, the legal separation of the races was adopted as a matter of police protection. It served to avoid the constant conflicts resulting from the contact of the rougher classes of the two races.[53] It kept apart the ignorant and the vicious of the two races and so made for harmony in the racial life of the community.[54] Residential segregation always had been the rule, but the desire to get away from the rougher and more ignorant classes and to be among the whites led certain prosperous and ambitious Negroes and mulattoes to move into white residential districts. Whether the motives impelling such actions on the part of the Negroes was a desire to assert their equality with the whites, or the perfectly laudable desire to live in better localities and to get their children away from the moral dangers which surrounded the predominantly Negro districts, their presence was equally offensive to the white residents. The uniform result of such actions on the part of the Negroes was the withdrawal of the whites, the consequent depreciation in the value of the property, and the section becoming a Negro settlement. Legal residential segregation grew up in order to restrain,

[53] In New Orleans, for example, where there existed a large number of free mulattoes, separate accommodations were provided long before the War.

[54] McCord, *The American Negro as a Dependent, Defective and Delinquent*, p. 273.

not the mass of the race but the ambitious Negroes and mulattoes who desired to escape from the race and associate with, and live among, the whites.

As the practice of racial segregation spread, it was presently seen that, in some ways at least, it was proving a real help to the Negroes. It kept the race together, prevented the loss by the race of its superior and talented individuals. It forced the Negroes back upon themselves, forced them to rely more upon themselves and less upon the whites, and it forced them to develop and to manage their own institutions and to develop their own social and economic life.[55] As they were forced to become more self-dependent, they gained in self-confidence and consequently in self-respect. In a negative way, the practice of segregation combined with the industrial and agricultural educational policy to build up an independent and self-reliant peasantry and middle-class group. Before the Negroes lay the greatest economic opportunity ever offered to the peasantry of any country in the world. The educational leaders sought to impress this fact upon the race; the segregation policy forced the Negroes to embrace the opportunity before them. To the extent that the Negroes became settled and industrious, they became prosperous. As they became prosperous they became contented, law-abiding, and valuable men in the community. Consequently, the segregation policy was further extended and advocated,[56] not alone as a defensive measure and because of the harmony it gave in the affairs of the races, but as the most effective legal

[55] E. G. Murphy, *The Schools of the People.* Evans, *Black and White in the Southern States,* p. 156.

[56] Frequently by the Negroes. For example: "Let us as a race not wait for the Caucasian to force us but let us segregate voluntarily in every particular. The white man has suggested it and now let us fol-

method, so far discovered, to help the Negroes to help themselves.

With the growth of a middle-class, chiefly through the operation of these two factors, and its increase in numbers and in importance in the affairs of the race, there is coming to be a new and a radically different type of adjustment between the races in the South.[57] This new adjustment tends to be a bi-racial one: a vertical division on race lines. The two races are separate in all those relations where opportunity for conflict seems likely to arise between individual members, and in all things social or that remotely imply social equality. Their residence districts are apart. They have separate accommodations when they travel. Their schools, churches, lodges, and places of entertainment and amusement are separate and distinct. Each race has its own organizations, and manages its own affairs. They coöperate or oppose each other as races on matters affecting the relations of the races. In matters of mutual concern, a conference between the representatives or leaders of the two races arranges for coöperative action. Each is held responsible for the individual behavior of the members of its own group. They may work for the same ends, independently but coöperatively; except, however, in the strictly

low it up. His prescription [proscription?] and boycotting will help us to get together, if we have an ounce of race pride." The *Conservative Counselor*, Waco, Texas, 9-2-1915. See, also, "Editorial Comment," The *Afro-American*, Baltimore, Maryland, 12-11-1915.

This view is of course almost as superficial as that of the militant mulattoes who violently oppose every tendency toward segregation. Both are surface views. The real ground on which the policy is to be defended, from the Negroes' point of view, is indicated below. See pp. 390 ff. Residential segregation was declared unconstitutional by a ruling of the United States Supreme Court 11-5-1917.

[57] The bi-racial adjustment is of course not anywhere complete; it is in the process of becoming.

business relation of employer and employee, the races need not come into contact; they remain separate groups. They live a life apart, beside each other and yet separate in all the affairs of social and community life.

The bi-racial arrangement—the separation of the Negroes from the whites and their independence in many of the affairs of life—created a need and supplied a place for the superior men of the race. Under the earlier conditions, the Negroes had looked to the whites as the superior and educated class and depended upon them for advice and leadership; they uniformly preferred the services of white professional and business men to the services of the professional and business men of their own race. To the extent that the races became separated and the Negroes gained in independence and developed a sense of racial pride and self-reliance, there was a place for an educated class within the race; there was a need for teachers and preachers, for physicians and lawyers, for business men and entertainers, and for all the host of other parasitic and semi-parasitic classes that go to make up a modern community. With the rise of a middle-class, the race was able to support a professional and leisure class; previously the educated Negro was an idler and a parasite. The isolation of the race forced the Negroes to depend upon their own educated men and so made a place for such men.

Within the Negro group and catering to their own people, the men superior by nature, by virtue of education, because of special training, because of natural shrewdness, because of the possession of property or by virtue of the possession of the elements of natural leadership, became the leaders of the race. The separation of the races freed the Negro professional and business men from the competition of the better trained and more efficient white men and consequently gave them an opportunity to rise out of all proportion to their native ability and training. The plane of competition became one on which they could hope to succeed. The older—the slave and reconstruction plan of adjustment—was an accommodation on horizontal lines. The white man was at the top, the black man was at the bottom. It was a caste distinction that prevented the rise of the capable individual out of his group. In the newer arrangement, the opportunity to rise was limited only by the ability and the industry of the individual man. There was no superior caste above him.

As has been previously pointed out in detail, the superior men of the race are, with scarcely the proverbial exception, mulattoes.[58] The segregation of the Negroes, the rise of a middle-class, and the consequent bi-racial adjustment of the races thus have made a place and furnished a vocation for the mulattoes. Unable to escape the race and unable to constitute a caste above the race, they remained with the race and became its real leaders.[59] They are the professional and business men of the race. They are the leaders in all the racial and inter-racial affairs. The bi-racial arrangement gives the mulatto the opportunity for a useful life and, at the same time, it allows him to remain

---

[58] J. R. Brackett, *The Negro in Maryland*, p. 94.

[59] ". . . Although resenting a classification which they consider illogical and unnatural, they have never been given any choice in the matter and they have, at last, come to acquiesce in the arrangement. What is the result? It is leading to the unification of all Afro-Americans as no personal inclination or mutual persuasion could have done. The 'colored' (mulatto) class, which contains the most intelligent and ambitious men of the race, has deliberately thrown its lot with the black, and set itself to the task of educating and training them for the great struggle which they believe is to come. . . ." W. P. Livingstone, "The West Indian and the American Negro," *North American Review*, Vol. 185, p. 646.

superior to his black fellows.

These Southern mulatto leaders, however, are men who, at least outwardly, consider themselves Negroes.[60] They are men who have given up, in practice if not in theory, the hopeless struggle for social recognition by the whites and identified themselves with the black group.[61] Their status is fixed; they are members of the Negro race. Social equality with the whites is out of the question and the denial of it ceases to disturb them. The success they make in life is in another direction and the amount of it depends upon themselves. They are men who have concealed, if they have not succeeded in overcoming, their aversion for the black man. They do not openly flaunt their superiority because of their white blood, and they find their life and their work among their darker and more backward fellows. The mulattoes, for the most part Southern mulattoes, have, in this new adjustment of the races, found their place as the real and natural leaders of the race. They are the men who teach the black man in the schools and in the Negro colleges, who preach to him from the pulpits, who manage his banks and business enterprises, who rise to prominence in all the social, political, and economic affairs of

[60] "I love my people and prefer to live among them. I am not ashamed of being a Negro." C. V. Roman, "Racial Self-respect and Racial Antagonism," *Atlanta Congress,* 1913, p. 445.

[61] The condition of the mulatto or educated Negro who has not yet reached this point in his development appears everywhere in the writings of the mulattoes. For example: ". . . there is to my mind no more pathetic side to this many sided question than the isolated position into which are forced the very colored people who most need and could best appreciate sympathetic coöperation; [the educated and upper classes] and their position grows tragic when the effort is made to couple them, whether or no, with the Negroes of the first class I mentioned [the lower classes]." Johnson, *The Autobiography of an Ex-colored Man,* p. 78.

the race. They, too, are the men who rob and defraud him in the lodges, who grow wealthy, through appealing to the Negro's desire to be like the white man, with nostrums to blanch the skin and straighten the hair, who gain wealth and distinction among their race by fostering, and catering to, the Negro's morbid interest in and superstitious fear of death and love of vulgar funeral display. But whether they guide and help the black man or fatten on his gullibility, they are in every respect the prominent men of the race and the leaders in the race's social affairs. Whether they are engaged in robbing the black man, preaching to him, healing his sick or burying his dead, and in spite of their concealed dislike and their contempt for the degraded black man, the mulattoes are endeavoring to raise him to a higher mental, moral, and industrial plane.

The organization takes on the form of a primary group relation. From the similarity of life and activities, come a similarity of sentiments and ideas. The mulattoes and other superior men become an integral part of the race, desirous of a respected place in the thoughts of the group and ambitious for an honored place in its counsels. The mulatto feels himself in alliance with the group and in the coöperation of common activities there arises a sympathetic understanding and appreciation which fuses the mulatto, in sentiments and attitudes, with the larger whole. He is identified with the black group, feels the mute longing of the common folk, feels himself a part of it, is moulded by it, and comes, little by little, to realize himself as a factor in the common life and purpose of the group. He ceases to be, in thought and feeling, a stranger among his people; he learns to appreciate them, ceases to be ashamed of his relationship to them, ceases to resent being classed with them. Their problems become his problems; their life his life. The mulatto thus ceases to be a problem within a problem; he becomes a functioning unit in the social life of an evolving people.

In the South, as elsewhere among the Negro people, the mulattoes enjoy a prestige because of their color; the Negroes readily accept them as superior men. The conditions of life for the Negroes are decidedly easier in the South than in other sections of the country and this is especially the case for the mulattoes and other men of business and professional training.[62] To the extent that they do a work for the good of the race and live an honest and industrious life, they are helped by the white man and do not have to meet his competition. Race prejudice and discrimination are less clearly manifested[63] than in sections of the country where the struggle for professional existence is somewhat more severe, and where the tolerance of racial shortcomings is less evident. There is no lack of

[62] It is to be remembered, of course, that in competition, the Southern trained Negro has proven his equality if not his superiority to the Northern trained Negro. See G. E. Haynes, *The Negro at Work in New York City*, pp. 50 ff.

[63] E. R. Turner, *The Negro in Pennsylvania*, p. 149.

Editorial, The *Free Lance*, 11-6-1915.

"Despite evidences of racial friction which crop out here and there, the relations existing between the individual Negro and the individual white man are often closer and better understood and more sympathetic than those obtaining in any community outside of the South." Booker T. Washington, *The Southern Workman*, quoted from the *Chicago Defender*, 12-19-1914.

"For years after the war the North went into a frenzy, especially during political campaigns, over outrages, real and alleged, upon their colored fellow-citizens in the South. In the North to-day the Negro has less chance to gain a livelihood above the very humblest levels than he had twenty-five years ago, and only in rare instances does education beyond the prime essentials benefit him in his struggles upward." *Boston Traveller*, 11-15-1915.

opportunity. There are fewer men in proportion to the number of the race who are trained and it is proportionately easier for the men of a little training and ability to rise to positions of importance within the group. The superior education of the mulattoes qualifies them for leadership; their superior ambition and greater self-confidence pushes them to the front. The mulatto, even though only slightly superior, is assured of success once he has cast his lot with the Negro people. His rôle on the Southern situation is the rôle of leadership.

The rôle of leadership is, of course, a peculiarly difficult one; the Negroes do not readily follow their own best leaders. The mass of the Negroes are ignorant, untrained in self-direction, and not awake to the importance of self-help and coöperative association. They are pretty generally unreliable and subconsciously recognize their own unreliability; bitter experience has made them more suspicious and distrustful of their own race than of the white. Petty jealousies among the leaders themselves are continually breaking out into factional strife. Public spirit and pride of race is still more a hope of certain individuals than a realization of the masses. It is the problem of the leaders of the race to organize this ignorant and distrustful peasant people, replace a bizarre idea of education by saner ones, teach them the need of industry and morality, and lead them to a respect for, and a belief in, their own race.

In those sections of the country where the Negroes are relatively less numerous, they have in general not been legally assigned a definite racial status in the community life. No special provisions have been made for their education. There are no restrictions on their place of residence. They are free to intermarry and otherwise associate with individuals of a different racial extraction to the extent of their desire and opportunity. There has been a refusal on the part of the white people to recognize publicly the presence of the Negroes as constituting a problem distinct from other social problems of the community life.[64] The policy has been rather to ignore their presence and to leave them to accommodate themselves individually as best they may to the social situation. Ostensibly at least, they stand on the same legal and social footing as other members of the population.

As a consequence of the absence of any restrictive or other legislation applying particularly to the Negro people, their greater individual freedom of choice and action, there is a less definite and uniform accommodation between the races and more of individual variation from the usual mode. The conditions of life, however, are markedly more difficult. There is more of prejudice and active discrimination in economic and industrial relations. The individual relations between members of the races are in general marked by less of personal friendliness; there is not the good-natured expectation of inefficiency and toleration of shiftlessness which marks the relations of the races in the South.[65] The Negro is in individual competition with men of the other race, and, in general, he has to measure up to their standard of efficiency and reliability in order to secure and retain employment. Among the Negro people of the North, therefore, there is more failure, dissatisfaction, complaint, more bitterness, more enforced idleness, more distress, poverty, and crime than in those sections of the country where the Negroes do not come into direct individual competition

[64] It has not, of course, been possible to live up to any such theory. See the *Negro Year Book,* pp. 365-67.

[65] This is due in large part to the fact that in the North the Negro is in the city, whereas in the South he is more generally a rural man.

with better trained and more energetic and ambitious rivals. Among those who have succeeded, however, there are more examples of conspicuous individual success, as measured by white standards, than where the competition is racial and not individual. The struggle for success is more difficult, the failures are more numerous, but the rewards of success are greater.

There is among the Negroes in the North an absence of unity and race solidarity. The numbers of the race are relatively small, widely scattered, unorganized, and without a common interest. It is predominantly an urban population and stands for the most part as a population of unskilled laborers dependent for the means of livelihood upon white employers.[66] Their tendency to congregate in one or a few sections of the cities and towns gives an appearance of unity which in reality does not exist; the residential segregation is a matter of economic necessity rather than a matter of choice. The race is divided into innumerable antagonistic groups, societies, orders, factions, cliques, and what not, endless in number and puzzling in complexity, whose mutual jealousy and distrust prevent any united, coöperative action. There is no leadership that has any considerable following and no program for racial progress that has the assent of more than a faction of the Negro group; there is nothing to hold the various factions together and the group is without any semblance of organized unity.

The superior men of the race, even more than in the South, are mulattoes. There is not, certainly, always a sharp and complete separation; there are occasional blacks among the educated section and by no means all the mu-

[66] See, for example, A. P. Comstock, "Chicago Housing Conditions: VI. The Problem of the Negro," The *American Journal of Sociology*, Vol. 18, pp. 241-57.

lattoes are in the non-laboring classes. But the occupational differentiation is pretty complete. Speaking generally, the successful group is a light-colored group, while the great uneducated mass is dark. Moreover, the individuals who have risen markedly above their fellows in success in any line are, with rarely an exception, mulattoes. The successful professional and business man are in almost every case men of mixed blood and generally men of relatively little Negro admixture. The same thing is true of the men prominent in every line of work. In education, the mulattoes are almost the only members of the Negro community who avail themselves of the school opportunities beyond the legal minimum. The prominent and educated men and women of the race are mulattoes and the mulatto group as a whole occupies a higher economic and intellectual status than do the darker colored groups.

The Northern mulattoes are, however, in spite of their superior education and position, without a definite rôle in the inter-racial life of the community. More than in the Southern section of the country, the mulattoes are separated in fact and in sympathy from the mass of the race. They are proud of their European blood, their smoother features, their "better" hair and their higher economic status; they are not always careful to conceal the fact. Frequently they live apart from the Negro community, find their social life among others of their kind, attend white churches or form congregations of their own class and color.[67] The upper class mulattoes are frequently without much acquaintance with the real Negroes. In their professional or business life, they are separated from the mass of the race and come often into very little contact with them even in a busi-

[67] See E. H. Abbott, "The South and the Negro," The *Outlook*, Vol. 77, pp. 367 ff.

ness way. Their idea of the Negro and their attitude toward him, is the idea and the attitude of the white man. The attitude is one of more or less kindly toleration and mild contempt which changes to active discrimination and positive hatred when the Negro assumes the attitude of an equal and seeks the privilege of social equality. In their public utterances the Negro may be idealized, but there is no desire or disposition on the part of the mulatto to have any intimate association with him.

Yet the mulattoes assume the rôle of spokesman for the race; they undertake to represent the Negro and to speak for him. Their superior education, their higher economic status as well as their greater individual success, and their more prominent position give plausibility to their assumption of leadership and allow them, rather than men who are closer to the race and better able to voice the feelings and attitudes of the inarticulate mass, to get themselves accepted as representatives of the Negroes. They appear as champions of the Negro at all times when there is profit or notoriety to be gained by so doing. They make incendiary speeches, draw up petitions and protests, appear before legislative and executive committees as the representatives of a people they only imperfectly represent. They are the men Mr. Washington had in mind when he wrote:[68]

> . . . there are others who claim that the Negro is too submissive. The latter insist that, if he had the courage to stand up and denounce his detractors in the same harsh and bitter terms that these persons use toward him, in a short time he would win the respect of the world, and the only obstacle to his progress would be removed.
>
> It is interesting, sometimes amusing, and sometimes

[68] *The Story of the Negro,* Vol. 1, pp. 190-91.

Rôle of the Mulatto in the United States 369

even pathetic, to note the conception of "bravery" and "courage" which some colored men, who put their faith in this solution of the Negro problem, occasionally apply to other members of their race. For a long time after freedom came, and the same is not infrequently true at the present time, any black man who was willing, either in print or in public speech, to curse and abuse the white man, easily gained for himself a reputation of great courage. He might spend thirty minutes or an hour once a year in that kind of "vindication" of his race, but he got the reputation of being an exceedingly brave man. Another man, who worked patiently and persistently for years in a Negro school, depriving himself of many of the comforts and necessities of life, in order to perform a service which would uplift his race, gained no reputation for courage. On the contrary, he was likely to be denounced as a coward by the "heroes," because he chose to do his work without cursing, without abuse, and without complaint.

The larger part of the present-day discussion of inter-race matters, the agitations for social and political rights and privileges, the fulminations against discriminations, the exaggerations of real and fancied wrongs, is not the work of Negroes. It is a small, widely scattered, light-colored and largely deracialized group of mulattoes who have not found their place in the bi-racial community life—who refuse to be Negroes and are refused the opportunity to be white—whose sentiments and attitudes find expression in the present-day agitations. The bitter, abusive tone of so much present-day Negro literature does not voice the attitude of the Negro; the real Negro is remarkably free from bitterness. The rank and file are intimately concerned with the daily problem of earning a living; they accept the social situation and their place therein more as a matter of fact than as a hardship. The abstract rights for which certain individuals and groups within the race contend interest them very little or not at all. The Negroes have given very little support to the so-called radical movements.[69] A native common sense leads them to a half-conscious recognition of the futility of systematically antagonizing the race upon which they are so largely dependent. The trend of sentiment has been away from, rather than towards, an advocacy of rights and privileges which they are not in a position to demand and which the opposite race seems less and less inclined to bestow upon them. There has been a pretty general acceptance by the more intelligent Negroes in all sections of the country of the Southern point of view.[70]

The agitations of the mulatto groups and individuals are, for obvious reasons, carried on in the name of the Negro, not in the name of the mulatto. The ends to be reached are such as concern the real Negroes very little. The agitations voice the bitterness of the superior mulattoes, of the deracialized men of education, culture, and refinement who resent and rebel against the intolerant social edict that excludes them from white society and classes them with the despised race. The demands resolve themselves in last analysis into a demand that all race distinctions be blotted out and that each man be accepted on the basis of his individual merit irrespective of his race or

---

[69] The National Association for the Advancement of the Colored People, the chief present-day association concerned with the political rights and the social ambitions of the Negroes, claims a membership of only 9,500. Of this membership many, perhaps the great majority, are white persons. Certainly the organization has always been financed and largely managed by white persons. See The *Crisis*, 3-1916, p. 225.

[70] Many leading Negroes who were earlier identified with the movement in opposition to the policies of Booker T. Washington, later went over to the constructive point of view. See, for e.g., John Daniels, *In Freedom's Birthplace*, p. 128.

color.[71] The result of the adoption of such a policy would be, of course, to allow the exceptional men of the race, that is the mulattoes, to escape from it and be accepted by and absorbed into the white race. The demands of the militant mulattoes thus amount to a plea for special privilege; it is a plea for themselves and not for the Negroes. They ask the opportunity to escape from the race toward which they feel much the same prejudice as does the white man. They are Negroes only by compulsion.

The inter-racial situation in the North is thus, in very large part, a caste arrangement. The mulattoes are the superior men and form, or tend to form, a separate and exclusive class above the race. They assume the rôle of spokesman for the race but they are not an integral part of it as are the mulatto leaders of the South. The Negroes resent, more or less, the mulattoes' assumption of superiority and their presuming to speak for a race with whom they neither live nor associate. At the same time, it is the desire of every ambitious Negro to secure admittance to the more exclusive circles and to escape from the black group. The mulattoes are rather outside the race, above it. They have not given up the hope of equality with the whites; they are not satisfied to be Negroes and to find their life and their work among the members of the race. They are contemptuous of the blacks who are socially below them and envious of the whites who are socially above them. The accommodation of the races is on horizontal lines with the educated and light-colored mulattoes standing between the blacks and the whites.

The arrangement, however, seems to lack the elements of permanence. The realization of the mulattoes' ambi-

[71] See, for example, "Editorial," The *Crisis*, 2-1914, pp. 186-87. Also, Katherine B. Davis, The *Crisis*, 6-1914, pp. 83-84.

tion is dependent upon a change of attitude on the part of the white population. Their recognition of the mulatto as superior to the black Negro would insure the permanence of the mulatto caste; it would give it a recognized place in the society.[72] Their granting of the demands for a complete removal of all distinctions based on race or color would allow the escape from the race of the superior and light colored individuals.[73] But curiously enough the rebellious attitude of the militant mulattoes against the habitual attitude of the white group and their agitations against discriminations, whether carried on by themselves or by their white sympathizers, which have for their real though seldom openly avowed and sometimes not consciously understood purpose the allowing of the superior, educated mulattoes to escape from the Negro race and to be absorbed into the white race—their protests and complaints and campaigns of bitterness and abuse—have an effect quite different from that desired. It tends to defeat its own object [74] and works ultimately to the profit of the Negro group as a whole rather than to that of the protesting group. Instead of influencing the white man to recognize the mulattoes as a superior type of man and to accept them on a rating different from that on which he accepts the mass of the race —as an individual regardless of race or color—the effect is to identify the complaining individuals more closely with the masses of the race; it tends to solidify the race and, in the thinking of the white man, to class the agitators with it. Its effect is not to break down the white man's antipathy and prejudice, but to make the feeling more acute and to

[72] The Jamaican solution of the race problem. See pp. 331-35 above.
[73] The Brazilian solution of the problem. See pp. 320-24 above.
[74] A fact frequently recognized by the Negroes themselves. See, for e.g., The *Kansas (City) Elevator* (A Negro Paper), 2-2-1916.

make more conscious and distinct the determination of the white people to preserve their ideals of racial and social purity.[75] It results in a stricter and a more conscious and purposeful drawing of the color line and a drawing of the line where it had previously not been drawn. In the effort to escape the race, the mulattoes become more than ever identified with it.[76] The segregation policy which exists in all lines everywhere in the South and less openly and frankly but frequently not less effectively in the North wherever the Negroes are numerous and troublesome, is in large part a reaction on the part of the white people against the militant mulattoes' efforts to achieve social equality with the whites.

Both the mulattoes and the Negroes stand to profit in the end by the agitation of the radical mulatto group for social and class recognition. The struggle for abstract rights is not productive of any important results in the way of removing racial prejudice or social discrimination; it has rather the contrary tendency. But it serves to identify the mulatto with the race and this is an advantage both to the black and to the yellow man. The black Negroes are the gainers by having their natural leaders thrust, even though it be against their will, back upon the race. The mulattoes are gainers in that they are thus forced to see and to embrace the great opportunity which the presence of the people of their own race affords them for a useful and a valuable life of real leadership. The horizon-

[75] "Race Separation Without Discrimination," *Outlook*, Vol. 86, p. 576.
[76] Evans, *Black and White in the Southern States*, p. 208.
". . . I am in grave doubt as to whether the greater part of the friction in the South is caused by the whites having a natural antipathy to Negroes as a race, or an acquired antipathy to Negroes in certain relations to themselves." Johnson, *The Autobiography of an Ex-colored Man*, p. 78.

tal accommodation—the caste system—of the North seems destined ultimately to transform itself, as the earlier caste system of the South has already largely done, into a vertical accommodation—a bi-racial system.

CHAPTER XIV

SUMMARY: PRESENT TENDENCIES

IN summarizing this study, emphasis should be placed on the fact that it has had to do with the mulatto as a social group rather than as a biological type. Mixture of blood, however important or unimportant it may be in itself, has not been the subject of inquiry and there is no assumption concerning its good or ill effects. But mixture of blood has been made the basis of class and caste distinctions. As a result of these distinctions—and possibly because of their mixed ethnic origin—various groups, physically distinguishable because of their mixed ancestry, have appeared, manifest a peculiar psychology and play a distinctive rôle in various inter-racial situations. It is with the status of one of these groups—the mulatto in the United States—with which this study has had principally to do. Without predicating or assuming anything with regard to the inherent mental superiority, inferiority, or equality of the members of the mixed-blood group, as compared with either element of their ethnic ancestry, inquiry was made concerning their origin and increase in numbers, their status in the general social situation, and their rôle in the inter-racial community life. So far as there has been any unavoidable presupposition concerning inherent mental racial capacity, it has been the presupposition of approximately equal mental possibility among the various human types and that such inequalities as may be found existent, culturally or otherwise, are rationally explainable on the assumption of inferior racial opportunity.

As preliminary to the main topic of inquiry, a survey was made of the chief of the mixed-blood groups which have appeared in other bi-racial situations. This survey was necessarily brief and, owing to the scanty, defective and frequently contradictory nature of the data available concerning these groups, the conclusions are highly tentative. In general, however, it may be said that mixed-blood individuals have appeared everywhere when two racial groups representing different cultural stages have been brought into contact. The size of these mixed-blood groups seems to have been dependent upon the races in contact, the relative numbers of the advanced and backward groups, the presence or absence of women of the advanced group and the class of the advanced in contact with the backward race. These mixed-blood groups are everywhere the result of illicit relations between the men of the superior and the women of the inferior group. Everywhere the women of lower races, if not actually seeking sexual relations with the men of the advanced race, nowhere show any pronounced repugnance to such association. The mixed-bloods as a group everywhere have formed, or tended to form, or been formed, into a separate class or caste standing somewhere between the two parent races. Judged from the point of view of the superior race, they have reached everywhere a social position superior to that of the mother race and nowhere have they achieved a position of equality with the advanced group. The superior individuals who have appeared among the lower racial groups have been, almost without exception, members of this mixed-blood class. The ambition of the mixed-bloods seems everywhere an ambition to be accepted into the advanced race and to escape from the lower group. Their actual rôle in the inter-racial situation is consequently dependent upon the attitude of the dominant group. Where no social color line has been formally drawn against them, they have tended to identify themselves with the superior race and themselves to draw a color line against the lower race or else to serve as a physiological tie between the extremes of the population during the process of its reduction to a mongrel unity. Where a color line has been drawn against them by the superior group in the population, they everywhere have tended to form an intermediate caste in the population. Where this caste has been more or less frankly recognized, it serves as a harmonizing group between the population extremes. Where it has not been recognized by the superior race, the caste seldom has been able to maintain itself and the mixed-blood individuals tend to unite their interests with, and become an upper-class among, the lower group.

Passing, then, to the mulatto in the United States, it was found that the intermixture of the races had gone on during the whole period that the races have been in contact on American soil. This mixture was particularly rapid during the colonial era owing to the scarcity of women of the white race and owing to the fact that the lack of any intolerant racial prejudice allowed the lower classes to associate, and freely intermix, with the Negro women. The mixture probably somewhat decreased during the period of national slavery owing to a bitter hatred that grew up between the Negroes and the lower-class whites and to the fact that the Negroes were under a stricter control. The intermixture also appears by statistical measurement to have gone on at a rate somewhat slower than was actually the case owing to the fact that much of it was with the mulatto rather than with the black girls. Since the Emancipation there has continued to be a rapid increase in the number of mulattoes.

The intermixture of the races in the United States has been almost exclusively outside the bounds of the marriage union. There has been a little intermarriage between the races, generally between lower-class white women and Negro or mulatto men. The number of such marriages, however, has been so small as to be entirely negligible in the consideration of race mixture. There has been a much larger amount of concubinage of Negro girls by white men. This form of sex relation was common in some sections during the slave regime and still exists to some extent. The great amount of the intermixture, however, has been of the nature of temporary associations implying absolutely nothing in the way of sentimental attachment on either side and being in point of fact nothing more than a satisfaction of the physical appetite of the individuals concerned. This form of association at present is most frequently between mulatto men and black girls, on the one hand, and between white men and mulatto girls, on the other.

As individuals, the mulattoes always have enjoyed opportunities somewhat greater than those enjoyed by the rank and file of the black Negroes. In slavery days, they were most frequently the trained servants and had the advantages of daily contact with cultured men and women. Many of them were free and so enjoyed whatever advantages went with that superior status. They were considered by the white people to be superior in intelligence to the black Negroes and came to take great pride in the fact of their white blood. They developed a tradition of superiority. This idea was accepted by the black Negroes and consequently the mulattoes enjoyed a prestige in the Negro group. Where possible, they formed a sort of mixed-blood caste and held themselves aloof from the black Negroes and

Summary: Present Tendencies

the slaves of lower station.

The mulattoes, at all times in the history of the Negro in America, have been the superior individuals of the race. Of the score or so of men of first-rate ability which the race has produced, not more than two at the most were Negroes of pure blood. Of the two hundred or so who have made the most noteworthy success in a business or professional way, all, with less than a dozen exceptions, are Negroes of mixed blood. Of some two hundred and forty-six persons, presumably the most successful and the best known men the race has produced, at least thirteen-fourteenths of them are men of mixed blood. Of the list of six hundred and twenty-seven names of persons compiled from the historical and biographical literature and including men of a distinctly lesser degree of note, only about one-ninth were even of approximately pure blood. The same condition was found to prevail in the examination of compilations of the leading men in the various professional and semi-professional pursuits; the professional men of the race are nearly all mulattoes as are the men who have succeeded in some form of artistic or semi-artistic endeavor. In the industrial and business world the same condition prevails; the men who have made any marked success are found to be in nearly every case from the mixed-blood group. It was further found that by taking large numbers of cases from any profession or pursuit and consequently tapping lower ranges of ability and success, the ratio of black men to mulattoes was increased. The higher the standard of success, the lower the per cent of full-blooded Negroes. This was the case as between different professions and within the ranks of the same profession; the ministry has a much higher per cent of full-blood Negroes than does the medical or the teaching profession; the higher positions in all the professions have been reached by mulattoes, very seldom by black Negroes. Speaking generally, the intellectual class of the race is composed of mulattoes; a black man in the class is a rather rare exception.

The rôle which these mixed-blood individuals have played in the inter-racial situation has varied with the time and the place. During the slavery period, they were the superior individuals; but they were not leaders. In the decade just preceding the Civil War, a few persons of Negro blood took a minor part in the anti-slavery agitation. During the Reconstruction Period, they were in some cases used by the white politicians, but had little independent part. After the War and the Reconstruction, there was a further separation between the superior mulattoes and the mass of the race; the tendency for them to form a caste within or just above the Negro group continued.

In the North, the mulattoes of education have tended to be agitators for equal social, civil, and political rights. They consider the ballot an inherent human right rather than an earned responsibility; consequently, they do not endeavor to fit the Negroes to meet the requirements of suffrage, but strive to force the abandonment of suffrage requirements. In social and civil affairs, they insist that equality of treatment is synonymous with identity of treatment. Their spirit is one of complaint and bitterness. They represent a grievance rather than a policy of constructive work. They emphasize what the law can do for the Negro and concern themselves very little with what the Negro can do for himself. They assume, moreover, the rôle of spokesman for the race though, as a whole, they neither understand nor represent the Negro. They do not live with the Negroes; they do not know the Negroes, and, in general, they do not know the condition of the race. They are widely separated in appearance and in sympathy from the mass of the Negro people. They are not even in close touch with the mass of the Negroes in the Northern States. They have not, as yet, found themselves nor their place in the general social life of the community.

In the South with the growth of industrial education and the rise of a middle-class within the Negro group, the mulattoes have taken their place as the natural leaders of the race. The bi-racial adjustment of the races has allowed the rise of men of superior ability and of training and has provided a place for them. These men are, in all but the exceptional cases, mulattoes and generally men of more white than black blood. The teaching of these Southern mulatto leaders is work and service. They emphasize what the Negroes can do to improve their condition and recognize that they will gain in efficiency and in strength of character by overcoming obstacles. They are close to the Negro; they are content to be classed with the race. They have abandoned any hope they may have entertained of being white men. They have their work and their place. Their social and consequently their psychological status is fixed, and there is, therefore, an almost entire absence of the bitterness which characterizes the Northern division of the mulatto group.

* * * * *

Any race, or group within a race, which is subjected to discrimination or persecution tends to take on the form of a nationality. The natural bonds of union within are strengthened by the opposition from without. A race consciousness and a race pride tend to develop as a defensive reaction. The struggle of races and of race groups is not so much an economic struggle as it is a struggle for self-respect and race preservation. As the group or race in contact with one of superior culture itself advances to a degree of culture, the innate desire of the members to isolate themselves from unpleasant stimulation and to enjoy the association of others of their kind, becomes strengthened by their consciousness that their presence is an unwelcome intrusion upon the desires of the other race. A developing consciousness of worth reinforces the innate tendency and the prideful reaction. The ostracized group develops a pride of accomplishment in an effort to offset the feeling of inferiority which the rejection by the superior group necessarily creates. The race or group escapes the unpleasant stimulation given by the latent or active hostility of the superior group by retiring within itself and endeavoring to become self-sufficient. This seems to be the tendency of the American Negro group in the present decade.

The obstacles to racial solidarity among the American Negroes, however, are very numerous and very real. Their isolation is nowhere complete; geographically they are settled among a more numerous white population on which, in very large measure, they are economically and culturally dependent. They lack a distinctive language, one of the most valuable focal points for the growth of such a sentimental complex, and, in the common language, there is no body of literature by members of the race that is in in any way distinctive, or in which a pride of achievement can center. Their religion is but a recent acquisition and in creed differs in no essential way from the religion of the white race. Their manners, customs, and habits of life are in no way distinctive. The race is without a history, or even a tradition of past greatness. Consequently, there are no historical names about which a popular tradition can grow. The only accomplishments of the race are modern ones; a generation into the past brings them against the bleak fact of slavery and beyond that lies the age-long condition from which enslavement by a civilized race was a mighty step. Color, the peculiarity of physical type, is the obvious basis for their nationality. But color is everywhere correlated with primitive and degraded people; it is a thing from which to escape, not a thing of which to be proud.

In spite, however, of the apparently insuperable obstacles in the way of a Negro nationality in America, the present tendency is clearly in that direction. It is toward an identification of the various creeds and a union of the various classes in the race; toward a feeling of pride in the growing accomplishments of the race and a consciousness of unity of interest. Whatever may be the limit that the tendency may finally reach, it is being promoted both designedly and undesignedly by both the whites and the blacks, and by forces from within and from without the race.

The isolation of the race through voluntary action on its part and through legal action on the part of the white race, is the most important single fact making for class consciousness and race solidarity. This isolation of the race is not a recent phenomenon. It is the legal recognition and enforcement of the separation and the extension of it to include every line of contact and every individual of the race which is the characteristic feature of the present policy. The degree to which the races are admittedly separate is somewhat different in different regions. Where the numbers of the race are small and their activities have not conflicted with the white man's idea of what the Negroes' attitude and behavior should be, they have, except in the proscription against social equality, met with no serious difficulty beyond the contempt-to-hatred attitude of their white neighbors. But wherever their numbers have become considerable, or their attitude has become assertive, the Negroes have met the non-intercourse policy of the dominant white man.

The present tendency is toward an increased application intensively and extensively of this segregation policy. Residential segregation is well-nigh universal. In the South, generally, it is enforced by state laws and city ordinances; in the North, by various means depending upon the local conditions.[1] In the school, the Negro child is separated from the white in all the states having a considerable black population. The number of Negro schools is increasing in the cities of the North. Where separate schools are not specially provided, the residential segregation in the Northern cities usually confines the Negro children to one or a few schools.[2] The churches and church organizations are generally separate and tend to become more independent in their development. The membership of most of the well-known secret societies is limited to white men. The clandestine lodges of the Negroes under similar names have nothing in common with the white organizations except the names[3] and the Negroes have organized many secret so-

---

[1] In Chicago the most effective technique seems to be a gentleman's agreement among the real estate men.

A recent ruling of the United States Supreme Court—November 5, 1917—holds all residential segregation laws to be unconstitutional. It will be of interest to note in how far this decision will modify the present tendency.

[2] It is still an open question and one just beginning to be investigated scientifically, whether or not the difference in mental ability of the races is sufficiently great to warrant their separate education as a matter of economy and educational policy. See, for e.g., M. J. Mayo, *The Mental Capacity of the American Negro*.

[3] See G. W. Crawford, *Prince Hall and His Followers*, for a recent effort by a mulatto to prove the legitimacy of Negro Masonry.

cieties under distinctive names. The social life of the races is everywhere separate and distinct.[4] Slowly the race is evolving its own group of business and professional men who cater exclusively to their own race while the white business and professional men tend to avoid the patronage of the Negroes.[5] In all lines and in all sections of the country, the tendency of the white people seems to be to force the Negro people back upon themselves and to allow them or to force them to develop their own institutions and racial life.

This policy on the part of the whites is supplemented by the desire of the rank and file of the Negroes themselves. An overwhelming majority of the Negroes accept racial separation as a simple and natural matter of fact.[6] It seldom concerns them in any concrete way and they are but little interested in abstract considerations. They live in Negro settlements as a matter of social choice and of economic necessity. They avail themselves thankfully of whatever school facilities are offered them; other things being equal, they generally prefer the separate schools.[7] They

[4] See O. Madden, "A Color Phase of Washington," The *World To-day*, Vol. 14, pp. 549-52.

[5] The largest department store in Chicago, for e.g., endeavors by inattentive treatment to discourage Negro patronage.

See reference to Hartman Furniture Company in the *Crisis*, 4-1915, p. 316. White bankers frequently refuse deposits of Negroes and direct them to institutions managed by members of their own race.

[6] See Maurice S. Evans, *Black and White in the Southern States*, pp. 144-45. What the Negro resents is, frequently, not so much the fact of segregation as the humiliating way in which the policy is enforced and the abusive tone of many of its advocates.

[7] "There is not the slightest doubt but that separate school systems, by giving colored children their own teachers and a sense of racial pride, are enabled to keep more colored children in school and take them through longer courses than mixed systems. The 100,000 Negroes of Baltimore have 600 pupils in the separate high school; New York, with

seek and prefer the society of their own class and color. The fact that they are unwelcome in the hotels and restaurants, in the theaters and other places of amusement and entertainment open to the whites, never comes within the experience of any but the very exceptional Negro. The exclusion policy of the whites is in line with the natural tendency of the blacks; it affects and offends the small class of educated and cultured individuals who have more in common, intellectually and otherwise, with the cultured whites, than they have with the mass of the Negro people.[8]

On the part of the leaders among the Negroes, there is an increasing amount of voluntary segregation in more places and in more lines. Separate schools are advocated and petitioned for: they open positions for the teachers. Professional and business men see it more and more to their advantage to promote a spirit of race solidarity.[9] To the extent to which this exists, they cease to be in competition with the business and professional men of the other race.[10] In increasing numbers they are going South, identifying themselves with the race, and finding their life and work among the black group. The opportunities for the educated and ambitious Negro or mulatto is greatest among the people of his own race.[11] Competition there is not so keen and the slightly superior individual can become an important and influential person. The matter of self-inter-

a larger colored population, has less than 200 in its mixed high schools." Editorial, *Crisis,* 2-1912, p. 184-85.

[8] See E. W. Blyden, *Christianity, Islam and the Negro Race,* pp. 168-69.

[9] Editorial, "Segregation—Let Her Come," The *Conservative Counselor,* Waco, Texas, 9-2-1915.

[10] See Editorial, "Paying for a Name," *Chicago, Illinois, Idea,* 9-9-1915.

[11] Booker T. Washington, "Why Should Negro Business Men Go South?" *Charities,* Vol. 15, pp. 17-19.

est ranges them on the side of the segregation policy where the rank and file always have been as a matter of choice. The acquisition of these men increases the feeling of importance on the part of the group and so increases its tendency toward unity. With the increase of racial unity, the opportunities for educated men in the race increase in number and importance, and this, in turn, attracts with increasing force the mulatto and other superior men of the race.

The self-respect as well as the self-interest of the educated Negro tends to the same end as the proscription of the white and the temperament of the blacks. Speaking generally, no Negro, regardless of color or training, is welcome in any social organization of cultured white people anywhere in America. In the semi-social and professional organizations, the same thing is in general true.[12] If the Negro is not barred from the medical, bar, teaching, and other professional associations, he never is made to feel that he is welcome. As a consequence, the Negro, to the extent of his culture and education, stays away when he finds that he is not wanted. It is the only action he can take and preserve his self-respect.[13]

By going South, the educated Negro is allowed to forget that he is denied privileges granted to others, that the race is looked upon as inferior and treated as alien. These are things which concern the individual very little. Aside from the professional agitator, they distress the Negro not at

[12] The action of the American Bar Association in regard to certain near-white Negroes who had been accepted into membership without the fact of their race being known to the Association is a case in point. See "The American Bar Association and the Negro," *Outlook,* Vol. 102, pp. 1-2; "Lawyers and the Color Line," *Literary Digest,* Vol. 45, p. 361; "The Color Line at the Bar," The *Nation,* Vol. 94, pp. 509-10.

[13] Editorial, The *Voice of the People,* Birmingham, Ala., 3-13-1915.

all. In the North, however, they are the constant refrain from which the only escape is an escape from the race. In the South, the educated Negro can escape this everlasting agitation about his status and his rights. There his social status is fixed and once he realizes and accepts this fact, it ceases to trouble him. He has his own group and he is definitely excluded from white society. The treatment in the matter is at least consistent and the mulatto, recognizing the impossibility of achieving a position of social equality, ceases to be concerned about it and loses his bitterness at being excluded. He is able to stop "thinking black." The morbid brooding over real and fancied wrongs gives place to a healthy thought about actual problems. The attitude of slavish dependence—the childish wail for others to right his wrongs—is replaced by an attitude of manly independence, a determination to face the world and to play a manly part therein. Agitation gives place to work; self-reliance replaces self-pity. He no longer lives "behind the veil"; he is dealing with objective reality. He becomes a useful man and, in proportion to his ability, a leader among his people.

Another thing making for the increase in this spirit of nationality is the growing literature of the race. This is a focal point about which the sentiments of the race can crystallize. As it increases in volume and in quality and comes to be more widely read, the sentiment of pride correspondingly increases. There is also some effort being made by the Negroes themselves to create a Negro history.[14] A tradition of musical genius already exists among the race and, outside musical circles, is generally accepted by the whites. The gift which so many Negroes have for effective public speaking is another thing of which the race is ex-

[14] See p. 216 above.

ceedingly proud. The point here is that regardless of the slender basis of fact upon which many of these things rest, they have an immense effect upon the thinking of the race. It is the opinion that a race has of itself that counts in the growth of a nationalistic spirit,[15] and the opinion of the best thinkers of the race is coming more and more to be that if the Negroes desire really to reach a full manhood they must reach it by being Negroes rather than by being weak imitations of white people.

Whether it be because of compulsion on the part of the whites or because of voluntary action on the part of the Negroes, there is an increasing segregation on the part of the Negroes and consequently an increasing tendency toward racial solidarity.

In this growing nationality, the mulattoes who have gone over to the race and cast their fortunes with it are the aristocracy. Broadly speaking, they are the only members of the race who are educated. Consequently, they now form the professional classes. For the most part, they are the property-owning members of the race [16] and most of the Negroes who have made any conspicuous success in a business or industrial way are members of the mulatto division. They are, then, the important men in the commercial and business affairs of the race. Their color or rather absence of color helps to qualify them for a social position among the élite. They have a confidence, born of their pride in their color and their more or less successfully concealed contempt

[15] The belief of the modern Greek, for example, and his boundless pride in the belief, that he is descended from the ancient historical race is not of any less social significance because of the mythological nature of the belief. Similarly, the Irish National movement is chiefly centered in religion, reinforced by myths of ancient greatness.

[16] See Booker T. Washington, "Negro Homes," *Century*, Vol. 76, pp. 71-79.

for a black skin, that the black man seldom attains. They have, and tend to maintain, an exclusive social status that is the despair and the envy of the black man.[17] Their superior economic position, their superior training, their light color and the tradition of superiority, all combine to make them the important and superior individuals in any racial group.

Certain consequences of this movement are fairly obvious. According as one judges these to be desirable or undesirable, one will be disposed to approve or oppose the nationalistic tendency.

Racial solidarity means an increased isolation of the Negro group. The bi-racial adjustment tends to keep the races apart. The further the Negroes develop a sense of nationality, the further do they voluntarily separate themselves from the white world. Direct individual competition between the members of the races tends to diminish. They receive less stimulation from the culture of the other race; they are isolated from that stimulation.[18] To the extent that this becomes true, the Negroes cease to measure their talents and accomplishments by the standards of the superior race. They do not compete with the white man. The isolation narrows their interests and their conceptions, for there is little with which to compare them and weigh their value. They do not need to measure up to the white man's standard; they can live and succeed on a lower plane of efficiency. They are more or less out of the stream of social advancement and the strenuous competition of modern life. This isolation means, of course, a slower advance

---

[17] See editorial, "Don't Blame All," The *Bee*, Washington, D. C., 1-30-1915. See, also, *Boston Reliance*, 3-13-1915.

[18] J. H. DeLoach, "The Negro as a Farmer," *Atlanta Congress*, 1913, p. 381.

on the part of the Negroes toward the standards and accomplishments of European civilization; but it also means a more normal development, a more gradual accommodation to ideas and standards that, by the great mass of the race, are at present neither appreciated nor understood. A gradual elevation of the race means less disorganization of the individual and of the group. The crises in the advance are less radical and the chances for a normal accommodation are greater. In brief, it means a slower but a more normal advance toward the ideals and standards of the white group.

The isolation consequent upon the formation of a nationality tends, in many ways, to inferior educational opportunity for the members of the race. To the extent that the schools are separated and the Negro schools in the hands of the race, the black children will get their schooling from mulatto teachers. These mulattoes are themselves but superficially and imperfectly trained men. The highest estimate would hardly place the number of college trained Negroes at five thousand.[19] They, for the most part, are the product of miserably inefficient Negro colleges. As long as these colleges exist with their present low standards—and the nationalistic tendency is to put them more and more in the hands of the race—the graduates, so far as schooling is concerned, will be equal, perhaps, to the graduate of the ordinary white high school. The teachers of the race will, at best, be graduates of these inferior colleges, and the masses of the race will be defectively trained just to the extent that they are isolated from the white

[19] C. H. McCord estimates the number of Negro college graduates from 1840 to 1909 as 3,853, and from 1910 to 1914 inclusive as 1,147, a total of 5,000 in all for the period of 75 years. *The American Negro as a Dependent, Defective and Delinquent*, p. 14.

race.[20] Under the nationalistic system, therefore, the black man will not make very rapid strides in educational advancement.

The growth of a nationality means the increasing competition on racial lines and the decreasing competition of individuals of the two races. Here, as elsewhere, competition is a selective process. The fact that individual differences are everywhere greater than race differences makes competition act against stratification on the basis of race and tends to put the individual, regardless of race, into the place for which he is best fitted. The racial competition results in forcing the mass of the race into the occupation, or small group of occupations, in which they are best fitted to survive, or for which no other group will compete. The displacement of the race from many vocations on which they once had a virtual monopoly has already gone very far. Mrs. Fannie Barrier Williams,[21] writing in 1905 in regard to the Negroes of Chicago, says on this point:[22]

> . . . In the matter of employment, the colored people of Chicago have lost in the last ten years nearly every occupation of which they once had almost a monopoly. There is now scarcely a Negro barber left in the business district. Nearly all the janitor work in the large

[20] "If such segregation led to the formation of Negro communities entirely apart from the life of the state and the current civilized life around them, with the prospect of personal and communal deterioration, I should be against it. But I can see no reason why it should be so. The best of the race would join the movement, the educated and trained would be available to keep the community life at a high standard, while the highest voluntary assistance and advice of the philanthropic whites would be willingly given. . . ." Evans, *Black and White in the Southern States*, p. 259.

[21] See p. 223 above.

[22] "Social Bonds in the 'Black Belt' of Chicago," *Charities*, Vol. 15, p. 43.

buildings has been taken away from them by the Swedes. White men and women as waiters have supplanted colered men in nearly all the first-class hotels and restaurants. Practically all the shoe polishing is now done by Greeks. Negro coachmen and expressmen and teamsters are seldom seen in the business districts. . . .

In the decade following, the Negroes still further lost ground. Not only in Chicago but throughout the country, the Negroes have been forced out of every occupation in which they have come into competition with another race. Only as roustabouts and rough laborers in the cities, and as agricultural laborers in the South, have the Negroes been able to hold their own.[23]

The growth of racial solidarity probably means a lessening of racial intermixture. The segregation and the voluntary isolation prevent, in large measure, the opportunity for it to take place. So long as the races are not isolated and remain on different cultural levels, intermixture will go on to the extent of the desire of the males of the superior race. Segregation does not lessen the tendency to intermix; it lessens the opportunity. On the other hand, the developing sense of race pride tends to the same end.[24] The Negro woman ceases to desire such relations when they come to mean disgrace instead of prestige. When the Negro provides as well for his wife as the white man does for his black or yellow concubine, there is also less disposition on the part of the race women to form such unions.[25] The

[23] E. C. Branson, "The Negro Working Out His Own Salvation," *Atlanta Congress*, 1913, p. 390. The exceptions to such generalizations are of course very numerous. In some cases the Negroes have been forced *up* instead of *out*.

[24] Thomas Nelson Page, *The Negro*, p. 291.

[25] See Editorial "Enemies Within Our Camp," The *Chicago Defender*, 4-22-1916.

vicious elements of the race, moreover, will be restrained by a sense of public disapproval and casual intermixture will decrease.

The growth of a nationalistic spirit may very conceivably mean an increase of friction between the races.[26] The increase of race pride and personal self-respect, until it reaches a stage beyond mere bumptiousness and braggadocio, has a tendency to bring the man into conflict with his social surroundings. The mulattoes going over to the Negroes and becoming their leaders contain a large per cent of disgruntled agitators.[27] So far, also, as the mulattoes are Northern men, they are unfamiliar with the Negro character and with the conditions of life in the South. That they are not always wise leaders may well be supposed. Their mistakes may increase racial strife unless restrained by the common sense of the members of the two races.[28] Some opponents of the segregation policy even predict race wars and revolutions—analogous, apparently, to the situation in the Latin-American countries which has been brought about, partly at least, by the adoption of an opposite policy—as the final outcome of the segregation policy.[29] Except for the placid disposition and the native common sense of the black man, the anarchistic teachings of some of the malcontents doubtless would result occasionally in rioting and the growth of a spirit of racial ill-will.

[26] S. D. McEnery, "Race Problem in the South," *Independent*, Vol. 55, p. 426.

[27] "There is, indeed, rather a tendency to racial solidarity in opposition to the whites on all questions whatsoever; . . . There is, moreover, a not rare belief among the whites that the preachers and leaders contribute to increase these tendencies and teach hostility rather than try to uplift the race morally." Page, *The Negro*, p. 304. See, also, p. 307.

[28] McCord, *The American Negro*, p. 109.

[29] "Segregation," *Crisis*, 12-1913.

Summary: Present Tendencies

The mulattoes at present are the leading men of the race and the indication is that they will become more and more so as time goes on. They have an immense start of the blacks and, granting that they have an equal amount of native ability, there is no immediate prospect of their losing the lead they now have, but every reason to believe that the gap will tend to widen. It is certainly being widened at the present time.

The mulattoes are the property-owning class among the race. Most of the business is conducted by them. They are the ones who own homes and other property. Whatever be the advance that the black man may make, the mulatto group with the aid of the accumulated capital is advancing in economic prosperity at even greater strides.

The mulattoes are at present the educated and the professional classes among the race. Moreover, at present they make the greatest use of the schools of a secondary and college character which provide education to members of the race. This means that, for a generation at least, the mulattoes will continue to be the intellectual group of the race.

The ideal of the Negro is a light-colored man. So long as the overwhelming majority of the notables of the race are yellow or near-white rather than brown or black, the ideal of the race will continue to be light rather than dark. With the growth of racial solidarity, these individuals are more and more included within the race where their light color is a distinct asset to them.[30] The ideal of the race tends to perpetuate the mulatto as a superior type.

The mulattoes are everywhere proud of their white re-

---

[30] This is true in spite of a species of "race pride" which seeks out black men for high positions and show purposes instead of seeking competence.

lationship and anxious to preserve it. Nearly every man of the group marries a woman lighter than himself. The number of prominent mulattoes with wives who are black, or even noticeably darker than themselves, are scarcely more numerous than those who have married white wives. The tendency, then, from generation to generation is for the intellectual part of the race to become lighter and lighter in color.

A very small number of very light mulattoes each year desert the race and become incorporated into the white race. This number tends to increase as successive generations of admixture of white blood lighten the color, straighten the hair, and smooth the features of the race. At present, however, the intermarriage of white women with mulattoes, as well as the illicit admixture of white blood, far more than counterbalances the losses to the group through such changes of racial status.

Furthermore, the mulatto group continually is being improved by the addition to it of the best blood of the Negro race. The black man of ability, in almost every case, marries into the mulatto caste; and his children, with whatever of their father's superior mentality they inherit, are mulattoes. So far as his superiority is inherited, it becomes an asset to the mulatto group. The black man of greatest ability, perhaps, of any black man in the race is married to a light-colored mulatto woman. The most widely known black man of the race has a wife who is near white. The black man who approached nearer to genius than any other man the race has produced, married a light mulatto. The rule is almost without an exception that the black man of consequence marries into the mulatto caste. The mulatto group thus, on the assumption of the transmission of superior mental capacity, tends to become not only a culturally but a biologically superior group.

The mulattoes are thus the vital point in the whole race problem. It is their ideas, their sentiments, and their attitudes, in so far as they identify themselves with the race, that tend to prevail. The fact needs to be recognized in any dealing with the race, or in any efforts for race betterment.

In any study and discussion of the race problem, scientific accuracy as well as a decent regard for simple truth requires that the writer indicate whether his discussion has to do with full-blooded Negroes or with the men of mixed blood. The failure to make this simple and elementary distinction, more than any other one thing, has made the vast bulk of the literature relating to the Negro in America either worthless or vicious.

INDEX TO NAMES OF MEN WHOSE ETHNIC ANCESTRY IS ANALYZED

Abbott, A. R., 228, 238.
Abbott, A. W., 247, 259.
Abbott, Granville S., 217.
Abner, David, 265.
Adams, Mrs. Agnes, 234.
Adams, Cyrus Field, 299.
Adams, John, 217.
Adams, J. W., 222.
Adams, Lewis, 238.
Adger, Robert, 229.
Aldridge, Ira, 196, 198, 288.
Alexander, John H., 228, 247.
Alexander, J. N. W., 254.
Alexander, M. S., 299.
Alexander, N. H., 297.
Alexander, William, 299.
Alexander, W. G., 222, 259.
Allen, B. F., 268.
Allen, G. W., 277.
Allen, Isaac B., 234.
Allen, Macon B., 234.
Allen, Richard, 191.
Allen, William G., 238.
Allensworth, Lt. Col. A., 247.
Allston, J. H., 234.
Allston, Philip J., 234, 298, 299.
Alstor, J. W., 277.
Ambush, James Enoch, 217.
Amiger, W. T., 266.
Amo, Anthony William, 189.
Anderson, C. H., 296, 298.
Anderson, Charles W., 203, 208, 253, 299.
Anderson, Duke William, 217.
Anderson, John C., 232.
Anderson, J. H., 225.
Anderson, Louis B., 228.
Anderson, Osborn Perry, 231.
Anderson, Major W. T., 247.
Andrews, W. T., 299.
Annibal, 189.
Annibal, Son of, 189.

Antoine, C. C., 220, 252.
Appo, William, 231.
Archer, H. E., 228, 266.
Archer, Mrs. Henrietta M., 228.
Armisted, E. H., 234.
Armstrong, William O., 234.
Arnett, B. W., 232.
Atkins, S. G., 225, 277.
Attway, W. A., 296, 299.
Attucks, Crispus, 197, 200.
Attwell Ernest, 238.
Attwell, Joseph S., 238.
Attwood, L. K., 238.
Augusta, A. T., 232, 247, 260.
Augustin, Peter, 229.
Avant, Henry, 299.

Bacote, S. W., 278.
Bagnall, Powhattan, 234.
Bailey, Grandmother, 229.
Bailey, J. B., 234.
Bailey, L. C., 257.
Baker, D. W., 297.
Baker, Gertrude M., 234.
Baker, Harry E., 225, 256.
Baker, T. Nelson, 270.
Baldwin, Maria L., 238.
Ballard, W. H., 299.
Banks, Charles, 208, 298, 299.
Banks, Mrs. Charles, 299.
Banks, J. B., 222.
Banks, Walden, 234.
Banneker, Benjamin, 189, 190, 196, 198, 199, 257.
Bannister, E. M., 220, 287.
Baptiste, George de, 239.
Barbadoes, James, 219.
Barnet, Mrs. Ida Wells, 201.
Barnett, Ferdinand L., 228.
Barrier, Anthony, 229.
Barrier, Miss Ella D., 222.
Bass, Charles T., 299.

399

Basset, E. D., 217, 251.
Beale, Mme. I. B., 299.
Beaman, Amon C., 229.
Beaman, Jehiel C., 234.
Beams, Charlotte, 217.
Beckett, W. W., 265.
Becraft, Maria, 217.
Bell, George, 232.
Bell, J. B., 299.
Bell, James M., 231.
Bell, L. A., 297.
Benjamin, Edgar P., 234.
Benjamin, L. W., 257.
Benjamin, Miss M. E., 257.
Benson, John J., 238.
Benson, William E., 238.
Bentley, C. E., 203, 209.
Bergen, Madam Flora B., 201.
Berry, E. C., 238, 299.
Bethune, Miss M. M., 266.
Bethune, Thomas, 220.
Bibb, J. D., 225.
Bigham, J. A., 285.
Binga, Jesse, 238, 299.
Bird, Frank K., 277.
Bishop, H. C., 203.
Black, Henry, 222.
Blackshear, E. L., 225, 268.
Blackwell, G. L., 277.
Blair, Henry, 258.
Blodgett, J. H., 299.
Blue, L., 257.
Bluitt, B. R., 260.
Blyden, Edward W., 199.
Bogle, Robert, 229.
Bonchet, Edward A., 270.
Bond, James, 239.
Bond, James A., 299.
Bond, Theophilus, 299.
Booker, Joseph A., 224, 265.
Booze, Eugene P., 299.
Boss, Hon. Harry, 200.
Bowen, Mrs. Ariel, 225.
Bowen, J. W. E., 203, 208, 299.
Bowler, Jack, 239.
Bowser, Mrs. Rosa D., 225.
Boyd, B., 239.
Boyd, Henry, 217.
Boyd, H. A., 299.
Boyd, Henry A., 295.
Boyd, R. F., 260, 299.
Boyd, R. H., 203, 208, 278 300.
Bradford James, 232.

Bragg, Fellow, 239.
Braggs, Geo. F., Jr., 225.
Braithwaite, William S., 200, 203, 208, 284.
Brawley, B. G., 203.
Brawley, E. M., 225.
Bray, J. A., 276.
Brooks, Charles H., 298, 300.
Brooks, Paul C., 234.
Brooks, W. H., 225.
Brown, Aaron, 277.
Brown, A. M., 239.
Brown, D. H., 300.
Brown, E. C., 296.
Brown, E. E., 234.
Brown, Henry, 257.
Brown, Henry E., 239.
Brown, Miss H. Q., 201, 203.
Brown, John M., 217.
Brown, Nellie, 220.
Brown, Richard L., 220.
Brown, Roscoe C., 260.
Brown, S. N., 225.
Brown, William Wells, 192, 200, 239.
Browne, Hugh M., 229.
Bruce, B. K., 196, 199, 250.
Bruce, Mrs. B. K., 203.
Bruce, John E., 203.
Bruce, Roscoe C., 203, 209, 252.
Bryan, Andrew, 19.
Bryant, Ira T., 203, 209, 277, 300.
Bryant, W. W., 234.
Buchanan, Noah, 252.
Buchanan, W. S., 267.
Buckner, George W., 253, 254.
Bugg, J. H., 239.
Bulkley, W. H., 203.
Bulkley, William L., 270.
Bundy, Richard W., 253.
Burkins, Eugene, 220, 257.
Burleigh, Harry T., 200, 203, 208.
Burns, Anthony, 220, 229.
Burr, Seymour, 234.
Burrell, W. P., 239.
Burroughs, George L., 239.
Burroughs, Miss Nannie H., 203, 266, 278, 300.
Burroughs, W. M., 300.
Burrows, William, 276.
Burwell, L. L., 239, 260.
Bush, Anita, 200.
Bush, Chester E., 300.

Index to Names

Bush, Mrs. Cora E., 300.
Bush, John E., 209, 239, 254, 298, 300.
Bush, Mrs. Olivia Ward, 234.
Bush, William H., 203.
Butler, H. R., 225, 260.

Cabaniss, J. A., 300.
Cain, R. H., 217, 251.
Caldwell, J. C., 277.
Caldwell, J. S., 203, 277.
Calhoun, A. R., 276.
Calhoun, R. C., 300.
Calloway, T. J., 300.
Campbell, J. B., 239.
Cannon, George E., 260.
Capitien, James Eliza John, 189.
Cardozo, F. L., 232.
Cardozo, T. W., 252.
Carey, Lott, 217.
Carey, Mary A. S., 217.
Carney, William H., 217.
Carr, James L., 203.
Carroll, Jacqueline, 234.
Carroll, Richard, 239, 300.
Carson, Simeon L., 260.
Carter, Rev. E. R., 222.
Carter, H. C., 252.
Carter, James G., 253, 300.
Carter, Lt. Louis A., 248.
Carter, R. A., 210, 275.
Carter, W. J., 203.
Carver, G. W., 210, 269.
Cato, 220.
Chappelle, Julius B., 234.
Chappelle, W. D., 225, 276.
Charles, H. M., 300.
Charlton, Melville, 220.
Chase, William Calvin, 224.
Chavis, John, 191.
Cheatham, H. P., 251.
Cherry, M. A., 257.
Chester, T. Morris, 232.
Chestnutt, C. W., 194, 195, 198, 203, 208, 284.
Chiles, Nick, 210.
Chosum, Melvin J., 296.
Chretien, Paul, 239.
Church, R. E. Jr., 209.
Church, R. R., 300.
Clark, Jonas, 234.
Clark, J. Milton, 234.
Clark, J. S., 268.
Clark, Peter H., 229.
Cleaves, N. C., 275.
Clement, G. C., 277.
Clinton, George W., 209, 277, 300.
Coard, B. T., Jr., 296.
Cobb, J. A., 253, 300.
Coggins, J. N. C., 278.
Cohen, Walter L., 300.
Coker, Daniel, 232.
Cole, Bob, 200, 234.
Cole, Rebecca J., 260.
Collier, N. W., 300.
Conner, James M., 276.
Cook, Elijah, 239.
Cook, Eliza Ann, 217.
Cook, George F. T., 199.
Cook, George W., 203, 210.
Cook, John F., Jr., 199.
Cook, John F., Sr., 199.
Cook, Will Marion, 203, 208.
Coolidge, J. S., 257.
Cooper, Mrs. Anna J., 228.
Cooper, E. J., 228.
Copeland, John Anthony, 231.
Coppin, Fanny M. Jackson, 199.
Coppin, L. J., 203, 209, 276.
Coppin, Thomas, 229.
Corbin, J. C., 232.
Cornell, A. C., 222.
Cornish, Alexander, 217.
Corrothers, James D., 220.
Cosey, A. A., 278.
Coshburn, Walter M., 222.
Coshburn, Mrs. W. M., 222.
Costin, Louisa Parke, 217.
Costin, Martha, 232.
Costin, William, 217.
Cottrell, Charles, 253.
Cottrell, Elias, 239, 275, 300.
Council, W. H., 222.
Coursey, Robert F., 234.
Courtney, S. E., 210, 260, 299, 300.
Covington, John, 300.
Cowan A. C., 300.
Cox, J. M., 226, 266.
Cox, W. Alexander, 235, 300.
Cox, W. W., 300.
Craft, Henry K., 239.
Crafts, William, 229.
Crafts, Mrs. William, 229.
Crawford, Joshua, 235.
Crogman, William Henry, 203, 209.
Cromwell, J. W., 226.

Index to Names

Crowdy, William, 235.
Crowther, Samuel, 239.
Crum, W. D., 239.
Crum, W. E., 235.
Crummel, Alexander, 196, 197, 199, 285.
Crummell, Boston, 239.
Cuffe, John, 218.
Cuffe, Paul, 196, 199.
Cugoano, Ottobah, 189.
Cummings, Harry S., 203.
Curtis, Bishop, 239.
Curtis, A. M., 203, 259, 260.
Curtis, James L., 200, 203.
Curtis, J. Webb, 228.
Custalo, William, 222.

Dabney, Austin, 239.
Dailey, Sam, 239.
Dailey, U. G., 260.
Dalton, Thomas, 235.
Dancey, J. C., 203, 209, 278.
Dandridge, Ann, 218.
Dangerfield, Newby, 231.
Daniels, Jim, 231.
Darden, J. H., 222.
Darden, John W., 260.
Davage, M. S., 278.
Davidson, Shelby, 257.
Davis, A. K., 220, 252.
Davis, Mrs. Belle, 300.
Davis, B. J., 209.
Davis, B. O., 209, 248.
Davis, Charles T., 300.
Davis, D. W., 226.
Davis, George W., 300.
Davis, Henrietta Vinton, 201.
Davis, I. D., 226.
Davis, Mrs. L. A., 222.
Davis, W. R., 257.
Day, J. Howard, 229.
Day, William Howard, 239.
Dean, Jennie, 239.
De Grasse, John V., 218, 260.
Delancey, Martin R., 230.
De Large, R. C., 220, 251.
De Mortie, Louise, 218, 235.
De Mortie, Mark, 235.
Dennison, F. A., 203, 209.
Derrick, W. B., 224.
Dett, R. N., 203.
Deveaux, John H., 239.
Dickerson, William F., 218.

Dickinson, J. H., 257.
Dickson, Rev. Moses, 239.
Diffay, J. O., 295.
Diggs, J. R. L., 270.
Dillon, Dr. Sadie, 239.
Dogan, M. W., 210, 266.
Dorsett, C. N., 239, 260.
Dorsey, Thomas L., 230.
Dossen, Vice-President, 240.
Douglass, Charles R., 230, 240.
Douglass, Frederick, 192, 196, 197, 198, 199, 200, 210, 252, 288.
Douglass, H. Ford, 230.
Douglass, J. H., 203.
Douglass, Lewis H., 230.
Douglass, W., 257.
Downing, George T., 230.
Downing, Thomas, 230.
Doyle, James, 258.
Draper, Garrison, 232.
Drew, Howard P., 200.
Drury, Theodore, 235.
Du Bois, W. E. B., 195, 197, 198, 200, 203, 207, 270, 284.
Dubuclet 240.
Duckery, Henry, 235.
Dudley, James B., 267.
Dumas, Alexandre, 188, 197, 200.
Dumas, A. W., 260.
Dunbar, Chas. B., 260.
Dunbar, Paul Laurence, 194, 195, 197, 198, 199, 200, 210, 224, 284, 285.
Dunbar, Mrs. Paul Laurence, 226.
Dungee, A. C., 300.
Dunlop, Alexander, 240.
Dunn, Oscar J., 220, 252.
Duprey, William, 235.
Durham, James, 189, 191, 196, 260.
Dyson, Walter, 285.

Earnest Louis, 222.
Easton, Hosea, 235.
Easton, Joshua, 235.
Edmonds, T. H., 257.
Eggleston, E. F., 240.
Elbert, S. G., 299, 300.
Elbert, Mrs. S. G., 300.
Ellerson, L. B., 226.
Elliot, R. B., 196, 199, 251.
Elliott, J. T., 299.
Elliott, T. J., 300.
Emanuel, J., 300.

Europe, James Resse, 200, 203.
Evans, Henry, 191.
Evans, Matilda A., 240.
Evans, Mrs. S. J., 228.
Evans, Wm. P., 300.

Ferguson, John C., 260.
Ferguson, Joseph, 260.
Ferguson, S. D., 203, 278.
Fields, W. R., 240.
Fisher, D. A., 257.
Fleet, John H., 218.
Flipper, Henry O., 247.
Flipper, J. S., 204, 276.
Floyd, Silas X., 220.
Ford, C. E., 300.
Ford, J. E., 210.
Forten, Miss Charlotte, 218.
Forton, James, 192, 258.
Fortune, T. Thomas, 195, 204, 208.
Fountain, W. A., 265.
France, Joseph J., 260.
Frances, J. W., 296.
Francis, J. R., 226, 228.
Francis, William, 189.
Franklin, G. W., 300.
Franklin, Nicholas, 218.
Frence, John B., 228.
Frierson, A. U., 226.
Fuller, S. C., 204, 208, 260.
Fuller, Mrs. S. C., See Meta Vaux Warrick.
Fuller, Thomas, 189, 190.
Furniss, Henry W., 204, 254.
Furniss, S. A., 300.

Gabriel, 218.
Gaones, John S., 240.
Gamble, H. F., 260.
Ganes, John F., 230.
Gardner, Eliza, 235.
Garland, C. N., 235, 260.
Garner, James E., 301.
Garner, J. H., 301.
Garnett, H. H., 196, 197, 199.
Garrett, Thomas, 220.
Gaskins, Nelson, 235.
Gates, George A., 301.
Gell, Monday, 220.
Geoffray, L'Islet, 189.
Gibbs, Miss Hattie, 222.
Gibbs, J. C., 219,

Gibbs, Miffin Wistar, 192, 301.
Gibson, G. W., 240.
Gilbert, F. H., 298, 301.
Gilbert, J. W., 226, 276.
Gilbert, M. W., 226, 276.
Gillian, C. W., 301.
Girideau, W. L., 301.
Gladden, Lt. W. W., 248.
Gleaves, R. H., 220, 252.
Gleed, Robert, 252.
Gloucester, John, 191.
Goddard, Julius B., 235.
Goiens, John W., 269.
Goler, W. H., 204, 265, 278.
Gomez, General Maximo, 228, 248.
Goodwin, G. A., 226.
Gordon, Henry, 240.
Gordon, James H., 301.
Gordon, Nora A., 222.
Gordon, Sarah, 240.
Gordon, W. C., 299, 301.
Graham, A. A., 301.
Grant, Bishop A., 224, 301.
Grant, George F., 235.
Gray, F. A., 301.
Gray, Miss Mary A., 301.
Gray, William, 240.
Green, Benjamin T., 240.
Green, Charles Henry, 232.
Green, E. E., 260.
Green, John, 224.
Green, Lt. J. E., 248.
Green, John P., 218.
Green, Shields, 231.
Green, S. W., 210.
Greener, R. T., 196, 197, 208, 220.
Gregory, J. M., 204.
Grigg, John A., 265.
Griggs, E. M., 296.
Griggs, Sutton E., 210, 278.
Grimes, Leonard, 218.
Grimké, Archibald H., 204, 208.
Grimké, F. J., 194, 204, 208.
Gross, F. W., 265.
Gross, William E., 240.
Groves, C. A., 301.
Groves, J. G., 301.
Groves, Marjory, 235.

Hackley, Mrs. E. A., 220.
Hale, W. J., 210, 267.
Hall, Mrs. Anna M., 218.
Hall, Charles H., 235,

Hall, G. C., 204, 208, 240, 259, 260, 299.
Hall, Primus, 230.
Hall, Prince, 240.
Hall, R. M., 240.
Hall, Walter P., 301.
Hamilton, R. T., 260.
Hamlett, J. A., 276.
Hamlin, J. A., 301.
Hamm, James R., 301.
Hansberry, E., 223.
Haralson, Jare, 240, 251.
Hargrave, F. S., 260.
Harlan, Robert, 232.
Harllee, N. W., 226.
Harper, Fenton, 240.
Harper, Frances E., 201.
Harper, Mrs. F. E. W., 192.
Harper, William A., 287.
Harris, Charles E., 235.
Harris, C. R., 277.
Harris, Mrs. Carol V., 301.
Harris, Gilbert C., 235, 301.
Harris, J. H., 301.
Harris, T. N., 240.
Harrison, Hazel, 220.
Harrod, W. A., 279.
Hart, Mrs., 228.
Hart, W. H. H., 204.
Hatcher, Henry A., 301.
Hatter, Allen, 301.
Havis, Ferdinand, 210.
Hawkins, J. R., 204, 209, 277, 301.
Hawkins, Mason A., 204.
Hawkins, T. S., 240.
Hawkins, W. Ashbie, 204.
Hayden, Lewis, 192.
Hayes, Alexander, 218.
Haynes, George E., 209, 270.
Haynes, Lemuel, 191, 196, 198.
Hayes, Roland W., 204.
Hayes, Thomas H., 299, 301.
Hazel, William A., 235.
Heard, W. H., 226, 276.
Hemmings, Robert, 235.
Hendley, Willie M., 269.
Henry, Sam, 252.
Henson, Josiah, 232.
Henson, Mathews, 200, 240.
Herndon, A. F., 210.
Hershaw, L. M., 204.
Hewin, J. T., 226.
Hewitt, W. V., 301.

Hewlett, E. M., 240.
Hibbler, John A., 301.
Higgins, W. H., 260.
Higiemonde, 188.
Hill, James, 252.
Hill, J. S., 296.
Hill, Mrs. L., 240.
Hill, L. P., 240.
Hills, J. Seth, 260.
Hilton, John T., 235.
Hilyer, A. F., 226, 257.
Hoagland, George, 301.
Hodges, M. Hamilton, 235.
Hogan, Ernest, 200.
Holloway, Richard, 240.
Holloway, T. B., 296.
Hollowell, William, 230.
Holly, J. T., 240.
Holmes, William E., 223, 265.
Hood, J. W., 204, 209, 277.
Holsey, L. H., 204, 275.
Holtzclaw, W. H., 301.
Hope, John, 204, 208, 265.
Hort, Mrs. Emma T., 223.
Horton, George, 232.
Hosier, Harry, 240.
Houston, R. C., 298.
Howard, A. C., 301.
Howard, Alexander S., 301.
Howard, E. C., 260.
Howard, P. W., 301.
Howell, G. M., 301.
Howell, S. A., 297.
Hubbard, A., 240.
Hubert, Z. T., 265.
Hudson, R. B., 278.
Hull, D. J., 265.
Hunt, A. H., 235.
Hunt, H. A., 226.
Hunt, William H., 224, 253.
Hunter, John E., 260.
Hunton, W. A., 204, 210.
Hurst, John E., 204, 209, 276.
Hurst, S. P., 301.
Hyer, The Sisters, 220.
Hyman, John, 240, 251.

Isaacs, E. W. D., 204, 278.
Ish, I. G., 224.

Jackson, A. B., 260, 299.
Jackson, A. D., 285.
Jackson, A. S., 277.

Index to Names

Jackson, Deal, 240.
Jackson, George H., 254.
Jackson, Jennie, 240.
Jackson, J. C., 299, 301.
Jackson, J. S., 278.
Jackson, Miss Lena T., 226.
Jackson, Mary C., 228.
Jackson, T. J., 296.
Jackson, William L., 232.
Jacobs, C. C., 278.
Jacobs, H. P., 252.
Jack, Uncle, 275.
Jamison, M. F., 275.
Janifer, J. T., 277.
Jason, W. C., 268.
Jasper, John, 240.
Jefferson, E. B., 301.
Jenifer, J. T., 204, 210.
Jenkins, O. C., 240.
Jenkins, S. J., 223.
Jennings, Cordelia A., 240.
Jennings, Mrs. Mary F., 240.
Johnson, 296.
Johnson, Mrs. A. E., 284.
Johnson, A. N., 301.
Johnson, Billy, 235.
Johnson, C. F., 210, 301.
Johnson, Elijah, 220.
Johnson, Harvey, 204.
Johnson, H. L., 204.
Johnson, H. T., 210.
Johnson, J. A., 204, 210, 276.
Johnson, J. O., 226.
Johnson, J. Rosamond, 200, 204, 209.
Johnson, John Thomas, 232.
Johnson, James W., 201, 204, 208, 226, 254.
Johnson, L. E., 240.
Johnson, Peter A., 260.
Johnson, Sol. C., 241.
Johnson, W. Bishop, 279.
Johnson, W. H., 301.
Johnson, W. I., 301.
Jones, Mme. (Black Patti), 201.
Jones, Absolom, 220.
Jones, A. D., 260.
Jones, E. M., 278.
Jones, E. P., 301.
Jones, Miss Hazel K., 302.
Jones, Henry, 229.
Jones, John, 230.
Jones, J. G., 241.

Jones, J. H., 226.
Jones, Joshua M., 276.
Jones, John W., 261.
Jones, Miles B., 260.
Jones, R. E., 204, 208, 278, 299, 302.
Jones, Scipio A., 210, 299, 302.
Jones, Sissieretta, 201.
Jones, T. W., 226, 302.
Jones, Wiley, 241.
Jordan, D. J., 226.
Jordan, L. G., 204, 209, 279, 302.
Josenberger, Mrs. Mary, 302.
Juan, 229.
Just, E. E., 204, 209.

Kealing, H. T., 195, 204, 209, 266.
Keatts, Chester W., 224.
Keatts, C. W., 302.
Kelly, James, 223.
Kennedy, W. A., 302.
Kenney, J. A., 241, 261.
Kerr, S., 226.
Kersey, Willis A., 302.
Keys, H. W., 302.
King, G. H., 223.
King, Horace, 223.
King, H. H., 302.
King, J. T., 223.
King, M. N., 223.
King, W. E., 209.
King, W. W., 223.
Knight, D. L., 302.
Knox, George L., 226.
Kyles, L. W., 278.

Lafon, Thomy, 220.
Lambert family, 241.
Lambert, William, 219.
Lane, Isaac, 241, 275.
Lane, J. F., 265.
Lane, Lunsford, 192, 193.
Lane, W. C., 235.
Laney, Lucy, 204.
Lankford, J. A., 302.
Langford, Sam, 207.
Langston, John M., 196, 197, 199, 251.
Lattimore, Andrew E., 235.
Latimer, George, 235.
Lavalette, W. A., 257.
Lawrence, W. P., 279.
Lawson, R. Augustus, 204.
Leary, John, S., 232.

Index to Names

Leary, Lewis S., 231.
Leary, Matthew, 241.
Leary, Matthew, Jr., 241.
Lee, Bertina, 220, 287.
Lee, B. F., 204, 208, 276.
Lee, Joseph, 235, 254.
Lee M. D., 278.
Lehman, M. J., 223.
Leile, George, 191.
Levy, J. R., 261, 302.
Lewis, A. L., 302.
Lewis, Edmonia, 201, 287.
Lewis, James, 204.
Lewis, J. H., 235, 302.
Lewis, John W., 296.
Lewis, M. N., 302.
Lewis, W. H., 201, 204, 207, 254.
Lewis, W. I., 226.
Lights, F. L., 297.
Lindsay, Samuel, 297.
Livingston, Lemuel W., 254.
Logan, Warren, 205, 210, 302.
Logan, Mrs. Warren, 226.
Loguen, Bishop, 218.
Long, Jefferson, 241, 251.
Loudin, F. J., 257.
Lovett, William C., 236.
Lovinggood, R. S., 266.
Lowe, J. I., 277.
Lowry, Samuel, 232.
Lowther, George W., 236.
Lucas, Sam, 201.
Lucas, W. W., 223, 278.
Lugrade, S. L., 241.
Lundy, Benjamin, 230.
Lynch, James, 252.
Lynch, John R., 205, 208, 248, 251.
Lynk, M. V., 266.
Lytle, Miss Lutie A., 228.

McCarthy, Anthony, 302.
McCarty, Owen, 241.
McCary, William, 252.
Maceo, 248.
McClennon, A. C., 261.
McClellan, G. M., 226.
McCord, Sam, 241.
McCoy, Benjamin M., 218.
McCoy, E., 205, 257.
McCoy, Elijah T., 198.
McCrorey, H. L., 265.
McCulloch, J. B., 302.
McDaniel, E. E., 302.

McDonald, J. Frank, 277.
McDonald, W. H., 296.
McDonough, David K., 261.
McDuffy, J. D., 302.
McGilbray, D. C., 302.
McKane, Cornelius, 236.
McKee, John, 220.
McKinley, J. Frank, 228.
McKinley, Whitfield, 254.
McKissack, E. H., 241, 302.
McKissack, Moses, 302.
Majors, W. L., 302.
Margetson, G. Reginald, 236.
Marshall, John R., 205.
Marshall, Napoleon B., 236.
Martin, J. A., 268.
Martin, J. C., 276.
Martin, John Sella, 236.
Martin, Martha and sister, 232.
Martin, William M., 228.
Mason, Cassius, 205.
Mason, Mrs. Lena, 226.
Mason, M. C. B., 226, 302.
Mason, U. G., 241.
Mathews, William E., 230.
Matthews, James C., 205.
Matthews, Victoria E., 241.
Matthews, W. Clarence, 236.
Matzeliger, J. E., 220, 257.
Maxwell, Leigh R., 223.
Merrick, John, 241.
Middleton, Charles H., 218.
Miles, Alexander, 228.
Miles, Mary E., 232.
Miller, Kelly, 194, 195, 201, 205, 207, 285, 302.
Miller, T. H., 241, 251.
Minton, F. J., 302.
Minton, Henry, 229.
Mitchell, Charlie L., 218.
Mitchell, John, 205.
Mitchell, John, Jr., 208.
Mitchell, Mrs. Nellie B., 236.
Mitchell, Robert, 279.
Mitchell, S. T., 232.
Mitchell, W. L., 297.
Mollison, W. E., 205.
Montgomery, Ben, 241.
Montgomery, I. T., 205, 208, 252, 302.
Montgomery, Thornton, 241.
Moody, O. L., 266.
Moore, A. M., 261.

Index to Names

Moore, Alice Ruth, 220.
Moore, Fred R., 209, 254.
Moore, G. W., 205, 278.
Moore, J. H., 276.
Moore, Lewis B., 205, 270.
Moore, T. Clay, 302.
Moorland, J. E., 205, 208.
Moreland, John F., 278.
Morgan, B. J., 302.
Morgan, Clement G., 236.
Morgan, J. H., 226.
Morris, Albert, 241.
Morris, E. C., 205, 208, 279, 302.
Morris, E. H., 194, 205, 208.
Morris, Freeman, 241.
Morris, J., 232.
Morris, Robert, 232.
Morris, W. R., 205.
Mosby, John M., 296.
Mossell, N. F., 205, 209, 261.
Moten, Lucy, 205.
Moton, R. R., 201, 205, 207, 269, 302.
Mott, Lucretia, 229.
Moultry, Francis J., 241.
Murphy, W. O., 302.
Murray, Daniel, 205.
Murray, G. W., 226, 251, 257.
Murray, J. L., 223.
Muse, Lindsay, 218.
Myers, Cyrus, 223.
Myers, George A., 241.
Myers, Stephen J., 230.

Nance, L., 257.
Napier, J. C., 205, 208, 254, 299, 302.
Napier, Mrs. J. C., 302.
Nash, Charles E., 241, 251.
Neighbors, W. D., 295, 302.
Nell, William, 232, 236.
Nelson, Dave, 302.
Nelson, Ida Gray, 228.
Nesbitt, F. M., 303.
Newby, Dangerfield, 231.
Newton, Osborn A., 236.
Nickens, Owen T. B., 241.
Norman, M. W. D., 223.
Nunn, Charles, 303.

O'Connell, Pezavia, 270.
O'Connor, 257.
Ogden, Peter, 241.

O'Harra, J. E., 231, 251.
O'Kelly, Berry, 303.
O'Kelley, C. G., 265.
Olandad, 189.
Olney, D. W., 226.
Oncles, Father, 205.
Osborn, Perry Anderson, 231.
Ossie, Keebe, 241.
Othello, 189.
Otis, Joseph E., 241.
Outlaw, John S., 261.
Owens, Mrs. R. C., 303.

Pace, Dinah, 241.
Page, Inman E., 268, 303.
Palmer, John H., 269.
Palmer, Loring B., 261.
Pamphlet, Gowan, 232.
Parker, James B., 224.
Parker, Inez C., 284.
Parks, H. B., 205, 276.
Parks, Thomas F., 303.
Parks, W. G., 279.
Parrish, C. H., 303.
Partee, W. E., 226.
Patrick, Thomas W., 236.
Patterson, Fred D., 303.
Patterson, Spenser, 303.
Paul, Thomas, 236.
Payne, Christopher H., 254.
Payne, D. A., 196, 199.
Payne, G. A., 265.
Payton, F. A., Jr., 303.
Pelham, R., 258.
Penn, I. G., 205, 209, 241, 278.
Penn, W. F., 261.
Pennington, J. W. C., 196.
Perdue, A. C., 303.
Perry, Christopher, 210.
Perry, C. W., 241.
Peters, "Dr.", 236.
Peters, E. S., 303.
Peters, John, 220.
Peters, Phyllis Wheatley, 189, 190, 196, 198, 199, 201, 202, 210, 284.
Peterson, B. H., 226.
Peterson, James T., 303.
Peterson, John, 241.
Pettey, Mrs., 226.
Pettiford, W. R., 303.
Phelps, Mrs. Mary Rice, 223.
Phillips, C. H., 205, 275.
Phillips, Henry L., 205.

Index to Names

Pickens, William, 208.
Pierce, Charles, 218.
Pinchback, Napoleon, 241.
Pinchback, P. B. S., 205, 209, 252, 253.
Pinheiro, Don T., 236.
Pitts, Coffin, 236.
Platt, Miss Ida, 223.
Pledger, William A., 224.
Plummer, "Elder," 236.
Poindexter, James, 218.
Pollard, L. M., 241.
Pompey, R. S., 269.
Ponton, M. M., 265.
Pope, James W., 236.
Porter, J. R., 226.
Porter, L. M., 303.
Porter, Maggie, 241.
Porter, Troy, 303.
Porter, W. M., 303.
Powell, B. F., 223.
Powell, Clayton, 201.
Powell, Holland, 279.
Pratt, Harry T., 303.
Price, J. C., 199, 241, 288.
Prillerman, Byrd, 268.
Prioleau, G. W., 248.
Procter, H. H., 209.
Prosser, 229.
Prout, John, 232.
Purcell, I. L., 226.
Purvis, C. B., 241, 261.
Purvis, Robert, 192, 196.
Purvis W. B., 220, 257.
Pushkin, Alexander, 188.

Quinn, William Paul, 218.

Rainey, J. H., 220, 251.
Rakestraw, W. M., 269.
Rankin, J. W., 277.
Ransier A. J., 220, 251, 252.
Ransom, R. C., 205, 209, 277.
Raphard, Father, 280.
Rapier, James T., 220, 251, 261.
Ray, Charles M., 230.
Ray, Charlotte. 241.
Ray, E. P., 257.
Ray, Peter Williams, 261.
Raymond, John T., 236.
Raymond, Theodore H., 236.
Reason, Charles L., 232.

Redmond, Sarah, 232.
Redmond, S. C., 241.
Redmond, S. D., 303.
Redwine, W. A., 296.
Reed, L. S., 242.
Reed, William L., 236.
Reeve, J. B., 205.
Reid, Dow, 242.
Reid, Frank, 242.
Remond, C. L., 192, 196.
Revels, Hiram R., 220, 250, 253.
Reynolds, H. H., 257.
Rich, William, 230.
Richards, Fannie, 233.
Richardson, A. St. George, 226.
Richey, C. V., 258.
Riddick, J. F., 297.
Ridley, Mrs. U. A., 242.
Rischer, H. K., 242.
Roberts, E. P., 209, 261.
Roberts, D. R., 233.
Roberts, Isaac L., 236.
Roberts, Thomas Wright, 218.
Roberson, W. E., 303.
Robinson, David R., 236.
Robinson, E. A., 298.
Robinson, G. T., 226.
Robinson, J. P., 224.
Robinson, Mrs. Leila, 303.
Robinson, Mrs. M. A., 223.
Robinson, R. G., 227.
Rock, David, 236.
Rock, John S., 242.
Rollins, Wade C., 303.
Roman, C. V., 209, 261.
Rosell, David, 261.
Ross, A. W., 230, 242.
Ross, John, 85.
Ross, J. O., 296, 303.
Rosser, L. E., 276.
Roundtree, P. C., 303.
Rucker, H. A., 205, 303.
Ruffin, G. L., 230.
Ruffin, Mrs. J. St. P., 205.
Ruffin, Stanley, 236.
Ruggles, David, 242.
Russell, G. P., 268.
Russell, James S., 242.
Russwurm, J. B., 192, 196.
Rutling, Thomas, 242.

Saffell, Mrs. Daisy, 303.
St. Benedict, The Moor, 242.

Index to Names

St. Pierre, John, 242.
Salem, Peter, 242.
Sampson, Benjamin, 242.
Sampson, B. K., 233.
Sampson, George M., 242.
Sampson, James D., 242.
Sancho, Ignatius, 189.
Sanders, D. J., 223.
Sanderson, Thomas, 242.
Sanford, J. M., 297.
Sanford, J. S., 304.
Sanifer, J. M., 242.
Saunders, M. P., 303.
Sawner, G. W. F., 303.
Sawner, Mrs. Lena, 303.
Sawyer, E. J., 303.
Scarborough, W. S., 198, 205, 208, 266.
Scarlett, John E., 236.
Scott, Emmett J., 205, 207, 298.
Scott, I. B., 205, 210, 278.
Scott, J. J., 296.
Scott, Lt. O. J. W., 248.
Scott, Walter, 242.
Scott, W. A., 303.
Scott, Wilkerson and Scott, 303.
Scott, William E., 205.
Scottron, S. R., 303.
Scruggs, B. E., 223.
Searcy, T. J., 303.
Sejour, Victor, 242.
Selika, Madam, 202.
Seme, Pixley Isaka, 242.
Shadd, Mary Ann, 233.
Shadwell, G. W., 303.
Shaffer, C. T., 205, 276.
Shaw, M. A. N., 236.
Shaw, Mrs. Mary E., 242.
Shepard, C. H., 261.
Shepherd, H. C., 303.
Sheppard, Mr., 242.
Sheppard, Ella, 242.
Sheppard, W. H., 242.
Shirley, Thomas, 229.
Shorter, James, 218.
Shorter, Mrs. J. A., 242.
Sidney, Thomas, 233.
Simms, S. William, 236.
Sims, W. H., 303.
Sinclair, 285.
Sinclair, William A., 220.
Singleton, David, 253.
Singleton, Huston, 223.
Slater, T. H., 261.
Smalls, Robert, 205, 251, 255.
Smiley, Charles H., 242.
Smith, Albretta Moore, 223.
Smith, Alfred, 242, 303.
Smith, Mrs. Amanda, 202.
Smith, B. S., 205.
Smith, Blanche, V., 236.
Smith, C. S., 205, 209, 276.
Smith, Eleanor A., 236.
Smith, Harriet, 237.
Smith, H. C., 205.
Smith, Mrs. Hannah G., 236.
Smith, Isaac H., 296, 304.
Smith, Joshua B., 237.
Smith, James McCune, 196, 242, 261.
Smith, Mary E., 237.
Smith, Mrs. M. E. C., 227.
Smith, R. L., 209, 304.
Smith, R. S., 227.
Smith, Stephen, 229.
Smith, Wilford H., 195, 304.
Smythe, John H., 227, 242.
Snow, Benjamin, 218.
Snowden, John Baptist, 233.
Spaulding, C. C., 304.
Sprague, Mrs. Rosetta D., 227.
Stafford, A. O., 220.
Stanley, Alexander, 242.
Stanley, Charles, 242.
Stanley, John, 242.
Stanley, John C., 242.
Stanley, J. P., 297.
Stanton, J. C., 276.
Starks, J. R., 276.
Steele, Carrie, 242.
Stephenson, J. B., 304.
Sterrs, Alexander, 242.
Sterrs, Willis E., 261.
Stevenson, William, 237.
Steward, T. G., 206, 209, 248.
Stewart, Austin, 218.
Stewart, F. A., 242, 261.
Stewart, G. W., 275.
Stewart, Logan H., 299.
Stewart, T. McCants, 233.
Still, Charity, 223.
Still, James, 237.
Still, Peter, 242.
Still, William, 192.
Stokes, A. J., 279.

Storum, James, 227.
Stout, R. S., 276.
Straker, D. A., 223.
Strauther, J. M., 304.
Street, H. Gordon, 237.
Stringer, T. W., 253.
Strong, J. W., 265.
Stubbs, Julian, 237.
Suggs, D. C., 243.
Sutton, E. H., 257.

Talbert, Mary B., 227.
Taliaferro, C. T., 304.
Talley, T. W., 227.
Tandy, H. A., 304.
Taniel, R. F., 297.
Tanner, B. T., 198, 206, 210, 276.
Tanner, Henry O., 194, 197, 198, 199, 200, 201, 206, 208, 210, 287.
Tate, W. A., 269.
Taylor, Hilliard, 304.
Taylor Major, 201.
Taylor, Marshall W., 218.
Taylor, Preston, 304.
Taylor, R. R., 243.
Taylor, S. Coleridge, 197, 201.
Taylor, W. L., 194.
Teamoh, Robert T., 237.
Terrell, Father of R. H., 233.
Terrell, Mrs. Mary Church, 202, 206.
Terrell, Mother of Mary C., 233.
Terrell, R. H., 206, 208, 253, 258.
Terrs, Holmes, 304.
Terry, Watt, 304.
Thomas, Alex S. 218.
Thomas, I. L., 278.
Thomas, James C., 243, 304.
Thomas, J. W., 304.
Thomas, Lillian J. B., 223.
Thompson, R. W., 227.
Thurman, Mrs. Lucy, 243.
Tibbs, Roy W., 220.
Tidrington, E. G., 304.
Tolton, Father Augustus, 280.
Toussaint, François Dominique, 189, 197, 248.
Townsend, A. M., 261, 266.
Townsend, J. M., 297.
Trotter, William H., 208.
Trotter, W. Monroe, 206, 237.

Troumontaine, Julian, 233.
Trower, John S., 243, 304.
Truth, Sojourner, 192, 196, 197, 199, 202.
Tubman, Harriet, 192.
Tucker, 261.
Tucker, A. L., 297.
Tucker, E. D., 304.
Tucker, T. de S., 227.
Tulane, Victor H., 243.
Tunnell, W. V., 206.
Turnbo, Mrs. Pope, 304.
Turner, Benjamin S., 243, 251.
Turner, C. H., 206, 210, 270.
Turner, H. M., 218, 247, 276.
Turner, M. W., 304.
Turner, Nat, 218.
Turner, Dihdwo, 237.
Tyler, Ralph W., 210, 255.
Tyree, Evans, 206, 210, 276.

Vachon, George B., 233.
Valladelid, Juan de, 239.
Vass, G. W., 206.
Vass, S. N., 278.
Vassa, Gustavus, 189.
Velar, N. T., 304.
Venegar, F. T., 268.
Vernon, W. T., 206, 209, 265, 304.
Vesey, Denmark, 218, 243.
Villa, Panco, 248.

Walder, Walter F., 237.
Waldron, J. Milton, 210.
Walker, 237.
Walker, Aida O., 201, 202, 288.
Walker, Mme. C. J., 201, 304.
Walker, David, 192, 196.
Walker, Edwin G., 237.
Walker, George, 201.
Walker, H. L., 227.
Walker, John W., 261.
Walker, Maggie B., 206.
Wall, Josiah T., 243, 251.
Wall, O. S. B., 243.
Wallace, A. G., 304.
Wallace, J. E., 265.
Wallace, T. W., 278.
Wallace, W. N., 227.
Waller, O. M., 227.
Walters, Alexander, 206, 208, 277.

Index to Names

Walton, L. P., 261.
Ward, E. E., 304.
Ward, S. R., 218, 243.
Ward, T. M. D., 218.
Warfield, W. A., 206, 210, 261.
Waring, J. H. N., 243.
Warner, A. J., 277.
Warrick, Meta Vaux, 220, 287.
Washington, Booker T., 194, 195, 196, 197, 198, 199, 200, 201, 210, 288, 298, 304.
Washington, Mrs. Booker T., 202.
Washington, J. W., 304.
Washington, Mrs. Margaret, 223.
Washington, Mrs. S. I. N., 237.
Watson, B. F., 277.
Wayman, A. W., 218.
Webb, John L., 304.
Wells, John W., 304.
Wells, Nelson, 218.
Welmon, Matthew, 304.
West, F. L., 269.
West, W. B., 223.
Westberry, R. W., 304.
Westons, 243.
Wharton, Heber E., 243.
Wheatland, Marcus F., 206.
Wheaton, J. F., 228.
Whipper, William, 192.
Whitaker, J. W., 227.
White, Clarence C., 206.
White, Fred, 206.
White, G. H., 206, 210, 251.
White, T. P., 233.
White, W. J., 233.
Whiting, J. L., 269.
Wier, Felix, 220.
Wilder, J. R., 227.
Wilkinson, G. C., 285.
Wilkinson, R. S., 268.
Williams, Bert, 196, 201, 206, 209, 288.
Williams, C. P., 304.
Williams, C. T., 209.
Williams, Charles W. M., 237.
Williams, Daniel H., 194, 198, 206, 207, 259, 261.
Williams, Mrs. D. H., 223.
Williams, E. C., 206.
Williams, Miss Emma Rose, 223.
Williams, Mrs. Fannie Barrier, 223.
Williams, G. G., 304.
Williams, George H., 198.
Williams, G. H. C., 268.
Williams, George Washington, 243.
Williams, J. A., 304.
Williams, J. B. L., 227.
Williams, J. M. P., 253.
Williams, J. S., 304.
Williams, P. B., 257.
Williams, R. S., 275.
Williams, Mrs. Sylvanie F., 223.
Williams, S. Laing, 304.
Williams, W. T. B., 206, 210.
Willis, E. D., 304.
Willis, Joseph, 275.
Wilson, Butler R., 237.
Wilson, Edward, 228.
Wilson, James H., 261.
Wilson, J. M., 253.
Wilson, T. J., 304.
Wilson, T. J., Jr., 304.
Windham, B. L., 304.
Windham, T. C., 304.
Winter, L., 305.
Wolff, James G., 237.
Wolff, James H., 237.
Wood, J. W., 278.
Wood, N. B., 228.
Wood, S. W., 305.
Woods, Granville T., 194, 195, 198, 257.
Woods, Lyates, 258.
Woods, R. C., 266.
Woodson, Ann, 233.
Woodson, C. G., 206, 209, 270.
Woodson, Emma J., 233.
Woodson, J. W., 206.
Work, Henry, 243.
Work, Monroe N., 206, 210.
Wormley, James, 233, 257.
Wormley, Mary, 218, 233.
Wormley, William, 218.
Wragg, J. P., 278.
Wright, Elizabeth E., 243.
Wright, E. J., 237.
Wright, Herbert R., 254.
Wright, John M., 298, 305.
Wright, Mrs. Minnie T., 237.
Wright, R. R., 206, 218, 268.
Wright, R. R., Jr., 206, 208, 270, 277.
Wright, Theodore S., 230.
Writt, John T., 305.
Wych, A. A., 261.

Wyche, R. P., 227.
Wynn, Robert D., 279.

Yates, Iola D., 237.
Yerb, William J., 254.

Young, Major Charles, 206, 208, 247, 248.
Young, James H., 228.
Young, Mrs. M. L., 305.
Young, Nathan B., 210, 268.

GENERAL INDEX

Abantus, 71.
Abolitionists, 342-344.
Achievement of Negroes, 183-184, 193.
Admixture of blood. *See* Amalgamation.
"Advance Guard," 194.
Africa, South, 71-77; Bastaards, 74-75; classes in, 75-76; color line in, 75; illicit sex relations, 75; intermarriage in, 75; mixed-blood people in, 72; mixture of races, 71; population of, 71; race prejudice in, 76; race separation in, 75.
Agitation, effect of, 371-374.
Agitators, mulatto, 346, 380-381.
Amalgamation, 17, 77, 86. *See, also,* Intermarriage, intermixture of races.
Ambition of mulatto, 315-318.
America, South, 33-51, 88.
American Indians. *See* Indians.
Anglo-Indians. *See* Eurasians.
Antipathy, race, 25, 317-319. *See, also,* Race prejudice.
Anti-slavery propaganda, 342.
Apache, 78.
Arabs, half-caste, 28.
Arawak Indians, 65.
Art, Negro in, 286-292.
Assimilation in ancient times, 26.
Attitude; of Northern mulattoes, 368-374; of races in Spanish America, 40-41; toward first American Negroes, 166-168.
Auxiliary wives, 22.

Backward race, definition of, 18.
Banks, Negro, 295-297, 307.
Bastaards, 71-75.
Biography of Negroes, 221-231, 237-245.
Bi-racial, 355, 358-360, 373-374.
Boston Negroes, 233-237.
Brazil, 27, 88.
Brazilian Negro, Roosevelt on, 323-324.
Business, Negro in, 293-307.
Business League, Negro, 289, 298-306, 307.

Cannibalism, 63.
Cascos, 13.
Caste, basis for, 19; accommodation to, 360, 371; in primitive society, 21.
Cherokee, 85.
Children, treatment of half-caste, 95-96.
Civilized Tribes, 81, 82, 84.
Class distinctions; in Cuba, 59; in Jamaica, 68; in Philippine Islands, 52-53; in Spain, 24; in Spanish America, 44-49; South Africa, 73.
Classes, influence of, on race intermixture, 90-92.
Color line; among American Indians, 85; among Negroes, 177-179; in Brazil, 36-37; in Cuba, 57; in Haiti, 63; in Jamaica, 67; in South Africa, 75; in Spanish America, 47.
Color prejudice; in Spanish America, 50; in Cuba, 60. *See, also,* Race prejudice.
Coloured, defined, 14.
Coloured peoples, 27; of Jamaica, 316; of South Africa, 27.
Comanche, 78.
Communication, effect on race intermixture, 16.
Competition, as affecting race prejudice, 101, 338.
Concubinage, 28-29; 139-144; 378.

Croatans, 81, 85.
Cuba, 57-60; color inferiority in, 325-326; mulatto in, 326.

Dance, 60, 88; orgiastic, 62.
Dentistry, Negro in, 262-263, 291.
Determination of racial type, 327.
Differentiation among slaves, 169-172.
Disorganization in South, 349.
Distribution of mulattoes, 113, 122-124.
Divide and Rule, policy of, 333.
Douglass, Frederick, 317.

Early American Negroes, 190-192.
Educated classes, 395.
Education of Negro, 339, 350; Woodson's, 231-233.
Eminent Negroes, 197-199.
Enfranchisement of Negroes, 350.
Escapement from the race, 396.
Eskimo half-castes, 27, 31-32, 316.
Ethnological distinctions, 47.
Eurasians, 26-31, 316.
Exclusion policy, 334-335.
Exogamy, 21.

Famous colored women, 201-202.
Famous Negroes, 199-201.
Fertility of mixed marriages, 83.
Foremost men of the race, 207-210.
Formation of primitive state, 97-98.
Free mulattoes, 176-177.
Free Negroes, 112-113.
Freedman's Bureau, 347.
French-Canadians, 77.

Greeks, 22.
Greenland, 31, 88.
Griffe, 12.
Griquas. *See* Bastaards.

Haiti, 61-65; civilization of, 61-62; classes in, 64; color line in, 63; dress, 65; education in, 63-65; marriage in, 62-64; political conditions, 62; population of, 63; presidents of, 65; race hatred in, 65; religion in, 62-63.

Half-breed; as a separate caste, 328-331; illegitimate origin of, 88; increase in numbers, 93-94; psychology of, 19; treatment of children, 95-96. *See,* also, Eurasians.
Hindu. *See* Eurasians.
Histories of the race, 216-220.
Hopi Indians, 80, 81.
Hybrid, variability of, 12.
Hybridization, 28.

Ideals of the Negro, 180-181.
Illicit sex relations, 145-155, 378; classes involved, 145-155; during colonial times, 144-155; effect of freedom on, 160-161; effect of slavery on, 158-160; indentured servants, 146-150; white women and Indians, 155; white women and Negroes, 153-155; slave owners and slaves, 145-146.
Immigrants in Spanish America, 38.
Indentured servants, 146-150.
India, 88.
Indians, 77-85; as slaves, 82; white crosses, 28; fertility of, 83; half-breed, 78-85, 317; Hopi, 81-82; intermixture, 77-79; Iroquois, 77-78; Navajo, 81; Negro intermixture, 82-83; Oklahoma, 81; Osage, 85; race problem among, 84-85; St. Regis, 81; Wyandots, 84.
Inquisition, 25.
Industrial education, 381.
Intermarriage, 69, 94-95, 127-139, 316, 378; classes involved, 130-131; 136-137; in Brazil, 36; in Greenland, 32; in South Africa, 75; in Spain, 24; in Spanish America, 48-50; laws concerning, 128-130, 134; Negro and Indian, 155-158.
Intermixture of races, 15-16, 393-394; among American Indians, 78-79; conditions determining, 88-93; effect of, on civilization, 17; in ancient world, 22-23; in Brazil, 33-38; in Cuba, 57-60; in Greenland, 31-33; in Haiti, 61-65; in India, 27-31; in

Jamaica, 65-71; in North American Indian group, 77-85; in Philippines, 51-54; in primitive society, 21-22; in Spain, 23-26; in Spanish America, 38-51; in South Africa, 71-77; in West Indies, 55-71; when a problem, 17-18.
Inventors, Negro, 256-259, 291.
Iroquois, 77-78.
Islam, policy of, 24.
Isolation, 359, 383, 390-391.

Jamaica, 65-71; classes, 66; education, 67; population, 66; relation of sexes, 67; separation of colors, 67-68; Spanish occupancy of, 65.
Johnson, Jack, 317.
Journalism, Negro in, 286, 291.

Kafirs, 73.
Key to race problem, 86-104.

Law, Negro in, 263-264, 291.
Leadership, Negro, 364, 366-367, 395.
Literature, Negro in, 282-286, 291; of Negroes, 388.
L'Ouverture. *See* Toussaint.

Mango, 13.
Manitoba, mixed-bloods in, 77.
Manumission, 339.
Marabon, 12.
Meamelouc, 12.
Medicine, Negro in, 259-263, 291.
Mestizo, 27, 33; Chinese, 27, 51-54, in Spanish America, 40; social position of, in Spanish America, 46-49; in Mexico, 44; Spanish, 27, 51-52.
Metif, 12.
Metis, 27, 33-38, 316-317; advance of, 320-323; characteristics of, 34-35.
Mexico, races in, 43-44.
Middle-class, growth of, 358.
Migrations, 14-15.
Ministry, Negroes in, 274-282, 291.
Miscegenation, 22; in Brazil, 33; in Greenland, 31-33; in India, 28. *See,* also, Intermarriage. Amalgamation. Intermixture of races.
Mixed-blood caste, 376.
Mixed-blood race. *See* Halfbreed.
Mixed-bloods as a cohesive force, 22.
Mixed marriages. *See* Intermarriage.
Mixture of blood, 22, 375.
Mongrel type, 28.
Moriscos, 24.
Mulattoes; as leaders, 341, 360-364; caste, 316; children of white women, 175-176; definition of, 11-14; Hall, 110; improvement of, 396-397; increase of, 118-122; key to race problem, 86-104; militant, 371; number of, 116-118; pride in color, 395-396; problem of, 19; sentiments of, 341, 343; societies, 340; superiority of, 339, 395.
Music, Negro in, 289-291.
Musical tradition, 388-389.
Mustifee, 13.
Mustifino, 13.

Natal. *See* South Africa.
National Association for the Advancement of the Colored People, 370.
Nationalities, composition of, 16.
Nationality; effect of, on economic competition, 392-393; effect of, on education, 391-392; effect of, on intermixture of races, 393; effect of, on isolation, 390-391; effect of, on race friction, 394; tendency toward, 383; sentiment of, in Roman colonies, 23.
Native policy in ancient times, 26-27.
Navajo, 81.
Negro aristocracy, 389-390.
Negro; Brazilian, 321; business league, 298-305; disappearance of, in Brazil, 38; Indian intermixture, 82; in history, 188-189; middle class, 353-359; politicians, 347-348.

Obstacles to race solidarity, 382-383.
Occupational differentiation, 339.
Octoroon, 13.
Oklahoma, 81.
Opportunities of mulattoes, 378.
Origin of mixed-bloods, 88, 376.
Osage, 85.

Persistence of negroid characteristics, 105.
Philippine Islands, 51-54.
Phoenicians, 22.
Physical appearance, as basis for class distinctions, 18-19.
Politicians, Negro, 346-347.
Politics, Negro in, 249-256, 291.
Polygamy, 62, 64.
Porto Rico, 56.
Portuguese, 88; in Brazil, 33ff.; in India, 28.
Prestige of mulattoes, 363.
Presuppositions, 375-376.
Professional classes, 395.
Property-owning class, 395.
Psychology of mixed-bloods, 19, 102-103.

Quadroon, 13.
Quarteron, 12.

Race; competition, 392-393; defined, 14; friction, 76, 394; harmony, 100; hatred, 48, 65; intermixture (*see* Intermixture of races); pride, 21; repugnance, 28; separation, 75, 385-386.
Race prejudice, 70; basis for, 18; as affected by numbers, 99-100; growth of, in American colonies, 167-168; in Philippines, 53; in South Africa, 76.
Race problem, 85; defined, 18-19; in Jamaica, 70; in Spain, 24.
Race solidarity, absence of, in North, 366-368; consequences of, 390ff. *See*, also, Nationality.
Races and classes in Spanish America, 40.
Races, relative tendency toward intermixture, 88-90.
Races; biological effect of crossing, 13; distribution of, in Spanish America, 42-43.
Reconstruction policy, 347.
Rizal, 53.
Rôle of mulatto, 104, 380-381, 338ff., 377, 315ff., 320.
Romans, mixture with subject peoples, 23.

Sacrata, 12.
St. Regis, 81.
Sambo, 13.
Sang-mele, 12.
Santo Domingo, 56.
Segregation, 355ff., 384-385.
Self-interest, 387-388.
Self-respect, 387.
Separation of colors in Jamaica, 68.
Sexual selection, 38.
Slave traffic, 106-107.
Slavery; domestic, 27; effect on race intermixture, 92-94; in Cuba, 57; in ancient times, 27; in West Indies, 55ff.; of Indians in Spanish America, 39.
Slaves; classes among, 172-173; distribution of, 108.
Snake worship, 63.
Social; classes in Cuba, 58-59; distinction in Jamaica, 68; equality, 319-320, 349; separation, *See* Color line.
Soldiers, Negro, 246-249, 291.
Southern mulatto leaders, 361ff.
Southern policy, 353ff.
Spain; mixture of races in, 23; race problem in, 24-25.
Spanish America, 33ff.
Spanish half-breeds, 317.
Statistics of mulattoes, 106.
Status of mixed-bloods, 96, 335-336; as affected by physical appearance, 98; as affected by cultural differences of races, 99; as slaves, 174-177; in Brazil, 33-38; in Cuba, 325-326; in India, 316, 328-330; in Greenland, 316; in Spanish America, 326-327; in Jamaica, 331-333.
Status of Negroes in North, 364ff.
Status of slaves, 167-168.
Students, Negro, 270-274.

Superior mulattoes, per cent of, 311-314.
Superiority of mulattoes, 101-102, 181, 187-188, 379.

"Talented Tenth," 196-197.
Teachers, Negro, 264-274, 291.
Toussaint, 64.
Tradition of mulatto superiority, 378-379.
Tuskegee. *See* Southern Policy.

"Uncle Tom's Cabin," 344.

Variability of mixed-bloods, 83-84.

Voluntary segregation, 386-387.
Voodooism, 62.

Waltz. *See* Dance.
Washington, policy of. *See* Southern policy.
West Indies, 55-71, 88.
"Whites by Law," 27.
"Who's Who in Colored America," 202-206.
Women, influence of, on race intermixture, 91-92.
Wyandots, 84.

Zambos, 33.

Milton Keynes UK
Ingram Content Group UK Ltd.
UKHW010138040324
438776UK00007B/1095

10th Anniversary Book
Selected Essays
from the
Vivekananda International Foundation

10th Anniversary Book
SELECTED ESSAYS
FROM THE
VIVEKANANDA INTERNATIONAL FOUNDATION

Edited by
**Lt Gen Gautam Banerjee,
PVSM, AVSM, YSM (Retd)**

Vivekananda International Foundation
New Delhi

Selected Essays from the Vivekananda International Foundation
Edited by Lt Gen Gautam Banerjee, PVSM, AVSM, YSM (Retd)

ISBN 978-81-942837-5-1

First Published in 2020

Copyright © Vivekananda International Foundation, New Delhi

All rights reserved. No part of this publication may be reproduced, stored in a retrieval system, or transmitted in any form or by any means, electronic, mechanical, photocopying, recording or otherwise, without the prior written permission of the Publisher.

Disclaimer: The views and opinions expressed in the book are the individual assertion of the Author. The Publisher does not take any responsibility for the same in any manner whatsoever. The same shall solely be the responsibility of the Author.

Published by
PENTAGON PRESS LLP
206, Peacock Lane, Shahpur Jat,
New Delhi-110049
Phones: 011-64706243, 26491568
Telefax: 011-26490600
email: rajan@pentagonpress.in
website: www.pentagonpress.in

Printed at Aegean Offset Printers, Greater Noida, U.P.

Contents

	Foreword	vii
	Editorial Note	ix
1.	State of the Economy: India and the World S. Gurumurthy	1
2.	India's Pakistan and China Policies Must be Based on Realism, not Hope Satish Chandra	18
3.	Arihant to India's Defence: Nuclear Triad Provides Credible Strategic Deterrence General N.C. Vij, PVSM, UYSM, AVSM	25
4.	India's Strategic Culture: Need for an Indian Narrative Arvind Gupta	28
5.	Where Economics and Strategy Intersect: A Political Economy Approach to Global Power Prabhat Prakash Shukla	46
6.	Rebooting India-Russia Ties Kanwal Sibal	75
7.	Information and Communication Technologies: Key to Transform India Davinder Kumar	82
8	Consecration of China's 'New Period' People's Liberation Army Gautam Banerjee	95

9	Missing Factors in India's Policy towards Pakistan *Tilak Devasher*	113
10	Afghanistan in Transition: Increasing Role of India *Gautam Mukhopadhaya and Lt Gen Ravi Sawhney*	129
11	Indus Water Treaty: An Appraisal *Maj Gen A.K. Chaturvedi*	142
12	Strategies for Enhancing India's Comprehensive National Power *Brig Rahul Bhonsle*	174
13	Japan's Changing Security Discourse through the Prism of its Deterrence Imperative *Prerna Gandhi*	199
14	Sister Nivedita's Ideas on Indian Nationhood and their Contemporary Relevance *Dr. Arpita Mitra*	227
15	Militancy in Kashmir: A Study *Abhinav Pandya*	260
	Index	291

*

Foreword

The Vivekananda International Foundation, popularly known as the VIF, completed ten years of its existence in December 2019. The objective of the founding of VIF was to bring about a change in the character of the strategic discourse in this country by building an Indian narrative and imbibing Indian civilisational values.

Over the last ten years, the VIF has provided a platform for intensive and vigorous discussions on a large number of important issues. We are happy to bring out a compilation of VIF's articles written over the last ten years covering subjects such as defence, diplomacy, economy, nationalism, terrorism and technology authored by prominent experts.

The articles are thought-provoking and indicate the evolution of strategic discourse in India.

New Delhi
Aug 2019

DR ARVIND GUPTA
Director,
Vivekananda International Foundation,
New Delhi

Editorial Note

A decade has gone by since the Vivekananda International Foundation or the VIF was founded under the patronage of the Vivekananda Kendra, the world-wide bearer of the great philosopher, thinker and nationalist Swami's legacy. The VIF was thus intended to develop as a repository of modern-day strategic thinking on the profound aspects of nation building to include national security and strategic studies, international relations and diplomacy, neighbourhood studies, governance and political studies, economic studies, and notably, historical and civilisational studies. What, however, distinguishes the founding of the VIF from other think-tanks is its spiritual roots which guide its objectives.

As the first decade of the second millennium was nearing its end, a group of dedicated nationalists, having served the national cause at the apex levels of governance, came together to devote their lives as private citizens to the continuation of their sole mission, that of building a spiritually and physically strong nation as envisioned by Swami Vivekananda. Committed to free the national narrative from a stranglehold of pacifist and self-depredating ideology—an ideology tainted by innate cynicism of the sublime idea of *Bharatvarsha*—the founding members of the VIF sought to marshal their outstanding intellect, extensive experience, deep knowledge and foresight to bring forth balanced, self-assured interpretations and analyses of strategic affairs concerning India. It was under such sublime objectives, mentored by the Vivekananda Kendra and its farsighted fraternity, that the VIF began its professional journey as a strategic think-tank. Well received in the strategic community, it was soon recognised as an intellectually well-endowed repository that was solely focused on propagating nation building ideas and options. That noble allegiance continues to pervade the VIF's functioning ever since.

Over the past decade, thanks to the inspiring fervour of its past and present guiding members, the VIF has charted an academically independent, if fiscally Spartan, path of research and analyses. Non-partisan and balanced strategic objectivity, and conformity with India's exalted native civilisational values being its fundamental competencies, it has earned a reputation for the highest level of credibility among national and international opinion as well as decision makers which include governments, strategists and academia. The Foundation has thus emerged as a reliable, and much valued thinking associate of the Indian State and its institutions, while visiting foreign delegates more or less mark it as an institution of compulsory call.

Since its inception, the VIF has been regularly disseminating a vast stream of analyses of key developments and decision dilemmas concerning the nation to its wide circle of associates and readers. Notably, due care is also taken to lead the analyses to prognoses, plausible options and recommendations for future courses of action to deal with the addressed situations. Besides round-table discussions, seminars, workshops, institutional visits, *Vimersha* talks and publication of books, monographs, and topical papers, the VIF website uploads have been the premier media through which these analyses are propagated. Thus, over the years, the VIF has come to possess a vast bank of content-rich, thought-provoking articles. The Editorial Committee's decision to commemorate the VIF's Tenth Anniversary by publishing a book containing selected articles from its mass of material was therefore apt.

The quest began with selection of articles of contemporary national concerns along with analyses and messages of continued applicability. A total of 15 articles mostly authored by the fraternity of VIF stalwarts were chosen for inclusion in this book. Even some of the recent contributors to the Foundation have been accommodated after due revision and editing to encourage strategic thinking. The topics chosen are diverse and, as the reader would find, the analyses are as concurrent as when the papers were written in the past few years. The authors, of course, are among the leading strategic thinkers of contemporary times—Shri S. Gurumurthy, Shri Satish Chandra, General N.C. Vij and Dr. Arvind Gupta, to mention just a few. Appropriately, works of many of the other noted authors, published exclusively and available on line and print, have not been repeated in this book. The reader might, however, find it odd that the VIF's founding mentor, Shri Ajit Doval, KC, does not figure in the Contents list—that is in deference to the sensitivity of the post of National Security Advisor that he holds.

The book is a combined effort of the VIF's Editor-in-Chief, the rest of the Editorial Committee and the Secretary, VIF. We are sanguine that the book will draw much interest among its readers.

Jai Hind

3, San Matin Marg
New Delhi
August 2109

Gautam Banerjee
Lieutenant General (Veteran)
Editor, VIF